KNIGHTS AND THEIR DAYS

# KNIGHTS AND THEIR DAYS

BY
DR. DORAN

Athens ‡ Manchester

Knights and their Days

Published by: Old Book Publishing Ltd

Book Cover Design: Old Book Publishing Ltd

Copyright © 2012 Old Book Publishing Ltd
All rights reserved.

**Title of original:** Knights and their Days

**Cover image:** *The Tournament at Cremorne Gardens.* Dressed as medieval knights, jousting London. According to Cremorne Gardens were popular pleasure gardens by the side of the River Thames in Chelsea, London. They lay between Chelsea Harbour and the end of the King's Road and flourished between **1845** to **1877**; today only a vestige survives, on the river at the southern end of Cheyne Walk.
**Date printed:** 18 July 1863

Originally published in 1856, Redfield, New York


**ISBN–10:** 1-78107-158-6
**ISBN–13:** 978-1-78107-158-8

# EDITOR'S NOTE

Old Book Publishing Ltd takes care in preserving the wording and images of the original books. For this reason we have invested in technology that enables us to enhance the quality of such reproduction. This investment helps overcome problems encountered when reproducing old books, such as stains, coloured paper, discolouration of ink, yellowed pages, see-through and onion skin type paper.

This reproduction book, produced from digital images of the original, may contain occasional defects such as missing pages or blemishes due to the original source content or were introduced by the scanning process.

These are scanned pages and the quality of print represents accurately the print quality of the original book, though we may have been able to enhance it.

As this book has been scanned and/or reformatted from the original we cannot guarantee that it is error-free or contains the full content of the original.

However, we believe that this work is culturally important, and despite its imperfections, have elected to bring it back into print as part of our commitment to the preservation of printed works.

Old Book Publishing

# KNIGHTS

## AND THEIR DAYS

### BY DR. DORAN

AUTHOR OF "LIVES OF THE QUEENS OF ENGLAND OF THE HOUSE OF HANOVER,"
"TABLE TRAITS," "HABITS AND MEN," ETC.

"Oh, 'tis a brave profession, and rewards
All loss we meet, with double weight of glory."
SHIRLEY *(The Gentleman of Venice.)*

REDFIELD
34 BEEKMAN STREET, NEW YORK
1856

TO

# PHILIPPE WATIER, ESQ.

IN MEMORY OF MERRY NIGHTS AND DAYS NEAR METZ AND THE
MOSELLE,

THIS LITTLE VOLUME

Is inscribed

BY HIS VERY SINCERE FRIEND,

THE AUTHOR.

# CONTENTS.

A FRAGMENTARY PROLOGUE . . . . . . . . . . . . . PAGE 9
THE TRAINING OF PAGES . . . . . . . . . . . . . . . . 30
KNIGHTS AT HOME . . . . . . . . . . . . . . . . . . . 36
LOVE IN CHEVALIERS, AND CHEVALIERS IN LOVE. . . . . . . 51
DUELLING, DEATH, AND BURIAL. . . . . . . . . . . . . 65
THE KNIGHTS WHO "GREW TIRED OF IT". . . . . . . . . 78
FEMALE KNIGHTS AND JEANNE DARC. . . . . . . . . . . 104
THE CHAMPIONS OF CHRISTENDOM . . . . . . . . . . . 113
SIR GUY OF WARWICK, AND WHAT BEFELL HIM . . . . . . 133
GARTERIANA . . . . . . . . . . . . . . . . . . . . 148
FOREIGN KNIGHTS OF THE GARTER . . . . . . . . . . . 170
THE POOR KNIGHTS OF WINDSOR, AND THEIR DOINGS . . . . 184
THE KNIGHTS OF THE SAINTE AMPOULE . . . . . . . . . 194
THE ORDER OF THE HOLY GHOST . . . . . . . . . . . . 200
JACQUES DE LELAING . . . . . . . . . . . . . . . . 208
THE FORTUNES OF A KNIGHTLY FAMILY . . . . . . . . . 228
THE RECORD OF RAMBOUILLET . . . . . . . . . . . . 263
SIR JOHN FALSTAFF . . . . . . . . . . . . . . . . . 276
STAGE KNIGHTS . . . . . . . . . . . . . . . . . . . 295
STAGE LADIES, AND THE ROMANCE OF HISTORY . . . . . . 312

## CONTENTS.

THE KINGS OF ENGLAND AS KNIGHTS; FROM THE NORMANS TO THE
    STUARTS . . . . . . . . . . . . . . . . . PAGE 329
"THE INSTITUTION OF A GENTLEMAN" . . . . . . . . . . . 351
THE KINGS OF ENGLAND AS KNIGHTS; THE STUARTS . . . . . . 358
THE SPANISH MATCH . . . . . . . . . . . . . . . . . . 364
THE KINGS OF ENGLAND AS KNIGHTS; FROM STUART TO BRUNSWICK 375
RECIPIENTS OF KNIGHTHOOD . . . . . . . . . . . . . . 388
RICHARD CARR, PAGE, AND GUY FAUX, ESQUIRE . . . . . . . 410
ULRICH VON HUTTEN . . . . . . . . . . . . . . . . . 420
SHAM KNIGHTS . . . . . . . . . . . . . . . . . . . . 439
PIECES OF ARMOR . . . . . . . . . . . . . . . . . . 455

THE

# KNIGHTS AND THEIR DAYS.

## A FRAGMENTARY PROLOGUE.

"La bravoure est une qualité innée, on ne se la donne pas."
NAPOLEON I.

DR. LINGARD, when adverting to the sons of Henry II., and their knightly practices, remarks that although chivalry was considered the school of honor and probity, there was not overmuch of those or of any other virtues to be found among the members of the chivalrous orders. He names the vices that were more common, as he thinks, and probably with some justice. Hallam, on the other hand, looks on the institution of chivalry as the best school of moral discipline in the Middle Ages: and as the great and influential source of human improvement. "It preserved," he says, "an exquisite sense of honor, which in its results worked as great effects as either of the powerful spirits of liberty and religion, which have given a predominant impulse to the moral sentiments and energies of mankind."

The custom of receiving arms at the age of manhood is supposed, by the same author, to have been established among the nations that overthrew the Roman Empire; and he cites the familiar passage from Tacitus, descriptive of this custom among the Germans. At first, little but bodily strength seems to have been required on the part of the candidate. The qualifications and the forms of investiture changed or improved with the times.

In a general sense, chivalry, according to Hallam, may be referred to the age of Charlemagne, when the Caballarii, or horsemen, became the distinctive appellation of those feudal tenants and allodial proprietors who were bound to serve on horseback. When these were equipped and formally appointed to their martial duties, they were, in point of fact, knights, with so far more incentives to distinction than modern soldiers, that each man depended on himself, and not on the general body. Except in certain cases, the individual has now but few chances of distinction; and knighthood, in its solitary aspect, may be said to have been blown up by gunpowder.

As examples of the true knightly spirit in ancient times, Mr. Hallam cites Achilles, who had a supreme indifference for the question of what side he fought upon, had a strong affection for a friend, and looked at death calmly. I think Mr. Hallam over-rates the bully Greek considerably. His instance of the Cid Ruy Diaz, as a perfect specimen of what the modern knight ought to have been, is less to be gainsaid.

In old times, as in later days, there were knights who acquired the appellation by favor rather than service; or by a compelled rather than a voluntary service. The old landholders, the Caballarii, or Milites, as they came to be called, were landholders who followed their lord to the field, by feudal obligation: paying their rent, or part of it, by such service. The voluntary knights were those "younger brothers," perhaps, who sought to amend their indifferent fortunes by joining the banner of some lord. These were not legally knights, but they might win the honor by their prowess; and thus in arms, dress, and title, the younger brother became the equal of the wealthy landholders. He became even their superior, in one sense, for as Mr. Hallam adds:—"The territorial knights became by degrees ashamed of assuming a title which the others had won by merit, till they themselves could challenge it by real desert."

The connection of knighthood with feudal tenure was much loosened, if it did not altogether disappear, by the Crusades. There the knights were chiefly volunteers who served for pay: all feudal service there was out of the question. Its connection with religion was, on the other hand, much increased, particularly among the Norman knights who had not hitherto, like the Anglo-Saxons, looked upon chivalric investiture as necessarily a religious ceremony. The crusaders made religious professors, at least, of all knights, and never was one of these present at the reading of the gospel, without holding the point of his sword toward the book, in testimony of his desire to uphold what it taught by force of arms. From this time the passage into knighthood was a solemn ceremony; the candidate was belted, white-robed, and absolved after due confession, when his sword was blessed, and Heaven was supposed to be its director. With the love of God was combined love for the ladies. What was implied was that the knight should display courtesy, gallantry, and readiness to defend, wherever those services were required by defenceless women. Where such was bounden duty—but many knights did not so understand it—there was an increase of refinement in society; and probably there is nothing overcharged in the old ballad which tells us of a feast at Perceforest, where eight hundred knights sat at a feast, each of them with a lady at his side, eating off the same plate; the then fashionable sign of a refined friendship, mingled with a spirit of gallantry. That the husbands occasionally looked with uneasiness upon this arrangement, is illustrated in the unreasonably jealous husband in the romance of "Lancelot du Lac;" but, as the lady tells him, he had little right to cavil at all, for it was an age since any knight had eaten with her off the same plate.

Among the Romans the word *virtue* implied both virtue and valor—as if bravery in a man were the same thing as virtue in a woman. It certainly did not signify among Roman knights that a brave man was necessarily virtuous. In more recent times the word gallantry has been made also to take a double meaning, implying not only courage in man, but his courtesy toward woman. Both in ancient and modern times, however, the words, or their meanings, have been much abused. At a more recent period, perhaps, gallantry was never better illustrated than when in an encounter by hostile squadrons near Cherbourg, the adverse factions stood still, on a knight, wearing the colors of his mistress, advancing from the ranks of one party, and challenging to single combat the cavalier in the opposite ranks who was the most deeply in love with his mistress. There was no lack of adversaries, and the amorous knights fell on one another with a fury little akin to love.

A knight thus slain for his love was duly honored by his lady and contemporaries. Thus we read in the history of Gyron le Courtois, that the chivalric king so named, with his royal cousin Melyadus, a knight, by way of equerry, and a maiden, went together in search of the body of a chevalier who had fallen *pour les beaux yeux* of that very lady. They found the body picturesquely disposed in a pool of blood, the unconscious hand still grasping the hilt of the sword that had been drawn in honor of the maiden. "Ah, beauteous friend!" exclaims the lady, "how dearly hast thou paid for my love! The good and the joy we have shared have only brought thee death. Beauteous friend, courteous and wise, valiant, heroic, good knight in every guise, since thou has lost thy youth for me in this manner, in this strait, and in this agony, as it clearly appears, what else remains for me to suffer for thy sake, unless that I should keep you company? Friend, friend, thy beauty has departed for the love of me, thy flesh lies here bloody. Friend, friend, we were both nourished together. I knew not what love was when I gave my heart to love thee," &c., &c., &c. "Young friend," continues the lady, "thou wert my joy and my consolation: for to see thee and to speak to thee alone were sufficient to inspire joy, &c., &c., &c. Friend, what I behold slays me, I feel that death is within my heart." The lady then took up the bloody sword, and requested Melyadus to look after the honorable interment of the knight on that spot, and that he would see her own body deposited by her "friend's" side, in the same grave. Melyadus expressed great astonishment at the latter part of the request, but as the lady insisted that her hour was at hand, he promised to fulfil all her wishes. Meanwhile the maiden knelt by the side of the dead knight, held his sword to her lips, and gently died upon his breast. Gyron said it was the wofullest sight that eye had ever beheld; but all courteous as Gyron was, and he was so to such a remarkable degree that he derived a surname from his courtesy, I say that in spite of his sympathy and gallantry, he appears to have had a quick eye toward making such profit as authors could make in those days, from ready writing upon subjects of interest. Before another word was said touching the interment of the two loyers, Gyron intimated that he would write a ballad upon them that should have a universal circulation, and be sung in all lands where there were gentle hearts and sweet voices. Gyron performed what he promised, and the ballad of "Absdlon and Cesala," serves to show what very rough rhymes the courteous poet could employ to illustrate a romantic incident. Let it be added that, however the knights may sometimes have failed in their truth, this was very rarely the case with the ladies. When Jordano Bruno was received in his exile by Sir Philip Sidney, he requited the hospitality by dedicating a poem to the latter. In this dedication, he says: "With one solitary exception, all misfortunes that flesh is heir to have been visited on me. I have tasted every kind of calamity but one, that of finding false a woman's love."

It was not every knight that could make such an exception. Certainly not that pearl of knights, King Arthur himself. What a wife had that knight in the person of Guinever? Nay, he is said to have had three wives of that name, and that all of them were as faithless as ladies well *could* be. Some assert that the described deeds of these three are in fact but the evil-doings of one. However this may be, I may observe summarily here what I have said in reference to Guinever in another place. With regard to this triple-lady, the very small virtue of one third of the whole will not salubriously leaven the entire lump. If romance be true, and there is more about the history of Guinever than any other lady—she was a delicious, audacious, winning, seductive, irresistible, and heartless hussy; and a shameless! and a barefaced! Only read "Sir Lancelot du Lac!" Yes, it can not be doubted but that in the voluminous romances of the old day, there was a sprinkling of historical facts. Now, if a thousandth part of what is recorded of this heart-bewitching Guinever be true, she must have been such a lady as we can not now conceive of. True daughter of her mother Venus, when a son of Mars was not at hand, she could stoop to Mulciber. If the king was not at home, she could listen to a knight. If both were away, esquire or page might speak boldly without fear of being unheeded; and if all were absent, in the chase, or at the fray, there was always a good-looking groom in the saddle-room with whom Guinever could converse, without holding that so to do was anything derogatory. I know no more merry reading than that same ton-weight of romance which goes by the name of "Sir Lancelot du Lac." But it is not of that sort which Mrs. Chapone would recommend to young ladies, or that Dr. Cumming would read aloud in the Duke of Argyll's drawing-room. It is a book, however, which a grave man a little tired of his gravity, may look into between serious studies and solemn pursuits — a book for a lone winter evening by a library-fire, with wine and walnuts at hand; or for an old-fashioned summer's evening, in a bower through whose foliage the sun pours his *adieu*, as gorgeously red as the Burgundy in your flask. Of a truth, a man must be "in a concatenation accordingly," ere he may venture to address himself to the chronicle which tells of the "bamboches," "fredaines," and "bombances," of Guinever the Frail, and of Lancelot du Lac.

We confess to having more regard for Arthur than for his triple-wife Guinever. As I have had occasion to say in other pages, "I do not like to give up Arthur!" I love the name, the hero, and his romantic deeds. I deem lightly of his light o'love bearing. Think of his provocation both ways! Whatever the privilege of chivalry may have been, it was the practice of too many knights to be faithless. They vowed fidelity, but they were a promise-breaking, word-despising crew. On this point I am more inclined to agree with Dr. Lingard than with Mr. Hallam. Honor was ever on their lips, but not always in their hearts, and it was little respected by them, when found in the possession of their neighbor's wives. How does Scott consider them in this respect, when in describing a triad of knights, he says,

> "There were two who loved their neighbor's wives,
> And one who loved his own."

Yet how is it that knights are so invariably mentioned with long-winded laudation by Romish writers — always excepting Lingard — when they desire to illustrate the devoted spirit of olden times? Is it that the knights were truthful, devout, chaste, God-fearing? not a jot! Is it because the cavaliers cared but for one thing, in the sense of having fear but for one thing, and *that* the devil?

To escape from being finally triumphed over by the Father of Evil, they paid largely, reverenced outwardly, confessed unreservedly, and were absolved plenarily. That is the reason why chivalry was patted on the back by Rome. At the same time we must not condemn a system, the principles of which were calculated to work such extensive ameliorations in society as chivalry. Christianity itself might be condemned were we to judge of it by the shortcomings of its followers.

But even Mr. Hallam is compelled at last, reluctantly, to confess that the morals of chivalry were not pure. After all his praise of the system, he looks at its literature, and with his eye resting on the tales and romances written for the delight and instruction of chivalric ladies and gentlemen, he remarks that the "violation of marriage vows passes in them for an incontestable privilege of the brave and the fair; and an accomplished knight seems to have enjoyed as undoubted prerogatives, by general consent of opinion, as were claimed by the brilliant courtiers of Louis XV." There was an especial reason for this, the courtiers of Louis XV. might be anything they chose, provided that with gallantry they were loyal, courteous, and munificent. Now loyalty, courtesy, and that prodigality which goes by the name of munificence, were exactly the virtues that were deemed most essential to chivalry. But these were construed by the old knights as they were by the more modern courtiers. The first took advantages in combat that would now be deemed disloyal by any but a Muscovite. The second would cheat at cards in the gaming saloons of Versailles, while they would run the men through who spoke lightly of their descent. So with regard to courtesy, the knight was full of honeyed phrases to his equals and superiors, but was as coarsely arrogant as Menschikoff to an inferior. In the same way, Louis XIV., who would never pass one of his own scullery-maids without raising his plumed beaver, could address terms to the ladies of his court, which, but for the sacred majesty which was supposed to environ his person, might have purchased for him a severe castigation. Then consider the case of that "first gentleman in Europe," George, Prince of Wales: he really forfeited his right to the throne by marrying a Catholic lady, Mrs. Fitzherbert, and he freed himself unscrupulously from the scrape by uttering a lie.

And so again with munificence; the greater part of these knights and courtiers were entirely thoughtless of the value of money. At the Field of the Cloth of Gold, for instance, whole estates were mortgaged or sold, in order that the owners might outshine all competitors in the brilliancy and quality of their dress. This sort of extravagance makes one man look glad and all his relatives rueful. The fact is that when men thus erred, it was for want of observance of a Christian principle; and if men neglect that observance, it is as little in the power of chivalry as of masonry to mend him. There was "a perfect idea" of chivalry, indeed, but if any knight ever realized it in his own person, he was, simply, nearly a perfect Christian, and would have been still nearer to perfection in the latter character if he had studied the few simple rules of the system of religion rather than the stilted and unsteady ones of romance. The study of the latter, at all events, did not prevent, but in many instances caused a dissoluteness of manners, a fondness for war rather than peace, and a wide distinction between classes, making aristocrats of the few, and villains of the many.

Let me add here, as I have been speaking of the romance of "Lancelot du Lac," that I quite agree with Montluc, who after completing his chronicle of the History of France, observed that it would be found more profitable reading than either Lancelot or Amadis. La Noue especially condemns the latter as corrupting the manners of the age. Southey, again, observes that these chivalric romances acquired their poison in France or in Italy. The Spanish and Portuguese romances he describes as free from all taint. In the Amadis the very well-being of the world is made to rest upon chivalry. "What would become of the world," it is asked in the twenty-second book of the Amadis, "if God did not provide for the defence of the weak and helpless against unjust usurpers? And how could provision be made, if good knights were satisfied to do nothing else but sit in chamber with the ladies? What would then the world become, but a vast community of brigands?"

Lamotte Levayer was of a different opinion. "Les armes," he says, when commenting upon chivalry and arms generally; "Les armes detruisent tous les arts excepté ceux qui favorisent la gloire."

In Germany, too, where chivalry was often turned to the oppression of the weak rather than employed for their protection, the popular contempt and dread of "knightly principles" were early illustrated in the proverb, "Er will Ritter an mir werden," He wants to play the knight over me. In which proverb, knight stands for oppressor or insulter. In our own country the order came to be little cared for, but on different grounds.

Dr. Nares in his "Heraldic Anomalies," deplores the fact that mere knighthood has fallen into contempt. He dates this from the period when James I. placed baronets above knights. The hereditary title became a thing to be coveted, but knights who were always held to be knights bachelors, could not of course bequeath a title to child or children who were not supposed in heraldry to exist. The Doctor quotes Sir John Ferne, to show that Olibion, the son of Asteriel, of the line of Japhet, was the first knight ever created. The personage in question was sent forth to battle, after his sire had smitten him lightly nine times with Japhet's falchion, forged before the flood. There is little doubt but that originally a knight was simply *Knecht*, servant of the king. Dr. Nares says that the Thanes were so in the north, and that these, although of gentle blood, exercised the offices even of cooks and barbers to the royal person. But may not these offices have been performed by the "unter Thans," or deputies? I shall have occasion to observe, subsequently, on the law which deprived a knight's descendants of his arms, if they turned merchants; but in Saxon times it is worthy of observation, that if a merchant made three voyages in one of his own ships, he was thenceforward the Thane's right-worthy, or equal.

Among the Romans a blow on the ear gave the slave freedom. Did the blow on the shoulder given to a knight make a free-servant of him? Something of the sort seems to have been intended. The title was doubtless mainly but not exclusively military. To dub, from the Saxon word *dubban*, was either to gird or put on, "don," or was to *strike*, and perhaps both may be meant, for the knight was girt with spurs, as well as stricken, or *geschlagen* as the German term has it.

There was striking, too, at the unmaking of a knight. His heels were then degraded of their spurs, the latter being beaten or chopped away. "His heels deserved it," says Bertram of the cowardly Parolles, "his heels deserved it for usurping of his spurs so long." The sword, too, on such occasions, was broken.

Fuller justly says that "the plainer the coat is, the more ancient and honorable." He adds, that "two colors are necessary and most highly honorable: three are very highly honorable; *four* commendable; *five* excusable; more disgraceful." He must have been a gastronomic King-at-Arms, who so loaded a "coat" with fish, flesh, and fowl, that an observer remarked, "it was well victualled enough to stand a siege." *Or* is the richest coloring, but, as Fuller again says, "Herbs *vert*, being natural, are better than *Or*." He describes a "*Bend* as the best *ordinary*, being a belt athwart," but a coat bruised with a bar sinister is hardly a distinction to be proud of. If the heralds of George the Second's time looked upon that monarch as the son of Count Königsmark, as Jacobite-minded heralds may have been malignant enough to do, they no doubt mentally drew the degrading bar across the royal arms, and tacitly denied the knighthood conferred by what they, in such foolish case, would have deemed an illegitimate hand.

Alluding to reasons for some bearings, Fuller tells us that, "whereas the Earls of Oxford anciently gave their 'coats' plain, quarterly *gules* and *or*, they took afterward in the first a *mullet* or *star-argent*, because the chief of the house had a falling-star, as it was said, alighting on his shield as he was fighting in the Holy Land."

It is to be observed that when treating of precedency, Fuller places knights, or "soldiers" with seamen, civilians, and physicians, and after saints, confessors, prelates, statesmen, and judges. Knights and physicians he seems to have considered as equally terrible to life; but in his order of placing he was led by no particular principle, for among the lowest he places "learned writers," and "benefactors to the public." He has, indeed, one principle, as may be seen, wherein he says, "I place first princes, good manners obliging all other persons to follow them, as religion obliges me to follow God's example by a royal recognition of that original precedency, which he has granted to his vicegerents."

The Romans are said to have established the earliest known order of knighthood; and the members at one time wore rings, as a mark of distinction, as in later times knights wore spurs. The knights of the Holy Roman Empire were members of a modern order, whose sovereigns are not, what they would have themselves considered, descendants of the Cæsars. If we only knew what our own Round Table was, and where it stood, we should be enabled to speak more decisively upon the question of the chevaliers who sat around it. But it is undecided whether the table was not really a house. At it, or in it, the knights met during the season of Pentecost, but whether the assembly was collected at Winchester or Windsor no one seems able to determine; and he would impart no particularly valuable knowledge even if he could.

Knighthood was a sort of nobility worth having, for it testified to the merit of the wearer. An inherited title should, indeed, compel him who succeeds to it, to do nothing to disgrace it: but preserving the lustre is not half so meritorious as creating it. *Knights bachelors* were so called because the distinction was conferred for some act of *personal* courage, to reward for which the offspring of the knight could make no claim. He was, in this respect, to them as though he had been never married. The knight bachelor was a truly proud man. The word *knecht* simply implied a servant, sworn to continue good service in honor of the sovereign, and of God and St. George. "I remain your sworn servant" is a form of epistolary valediction which crept into the letters of other orders in later times. The manner of making was more theatrical than at the present time; and we should now smile if we were to see, on a lofty scaffold in St. Paul's, a city gentleman seated in a chair of silver adorned with green silk, undergoing exhortation from the bishop, and carried up between two lords, to be dubbed under the sovereign's hand, a good knight, by the help of Heaven and his patron saint.

In old days belted earls could create knights. In modern times, the only subject who is legally entitled to confer the honor of chivalry is the Lord Lieutenant of Ireland; and some of his "subjects" consider it the most terrible of his privileges. The attempt to dispute the right arose, perhaps, from those who dreaded the exercise of it on themselves. However this may be, it is certain that the *vexata questio* was finally set at rest in 1823, when the judges declared that the power in question undoubtedly resided in the Lords Lieutenant, since the Union, as it did in the viceroys who reigned vicariously previous to that period. According to the etiquette of heraldry, the distinctive appellation "Sir" should never be omitted even when the knight is a noble of the first hereditary rank. "The Right Honorable Sir Hugh Percy, Duke of Northumberland," would have been the proper heraldic defining of his grace when he became Knight of the Garter, for it is a rule that "the greater dignity doth never drown the lesser, but both stand together in one person."

A knight never surrendered his sword but to a knight. "Are you knight and gentleman?" asked Suffolk, when, four hundred years ago, he yielded to Regnault: "I am a gentleman," said Regnault, "but I am not yet a knight." Whereupon Suffolk bade him kneel, dubbed him knight, received the accustomed oaths, and then gave up his old sword to the new chevalier.

Clark considered that the order was degraded from its exclusively military character, when membership was conferred upon gownsmen, physician, burghers, and artists. He considered that civil merit, so distinguished, was a loss of reputation to military knights. The logic by which he arrives at such a conclusion is rather of the loosest. It may be admitted, however, that the matter has been specially abused in Germany. Monsieur About, that clever gentleman, who wrote "Tolla" out of somebody else's book, very pertinently remarks in his review of the fine-art department of the Paris Exhibition, that the difference between English and German artists is, that the former are well-paid, but that very few of them are knights, while the latter are ill-paid and consequently ill-clothed; but, for lack of clothes, have abundance of ribands.

Dr. Nares himself is of something of the opinion of Clark, and he ridicules the idea of a chivalric and martial title being given to brewers, silversmiths, attorneys, apothecaries, upholsterers, hosiers, tailors, &c. He asserts that knighthood should belong only to military members: but of these no inconsiderable number would have to be unknighted, or would have to wait an indefinite time for the honor were the old rule strictly observed, whereby no man was entitled to the rank and degree of knighthood, who had not actually been in battle and captured a prisoner with his own hands. With respect to the obligation on knights to defend and maintain all ladies, gentlewomen, widows, and orphans; the one class of men may be said to be just as likely to fulfil this obligation, as the other class.

France, Italy, and Germany, long had their forensic knights, certain titles at the bar giving equal privileges; and the obligations above alluded to were supposed to be observed by these knights—who found esquires in their clerks, in the forensic war which they were for ever waging in defence of right. Unhappily these forensic chevaliers so often fought in defence of wrong and called it right, that the actual duty was indiscriminately performed or neglected.

It has often been said of "orders" that they are indelible. However this may be with the clergy, it is especially the case with knights. To whatever title a knight might attain, duke, earl, or baron, he never ceased to be a knight. In proof too that the latter title was considered one of augmentation, is cited the case of Louis XI., who, at his coronation, was knighted by Philip, Duke of Burgundy. "If Louis," says an eminent writer (thus cited by Dr. Nares), "had been made duke, marquis, or earl, it would have detracted from him, all those titles being in himself."

The crown, when it stood in need of the chivalrous arms of its knights, called for the required feudal service, not from its earls as such, but from its barons. To every earldom was annexed a barony, whereby their feudal service with its several dependent duties was alone ascertained. "That is," says Berington, in his Henry II., "the tenure of barony and not of earldom constituted the legal vassal of the crown. Each earl was at the same time a baron, as were the bishops and some abbots and priors of orders."

Some of these barons were the founders of parish churches, but the terms on which priest and patron occasionally lived may be seen in the law, whereby patrons or feudatarii killing the rector, vicar, or clerk of their church, or mutilating him, were condemned to lose their rights; and their posterity, to the fourth generation, was made incapable of benefice or prelacy in religious houses. The knightly patron was bound to be of the same religious opinions, of course, as his priest, or his soul had little chance of being prayed for. In later times we have had instances of patrons determining the opinions of the minister. Thus as a parallel, or rather in contrast with measures as they stood between Sir Knight and Sir Priest, may be taken a passage inserted in the old deeds of the Baptist chapel at Oulney. In this deed the managers or trustees injoined that "no person shall ever be chosen pastor of this church, who shall differ in his religious sentiments from the Rev. John Gibbs of Newcastle. It is rather a leap to pass thus from the baronial knights to the Baptist chapels, but the matter has to do with my subject at both extremities. Before leaving it I will notice the intimation proudly made on the tombstone in Bunhill Fields Cemetery, of Dame Mary Page, relict of Sir George Page. The lady died more than a century and a quarter ago, and although the stone bears no record of any virtue save that she was patient and fearless under suffering, it takes care to inform all passers-by, that this knight's lady, "in sixty-seven months was tapped sixty-six times, and had taken away two hundred and forty gallons of water, without ever repining at her case, or ever fearing its operation." I prefer the mementoes of knight's ladies in olden times which recorded their deeds rather than their diseases, and which told of them, as White said of Queen Mary, that their "knees were hard with kneeling."

I will add one more incident, before changing the topic, having reference as it has to knights, maladies, and baptism. In 1660, Sir John Floyer was the most celebrated knight-physician of his day. He chiefly tilted against the disuse of baptismal immersion. He did not treat the subject theologically, but in a sanitary point of view. He prophesied that England would return to the practice as soon as people were convinced that cold baths were safe and useful. He denounced the first innovators who departed from immersion, as the destroyers of the health of their children and of posterity. Degeneracy of race, he said, had followed, hereditary diseases increased, and men were mere carpet-knights unable to perform such lusty deeds as their duly-immersed forefathers.

There are few volumes which so admirably illustrate what knights *should* be, and what they sometimes were *not*, as De Joinville's Chronicle of the Crusades of St. Louis—that St. Louis, who was himself the patron-saint of an order, the cross of which was at first conferred on princes, and at last on perruquiers. The faithful chronicler rather profanely, indeed, compares the royal knight with God himself. "As God died for his people, so did St. Louis often peril his life, and incurred the greatest dangers, for the people of his kingdom." After all, this simile is as lame as it is profane. The truth, nevertheless, as it concerns St. Louis, is creditable to the illustrious king, saint, and chevalier. "In his conversation he was remarkably chaste, for I never heard him, at any time, utter an indecent word, nor make use of the devil's name; which, however, now is very commonly uttered by every one, but which I firmly believe, is so far from being agreeable to God, that it is highly displeasing to him." The King St. Louis, mixed water with his wine, and tried to force his knights to follow his example, adding, that "it was a beastly thing for an honorable man to make himself drunk." This was a wise maxim, and one naturally held by a son, whose mother had often declared to him, that "she would rather he was in his grave, than that he should commit a mortal sin." And yet wise as his mother, and wise as her son was, the one could not give wise religious instructors to the latter, nor the latter perceive where their instruction was illogical. That it *was* so, may be discerned in the praise given by De Joinville, to the fact, that the knightly king in his dying moments "called upon God and his saints, and *especially* upon St. James, and St. Genevieve, *as his intercessors.*"

It is interesting to learn from such good authority as De Joinville, the manner in which the knights who followed St. Louis prepared themselves for their crusading mission. "When I was ready to set out, I sent for the Abbot of Cheminon, who was at that time considered as the most discreet man of all the White Monks, to reconcile myself with him. He gave me my scarf, and bound it on me, and likewise put the pilgrim's staff in my hand. Instantly after I quitted the castle of Joinville, without even re-entering it until my return from beyond sea. I made pilgrimages to all the holy places in the neighborhood, such as Bliecourt, St. Urban, and others near to Joinville. I dared never turn my eyes that way, for fear of feeling too great regret, and lest my courage should fail on leaving my two fine children, and my fair castle of Joinville, which I loved in my heart." "One touch of nature makes the whole world kin," and here we have the touch the poet speaks of. Down the Saône and subsequently down the Rhone, the crusaders flock in ample vessels, but not large enough to contain their steeds, which were led by grooms along the banks. When all had re-embarked at Marseilles and were fairly out at sea, "the captain made the priests and clerks mount to the castle of the ship, and chant psalms in praise of God, that he might be pleased to grant us a prosperous voyage." While they were singing the *Veni Creator* in full chorus, the mariners set the sails "in the name of God," and forthwith a favorable breeze sprang up in answer to the appeal, and knights and holy men were speedily careering over the billows of the open sea very hopeful and exceedingly sick. "I must say here," says De Joinville, who was frequently so disturbed by the motion of the vessel, so little of a knight, and so timid on the water as to require a couple of men to hold him as he leant over the side in the helpless and unchivalrous attitude of a cockney landsman on board a Boulogne steamer—"I must say," he exclaims—sick at the very reminiscence, "that he is a great fool who shall put himself in such dangers, having wronged any one, or having any mortal sins on his conscience; for when he goes to sleep in the evening, he knows not if in the morning he may not find himself under the sea."

This was a pious reflection, and it was such as many a knight, doubtless, made on board a vessel, on the castle of which priests and clerks sang *Veni Creator* and the mariners bent the sail "in the name of God." But whether the holy men did not act up to their profession, or the secular knights cared not to profit by their example, certain it is that in spite of the saintly services and formalities on board ship, the chevaliers were no sooner on shore, than they fell into the very worst of practices. De Joinville, speaking of them at Damietta, remarks that the barons, knights, and others, who ought to have practised self-denial and economy, were wasteful of their means, prodigal of their supplies, and addicted to banquetings, and to the vices which attend on over-luxuriant living. There was a general waste of everything, health included. The example set by the knights was adopted by the men-at-arms, and the debauchery which ensued was terrific. The men were reduced to the level of beasts, and wo to the women or girls who fell into their power when out marauding. It is singular to find De Joinville remarking that the holy king was obliged "to wink at the greatest liberties of his officers and men." The picture of a royal saint winking at lust, rapine, and murder, is not an agreeable one. "The good king was told," says the faithful chronicler, "that at a stone's throw round his own pavilion, were several tents whose owners made profit by letting them out for infamous purposes." These tents and tabernacles of iniquity were kept by the king's own personal attendants, and yet the royal saint winked at them! The licentiousness was astounding, the more so as it was practised by Christian knights, who were abroad on a holy purpose, but who went with bloody hands, unclean thoughts, and spiritual songs to rescue the Sepulchre of Christ from the unworthy keeping of the infidel. Is it wonderful that the enterprise was ultimately a failure?

De Joinville himself, albeit purer of life than many of his comrades, was not above taking unmanly advantage of a foe. The rule of chivalry, which directed that all should be fair in fight, was never regarded by those chivalrous gentlemen when victory was to be obtained by violating the law. Thus, of an affair on the plains before Babylon, we find the literary swordsman complacently recording that he " perceived a sturdy Saracen mounting his horse, which was held by one of his esquires by the bridle, and *while he was putting his hand on his saddle to mount*, I gave him," says De Joinville, "such a thrust with my spear, which I pushed as far as I was able, that he fell down dead." This was a base and cowardly action. There was more of the chivalrous in what followed: "The esquire, seeing his lord dead, abandoned master and horse; but, watching my motions, on my return struck me with his lance such a blow between my shoulders as drove me on my horse's neck, and held me there so tightly that I could not draw my sword, which was girthed round me. I was forced to draw another sword which was at the pommel of my saddle, and it was high time; but when he saw I had my sword in my hand, he withdrew his lance, which I had seized, and ran from me."

I have said that this knight who took such unfair advantage of a foe, was more of a Christian nevertheless than many of his fellows. This is illustrated by another trait highly illustrative of the principles which influenced those brave and pious warriors. De Joinville remarks that on the eve of Shrove-tide, 1249, he saw a thing which he "*must* relate." On the vigil of that day, he tells us, there died a very valiant and prudent knight, Sir Hugh de Landricourt, a follower of De Joinville's own banner. The burial service was celebrated; but half-a-dozen of De Joinville's knights, who were present as mourners, talked so irreverently loud that the priest was disturbed as he was saying mass. Our good chronicler went over to them, reproved them, and informed them that "it was unbecoming gentlemen thus to talk while the mass was celebrating." The ungodly half-dozen, thereupon, burst into a roar of laughter, and informed De Joinville, in their turn, that they were discussing as to which of the six should marry the widow of the defunct Sir Hugh, then lying before them on his bier! De Joinville, with decency and common sense "rebuked them sharply, and said such conversation was indecent and improper, for that they had too soon forgotten their companion." From this circumstance De Joinville tries to draw a logical inference, if not conclusion. He makes a sad confusion of causes and effects, rewards and punishments, practice and principle, human accidents and especial interferences on the part of Heaven. For instance, after narrating the mirth of the knights at the funeral of Sir Hugh, and their disputing as to which of them should woo the widow, he adds: "Now it happened on the morrow, when the first grand battle took place, although we may laugh at their follies, that of all the six not one escaped death, and they remained unburied. The wives of the whole six re-married! *This* makes it credible that God leaves no such conduct unpunished. With regard to myself *I fared little better*, for I was grievously wounded in the battle of Shrove Tuesday. I had besides the disorder in my legs and mouth before spoken of, and such a rheum in my head it ran through my mouth and nostrils. In addition I had a double fever called a quartan, from which God defend us! And with these illnesses was I confined to my bed for half of Lent." And thus, if the married knights were retributively slain for talking about the wooing of a comrade's widow, so De Joinville himself was somewhat heavily afflicted for having undertaken to reprove them! I must add one more incident, however, to show how in the battle-field the human and Christian principle was not altogether lost.

The poor priest, whom the wicked and wedded knights had

interrupted in the service of the mass by follies, at which De Joinville himself seems to think that men *may*, perhaps, be inclined to laugh, became as grievously ill as De Joinville himself. "And one day," says the latter, "when he was singing mass before me as I lay in my bed, at the moment of the elevation of the host I saw him so exceedingly weak that he was near fainting; but when I perceived he was on the point of falling to the ground, I flung myself out of bed, sick as I was, and taking my coat, embraced him, and bade him be at his ease, and take courage from Him whom he held in his hand. He recovered some little; but I never quitted him till he had finished the mass, which he completed, and this was the last, for he never celebrated another, but died; God receive his soul!" This is a pleasanter picture of Christian chivalry than any other that is given by this picturesque chronicler.

Chivalry, generally, has been more satirized and sneered at by the philosophers than by any other class of men. The sages stigmatize the knights as mere boasters of bravery, and in some such terms as those used by Dussaute, they assert that the boasters of their valor are as little to be trusted as those who boast of their probity. "Defiez vous de quiconque parle toujours de sa probité comme de quiconque parle toujours de bravoure."

It will not, however, do for the philosophers to sneer at their martial brethren. Now that Professor Jacobi has turned from grave studies for the benefit of mankind, to the making of infernal machines for the destruction of brave and helpless men, at a distance, that very unsuccessful but would-be homicide has, as far as he himself is concerned, reduced science to a lower level than that occupied by men whose trade is arms. But this is not the first time that philosophers have mingled in martial matters. The very war which has been begun by the bad ambition of Russia, may be traced to the evil officiousness of no less a philosopher than Leibnitz. It was this celebrated man who first instigated a European monarch to seize upon a certain portion of the Turkish dominion, whereby to secure an all but universal supremacy.

The monarch was Louis XIV., to whom Leibnitz addressed himself, in a memorial, as to the wisest of sovereigns, most worthy to have imparted to him a project at once the most holy, the most just, and the most easy of accomplishment. Success, adds the philosopher, would secure to France the empire of the seas and of commerce, and make the French king the supreme arbiter of Christendom. Leibnitz at once names Egypt as the place to be seized upon; and after hinting what was necessary, by calling his majesty a "miracle of secresy," he alludes to further achievements by stating of the one in question, that it would cover his name with an immortal glory, for having cleared, whether for himself or his descendants, "the route for exploits similar to those of Alexander."

There is no country in the memorialist's opinion the conquest of which deserves so much to be attempted. As to any provocation on the part of the Turkish sovereign of Egypt, he does not pause to advise the king even to feign having received cause of offence. The philosopher goes through a *resumé* of the history of Egypt, and the successive conquests that had been made of, as well as attempts against it, to prove that its possession was accounted of importance in all times; and he adds that its Turkish master was just then in such debility that France could not desire a more propitious opportunity for invasion. This argument shows that when the Czar Nicholas touched upon this nefarious subject, he not only was ready to rob this same "sick man," the Turk, but he stole his arguments whereby to illustrate his opinions, and to prove that his sentiments were well-founded.

"By a single fortunate blow," says Leibnitz, "empires may be in an instant overthrown and founded. In such wars are found the elements of high power and of an exalted glory." It is unnecessary to repeat all the seductive terms which Leibnitz employs to induce Louis XIV. to set his chivalry in motion against the Turkish power. Egypt he calls "the eye of countries, the mother of grain, the seat of commerce." He hints that Muscovy was even then ready to take advantage of any circumstance that might facilitate her way to the conquest of Turkey. The conquest of Egypt then was of double importance to France. Possessing *that*, France would be mistress of the Mediterranean, of a great part of Africa and Asia, and "the king of France could then, by incontestable right, and with the consent of the Pope, assume the title of Emperor of the East." A further bait held out is, that in such a position he could "hold the pontiffs much more in his power than if they resided at Avignon." He sums up by saying that there would be on the part of the human race, "an everlasting reverence for the memory of the great king to whom so many miracles were due!" "With the exception of the philosopher's stone," finally remarks the philosopher, "I know nothing that can be imagined of more importance than the conquest of Egypt."

Leibnitz enters largely into the means to be employed, in order to insure success; among them is a good share of mendacity; and it must be acknowledged that the spirit of the memorial and its objects, touching not Egypt alone, but the Turkish empire generally, had been well pondered over by the Czar before he made that felonious attempt in which he failed to find a confederate.

The original of the memorial, which is supposed to have been presented to Louis XIV. just previous to his invasion of Holland — and, as some say, more with the intention of diverting the king from his attack on that country, than with any more definite object — was preserved in the archives of Versailles till the period of the great revolution. A copy in the handwriting of Leibnitz was, however, preserved in the Library at Hanover. Its contents were without doubt known to Napoleon when he was meditating that Egyptian conquest which Leibnitz pronounced to be so easy of accomplishment; a copy, made at the instance of Marshal Mortier for the Royal Library in Paris, is now in that collection.

The suggestion of Leibnitz, that the seat, if not of universal monarchy, at least of the mastership of Christendom, was in the Turkish dominions, has never been forgotten by Russia; and it is very possible that some of its seductive argument may have influenced the Czar before he impelled his troops into that war, which showed that Russia, with all its boasted power, could neither take Silistria nor keep Sebastopol.

But in this fragmentary prologue, which began with Lingard and ends with Leibnitz, we have rambled over wide ground. Let us become more orderly, and look at those who were to be made knights.

## THE TRAINING OF PAGES.

> "What callest thou Page? What is its humor?
> Sir; he is *Nobilis ephebus,* and
> *Puer regius,* student of Knighthood,
> Breaking hearts and hoping to break lances."—*Old Play.*

I HAVE in another chapter noticed the circumstance of knighthood conferred on an Irish prince, at so early an age as seven years. This was the age at which, in less precocious England, noble youths entered wealthy knights' families as pages, to learn obedience, to be instructed in the use of weapons, and to acquire a graceful habit of tending on ladies. The poor nobility, especially, found their account in this system, which gave a gratuitous education to their sons, in return for services which were not considered humiliating or dishonorable. These boys served seven years as pages, or varlets—sometimes very impudent varlets—and at fourteen might be regular esquires, and tend their masters where hard blows were dealt and taken—for which encounters they "riveted with a sigh the armor they were forbidden to wear."

Neither pages, varlets, nor household, could be said to have been always as roystering as modern romancers have depicted them. There was at least exceptions to the rule—if there was a rule of roystering. Occasionally, the lads were not indifferently taught before they left their own homes. That is, not indifferently taught for the peculiar life they were about to lead. Even the Borgias, infamous as the name has become through inexorable historians and popular operas, were at one time eminently respectable and exemplarily religious. Thus in the household of the Duke of Gandia, young Francis Borgia, his son, passed his time "among the domestics in wonderful innocence and piety." It was the only season of his life, however, so passed. Marchangy asserts that the pages of the middle ages were often little saints; but this could hardly have been the case since "espiègle comme un page," " hardi comme un page," and other illustrative sayings have survived even the era of pagedom. Indeed, if we may believe the minstrels, and they were often as truth-telling as the annalist, the pages were now and then even more knowing and audacious than their masters. When the Count Ory was in love with the young Abbess of Farmoutier, he had recourse to his page for counsel.

> "Hola! mon page, venez me conseiller,
> L'amour me berce, je ne puis sommeiller;
> Comment me prendre pour dans ce couvent entrer?"

How ready was the ecstatic young scamp with his reply :—

> "Sire il faut prendre quatorze chevaliers,
> Et tous en nonnes il vous les faut habiller,
> Puis, à nuit close, à la porte il faut heurter."

What came of this advice, the song tells in very joyous terms, for which the reader may be referred to that grand collection the "Chants et Chansons de la France."

On the other hand, Mr. Kenelm Digby, who is, be it said in passing, a painter of pages, looking at his object through pink-colored glasses, thus writes of these young gentlemen, in his "Mores Catholici."

"Truly beautiful does the fidelity of chivalrous youth appear in the page of history or romance. Every master of a family in the middle ages had some young man in his service who would have rejoiced to shed the last drop of his blood to save him, and who, like Jonathan's armor-bearer, would have replied to his summons: 'Fac omnia quæ placent animo tuo; perge quo cupis; et ero tecum ubicumque volueris.' When Gyron le Courtois resolved to proceed on the adventure of the *Passage perilleux*, we read that the valet, on hearing the frankness and courtesy with which his lord spoke to him, began to weep abundantly, and said, all in tears, 'Sire, know that my heart tells me that sooth, if you proceed further, you will never return; that you will either perish there, or you will remain in prison; but, nevertheless, nothing shall prevent me going with you. Better die with you, if it be God's will, than leave you in such guise to save my own life;' and so saying, he stepped forward and said, 'Sire, since you will not return according to my advice, I will not leave you this time, come to me what may.' Authority in the houses of the middle ages," adds Mr. Digby, "was always venerable. The very term *seneschal* is supposed to have implied 'old knight,' so that, as with the Greeks, the word signifying 'to honor,' and to 'pay respect,' was derived immediately from that which denoted old age, πρεσβεύω being thus used in the first line of the Eumenides. Even to those who were merely attached by the bonds of friendship or hospitality, the same lessons and admonitions were considered due. John Francis Picus of Mirandola mentions his uncle's custom of frequently admonishing his friends, and exhorting them to a holy life. 'I knew a man,' he says, 'who once spoke with him on the subject of manners, and who was so much moved by only two words from him, which alluded to the death of Christ, as the motive for avoiding sin, that from that hour, he renounced the ways of vice, and reformed his whole life and manner.'"

We smile to find Mr. Digby mentioning the carving of angels in stone over the castle-gates, as at Vincennes, as a proof that the pages who loitered about there were little saints. But we read with more interest, that "the Sieur de Ligny led Bayard home with him, and in the evening preached to him as if he had been his own son, recommending him to have heaven always before his eyes." This is good, and that it had its effect on Bayard, we all know; nevertheless that chevalier himself was far from perfect.

With regard to the derivation of *Seneschal* as noticed above, we may observe that it implies "old man of skill." Another word connected with arms is "Marshal," which is derived from *Mar*, "a horse," and *Schalk*, "skilful," one knowing in horses; hence "Maréchal ferrant," as assumed by French farriers. *Schalk*, however, I have seen interpreted as meaning "servant." Earl Marshal was, originally, the knight who looked after the royal horses and stables, and all thereto belonging.

But to return to the subject of education. If all the sons of noblemen, in former days, were as well off for gentle teachers as old historians and authors describe them to have been, they undoubtedly had a great advantage over some of their descendants of the present day. In illustration of this fact it is only necessary to point to the sermons recently delivered by a reverend pedagogue to the boys who have the affliction of possessing him as headmaster. It is impossible to read some of these whipping sermons, without a feeling of intense disgust. Flagellation is there hinted at, mentioned, menaced, caressed as it were, as if in the very idea there was a sort of delight. The worst passage of all is where the amiable master tells his youthful hearers that they are noble by birth, that the greatest humiliation to a noble person is the infliction of a blow, and that nevertheless, he, the absolute master, may have to flog many of them. How the young people over whom he rules, must love such an instructor! The circumstance reminds me of the late Mr. Ducrow, who was once teaching a boy to go through a difficult act of horsemanship, in the character of a page. The boy was timid, and his great master applied the whip to him unmercifully. Mr. Joseph Grimaldi was standing by, and looked very serious, considering his vocation. "You see," remarked Ducrow to Joey, "that it is quite necessary to *make an impression* on these young fellows."—"Very likely," answered Grimaldi, dryly, "but it can hardly be necessary to make *the whacks* so hard!"

The discipline to which pages were subjected in the houses of knights and noblemen, does not appear to have been at all of a severe character. Beyond listening to precept from the chaplain, heeding the behests of their master, and performing pleasant duties about their mistress, they seem to have been left pretty much to themselves, and to have had, altogether, a pleasant time of it. The poor scholars had by far a harder life than your "Sir page." And this stern discipline held over the pale student continued down to a very recent, that is, a comparatively recent period. In Neville's play of "The Poor Scholar," written in 1662, but never acted, the character of student-life at college is well illustrated. The scene lies at the university, where Eugenes, jun., albeit he is called "the poor scholar," is nephew of Eugenes, sen., who is president of a college. Nephew and uncle are at feud, and the man in authority imprisons his young kinsman, who contrives to escape from du-rance vile, and to marry a maiden called Morphe. The fun of the marriage is, that the young couple disguise themselves as country lad and lass, and the reverend Eugenes, sen., unconsciously couples a pair whom he would fain have kept apart. There are two other university marriages as waggishly contrived; and when the ceremonies are concluded, one of the newly-married students, bold as any page, impudently remarks to the duped president, "Our names are out of the butteries, and our persons out of your dominions." The phrase shows that, in the olden time, an "ingenuus puer" at Oxford, if he were desirous of escaping censure, had only to take his name off the books. But there were worse penalties than mere censure. The author of "The Poor Scholar" makes frequent allusion to the whipping of undergraduates, stretched on a barrel, in the buttery. There was long an accredited tradition that Milton had been thus degraded. In Neville's play, one of the young Benedicks, prematurely married, remarks, "Had I been once in the butteries, they'd have their rods about me." To this remark Eugenes, jun., adds another in reference to his uncle the president, "He would have made thee ride on a barrel, and made you show your fat cheeks." But it is clear that even this terrible penalty could be avoided by young gentlemen, if they had their wits about them; for the fearless Aphobos makes boast, "My name is cut out of the college butteries, and I have now no title to the mounting a barrel."

Young scions of noble houses, in the present time, have to endure more harsh discipline than is commonly imagined. They are treated rather like the buttery undergraduates of former days, than the pages who, in ancient castles, learned the use of arms, served the Chatellaine, and invariably fell in love with the daughters. They who doubt this fact have only to read those Whipping Sermons to which I have referred. Such discourses, in days of old, to a body of young pages, would probably have cost the preacher more than he cared to lose. In these days, such sermons can hardly have won affection for their author. The latter, no doubt, honestly thought he was in possession of a vigorously salubrious principle; but there is something ignoble both in the discipline boasted of, and especially in the laying down the irresistible fact to young gentlemen that a blow was the worst offence that could be inflicted on persons of their class, but that *he* could and would commit such assault upon them, and that gentle and noble as they were, they dared not resent it!"

The pages of old time occasionally met with dreadful harsh treatment from their chivalrous master. The most chivalrous of these Christian knights could often act cowardly and unchristianlike. I may cite, as an instance, the case of the great and warlike Duke of Burgundy, on his defeat at Muret. He was hemmed in between ferocious enemies and the deep lake. As the lesser of two evils, he plunged into the latter, and his young page leaped upon the crupper as the Duke's horse took the water. The stout steed bore his double burden across, a breadth of two miles, not without difficulty, yet safely. The Duke was, perhaps, too alarmed himself, at first, to know that the page was hanging on behind; but when the panting horse reached the opposite shore, sovereign Burgundy was so wroth at the idea that the boy, by clinging to his steed, had put the life of the Duke in peril, that he turned upon him and poignarded the poor lad upon the beach. Lassels, who tells the story, very aptly concludes it with the scornful yet serious ejaculation, "Poor Prince! thou mightest have given another offering of thanksgiving to God for thy escape, than this!" But "Burgundy" was rarely gracious or humane. "Carolus Pugnax," says Burton, in his Anatomy of Melancholy, "made Henry Holland, late Duke of Exeter, exiled, run after his horse, like a lackey, and would take no notice of him." This was the English peer who was reduced to beg his way in the cities of Flanders.

Of pages generally, we shall have yet to speak incidentally— meanwhile, let us glance at their masters at home.

## KNIGHTS AT HOME.

"Entrez Messieurs; jouissez-vous de mon coin-de-feu. Me voilà, chez moi!"—*Arlequin à St. Germains.*

RITTER ERIC, of Lansfeldt, remarked, that next to a battle he dearly loved a banquet. We will, therefore, commence the "Knight at Home," by showing him at table. Therewith, we may observe, that the Knights of the Round Table appear generally to have had very solid fare before them. King Arthur— who is the reputed founder of this society, and who invented the table in order that when all his knights were seated none could claim precedency over the others—is traditionally declared to have been the first man who ever sat down to a whole roasted ox. Mr. Bickerstaff, in the "Tatler," says that "this was certainly the best way to preserve the gravy;" and it is further added, that "he and his knights set about the ox at his round table, and usually consumed it to the very bones before they would enter upon any debate of moment."

They had better fare than the knights-errant, who

> "as some think,
> Of old, did neither eat nor drink,
> Because when thorough deserts vast,
> And regions desolate they passed,
> Where belly-timber above ground,
> Or under, was not to be found,
> Unless they grazed, there's not one word
> Of their provision on record:
> Which made some confidently write,
> They had no stomachs but to fight."

This, however, is only one poet's view of the dietary of the errant gentlemen of old. Pope is much nearer truth when he says, that—

> "In days of old our fathers went to war,
> Expecting sturdy blows and scanty fare,
> Their beef they often in their morion stewed,
> And in their basket-hilt their beverage brewed."

—that basket-hilt of which it is so well said in Hudibras, that—

> "it would hold broth,
> And serve for fight and dinner both."

The lords and chivalric gentlemen who fared so well and fought so stoutly, were not always of the gentlest humor at home. It has been observed that Piedmontese society long bore traces of the chivalric age. An exemplification is afforded us in Gallenga's History of Piedmont. It will serve to show how absolute a master a powerful knight and noble was in his own house. Thus, from Gallenga we learn that Antonio Grimaldi, a nobleman of Chieri, had become convinced of the faithlessness of his wife. He compelled her to hang up with her own hand her paramour to the ceiling of her chamber; then he had the chamber walled up, doors and windows, and only allowed the wretched woman as much air and light, and administered with his own hand as much food and drink, as would indefinitely prolong her agony. And so he watched her, and tended her with all that solicitude which hatred can suggest as well as love, and left her to grope alone in that blind solitude, with the mute testimony of her guilt—a ghastly object on which her aching eyes were riveted, day by day, night after night, till it had passed through every loathsome stage of decomposition. This man was surely worse in his vengeance than that Sir Giles de Laval, who has come down to us under the name of Blue-Beard.

This celebrated personage, famous by his pseudonym, was not less so in his own proper person. There was not a braver knight in France, during the reigns of Charles VI. and VII., than this Marquis de Laval, Marshal of France. The English feared him almost as much as they did the Pucelle. The household of this brave gentleman was, however, a hell upon earth; and licentiousness, blasphemy, attempts at sorcery, and, more than attempts at, very successful realizations of, murder were the little foibles of this man of many wives. He excelled the most extravagant monarchs in his boundless profusion, and in the barbaric splendor of his court or house: the latter was thronged with ladies of very light manners, players, mountebanks, pretended magicians, and as many cooks as Julian found in the palace of his predecessor at Constantinople. There were two hundred saddle-horses in his stable, and he had a greater variety of dogs than could now be found at any score of "fanciers" of that article. He employed the magicians for a double purpose. They undertook to discover treasures for his use, and pretty handmaids to tend on his illustrious person, or otherwise amuse him by the display of their accomplishments. Common report said that these young persons were slain after a while, their blood being of much profit in making incantations, the object of which was the discovery of gold. Much exaggeration magnified his misdeeds, which were atrocious enough in their plain, unvarnished infamy. At length justice overtook this monster. She did not lay hold of him for his crimes against society, but for a peccadillo which offended the Duke of Brittany. Giles de Laval, for this offence, was burnt at Nantes, after being strangled—such mercy having been vouchsafed to him, because he was a gallant knight and gentleman, and of course was not to be burnt alive like any petty villain of peasant degree. He had a moment of weakness at last, and just previous to the rope being tightened round his neck, he publicly declared that he should never have come to that pass, nor have committed so many excesses, had it not been for his wretched education. Thus are men, shrewd enough to drive bargains, and able to discern between virtue and vice, ever ready, when retribution falls on them at the scaffold, to accuse their father, mother, schoolmaster, or spiritual pastor. Few are like the knight of the road, who, previous to the cart sliding from under him, at Tyburn, remarked that he had the satisfaction, at least, of knowing that the position he had attained in society was owing entirely to himself. "May I be hanged," said he, "if that isn't the fact." The finisher of the law did not stop to argue the question with him, but, on cutting him down, remarked, with the gravity of a cardinal before breakfast, that the gentleman had wronged the devil and the ladies, in attributing his greatness so exclusively to his own exertions.

I have said that perhaps Blue-Beard's little foibles have been exaggerated; but, on reflection, I am not sure that this pleasant hypothesis can be sustained. De Laval, of whom more than I have told may be found in Mezeray, was not worse than the Landvogt Hugenbach, who makes so terrible a figure in Barante's " Dukes of Burgundy." The Landvogt, we are told by the last-named historian, cared no more for heaven than he did for anybody on earth. He was accustomed to say that being perfectly sure of going to the devil, he would take especial care to deny himself no gratification that he could possibly desire. There was, accordingly, no sort of wild fancy to which he did not surrender himself. He was a fiendish corruptor of virtue, employing money, menaces, or brutal violence, to accomplish his ends. Neither cottage nor convent, citizen's hearth nor noble's château, was secure from his invasion and atrocity. He was terribly hated, terribly feared—but then Sir Landvogt Hugenbach gave splendid dinners, and every family round went to them, while they detested the giver.

He was remarkably facetious on these occasions, sometimes ferociously so. For instance, Barante records of him, that at one of his pleasant soirées he sent away the husbands into a room apart, and kept the wives together in his grand saloon. These, he and his myrmidons despoiled entirely of their dresses; after which, having flung a covering over the head of each lady, who dared not, for her life, resist, the amiable host called in the husbands one by one, and bade each select his own wife. If the husband made a mistake, he was immediately seized and flung headlong down the staircase. The Landvogt made no more scruple about it than Lord Ernest Vane when he served the Windsor manager after something of the same fashion. The husbands who guessed rightly were conducted to the sideboard to receive congratulations, and drink various flasks of wine thereupon. But the amount of wine forced upon each unhappy wretch was so immense, that in a short time he was as near death as the mangled husbands, who were lying in a senseless heap at the foot of the staircase.

They who would like to learn further of this respectable individual, are referred to the pages of Barante. They will find there that this knight and servant of the Duke of Burgundy was more like an incarnation of the devil than aught besides. His career was frightful for its stupendous cruelty and crime; but it ended on the scaffold, nevertheless. His behavior there was like that of a saint who felt a little of the human infirmity of irritability at being treated as a very wicked personage by the extremely blind justice of men. So edifying was this chivalrous scoundrel, that the populace fairly took him for the saint he figured to be; and long after his death, crowds flocked to his tomb to pray for his mediation between them and God.

The rough jokes of the Landvogt remind me of a much greater man than he — Gaston de Foix, in whose earlier times there was no lack of rough jokes, too. The portrait of Gaston, with his page helping to buckle on his armor, by Giorgione da Castel Franco, is doubtless known to most of my readers — through the engraving, if not the original. It was formerly the property of the Duke of Orleans; but came, many years ago, into the possession, by purchase, of Lord Carlisle. The expression of the page or young squire who is helping to adjust Gaston's armor is admirably rendered. That of the hero gives, perhaps, too old a look to a knight who is known to have died young.

This Gaston was a nephew of Louis XII. His titles were Duke of Nemours and Count d'Etampes. He was educated by his mother, the sister of King Louis. She exulted in Gaston as one who was peculiarly her own work. "Considering," she says, "how honor became her son, she was pleased to let him seek danger where he was likely to find fame." His career was splendid, but proportionally brief. He purchased imperishable renown, and a glorious death, in Italy. He gained the victory of Ravenna, at the cost of his life; after which event, fortune abandoned the standard of Louis; and Maximilian Sforza recovered the Milanese territories of his father, Ludovic. This was early in the sixteenth century.

But it is of another Gaston de Foix that I have to speak. I have given precedence to one bearer of the name, because he was the worthier man; but the earlier hero will afford us better illustrations of the home-life of the noble knights who were sovereigns within their own districts. Froissart makes honorable mention of him in his "Chronicle." He was Count de Foix, and kept court at Ortez, in the south of France. There assembled belted knights and aspiring 'squires, majestic matrons and dainty damsels. When the Count was not on a war-path, his house was a scene of great gayety. The jingle of spurs, clash of swords, tramp of iron heels, virelays sung by men-at-arms, love-songs hummed by audacious pages, and romances entoned to the lyre by minstrels who were masters in the art—these, with courtly feasts and stately dances, made of the castle at Ortez anything but a dull residence. Hawking and hunting seem to have been "my very good Erle's" favorite diversion. He was not so much master of his passions as he was of his retainers; and few people thought the worse of him simply because he murdered his cousin for refusing to betray his trust, and cut the throat of the only legitimate son of the Earl.

We may form some idea of the practical jests of those days, from an anecdote told by Froissart. Gaston de Foix had complained, one cold day, of the scanty fire which his retainers kept up in the great gallery. Whereupon one of the knights descended to the court-yard, where stood several asses laden with wood. One of them he seized, wood and ass together, and staggering up-stairs into the gallery, flung the whole, the ass heels uppermost, on to the fire. "Whereof," says Froissart, "the Earl of Foix had great joy, and so had all they that were there, and had marvel of his strength, how he alone came up all the stairs with the ass and the wood on his neck."

Gaston was but a lazy knight. It was high noon, Froissart tells us, before he rose from his bed. He supped at midnight; and when he issued from his chamber to proceed to the hall where supper was laid, twelve torches were carried before him, and these were held at his table "by twelve varlets" during the time that supper lasted. The Earl sat alone, and none of the knights or squires who crowded round the other tables dared to speak a word to him unless the great man previously addressed him. The supper then must have been a dull affair.

The treasurer of the Collegiate Church of Chimay relates in a very delicate manner how Gaston came to murder his little son. Gaston's wife was living apart from her husband, at the court of her brother, the King of Navarre, and the "little son" in question was residing there on a visit to his mother. As he was on the point of returning, the king of Navarre gave him a powder, which he directed the boy to administer to his father, telling him that it was a love-powder, and would bring back his father's affection for the mother. The innocent boy took the powder, which was in fact poison; and a night or two after his return to Ortez, an illegitimate son of Gaston found it in the boy's clothes. The baseborn lad informed against his brother, and when Gaston had given the powder to a dog, which immediately died, he could scarcely be kept from poniarding his son upon the spot. The poor child was flung into a dungeon, where, between terror and despair, he refused to take any food. Upon being told of this, the earl entered the chamber in which the boy was confined, " he had at the same time a little knife in his hand, to pare withal his nails . . . . In great displeasure he thrust his hand at his son's throat, and the point of his knife a little entered into his throat into a certain vein; and the earl said, 'Ah, traitor, why dost thou not eat thy meat?' and therewith the earl departed without any more doing or saying." Never was brutal murder more daintily glozed over, but Froissart is so afraid that he may not have sufficiently impressed you with a conviction of its being a little accident, that he goes on to say "The child was abashed, and afraid of the coming of his father, and was also feeble of fasting, and the point of the knife a little entered into his throat, into a certain vein of his throat; and so [he] fell down suddenly *and died!*"

The rascally sire was as jolly after the deed as before it; but he too one day "fell down suddenly and died." He had overheated himself with hunting, and in that condition bathed in cold water as soon as he reached home. The description of the whole of this domestic scene is one of the most graphic in Froissart, but it is too long for quotation. It must suffice that the vast possessions of the count fell into the hands of that villanous illegitimate son, Sir Jenbayne de Foix. The latter was one of the six knights who, with Charles VI., entered a ball-room disguised as satyrs, and fast chained together. Some one, who is supposed to have owed no good-will to the king, flung a torch into the group. Their inflammable dresses immediately caught fire, and Sir Jenbayne de

Foix was one of those who was burned to death. The king himself, as is well known, had a very narrow escape.

Perhaps one of the chief home pleasures enjoyed by knights when not engaged in war, was the pleasure of the chase. Idle country gentlemen now resemble their chivalrous ancestors in this respect, and for want of or distaste for other vocations, spend three fourths of their rural time in the fields. In the old days too, as ever, there were clerical gentlemen very much addicted to hunting and moreover not less so to trespassing. These were not reverend rectors on their own thorough-breds, or curates on borrowed ponies, but dignified prelates—even archbishops. One of the latter, Edmund, archbishop of Canterbury, in the beginning of the thirteenth century, presumed to hunt without permission, on the grounds of a young knight, the Earl of Arundel, a minor. On the day the Earl came of age, he issued a prohibition against the archiepiscopal trespasser, and the latter in return snapped his fingers at the earl, and declared that his way was as legally open to any chase as it was free into any church. Accordingly, the right reverend gentleman issued forth as usual, with hounds and horses, and a "numerous meet" of clerical friends and other followers, glad to hunt in such company. Their sport, however, was spoiled by the retainers of the young earl. These, in obedience to their master's orders, called off the dogs, unstopped the earths, warned off the riders, and laughed at the ecclesiastical thunder of the prelate, flung at them in open field. Edmund, finding it impossible to overcome the opposition of the men, addressed himself to the master, summarily devoting him *ad inferos* for daring to interfere with the prelatic pastimes. Nothing daunted, the young earl, who would gladly have permitted the archbishop to hunt in his company, whenever so disposed, but who would not allow the head of the church in England to act in the woods of Arundel as as if he were also lord of the land, made appeal to the only competent court—that of the Pope. The contending parties went over and pleaded their most respective causes personally; the earl with calmness, as feeling that he had right on his side; Edmund with easy arrogance, springing from a conviction that the Pontiff would not give a layman a triumph over a priest. The archbishop, however, was mistaken. He not only lost his cause, but he was condemned in the expenses; and if any one thinks that this decree checked him in trespassing, such an idea would show that the holder of it knew little of the spirit which moved prelates fond of hunting. The archbishop became the most confirmed poacher in the country; and if he did not spoil the knight's sport by riding in advance of the hounds with a red herring, he had resort to means as efficacious for marring the pleasures of others in the chase. He affected, too, to look down upon the earl as one inferior to him in degree, and when they encountered at court, the prelate exhibited no more courtesy toward the gallant knight than was manifested by Lord Cowley in Paris toward the English Exhibition Commissioners, when the mere men of intellect were kept at what the peer thought a proper distance by the mere men of rank.

There is, however, no lack of instances of young knights themselves being brought up in arrogance and wilfulness. This sort of education lasted longer, perhaps, in France than elsewhere. As late as the last century this instruction prevailed, particularly where the pupil was intended for the army. Thus, the rearing of the little Vidame d'Amiens affords us an illustration. He was awkward and obstinate, but he might have been cured of both defects, had his mother been permitted to have some voice in his education. She was the last to be consulted, or rather, was never consulted at all. The more the little man was arrogant, the more delighted were his relatives with such manifestation of his spirit; and one day, when he dealt to his aunt, the Marquise de Belliere Plessis, a box of the ear which sent the old lady staggering, her only remark was, "My dear, you should never strike me with the left hand." The courteous Vidame mortally hated his tutor, and expressed such a desire to kill him, that the pedagogue was asked to allow the little savage to believe that he had accomplished the desired act of homicide. Accordingly, a light musket was placed in the boy's hands, from which the ball had been drawn, unknown to him, and with this, coming suddenly upon his instructor, who feigned the surprise he did not feel, the Vidame discharged the piece full at the breast of his monitor and friend.. The servile sage pretended to be mortally wounded, and acted death upon the polished floor. He was quietly got rid of, and a pension of four hundred francs, just sixteen pounds a year, rewarded his stupid servility. The little chevalier was as proud as Fighting Fitzgerald of having, as he supposed, "killed his man."

Let us return to earlier times for illustrations of the knight at home, and also abroad. There is no lack of such illustration in the adventures of Fulke Fitzwarren. Fulke was one of the outlawed barons of the reign of King John. In his youth, he was brought up with the four sons of King Henry; he was much beloved by them all, except John. "It happened that John and Fulke were sitting all alone in a chamber playing at chess; and John took the chess-board, and struck Fulke with a great blow. Fulke felt himself hurt, raised his foot and struck John in the middle of the stomach; and his head flew against the wall, and he became all weak, and fainted. Fulke was in consternation; but he was glad that there was nobody in the chamber but they two, and he rubbed John's ears, who recovered from his fainting fit, and went to the king his father, and made a great complaint. 'Hold your tongue, wretch,' said the king, 'you are always quarrelling. If Fulke did anything but good to you, it must have been by your own desert;' and he called his master, and made him beat him finely and well for complaining. John was much enraged against Fulke, so that he could never afterward love him heartily."

The above, as has been remarked, evinces how little respect there was in those early times for royal authority and the doctrine of non-resistance. But it may be observed, that even in these more polite times, were the heir-apparent to strike a playfellow, his royal highness would probably meet in return with as ready-handed, if not quite so rough a correction as was inflicted upon John. The latter could not forgive a bold companion of his boyhood, as James I. did, in subsequent times, with regard to "Jamie Slates." On the contrary, when John became king, he plotted with as unscrupulous a person as himself, to deprive Fulke of his estate. The conversation between the king and his confederate, Moris de Powis, was overheard; and what came of it is thus told in the history of Fulke Fitzwarren, as edited by Thomas Wright Esq., for the Warton Club:—

"There was close by a knight who had heard all the conversation between the king and Moris, and he went in haste to Sir

Fulke, and told him that the king was about to confirm by his charter, to Sir Moris, the lands to which he had right. Fulke and his four brothers came before the king, and prayed that they might have the common law and the lands to which they had claim and right, as the inheritance of Fulke; and they prayed that the king would receive from them a hundred pounds, on condition that he should grant them the award of his court of gain and loss. The king told them that what he had granted to Sir Moris, he would hold to it whoever might be offended or who not. At length Sir Moris spoke to Sir Fulke, and said, 'Sir Knight, you are a great fool to challenge my lands; if you say that you have a right to White-Town, you lie; and if we were not in the king's presence I would have proved it on your body.' Sir William, Fulke's brother, without a word more, sprang forward and struck Sir Moris with his fist in the middle of his face, that it became all bloody; knights interfered that no more hurt was done; then said Sir Fulke to the king: 'Sir King, you are my liege-lord, and to you was I bound by fealty, as long as I was in your service, and as long as I held the lands of you; and you ought to maintain me in right, and you fail me in right and common law; and never was he good king who denied his frank tenants law in his court; wherefore I return you your homages:' and with this word, he departed from the court and went to his hostel."

Fulke was most unjustly exiled, but after a while he returned to England, wandered about in various disguises, and at length, with a ripe project, settled down as a collier or charcoal-burner in Windsor Forest. I will once more draw from Mr. Wright's edition of this knightly biography for what ensued.

"At length came the king with three knights, all on foot to Fulke, where he was arranging his fire. When Fulke saw the king, he knew him well enough, and he cast the fork from his hand and saluted his lord and went on his knees before him very humbly. The king and his three knights had great laughter and game at the breeding and bearing of the collier. They stood there very long. 'Sir Vilain,' said the king, 'have you seen no stag or doe pass here?' 'Yes, my lord, awhile ago.' 'What beast did you see?' 'Sir, my lord, a horned one; and it had long horns.' 'Where is it?' 'Sir, my lord, I know very well how to lead you to where I saw it.' 'Onward then, Sir Vilain, and we will follow you.' 'Sir,' said the collier, 'shall I take my fork in my hand? for if it were taken I should have thereby a great loss.' 'Yea, Vilain, if you will.' Fulke took the great fork of iron in his hand and led the king to shoot; for he had a very handsome bow. 'Sir, my lord,' said Fulke, 'will you please to wait, and I will go into the thicket and make the beast come this way by here?' 'Yea,' said the king. Fulke did hastily spring into the thick of the forest; and commanded his company hastily to seize upon King John, for 'I have brought him there only with three knights; and all his company is on the other side of the forest.' Fulke and his company leaped out of the thicket, and rushed upon the king and seized him at once. 'Sir King,' said Fulke, 'now I have you in my power, such judgment I will execute on you as you would on me, if you had taken me.' The king trembled with fear for he had great dread of Fulke."

There is here, perhaps, something of the romantic history, but with a substantiality of truth. In the end, Fulke, who we are told was really one of the barons to whom we owe Magna Charta, and who was anathematized by the pope, and driven into exile again and again, got the better of all his enemies, pope and king included. There are two traditions touching his death. One is, that he survived to the period of the battle of Lewes, where he was one of a body of Henry the Third's friends who were drowned in the adjacent river. The other tells a very different story, and is probably nearer the truth. We are inclined to think with Mr. Wright, the editor of the biographical history in question, that he who was drowned near Lewes, was the son of Fulke. We add the following account, less because of its detail touching the death of the old knight than as having reference to how knights lived, moved, and had their being, in the period referred to:—

"Fulke and Lady Clarice his wife, one night, were sleeping together in their chamber; and the lady was asleep, and Fulke was awake, and thought of his youth; and repented much in his heart for his trespasses. At length, he saw in the chamber so great a light, that it was wonderful; and he thought what could it be? And he heard a voice, as it were, of thunder in the air, and it said:—'Vassal, God has granted thy penance, which is better here than elsewhere.' At that word the lady awoke, and saw the great light, and covered her face for fear. At length this light vanished. And after this light Fulke could never see more, but he was blind all his days. Then Fulke was very hospitable and liberal, and he caused the king's road to be turned through his hall at his manor of Alleston, in order no stranger might pass without having meat or lodging, or other honor or goods of his. This Fulke remained seven years blind, and suffered well his penance. Lady Clarice died and was buried at the New Abbey; after whose death Fulke lived but a year, and died at the White-town; and in great honor was he interred at the New Abbey—on whose soul may God have mercy. Near the altar is the body. God have mercy on us all, alive and dead. Amen!"

The religious sentiment was strong in all Norman knights, but not more so, perhaps, than in the wild chivalry of North America, when first its painted heroes heard of the passion and death of Christ. Charlevoix tells us of an Iroquois, who, on hearing of the crucifixion, exclaimed with the feeling of a Christian crusader, "Oh, if I had been there!" Precisely such an exclamation was once made by a Norman knight, as he listened to a monk narrating the great sacrifice on Mount Calvary. The more savage warrior, however, has always had the more poetical feeling. Witness the dying request of a young Indian chief, also noticed by Charlevoix. The dying victor asked to be buried in a blue robe, because that was the color of the sky: the fashion, with many Norman knights, of being interred in a robe and cowl of a monk, had far less of elevated feeling for its motive.

Having shown something of what the knight did at home, let us contemplate also what he taught there, by precept, if not by example. There was a knight who was known by the title of "the White Knight," whose name was De la Tour Landay, who was a contemporary of Edward the Black Prince, and who is supposed to have fought at Poictiers. He, is, however, best known, or at least equally well known, as the author of a work entitled "Le Livre du Chevalier de la Tour Landay." This book was written, or dictated by him, for the especial benefit of his two daughters, and for the guidance of young ladies generally. It is extremely indelicate in parts, and in such wise gives no very favorable idea of the young ladies who could bear such instruction as is here imparted. The Chevalier performed his authorship after a very free and easy fashion. He engaged four clerical gentlemen, strictly designated as "two priests and two clerks," whose task it was to procure for him all the necessary illustrative materials, such as anecdotes, apophthegms, and such like. These were collected from all sources, sacred and profane—from the Bible down to any volume, legendary or historical, that would suit his purpose. These he worked mosaically together, adding such wise saw, moral, counsel, or sentiment, as he deemed the case most especially required;—with a sprinkling of stories of his own collecting. A critic in the "Athenæum," commenting upon this curious volume, says with great truth, that it affords good materials for an examination into the morals and manners of the times. "Nothing," says the reviewer, "is urged for adoption upon the sensible grounds of right or wrong, or as being in accordance with any admitted moral standard, but because it has been sanctified by long usage, been confirmed by pretended miracle, or been approved by some superstition which outrages common sense."

In illustration of these remarks it is shown how the Chevalier recommends a strict observation of the meagre days, upon the ground that the dissevered head of a soldier was once enabled to call for a priest, confess, and listen to the absolution, because the owner of the head had never transgressed the Wednesday and Friday's fasts throughout his lifetime. Avoidance of the seven capital sins is enjoined upon much the same grounds. Gluttony, for instance, is to be avoided, for the good reason, that a prattling magpie once betrayed a lady who had eaten a dish of eels, which her lord had intended for some guests whom he wished particularly to honor. Charity is enjoined, not because the practice thereof is placed by the great teacher, not merely above Hope, but before Faith, but because a lady who, in spite of priestly warning, gave the broken victuals of her household to her dogs rather than to the poor, being on her death-bed, was leaped upon by a couple of black dogs, and that these having approached her lips, the latter became as black as a coal. The knight the more insists upon the proper exercise of charity, seeing that he has unquestionable authority in support of the truth of the story. That is, he knew a lady that had known the defunct, and who said she had seen the dogs. Implicit obedience of wives to husbands is insisted on, with a forcibly illustrative argument. A burgher's wife had answered her lord sharply, in place of silently listening to reproof, and meekly obeying his command. The husband, thereupon, dealt his wife a blow with his clenched fist, which smashed her nose, and felled her to the ground. "It is reason and right," says the mailed Mrs. Ellis of his time, "that the husband should have the word of command, and it is an honor to the good wife to hear him, and hold her peace, and leave all high talking to her lord; and so, on the contrary, it is a great shame to hear a woman strive with her husband, *whether right or wrong*, and especially before other people." Publius Syrus says, that a good wife commands by obeying, but the Chevalier evidently had no idea of illustrating the Latin maxim, or recommending the end which it contemplates. The knight places the husband as absolute lord; and his doing so, in conjunction with the servility which he demands on the part of the wife, reminds me of the saying of Toulotte, which is as true as anything enjoined by the moralizing knight, namely, that "*L'obéissance aux volontés d'un chef absolu assimile l'homme à la brute.*" This, with a verbal alteration, may be applied as expressive of the effect of the knight's teaching in the matter of feminine obedience. The latter is indeed in consonance with the old heathen ideas. Euripides asserts, that the most intolerable wife in the world is a wife who philosophizes, or supports her own opinion. We are astonished to find a Christian knight thus agreed with a heathen poet — particularly as it was in Christian times that the maxim was first published, which says, "*Ce que femme veut, Dieu le veut !*"

This sentiment reminds me, that it is time to show how the knight was affected by the tender passion, how it was sometimes his glory and sometimes his shame. He was sometimes the victim, and at others the victimizer.

# LOVE IN CHEVALIERS, AND CHEVALIERS IN LOVE.

> "How pleasing are the steps we lovers make,
> When in the paths of our content we pace
> To meet our longings!"—*The Hog hath Lost his Purse.*

BUTLER, in his Hudibras (part iii. cant. 1), has amusingly illustrated the feeling which moved knights-errant, and the particular object they had in view: "the ancient errant knights," he says:—

> "Won all their ladies' hearts in fights,
> And cuts whole giants into fritters,
> To put them into amorous twitters;
> Whose stubborn bowels scorned to yield,
> Until their gallants were half killed:
> But when their bones were drubbed so sore
> They durst not win one combat more,
> The ladies' hearts began to melt,
> Subdued by blows their lovers felt.
> So Spanish heroes with their lances
> At once wound bulls and ladies' fancies."

However willing a knight may have been to do homage to his lady, the latter, if she truly regarded the knight, never allowed his homage to her to be paid at the cost of injury to his country's honor or his own. An instance of this is afforded us in the case of Bertrand de Guesclin. There never was man who struck harder blows when he was a bachelor; but when he went a wooing, and still more after he had wed the incomparable Tiphania, he lost all care for honor in the field, and had no delight but in the society of his spouse. The lady, however, was resolved that neither his sword nor his reputation should acquire rust through any fault or beauty of hers. She rallied him soundly on his home-keeping propensities, set them in contrast with the activity of his bachelor-days, and the renown acquired by it, and forthwith talked him out of her bower and into his saddle.

The English did not profit by the lady's eloquence, for our forefathers never had a more gallant or more difficult adversary to deal with than Bertrand. Living, his name was a terror to them; and dying, he had the sympathy of those who had been his foes. Charles V. made him Constable of France, and appointed him a grave at the foot of his own royal tomb. De Guesclin would never have been half the man he was but for the good sense of his wife Tiphania.

There are many instances in romance which would seem to imply, that so strained was the sentiment which bound knights to respect ladies, it compelled them not to depart therefrom even in extreme cases, involving lightness of conduct and infidelity. The great northern chiefs, who were a sort of very rough knights in their way, were, however, completely under the distaff. Their wives could divorce themselves at will. Thus, in Erysbiggia Saga we read of Borck, an Icelandic chief, who, bringing home a guest whom his wife not only refused to welcome, but attempted to stab, administered such correction to his spouse in return, that the lady called in witnesses and divorced herself on the spot. Thereupon the household goods were divided among them, and the affair was rapidly and cheaply managed without the intervention of an Ecclesiastical Court. More modern chivalry would not have tolerated the idea of correcting even a faithless, much less a merely angry spouse. Indeed, the amatory principle was quite as strong as the religious one; and in illustration thereof, it has been remarked that the knight must have been more than ordinarily devout who had God on his *right* hand (the place of honor), and his lady on his *left*.

To *ride at the ring* was then the pleasantest pastime for knights; and ladies looked on and applauded the success, or laughed at the failures. The riding, without attempting to carry off the ring, is still common enough at our fairs, for children; but in France and Germany, it is seriously practised in both its simple and double forms, by persons of all ages, who glide round to the grinding of an organ, and look as grave as if they were on desperate business.

It is an undoubted matter of fact, that although a knight was bound to be tender in his gallantry, there were some to be found whose wooing was of the very roughest; and there were others who, if not rough, were rascally.

The old Rue des Lombards, in Paris, was at one time occupied exclusively by the "professed pourpoint-makers," as a modern tailor might say. They carried on a flourishing trade, especially in times when men, like Bassompierre, thought nothing of paying, or promising to pay, fourteen thousand crowns for a pourpoint. When I say the street was thus occupied exclusively, I must notice an exception. There were a few other residents in it, the Jew money-lenders or usurers; and when I hear the old French proverb cited "patient as a Lombard," I do not know whether it originally applied to the tailors or the money-lenders, both of whom were extensively cheated by their knightly customers. Here is an illustration of it, showing that all Jessicas have not been as lucky as Shylock's daughter, and that some Jews have been more cruelly treated than Shylock's daughter's father—whom I have always considered as one of the most ill-used of men.

In the Rue des Lombards there dwelt a wealthy Jew, who put his money out at interest, and kept his daughter under lock and key at home. But the paternal Jew did not close his shutters, and the Lombard street Jessica, sitting all day at the window, attracted the homage of many passers-by. These were chiefly knights who came that way to be measured for pourpoints; and no knight was more attracted by the black eyes of the young lady in question, than the Chevalier Giles de Pontoise. That name indeed is one of a celebrated hero of a burlesque tragedy, but the original knight was "*my* Beverley."

Giles wore the showiest pourpoint in the world; for which he had obtained long credit. It struck him that he would call upon the Jew to borrow a few hundred pistoles, and take the opportunity to also borrow the daughter. He felt sure of succeeding in both exploits; for, as he remarked, if he could not pay the money he was about to borrow, he could borrow it of his more prudent relatives, and so acquit himself of his debt. With regard to the lady, he had serenaded her, night after night, till she looked as ready to leap down to him as the Juliets who played to Barry's Romeo;—and he had sung "Ecco ridente il sole," or what was then equivalent to it, accompanied by his guitar, and looking as ridiculous the while, without being half so silvery-toned as Rubini in Almaviva, warbling his delicious nonsense to Rosina. Our Jew, like old Bartolo, was destined to pay the musician.

Giles succeeded in extracting the money required from the usurer, and he had like success in inducing the daughter to trust to his promises. He took the latter to Pontoise, deceived her by a mock-marriage, and spent all that he had borrowed from the father, in celebrating his pretended nuptials with the daughter. There never was a more recreant knight than Giles de Pontoise.

However, bills will become due, if noble or simple put their names to them, and the Jew claimed at once both his debt and his daughter. He failed in obtaining his money, but the lady he carried off by violence, she herself exhibiting considerable reluctance to leave the Château de Pontoise for the paternal dungeon in the Rue des Lombards.

This step brought Giles to a course of reflection. It was not of that quality which his confessor would have recommended, but rather of a satanic aspect. "In the usurer's house," thought Giles, "live the tailor to whom I am indebted for my pourpoint, the Jew who holds my promise to pay, and the pretty daughter of whom I have been so unjustly deprived. I will set fire to the house. If I burn tailor, money-lender, and the proofs of my liabilities, I shall have done a good night's work, if I therewith can carry off little Jessica."

Thereupon, Giles went down to the Rue des Lombards, and with such aid as was then easily purchasable, he soon wrapped the Jew's dwelling in flames. Shylock looked to his papers and money-bags. The knight groped through the smoke and carried off the daughter. The Jew still held the promissory note of the Knight of Pontoise, whose incendiary act, however, had destroyed half of one side of the Rue des Lombards. Therewith had perished reams of bonds which made slaves of chevaliers to Jew money-lenders. "*Sic vos non vobis*," thought Giles, "but at all events, if he has my bill, I have possession of Jessica."

The Jew held as much to his daughter as to his ducats. He persecuted the pretended husband with a pertinacity which eventually overcame Giles de Pontoise. A compromise was effected.

The knight owed the usurer three thousand golden crowns, and had stolen from him his only daughter. Giles agreed to surrender his "lady," on condition that the money-lender should sign an acquittance of the debt. This done, the Jew and daughter walked homeward, neither of them well satisfied with the result of their dealings with a knight.

The burnt-out Lombarder turned round at the threshold of the knight's door, with a withering sneer, like Edmund Kean's in Shylock when he was told to make haste and go home, and begin to be a Christian. "It is little but sorrow I get by you, at all events," said the Jew to the Chevalier.

"Do you make so light of your grandson?" asked Giles. And with this Parthian dart he shut his door in the face of the trio who were his victims.

This knight was a victimizer; but below we have an illustration of knights victimized through too daring affection.

The great Karloman may be said to have been one of those crowned knights who really had very little of the spirit of chivalry in him, with respect to ladies. He married, successfully, two wives, but to neither did he allow the title of Empress. It is, however, not with his two wives, but his two daughters and their chevaliers *par amours*, with whom we have now to do.

In the Rue de la Harpe, in Paris, may be seen the remains, rather than the ruins, of the old building erected by the Emperor Julian, and which was long known by the name of the "old palace." It served as a palace about a thousand years and half a century ago, when one night there drew up before it a couple of knights, admirably mounted, and rather roughly escorted by a mob, who held up their lanterns to examine the riders, and handled their pikes as if they were more ready to massacre the knights than to marshal them.

All the civility they received on this February night was of a highly equivocal nature. They were admitted, indeed, into the first and largest court of the palace, but the old seneschal locked and barred the gate behind them. An officer too approached to bid them welcome, but he had hardly acquitted himself of his civil mission when he peremptorily demanded of them the surrender of their swords.

"We are the King's own messengers," said one of the knights, rather puzzled at the reception vouchsafed to them;—"and we have, moreover, a despatch to deliver, written in our gracious master's own hand," remarked the second knight.

"Vive Louis le Debonnaire!" exclaimed the seneschal; "how fares it with our sovereign?"

"As well as can be," was the reply, "with a monarch who has been engaged six whole weeks at Aix, in burying his father and predecessor, Charlemagne. Here is his missive." This missive was from Louis the Frolicsome, or Louis the Good-Natured, or Louis of Fair Aspect. He was morose, wittily disposed, and ill-featured;—but then the poet-laureate had given him his fine name; and the king wore it as if it had been fairly won. He had clipped, shaved, and frocked, all his natural brothers, and then shut them up in monasteries. He had no more respect for treaties than he had for Mohammed, and by personal example he taught perjury and rebellion to those whom he cruelly punished when they imitated their exalted instructor. The seneschal perused the letter addressed to him by his royal correspondent, and immediately requested the two knights to enter the palace itself.

They were ushered into a lofty-arched apartment on the ground floor, which ordinarily served as an ante-room for the guards on duty; it was for the moment, however, empty. They who have visited the old Palais de Thermes, as it is called, have, doubtlessly, remarked and admired this solid relic of the past.

After entering, the seneschal once more lifted the despatch to the flambeau, read it through, looked at the seal, then at the knights, coughed uneasily, and began to wear an air of dislike for some duty imposed upon him. He repeated, as if he were learning by rote, the names Raoul de Lys and Robert de Quercy. "Those are our names," observed the first; "we have ridden hither by the king's orders to announce his coming; and having done so, let us have fire and food, lest we be famished and frozen before he arrives."

"Hem!" muttered the seneschal, "I am extremely sorry; but, according to this letter, you are my prisoners, and till to-morrow you must remain in this apartment;" and, seeing them about to remonstrate, he added, "You will be quite at liberty here, except, of course, that you cant't get out; you will have separate quarters to-morrow."

It was in vain that they inquired the reason for their detention, the nature of the charge alleged against them, or what they had further to expect. The seneschal dryly referred them to the monarch. He himself knew nothing more than his orders, and by them he was instructed to keep the two friends in close confinement till the sovereign's arrival. "On second thoughts," said the seneschal, "I must separate you at once. There is the bell in the tower of St. Jacques ringing midnight, and to-morrow will be upon us, before its iron tongue has done wagging. I really must trouble one of you gentlemen to follow me." The voice was not so civil as the words, and after much parleying and reluctance, the two friends parted. Robert bade Raoul be of good cheer; and Raoul, who was left behind, whispered that it would be hard, indeed, if harm was to come to them under such a roof.

The roof, however, of this royal palace, looked very much like the covering of a place in which very much harm might be very quietly effected. But there were dwelling there two beings who might have been taken for spirits of good, so winning, so natural, and so loveable were the two spirits in question. They were no other than the two daughters of Charlemagne, Gisla and Rotrude. The romancers, who talk such an infinite deal of nonsense, say of them that their sweet-scented beauty was protected by the prickles of principle. The most rapid of analysers may see at once that this was no great compliment to the ladies. It was meant, however, to be the most refined flattery; and the will was accepted for the deed.

Now, the two knights loved the two ladies, and if they had *not*, neither Father Daniel nor Sainte Foix could have alluded to their amorous history; nor Father Pasquale, of the Convent of the Arminians in Venice, have touched it up with some of the hues of romance, nor Roger de Beauvoir have woven the two together, nor unworthy ægomet have applied it to the illustration of daring lovers.

These two girls were marvellously high-spirited. They had

been wooed by emperors; but feeling no inclination to answer favorably to the wooing, Charlemagne generously refused to put force upon their affections, and bade them love only where their hearts directed them. This "license" gave courage to numberless nobles of various degrees, but Rotrude and Gisla said nay to all their regular advances. The Princesses were, in fact, something like Miss Languish, thought love worth nothing without a little excitement, and would have considered elopement as the proper preceder of the nuptial ceremony. Their mother, Hildegarda, was an unexceptional woman, but, like good Queen Charlotte, who let her daughters read Polly Honeycombe as well as Hannah More, she was a little confused in the way she taught morals, and the young Princesses fell in love, at the first opportunity, with gallant gentlemen of — as compared with princesses — rather low degree. In this respect, there is a parallel between the house of Karloman and some other houses of more modern times.

Louis le Debonnaire had, as disagreeable brothers will have, an impertinent curiosity respecting his sisters' affairs. He was, here, the head of his family, and deemed himself as divinely empowered to dispose of the hearts of these ladies, as of the families and fortunes of his people. He had learned the love-passages that had been going on, and he had hinted that when he reached the old palace in Paris, he would make it as calmly cold as a cloister, and that there were disturbed hearts there, which should be speedily restored to a lasting tranquillity. The young ladies did not trouble themselves to read the riddle of a brother who was for ever affecting much mystery. But they prepared to welcome his arrival, and seemed more than ordinarily delighted when they knew that intelligence of his approaching coming had been brought by the two knights then in the castle.

Meanwhile, Raoul de Lys sat shivering on a stone bench in the great guard-room. He subsequently addressed himself to a scanty portion of skinny wild boar, very ill-cooked; drank, with intense disgust, part of a flask of hydromel of the very worst quality; and then having gazed on the miniature of Rotrude, which he took from beneath the buff jerkin under his corslet, he apostrophized it till he grew sleepy, upon which he blew out his lamp, and threw himself on an execrably hard couch. He was surprised to find that he was not in the dark. There was very good reason for the contrary.

As he blew out his lamp, a panel in the stone wall glided noiselessly open, and Robert de Quercy appeared upon the threshold—one hand holding a lamp, the other leading a lady. The lady was veiled; and she and the knight hurriedly approached Raoul, who as hurriedly rushed forward to meet them. He had laid his armor by; and they who recollect Mr. Young in Hotspur, and how *he* looked in tight buff suit, before he put his armor on, may have some idea of the rather ridiculous guise in which Raoul appeared to the lady. But she was used to such sights, and had not time to remark it even had she not been so accustomed.

Raoul observing that Robert was accompanied only by Gisla, made anxious inquiry for Rotrude. Gisla in a few words told him that her sister would speedily be with them, that there was certain danger, even death, threatening the two cavaliers, and probable peril menacing—as Gisla remarked, with a blush—those who loved them. The King, she added, had spoken angrily of coming to purify the palace, as she had heard from Count Volrade, who appears to have been a Polonius, as regards his office, with all the gossip, but none of the good sense, of the old chamberlain in Denmark.

"Death to us!" exclaimed Robert. "Accursed be the prince who transgresses the Gospel admonition, not to forget his own or his father's friends." "We were the favored servants of Charlemagne," said Raoul. "We were of his closest intimacy," exclaimed Robert. "Never," interrupted Raoul, "did he ascend his turret to watch the stars, without summoning us, his nocturnal pages, as he called us, to his side." "He dare not commit such a crime; for the body of Charlemagne is scarcely sealed down in its tomb; and Louis has not a month's hold of the sceptre."

"He holds it firmly enough, however, to punish villany," exclaimed Louis himself, as he appeared in the doorway leading to a flight of stone stairs by which Gisla had indicated the speedy appearance of Rotrude.

And here I would beseech my readers to believe that if the word "tableau!" ought to be written at this situation, and if it appears to them to be too melo-dramatic to be natural, *I* am not in fault. I refer them to all the histories and romances in which this episode in knightly story is told, and in all they will find that Louis makes his appearance exactly as I have described, and precisely like Signor Tamburini in the great scene of Lucrezia Borgia.

Louis having given expression to his startling bit of recitative, dragged forward Rotrude, whom he had held behind him, by the wrist. The background was occupied by four guards, wearing hoods; and I can not think of them without being reminded of those same four old guards, with M. Desmousseaux at their head, who always represented the Greek or Roman armies upon the stage of the Théâtre Français, when Talma was the Nero or the Sylla, the Orestes or the Capitolinus of the night.

With some allusion to Rotrude as a sacred dove, and to himself as a bird-catcher, Louis handed his sister to a stone bench, and then grew good-natured in his remarks. This sudden benevolence gave a chill to the entire company. They turned as pale as any Russian nobleman to whom Nicholas was extraordinarily civil.

"We know the winding passages of the palace of Thermes," said Louis, laughingly, "as well as our sisters; and I have not gone through them to-night for the purpose of terrifying the sister whom I encountered there, or the other sister whom I see here. I am a kind-hearted brother, and am marvellously well-disposed. I need only appeal to these four gentlemen of my guard, who will presently take off their hoods, and serve as witnesses this night in a little ceremony having reference to my dear Rotrude."

"A ceremony! this night!" exclaimed the two princesses.

"Ay, by the nails of the cross! Two ceremonies. You shall both be married forthwith. I will inaugurate my reign by a double wedding, here in the old palace of Thermes. You, Gisla, shall espouse Robert, Count de Quercy, and you, Rotrude, shall wed with Raoul, Baron de Lys. You might have aimed higher, but they are gallant gentlemen, friends of my deceased sire; and, by my sooth, the nuptials shall not lack state and ceremony! Here are our wedding-gifts to the bridegrooms."

He pointed to two showy suits of armor, the pieces of which were carried by the four guards. The knights were in a dream of delight. They vowed eternal gratitude to the most noble of emperors and unparalleled of brothers.

"We have no great faith in human gratitude," said Louis, "and shall not expect from you more than is due. And you, my sisters," added he, "retire for awhile; put on what you will; but do not tarry here at the toilette of men-at-arms, like peasant-girls looking at the equipping of two pikemen."

The two princesses withdrew; and there would have been a smile upon their lips, only that they suspected their brother. Hoping the best, however, they kissed the tips of their rosy fingers to the knights, and tripped away, like two pets of the ballet. They were true daughters of their sire, who reckoned love-passages as even superior to stricken fields. He was not an exemplary father, nor a faithful husband. His *entourage* was not of the most respectable; and in some of his journeys he was attended by the young wife of one of his own cavaliers, clad in cavalier costume. It was a villanously reprobate action, not the less so that Hermengarde was living. The mention of it will disgust every monarch in Europe who reads my volume; and I am sure that it will produce no such strong sensation of reproof anywhere as in the bosom of an admirable personage "over the water."

The two princesses, then, had not so much trouble from the prickles of principle as the romances told of them. But, considering the example set them by their imperial father, they were really very tolerable princesses, under the circumstances.

"Don your suits, gentlemen!" exclaimed the king.

The four guards advanced with the separate pieces of armor, at which the two knights gazed curiously for a moment or two, as two foxes might at a trap in which lay a much-desired felicity. They were greatly delighted, yet half afraid. The monarch grew impatient, and the knights addressed themselves at once to their adornment. They put aside their own armor, and with the assistance of the four mute gentlemen-at-arms they fitted on the *brassards* or arm-pieces, which became them as though the first Milainer who ever dressed knight had taken their measure. With some little trouble they were accoutred, less as became bridegrooms than barons going to battle; and this done, they took their seats, at a sign from the king, who bade the four gentlemen come to an end with what remained of the toilette.

The knights submitted, not without some misgiving, to the services of the four mysterious *valets!* and, in a short time, the preparations were complete, even to the helmet with the closed visor. This done, the knights took their places, or were led rather to two high-backed oaken chairs. As soon as they were seated there, the four too-officious attendants applied their hands to the closed head-pieces; and in a very brief space the heads of the cavaliers sunk gently upon their breasts, as if they were in deep slumber or as deep meditation.

Two o'clock rang out from the belfry of St. Jacques, as the two brides entered. The king pointed with a smile to the bridegrooms, and left the apartment with his attendants. The ladies thought that the lovers exhibited little ardor or anxiety to meet them; for they remained motionless on their oaken chairs. The daughters of Charlemagne advanced, half-timidly, half-playfully; and, at length, finding the knights not disposed to address them, gently called to each by his name. Raoul and Robert continued motionless and mute. They were in fact dead. They had been strangled or suffocated in a peculiar sort of armor, which had been sent to Charlemagne from Ravenna, in return for a jewelled vase presented by that emperor to the ancient city. "In 1560," says Monsieur Roger de Beauvoir, himself quoting an Italian manuscript, there were several researches made in this part of the palace of Thermes, one result of which was the discovery of a 'casque à soufflet,' all the openings in which could be closed in an instant by a simple pressure of the finger on a spring. At the same instant the lower part of the neck-piece tightened round the throat, and the *patient* was disposed of. In this helmet," adds the author, "was found the head of a man, well preserved, with beard and teeth admirable for their beauty." I think, however, that in this matter M. de Beauvoir proves a little too much.

Father Daniel, in his history notices the vengeance of Louis le Debonnaire against two young nobles who were, reputedly, the lovers of Gisla and Rotrude. The details of the act of vengeance have been derived from an Italian source; and it is said that an Italian monk, named Pagnola, had some prominent part in this dreary drama, impelled thereto by a blow dealt to him at the hands of Raoul, by way of punishment for some contemptuous phrases which the monk had presumed to apply to the great Charlemagne.

## LOVE IN CHEVALIERS, AND CHEVALIERS IN LOVE.

Love and sword-blades seem to have been as closely connected as "Trousseaux et Layettes," which are always named together in the shop-fronts of a Parisian "Lingere." There was once an ample field for the accommodation of both the sentiments of love and bravery in the old Chaussée d'Antin, when it was merely a *chaussée* or highway, and not the magnificent street it now is. It was, down even to comparatively modern times, the resort of lovers of every degree, from dukes and duchesses to common dragoons and dairymaids. They were not always, however, under this strict classification.

But whatever classification or want of it there may have been, there was a part of the road which was constantly the scene of bloody encounters. This was at the narrow bridge of Arcans. Here if two cavaliers met, each with a lady at his side, it was a matter of honor not to give way. On the contrary, the latter was to be forced at the point of the sword. While the champions were contending, the ladies would scarcely affect to faint; they would stand aside, remain unconcerned on their jennets or mules, till the two simpletons had pinked one another; or lounge in their cumbrous coaches till the lovers limped back to them.

It was on this bridge, of which no vestige now remains, not even in a museum, that the Count de Fiesque one evening escorting Madame de Lionne, encountered M. de Tallard, who was chaperoning Louison d'Arquien. Each couple was in a carriage, and neither would make way for the other to pass. Thereupon the two cavaliers leaped from their coaches, drew their swords, planted their feet firmly on the ground, and began slashing at each other like two madmen, to the great delight of a large crowd who enjoyed nothing so much as the sight of two noble gentlemen cutting one another's throats.

The ladies, meanwhile, flourished their handkerchiefs from their respective carriage-windows, for the encouragement of their champions. Now and then each laughed aloud when her particular friend had made a more than ordinary successful thrust; and each was generous enough to applaud any especial dexterity, even when her own lover thereby bloodily suffered. The two foolish fellows only poked at each other with the more intensity. And when they had sufficiently slit their pourpoints and slashed their sleeves, the ladies, weary of waiting any longer for a more exciting denouement, rushed between the combatants, like the Sabine ladies between the contending hosts; each gentleman gallantly kissed the lady who did not belong to him; and the whole four gayly supped together, as though they had been the best friends in the world.

This incident fairly brings us to the questions of duelling and death, as illustrated by chivalry.

# DUELLING, DEATH AND BURIAL.

"Le duel, ma mie, ne vaut pas un duo, de Lully."
CRISPIN MOURANT.

As an effect of chivalry, duelling deserves some passing notice. Its modern practice was but an imitation of chivalric encounters, wherein the issue of battle was left to the judgment of God.

Bassompierre dates the origin of duelling (in France) from the period of Henri II. Previous to that king's reign, the quarrels of gentlemen were determined by the decree of the constable and marshals of France. These only allowed knightly encounters in the lists, when they could not of themselves decide upon the relative justice and merits of the dispute.

"I esteem him no gentleman," said Henri one day, "who has the lie given him, and who does not chastise the giver." It was a remark lightly dropped, but it did not fall unheeded. The king in fact encouraged those who resorted, of their own will, to a bloody arbitrament of their dissensions; and duelling became so "fashionable," that even the penalty of death levelled against those who practised it, was hardly effectual enough to check duellists. At the close of the reign of Henri IV. and the commencement of that of Louis XIII. the practice was in least activity; but after the latter period, as the law was not rigorously applied, the foolish usage was again revived; and sanguinary simpletons washed out their folly in blood.

But duelling has a more remote origin than that ascribed to it by Bassompierre. Sabine, in his "Dictionary of Duelling," a recently-published American work, dates its rise from the challenge of the Philistine accepted by David! However this may be, it is a strange anomaly that an advocate for the savage and sinful habit of duelling has appeared in that France which claims to be the leader of civilization. Jules Janin has, among his numberless *feuilletons* published three reasons authorizing men to appeal to single combat. The above M. Janin divides the world into three parts — a world of cravens; a world in which opinion is everything; and a world of hypocrites and calumniators. He considers the man who has not the heart to risk his life in a duel, as one lost in the world of cravens, because the legion of cowards by whom he is surrounded will assume courage at his expense.

Further, according to our gay neighbor's reasoning, the man is lost in this world, in which opinion is everything, who will not seek to obtain a good opinion at the sword's point.

Again, says M. Janin, the man is lost in this world of hypocrites and calumniators who will not demand reparation, sword in hand, for the calumnies and malicious reports to which he has been exposed. It would be insulting to the common sense of my readers to affect to point out to them the rottenness of reasons like these. They could only convince such men as Buckingham and Alfieri, and others in circumstances like theirs; Buckingham after killing Lord Shrewsbury at Barnes, and pressing the head of Lady Shrewsbury on his bloody shirt; and Alfieri, who, after a vile seduction, and very nearly a terrible murder in defence of it, went home and slept more peacefully than he had ever slept before: "dopo tanto e si stranie peripizie d'un sol giorno, non ho dormito mai d'un sonno piu tenace e piu dolce." Alfieri would have agreed with M. Janin, that in duelling lay the safeguard of all that remains to us of civilization. But how comes it then that civilization is thus a wreck, since duelling has been so long exercising a protective influence over it?

However few, though dazzling, were the virtues possessed by the chivalrous heroes of ancient history, it must be conceded to them, that they possessed that of valor, or a disregard of life, in an eminent degree. The instances of cowardice are so rare that they prove the general rule of courage; yet these men, with no guides but a spurious divinity and a false philosophy, never dreamed of having recourse to the duel, as a means of avenging a private wrong. Marius, indeed, was once challenged, but it was by a semi-barbarous Teutonic chief, whom the haughty Roman recommended, if he were weary of his life to go and hang himself.

Themistocles, too, whose wisdom and courage the most successful of our modern gladiators may admire and envy, when Eurybiades threatened to give him a blow, exclaimed, "Strike, but hear me!" Themistocles, it must be remembered, was a man of undaunted courage, while his jealous provoker was notorious for little else but his extreme cowardice.

But, in truth, there have been brave men in all countries, who have discouraged this barbarous practice. A Turkish pacha reminded a man who had challenged a fellow Spahi, that they had no right to slay one another while there were foes to subdue. The Dauphin of Viennois told the Count of Savoy, who had challenged him, that he would send the count one of his fiercest bulls, and that if the count were so minded, his lordship of Savoy might test his prowess against an antagonist difficult to overcome. The great Frederick would not tolerate the practice of duelling in his army; and he thoroughly despised the arguments used for its justification. A greater man than Frederick, Turenne, would never allow himself to be what was called "concerned in an affair of honor." Once, when the hero of Sintzheim and the Rhine had half drawn his sword to punish a disgusting insult, to which he had been subjected by a rash young officer, he thrust it back into the sheath, with the words: "Young man, could I wipe your blood from my conscience with as much ease as I can this filthy proof of your folly from my face, I would take your life upon the spot."

Even the chivalrous knights who thought duelling a worthy occupation for men of valor, reduced opportunities for its practice to a very small extent. Uniting with the church, they instituted the *Savior's Truce*, by which duels were prohibited from Wednesday to the following Monday, because, it was said, those days had been consecrated by our Savior's Passion. This, in fact, left only Tuesday as a clear day for settling quarrels by force of arms.

There probably never existed a mortal who was opposed by more powerful or more malignant adversaries than St. Augustin was. His great enemies the Donatists never, it is true, challenged him to any more dangerous affray than a war of literary controversy. But it was in answer to one of their missiles hurled against him, in the form of an assertion, that the majority of authors was on their side, he aptly told them that it was the sign of a cause destitute of truth when only the erring authority of many men could be relied on.

The Norman knights or chiefs introduced the single combat among us. It is said they were principally men who had disgraced themselves in the face of the enemy, and who sought to wipe out the disgrace in the blood of single individuals. It is worthy of remark too, that when king and sovereign princes had forbidden duelling, under the heaviest penalties, the popes absolved the monarchs from their vows when the observance of them would have put in peril the lives of offending nobles who had turned to Rome in their perplexity, and who had gained there a reputation for piety, as Hector did, who was esteemed so highly religious, for no other reason than that he had covered with rich gifts the altar of the father of Olympus.

Supported by the appearance that impunity was to be purchased at Rome, and encouraged by the example of fighting-cardinals themselves, duelling and assassination stalked hand in hand abroad. In France alone, in the brief space of eighteen years, four thousand gentlemen were killed in *rencontres*, upon quarrels of the most trivial nature. In the same space of time, not less than fourteen thousand pardons for duelling were granted. In one province alone, of France, in Limousin, one hundred and twenty gentlemen were slain in six months—a greater number than had honorably fallen in the same period, which was one of war, in defence of the sovereign, their country, and their homes. The term *rencontre* was used in France to elude the law. If gentlemen "met" by accident and fought, lawyers pleaded that this was not a *duel*, which required preliminaries between the two parties. How frequent the *rencontres* were, in spite of the penalty of death, is thus illustrated by Victor Hugo, in his *Marion Delorme*:—

> "Toujours nombre de duels, le trois c'était d'Angennes
> Contre d'Arquien, pour avoir porté du point de Gènes.
> Lavarde avec Pons s'est rencontré le dix,
> Pour avoir pris à Pons la femme de Sourdis.
> Sourdis avec Dailly pour une du théâtre
> De Mondorf. Le neuf, Nogent avec Lachâtre,
> Pour avoir mal écrit trois vers de Colletet.
> Gorde avec Margaillan, pour l'heure qu'il était.

> D'Himière avec Gondi, pour le pas à l'église.
> Et puis tous les Brissac avec tous les Soubise,
> A propos d'un pari d'un cheval contre un chien.
> Enfin, Caussade avec Latournelle, pour rien.
> Pour le plaisir, Caussade a tué Latournelle.

Jeremy Taylor denounced this practice with great earnestness, and with due balancing of the claims of honor and of Christianity. "Yea; but flesh and blood can not endure a blow or a disgrace. Grant that too; but take this into the account: flesh and blood shall not inherit the kingdom of God."

What man could endure for honor's sake, however, is shewn in the Memoirs of the Sieur de Pontis, who, in the seventeenth century, was asked to be second to a friend, when duels were punishable by death to all parties concerned in them. The friend of De Pontis pressed it on him, as a custom always practised among friends; and his captain and lieutenant-colonel did not merely permit, but ordered him to do what his friend desired.

Boldly as many knights met death, there were not a few who did their best, and that very wisely, to avoid "the inevitable."

Valorously as some chevaliers encountered deadly peril, the German knights, especially took means to avoid the grisly adversary when they could. For this purpose, they put on the *Nothhemd* or shirt of need. It was supposed to cover the wearer with invulnerability. The making of the garment was a difficult and solemn matter. Several maidens of known integrity assembled together on the eve of the Nativity, and wove and sewed together this linen garment, in the name of the devil! On the bosom of the shirt were worked two heads; one was long-bearded and covered with the knightly helmet, the other was savage of aspect, and crowned like the king of demons. A cross was worked on either side. How this could save a warrior from a mortal stroke, it would be difficult to say. If it was worn over the armor, perhaps the helmeted effigy was supposed to protect the warrior, and the demoniacal one to affright his adversary. But then, this shirt similarly made and adorned, was woven by ladies when about to become mothers of knights or of common men. What use it could be in such case, I leave to the "*commères*" to settle. My own vocation of "gossip" will not help me to the solution.

But if chivalry had its shirts of need in Germany, to save from death, in England and France it had its "mercy-knives" to swiftly inflict it. Why they were so called I do not know, for after all they were only employed in order to kill knights in full armor, by plunging the knife through the bars of the visor into the eye. After the battle of Pavia, many of the French were killed with pickaxes by the peasantry, hacking and hewing through the joints of the armor.

How anxious were the sires of those times to train their children how best to destroy life! This was more especially the case among what were called the "half-christened Irish" of Connaught. In this province, the people left the right arms of their male infants unchristened. They excepted that part coming under the divine influences of baptism, in order that the children, when grown to the stature of fighting men, might deal more merciless and deadly blows. There was some such superstitious observance as this, I think, in ancient Germany. It can not be said, in reference to the suppressing of this observance, as was remarked by Stow after the city authorities had put down the martial amusement of the London apprentices—contending against one another of an evening with cudgels and bucklers, while a host of admiring maids as well as men stood by to applaud or censure—that the open pastime being suppressed, worse practice within doors probably followed.

Stout fellows were some of the knights of the romantic period, if we may believe half that is recorded of them. There is one, Branor le Brun, who is famous for having been a living Quintain. The game so called consists of riding at a heavy sack suspended on a balanced beam, and getting out of its way, if possible, before the revolving beam brought it round violently against the back of the assailant's head. When Palamedes challenged old Branor, the aged knight rather scornfully put him aside as an unworthy yet valiant knight. Branor, however, offered to sit in his saddle motionless, while Palamedes rode at him, and got unhorsed by Branor's mere inert resistance. I forget how many knights Branor le Brun knocked over their horses' cruppers, after this quiet fashion.

It was not all courtesy in battle or in duel. Even Gyron, who was called the "courteous," was a very "rough customer" indeed, when he had his hand on the throat of an antagonist. We hear of him jumping with all his force upon a fallen and helpless foe, tearing his helmet from its fastenings by main force, battering the knight's face with it till he was senseless, and then beating on his head with the pommel of his sword, till the wretched fellow was dead. At this sort of pommelling there was never knight so expert as the great Bayard. The courtesy of the most savage in fight, was however undeniable when a lady was in the case. Thus we hear of a damsel coming to a fountain at which four knights were sitting, and one of them wishes to take her. The other three object, observing that the damsel is without a knight to protect her, and that she is, therefore, according to the law of chivalry, exempt from being attacked. And again, if a knight slew an adversary of equal degree, he did not retain his sword if the latter was a gift from some lady. The damsel, in such case, could claim it, and no knight worthy of the name would have thought of refusing to comply with her very natural request. Even ladies were not to be won, in certain cases, except by valor; as Arthur, that king of knights, would not win, nor retain, Britain, by any other means. The head of Bran the Blessed, it may be remembered, was hidden in the White Hill, near London, where, as long as it remained, Britain was invulnerable. Arthur, however removed it. He scorned to keep the island by any other means than his own sword and courage; and he was ready to fight any man in any quarrel.

Never did knight meet death more nobly than that Captain Douglas, whose heroism is recorded by Sir William Temple, and who "stood and burnt in one of our ships at Chatham, when his soldiers left him, because it never should be said a Douglas quitted his post without orders." Except as an example of heroic endurance, this act, however, was in some degree a mistake, for the state did not profit by it. There was something more profitable in the act of Von Speyk, in our own time. When hostilities were raging between Holland and Belgium, in 1831, the young Dutch captain, just named, happened to be in the Scheldt, struggling in his gun-boat against a gale which, in spite of all his endeavors and seamanship, drove him ashore, under the guns of the Belgians. A crowd of Belgian volunteers leaped aboard, ordered him to haul down his colors and surrender. Von Speyk hurried below to the magazine, fell upon his knees in prayer, flung a lighted cigar into an open barrel of powder, and blew his ship to atoms, with nearly all who were on board. If he, by this sacrifice, prevented a Dutch vessel from falling into the enemy's power, he also deprived Holland of many good seamen. The latter country, however, only thought of the unselfish act of heroism, in one who had been gratuitously educated in the orphan house at Amsterdam, and who acquitted his debt to his country, by laying down his life when such sacrifice was worth making. His king and countrymen proved that they could appreciate the noble act. The statue of Von Speyk was placed by the side of that of De Ruyter, and the government decreed that as long as a Dutch navy existed there should be *one* vessel bearing the name of Von Speyk.

To return to the knights of earlier days, I will observe that indifferent as many of them were to meeting death, they, and indeed other men of note, were very far from being so as to the manner in which they should be disposed of *after* death. In their stone or marble coffins, they lay in graves so shallow that the cover of the coffin formed part of the pavement of the church. Whittingham, the Puritan Dean of Durham, took up many of their coffins and converted them into horse or swine troughs. This is the dean who is said to have turned the finely-wrought holy-water vessels into salting-tubs for his own use.

Modern knights have had other cares about their graves than that alluded to above. Sir William Browne, for instance, one of George II.'s knights, and a medical man of some repute, who died in 1770, ordered by his will that when his coffin was lowered into the grave, there should be placed upon it, "in *its* leathern case or coffin, my pocket Elzevir Horace, comes viæ vitæque dulcis et utilis, worn out with and by me." There was nothing more unreasonable in this than in a warrior-knight being buried with all his weapons around him. And, with respect to warrior-knights and what was done with them after death, I know nothing more curious than what is told us by Stavely on the authority of Streder. I will give it in the author's own words.

"Don John of Austria," says Stavely, "governor of the Netherlands for Philip II. of Spain, dying at his camp at Buge" (Bouges, a mile from Namur), " was carried from thence to the great church at Havre, where his funeral was solemnized and a monument to posterity erected for him there by Alexander Farnese, the Prince of Parma. Afterward his body was taken to pieces, and the bones, packed in mails, were privately carried into Spain, where, being set together with small wires, the body was rejointed again, which being filled or stuffed with cotton, and richly habited, Don John was presented to the King, entire, leaning upon his commander's staff, and looking as if he were alive and breathing. Afterward the corpse being carried to the Church of St. Laurence, at the Escurial, was there buried near his father, Charles V., with a fitting monument erected for him."

Considering that there was, and is, a suspicion that Philip II. had poisoned his kinsman, the interview must have been a startling one. But Philip II. was not, perhaps, so afraid of dead men as the fourth Spanish king of that name. Philip IV., by no means an unknightly monarch, was born on a Good Friday, and as there is a Spanish superstition that they who are born on that day see ghosts whenever they pass the place where any one has been killed or buried, who died a violent death, this king fell into a habit of carrying his head so high, in order to avoid seeing those spirits, that his nose was continually *en l'air*, and he appeared to see nobody.

Romance, and perhaps faithful history, are full of details of the becoming deaths of ancient knights, upon the field. I question, however, if even Sir Philip Sidney's was more dignified than that of a soldier of the 58th infantry, recorded in Nichols's " Anecdotes of the Eighteenth Century." A straggling shot had struck him in the stomach. As he was too dreadfully wounded to be removed, he desired his comrades would pray by him, and the whole guard knelt round him in prayer till he died. Bishop Hurd remarked, when this was told him, that " it was true religion." There was more of religion in such sympathy than there was of taste in the condolence of Alnwick, on the death of Hugh, Duke of Northumberland — a rather irascible officer, and Knight of the Garter. " O," cried the Alnwick poet —

> " O rueful sight! Behold, how lost to sense
> The millions stand, suspended by suspense!"

But all fruitlessly were the millions so suspended, for as the minstrel remarked in his Threnodia—

"When Time shall yield to Death, Dukes must obey."

"Dying in harness," is a favorite phrase in chivalric annals to illustrate the bravery of a knight falling in battle, "clothed in complete steel." So to die, however, was not always to die in a fray. Hume says of Seward, Earl of Northumberland, that there are two circumstances related of him, "which discover his high sense of honor and martial disposition. When intelligence was brought to him of his son Osborne's death, he was inconsolable till he heard the wound was received on his breast, and that he had behaved with great gallantry in the action. When he found his own death approaching, he ordered his servants to dress him in a complete suit of armor, and sitting erect on the couch, with a spear in his hand, declared that in that position, the only one worthy of a warrior, he would patiently await the fatal moment."

> See how the chief of many a field
>   Prepares to give his latest breath;
> And, like a well-trimmed warrior, yield
>   Becomingly t' impending death—
> That one, stern conqueror of all,
>   Of chieftain in embattled tower,
> Of lord within his ancient hall,
>   And maiden in her trellised bower.
>
> To meet that surest of all foes,
>   From off his soft and pillowed bed,
> With dignity old Seward rose,
>   And to a couch of state was led.
> Fainting, yet firm of purpose there,
>   Stately as monarch on his throne,
> Upright he sat, with kingly air,
>   To meet the coming foe, alone.
>
> "Take from these limbs," he weakly cried,
>   "This soft and womanish attire;
> Let cloak and cap be laid aside—
>   Seward will die as died his sire:
> Not clad in silken vest and shirt,
>   Like princes in a fairy tale;
> With iron be these old limbs girt—
>   My vest of steel, my shirt of mail.

## DUELLING, DEATH AND BURIAL.

"Close let my sheaf of arrows stand;
   My mighty battle-axe now bring;
My ashen spéar place in my hand;
   Around my neck my buckler sling.
Let my white locks once more be pressed
   By the old cap of Milan steel;
Such soldier's gear becomes them best —
   They love their old defence to feel.

"'Tis well! Now buckle to my waist
   My well-tried gleaming blade of Spain
My old blood leaps in joyful haste
   To feel it on my thigh again.
And here this pendent loop upon,
   Suspend my father's dagger bright;
My spurs of gold, too, buckle on —
   Or Seward dies not like a knight."

'Twas done. No tear bedimmed his eyes —
   His manly heart had ne'er known fear;
It answered not the deep-fetched sighs
   Of friends and comrades standing near.
Death was upon him : that grim foe
   Who smites the craven as the brave.
With patience Seward met the blow —
   Prepared and willing for the grave.

The manner of the death, or rather of the dying of Seward, Earl of Northumberland, was in part, unconsciously, imitated by the great Mansfeldt. When the career of the latter was nearly at its close, his fragile frame was already worn' out by excess of action — his once stout soul irritated by disappointment, and his former vigorous constitution shattered by the ravages of a disease which had long preyed on it in secret. The erst gallant knight lay helpless in the miserable village of Zara, in Dalmatia. As he found his last moment drawing near, he put on one of his richest uniforms, and girded his favorite sword to his side. It was the one he most constantly carried in battle. Thus accoutrep, he summoned his chief officers to attend him. He was held up by the two whom he most wished to distinguish, because of their unwavering fidelity. Thus upheld, he exhorted all to go on, unwearied, in the path of glory; and, living or dying, never to bate a breath of inveterate hatred for Austria — whose government has been accursed in all time, since there has been an Austria, for its unmitigated infamy. "With the indifference of a man preparing for a journey of no extraordinary importance," thus speaks Naylor, when describing the scene, "he continued tranquilly to converse with his friends to the latest moment of his existence. His body was interred with military pomp at Spalatio, in Dalmatia, at the expense of the Venetians. Thus was the emperor delivered from an enemy who, though often defeated, never ceased to be formidable; and whose transcendent genius was so fertile in resources, that, without the smallest funds to support the expenses of war, he maintained an honorable contest during seven campaigns against the most powerful monarchs in Europe."

>His hour at length is come :
>The hero of a hundred fields,
>Who never yielded, only yields
>    To Him who rules the tomb.
>
>He whose loud trumpet's blast,
>Carried upon the trembling gale
>The voice of death o'er hill and dale,
>    Is struck himself at last.
>
>The same who, but of late,
>Serenely saw destruction hurled,
>And slaughter sweeping through the world,
>    Serenely meets his fate.
>
>The spirit of the brave,
>That led him o'er the embattled plain
>'Gainst lines of foes, o'er countless slain,
>    Waits on him to the grave.
>
>And with his latest breath
>The warrior dons his proud array,
>Prepared to meet, and to obey,
>    His last commander — Death!
>
>The mournful tears and sighs
>Fall not for him who, like the swan,
>Wears his best plumes, sings sweetly on,
>    Sounds his last song — and dies!

With regard to the burial of knights, we may observe that, down to a comparatively late period the knights and barons of England were buried with much solemn splendor. At the obsequies of a baron, there was an official present who wore the armor of the defunct, mounted a horse in full trappings, and carried the banner, shield, and helmet, of the deceased. So, in Henry the Eighth's time, Lord William Courtney was buried with the ceremonies observed at the funeral of an earl, to which rank it had been the king's intention to elevate him. On this occasion Sir Edmund Carew, a gallant knight, rode into the church in full armor, with the point of his battle-axe downward — a token, like a reversed torch, of death.

The latest instance I have met with of a union of ancient and modern customs at the burial of a knight, occurred at Treves, in 1781, at the interment of the Teutonic knight, General Frederick Casimir. This gallant soldier's charger was led to the brink of the grave in which the body had just been deposited; the throat of the steed was swiftly cut by an official, and the carcass of the horse was flung down upon the coffin of the knight. Such sacrifices were once common enough. At the funerals in England of cavalry soldiers, or of mounted officers, the horse is still processionally conducted to the brink of the grave, but we are too wisely economical to leave him there, or to fling him into it.

Where chivalry had great perils and temptations, we need not be surprised to find that there were many scions of noble houses who either declined to win spurs by encountering mortal danger, or who soon grew weary of making the attempt. Let us, then, consider the unambitious gentlemen who grew "tired of it."

## THE KNIGHTS WHO GREW "TIRED OF IT."

> "How blest are they that waste their weary hours
> In solemn groves and solitary bower
> Where neither eye nor ear
> Can see or hear
> The frantic mirth
> And false delights of frolic earth;
> Where they may sit and pant,
> And breathe their pursy souls;
> Where neither grief consumes, nor gaping want
> Afflicts, nor sullen care controls!
> Away false joys! Ye murder where ye kiss;
> There is no heaven to that, no life to this."
> FRANCIS QUARLES.

As marriage or the cloister was the alternative submitted to most ladies in the days of old, so young men of noble families had small choice but between the church and chivalry. Some, indeed, commenced with arms, won knightly honors, cared nothing for them when they had obtained the prize, and took up the clerical profession, or entered monasteries. There are many distinguished examples. There was first St. Mochua or Cluanus, who, after serving in arms with great distinction, entered a monastery and took to building churches and establishing cities. Of the former he built no less than thirty; and he passed as many years in one church as he had built of churches themselves. He was the founder of one hundred and twenty cells. He is to be looked upon with respect. Old warriors in our own days are often moved by the same impulse which governed Mochua; and when we see retired admirals taking the chair at meetings where Dr. Cumming is about to exhibit; or infirm major-generals supporting, with unabated mental energy, their so-called Puseyite pastors, we only look upon men who, acting conscientiously, are worthy of respect, and are such Mochuas as modern times and circumstances will admit of.

We have another example in Adelard, the cousin of Charlemagne. He was a gay and gallant chevalier at his imperial cousin's court, and there was no stouter wielder of a sword in all the army; but Alard, or Adelard, grew weary of camp and court alike. He fled from some very pretty temptations in the one, as well as great perils in the other. The young prince, he was only twenty, took the monastic habit at Corbie, where he was employed as a gardener, and spoiled cartloads of vegetables before he got his hand and his thoughts to his new profession. He was occasionally busy too in the kitchen, but not to the visible gratification of the monks. Charlemagne often insisted on his appearing at court, where at last he held one or two high offices; and, when he left, wrote a book for the guidance of courtiers generally, by which the latter as little profited, say wicked wits, as other nobility, for whom a nation has long prayed that grace, wisdom, and understanding might be their portion. St. Adelard, for the imperial knight was canonized, lived to be the chief authority in the monastery where he had commenced as cook and gardener, and St. Gerard composed an office in his honor, in gratitude for having been cured of a violent headache through the saint's interposition. This seems to me one of the oddest ways of showing gratitude for a small service that I ever heard of.

I believe that St. Cedd, Bishop of London, in very early days, was also of a family whose profession was military. When or why he entered the church I do not know; but he has some connection with military matters in the fact that Tilbury Fort occupies part of the site of a monastery which St. Cedd had founded, in which he resided, and which was the pride of all the good people in the then pleasant and prosperous city of Tillabury.

Touching St. Aldric, Bishop of Mans, there is no doubt whatever. He was of a noble family, and commenced life at twelve years old, as page to Louis le Debonnaire, at the court of Charlemagne. He was speedily sick of the court, and as speedily sick of the camp. At the age of twenty-one he withdrew to Metz, entered the clerical profession, and became chaplain and confessor to the sovereign whom he had once served as page. His military training made him a very sharp disciplinarian during the quarter of a century that he was bishop; and it is only to be regretted that he had not some influence over the king whose conscience he directed, and of whom a legend will be found in another part of this volume.

There was a second son of Eric, King of Denmark, known by the name of St. Knudt or Canute. He was Duke of Schleswig, and was much more of a monk than a duke. He was canonized accordingly for his virtues. He had a rough way of joking. His knights were nothing better than robbers and pirates, and he resolved to make them forswear violence and live peaceably. They represented, in vain, that they had a right to live as became knights, which Canute did not dispute; he simply dissented from the construction of the right as set down by the knights themselves. To prevent all mistakes on the matter, he one day condemned seven of these gentlemen to be hanged for acts of piracy. One of these exclaimed that, "fitting as the sentence might be for his fellows, there must necessarily be exemption for him." He was like the German corporal in the "Etoile du Nord," who can very well understand that it is quite proper that a man should be hanged, but could *not* comprehend that *he* himself should be the man. The Schleswig knight claimed special exemption on the ground that he was a kinsman of Canute. The latter allowed that this entitled him to some distinction, and the saintly duke hung his cousin six feet higher than any of his accomplices.

We come back more immediately to a knight who grew tired of his vocation, in the person of Nathalan, a Scottish noble of the fifth century. He sold arms, horses, and estate, divided the proceeds among the poor, and devoted himself to preparations for ordination, and the cultivation of vegetables. He bears a highly respectable reputation on the roll of Bishops of Aberdeen.

We meet with a man more famous, in Peter of Sebaste, whose pedigree showed more heroes than could be boasted by any of Peter's contemporaries. He is not an example, indeed, of a man quitting the camp for the cloister; but he and two of his brothers exhibit to us three individuals who might have achieved great worldly profit, by adopting arms as a vocation, but who preferred the Church, and became, all three, bishops.

We have a similar example in the Irish St. Felan. His high birth and great wealth would have made him the flower of Irish chivalry, but he selected another profession, and despising chivalry, entered the Church. He went *a Mundo ad Mundum*, for it was from the hands of Abbot Mundus that he received the monastic habit. Thus, as it was wittily said, the world (Mundus) at once drove and drew him into the Church. It is clear, however, that, like the old war-horse, he pricked up his ears at the sound of battle, and took an interest in stricken fields. To such conclusion we must come, if it be true, as is asserted of him, that the battle of Bannockburn, in 1314, was won by Bruce through the saint's especial intercession. The Dukes of Normandy owed equal obligations to St. Vaneng, who unbuckled the armor from his aristocratic loins, to cover them with a frock; and built churches for the Normans, where he offered up continual prayer for the Norman dukes.

Then again, there was William Berringer, of the family of the Counts of Nevers. No persuasion could induce the handsome William to continue in the career he had embraced, the career of chivalry and arms. His uncle, Peter the Hermit, may have had considerable influence over him, and his change of profession was by no means unprofitable, for the once horse-loving William became Archbishop of Bourges: and he defended the rights of his Church against kings and councils with as much boldness, zeal, and gallantry, as any knight could have exhibited against the stoutest of assailants.

Among our English saints, the one who most nearly resembles him is St. Egwin, who was of the royal blood of the Mercian kings, and who, after a short trial of the profession of arms, retired to the cloister, but was ultimately raised to the see of Worcester. The spirit of the man may perhaps be seen through the legend which says that on setting out on a penitential pilgrimage to Rome, he put iron shackles on his legs, the key of which shackles he flung into the Avon. This is very possible; but when we are told that on requiring the key at a subsequent period, he found it inside a fish, we see that the author of the legend has plagiarized from the original constructor of the story of Polycrates and his ring.

St. Egwin was far less a benefactor to his fellow-men that St. Benedict Biscop, a noble knight of the court of Oswi, the pious king of the Northumbrians. When Benedict, or Bennet, as he is familiarly called, retired from the profession of arms to follow that of the Church, he continued quite as active, and twice as useful, as he had been before. He was a great traveller, spent and gave liberally, and brought over with him, from the continent, workers in stone to erect that monastery at Weremouth which, in its ruins, commemorates his name and deeds. He also brought from France the first glaziers who ever exercised the art of glass-making in England. Altogether St. Bennet is one of those who find means to effect good to others, whatever may be the position they are in themselves.

Aelred of Ridal was a man of similar quality. He was a young North-of-England noble, when he figured as the handsomest cavalier at the court of that "sair saint to the Church," the Scottish king, David. He was remarkable for his good temper, and was as well-disciplined a monk as he had been a military man; for when he once happened to inadvertently break the rule of permanent silence, which prevailed in the monastery at Ridal, into which he entered at the age of twenty-five, he became so horror-stricken that he was eager to increase the penalty put upon him in consequence. He had only dropped a single word in the garden, to a monk who, like himself, had been a knight, but who gave him in return so edifying a scowl, that in an instant poor Aelred felt all the depth of his unutterable iniquity, and accounted himself as criminal as if he had set fire to the neighboring nunnery. He never afterward allowed himself the indulgence of reading his favorite Cicero, but confined his reading to his own work "On Spiritual Friendship," and other books of a similar description.

The great St. Hilary was another of the men of noble family following arms as a vocation, who gave up the profession for that of the Church, and prospered remarkably in consequence. St. Felix of Nola affords us an additional illustration of this fact. This noble young soldier found no happiness in the business of slaughtering, and all the sophistry in the world could not persuade him that it was honorable. "It is a disgusting business," said the Saint, "and as I can not be Felix [happy] in performing it, I will see if I can not be Felix in the Church;" and the punning saint found what he sought.

There is something more wonderful in the conversion of St.

Maurus. He was the son of a nobleman, had St. Benedict for a tutor, and was destined to the career of arms. The tutor, however, having awoke him one night, and sent him to pick a monk out of the river, whom Benedict, in a dream, had seen fall in, Maurus, although no swimmer, obeyed, walked upon the surface of the water, pulled out the struggling monk, walked back with him, arm-in-arm, to the shore, and immediately concluded that he was called to another vocation than that of arms. As for St. John Calybyte, he would not be a soldier, but ran away from home before his wealthy sire could procure him a commission, and only returned to stand, disguised as a mendicant, in front of his father's house, where he received alms till he died. A curious example of idiosyncrasy. St. Honoratus was wiser. He was of a consular family; but, in declining the military profession, he addressed himself with sincerity to be useful in the Church; and the well-deserved result was that he became Archbishop of Arles. St. Anthony, the patriarch of monks, made still greater sacrifices, and chose rather to be a hermit than a commander of legions. St. Sulpicius, the Debonnair, was both rich and good-looking, but he cared less for helmet and feathers than for cord and cowl, and the archbishopric of Bourges rewarded his self-denial. There was more than one King Canute too, who, though not surrendering royalty and generalship of armies, seemed really more inclined, and indeed more fitted, to be studious monks than chivalrous monarchs. Wulstan of Worcester was far more decided, for finding himself, one night, most warmly admiring the young lady who was his *vis-à-vis* in a dance, the gallant officer was so shocked at the impropriety, that he made it an excuse for taking to the cowl forthwith. He did not so ill by the exchange, for the cowl brought him to the mitre at Worcester.

St. Sebastian was a far bolder man, seeing that although he hated a military life, he, to the very utmost, did his duty in that state of life to which it had pleased God to call him; and if half be true of what is told of him, there never was knight of the actual days of chivalry who performed such bold and perilous actions as St. Sebastian. What was a cavalier, pricking against a dragon, to a Roman officer preaching Christianity to his men, under Diocletian?

In later days we meet with St. Raymund of Pennafort, the wealthy young lord, who, rather than serve for pay or plunder, went about teaching philosophy for nothing. St. John, the Patriarch of Alexandria, might have been known as a conqueror, but he preferred being handed down, under the title of the Almoner. He was like that St. Cadoc who chose rather to be abbot *in*, than prince *of*, Wales. St. Poppo of Stavelo exhibited similar humility. He was rapidly rising in the Flandrian army when he suddenly sunk into a cell, and became a sort of Flemish John Wesley. He preached against all tournaments, but only succeeded in abolishing the very exciting combats between a knight and a bear, which were greatly patronized by Flemish ladies, and at which parties staked great sums upon their favorite animal.

St. Francis of Sales, on the other hand, that gentlemanly saint, was saved from the knightly career which his noble birth seemed to promise him, by a vow made by his mother, before he was born. She was resolved that he should be a saint and not a soldier, and as all things went as the lady desired, she placed her son in a position direct for the Church, and the world certainly lost nothing by the matron's proceeding. I respect St. Francis of Sales all the more that he had small human failings, and did not scatter damnation over men whom he saw in a similar concatenation. Sulpicius Severus was, in many respects, like him, save that he had some experience of a soldier's life. But he laid down the sword for the pen, and gave us that admirable historical romance, in which he details so graphically the life of another noble warrior, who quitted the command of soldiers, to take up the teaching of men — St. Martin of Tours.

There was a lady, St. Aldegonde, of the royal blood of France, in the seventh century, who at least encouraged young knights to abandon their fancied vocation, and assume that of monks or friars. She was, most undeservedly, I dare say, assailed by scandalizing tongues accordingly. Indeed, I never heard of lady more persecuted in this way, except perhaps this particular lady's namesake, who once belonged to the gay *troupe* of the Variétés, and to whom the most rattling of *chansonniers* alluded, in the line of a song, which put the significant query of

>  Que fait Aldegonde avec le monde entier ?

One of the most remarkable features in the characters of many of these young nobles who were disinclined to take up arms, or who laid them down for the religious vocation, is the dread they entertained of matrimony. In illustration of this fact, I may notice the case of St. Silvin of Auchy. There was not a gayer or braver knight at the court of Childeric II., nor a more welcome wooer among the ladies. In due time he proposed to a noble maiden, who was in a flutter of happiness at the thought of carrying off such a bachelor from a host of competitors. The wedding was brilliant, up to the conclusion of the ceremony. That over, no persuasion could induce the bridegroom to go to the breakfast. As he had been brought to the altar, there he was resolved to remain. He denounced all weddings as wicked vanities, and darting out of the church-door, left bride and bridal party to take what course they would. There was no end of conjectures as to the cause of the sudden fright which had seized upon the young bridegroom. The latter set it down to inspiration, and as he took to the cowl and led a most exemplary life, no one presumed to doubt it, except the bride and her relations.

The case of St. Licinius is easier of explanation. He was the most rollicking knight-bachelor at the court of Clotaire I. It must, however, be said for him that he sowed his wild oats early, and fought none the less stoutly for going to mass daily, and confessing once a quarter. He was rich, and had a maiden neighbor who was richer. The families of knight and maiden were united in thinking that the estates of the two, encircled in one ring fence, would be one of the most desirable of consummations. The maiden was nothing loath, the knight alone was reluctant. He too, had his doubts about the excellence of marriage, and it was only with very considerable difficulty he was brought to woo the lady, who said "Yes" before the plume in his bonnet had touched the ground when he made his bow to her. The wedding-day was fixed, and as the old epitaph says, "wedding-clothes provided." On the eve of the eventful day, however, Licinius, on paying a visit to the bride, found her suddenly attacked with leprosy. The doctor protested that it would be nothing, but Licinius declared that it was a warning which he dared not neglect. He looked at the leprous lady, muttered the word "unpleasant," and at once betook himself, not to active military life, but to a religious mission. In this occupation he is alleged to have performed such miracles as to deserve canonization, if only the half of them were true.

Now, a bride afflicted with leprosy may fairly be said to be an unpleasant sight. Licinius may even be considered authorized to hesitate in performing his promise, if not in altogether declaring off. We can not say as much in extenuation of another knight who broke his word to a lady, and was clapped into the Roman calendar of deified men. This gentleman in question had a rather unchristian-sounding name. He was called Abraham of Chiduna. At tilt and tournament, and in tented field, there was no cavalier who sat more perfectly in saddle, or handled his lance and wielded his battle-axe with more terrible effect. He was of noble birth, of course; was wealthy, somewhat addicted to light living, in his salad days, but a man who lived soberly enough when those were over. He then resolved to marry, and he had the "good taste," if one may use a term which, we are told, belongs to the literary milliner's vocabulary, to offer himself to, and ask the hand of a very pious maiden with a highly satisfactory dower. The required conclusion was soon come to, and one fine spring morning saw the two principals and their respective friends in church. The knight, it is true, was the last to arrive, and he had been, previously, as unwilling to get up and be married, as Master Barnardine was to get up and be hanged. He was finally brought to the altar, and after some little delay, such as searching for the ring which he had misplaced, and only recovered after much search, the nuptial knot was tied. When this had been accomplished, surrounding friends approached to offer their congratulations; but the icy Abraham coldly waved them back, and announced his determination, then and there, to end his short-lived married state. As he immediately rushed into the wood which was in the vicinity of the church, there was a universal cry that he contemplated suicide. The bride was conveyed home amid much sympathy, and a general but an ineffectual search was made for the "groom." Yet, not altogether ineffectual, for at the end of seventeen days he was discovered, offering up his orisons, in the midst of a marsh. There he had been, he said, for a fortnight, and there he declared he would remain, unless those who sought him consented to the terms he should propose. These were, that he should be allowed to retire to a cell which should be entirely walled up, save a small square aperture for a window. The agreement was ratified, and Abraham was shut up according to his desire; and by a long life of seclusion, passed in preaching to all who approached the window, and taking in all they brought through the same aperture, Abraham has had "Beatus" attached to his name, and that name has been recorded upon the roll of saints.

If there be any reader who objects to this story as unnatural, I would remark to the same, that similar incidents may be met with in our own time. In proof thereof I will briefly relate an anecdote which was told me by the reverend father of a legal knight, who was himself the officiating minister at the ceremony of which I am about to speak.

To the clergyman of a pretty village in Wales, due notice had been given, and all preliminary legal observances having been fulfilled, he awaited in his vestry, ready to marry an ex-sergeant and one of the girls of the village. The canonical hours were fast gliding away, and yet the priest was not summoned to the altar. By certain sounds he could tell that several persons had assembled in the church, and he had two or three times seen a pretty face peeping in at the vestry-door, with a look upon it of pleasure to see that he was still there, and of perplexity as if there was something to be told which only waited to be asked for. At half-past eleven the face again peeped in, whereupon the clergyman invited the owner of it to approach nearer. The invitation was obeyed, and the clergyman inquired the reason for the unusual delay, remarking at the same time, that if the parties were not speedily prepared it would be too late to perform the ceremony that day.

"Well sir," said the nymph, "I was about asking your advice. I am the bride's sister; and there is a difficulty—"

"What is it?" asked the priest.

"Just this, sir," said Jenny. "Sergeant Jones has promised to marry sister Winnifred if father will put down five pounds. Father agrees; but he says that if he puts down the money before the marriage, the sergeant will walk off. And the sergeant will not come up to be married till the money is put down. So, you see, sir, we are in a terrible difficulty; and we want you to propose a method to get us out of it."

"There is nothing easier," said the minister; "let your father put the money into the hands of a trusty third person, who will promise to place it in the sergeant's possession as soon as he has married your sister."

Jenny Morgan saw the excellence of the device in a moment, rushed back to the bridal parties, and they showed their appreciation of the clergyman's suggestion, by crowding to the altar as soon as the preliminary proceeding recommended to them had been accomplished. At length the clergyman came to the words, "Wilt thou have this woman to thy wedded wife?"

"Jack," said the ex-sergeant, looking round at the stake-holder, "have you got the cash?"

"All right!" nodded Jack.

"Then I will," said the sergeant; "and now, Jack, hand over the *tin*."

The agreement was rigidly fulfilled; but had not the minister thought of the means which solved the difficulty, Sergeant Jones would have been nearly as ungallant to his lady as Abraham, Silvin, and Licinius, had been to theirs.

But to return to Abraham. I have said this knight, on assuming his monkly character, had caused himself to be walled up in his cell. I have my suspicions, however, that it was a theatrical sort of wall, for it is very certain that the saint could pass through it. Now, there resided near him a lady recluse who was his "niece," and whose name was Mary. The two were as inseparable as the priest Lacombe and Madame Guyon; and probably were as little deserving of reproach. This Mary was the original of "Little Red Riding Hood." She used to convey boiled milk and butter, and other necessary matters to her uncle Abraham. Now it happened that the ex-knight used also to be visited by a monk whose name was Wolf, or who, at all events, has been so called by hagiographers, on account of his being quite as much of a beast as the quadruped so called. The monk was wont to fall in with Mary as she was on her way to her uncle's cell with pleasant condiments under a napkin, in a wicker-basket. He must have been a monk of the Count Ory fashion, and he was as seductive as Ponchard, when singing " Gentille Annette" to the " Petit Chaperon Rouge," in Boieldieu's Opera. The result was, that the monk carried off Mary to a neighboring city — Edessa, if I remember rightly — and if I am wrong, Mr. Mitchell Kemble will, perhaps, set me right, in his bland and gentleman-like way. The town-life led by these two was of the most disgraceful nature; and when the monk had grown tired of it, he left Mary to lead a worse, without him. Mary became the " Reine Pomare," the " Mogadore," the " Rose Pomponne" of Edessa, and was the terror of all families where there were elder sons and latch-keys. Her doings and her whereabouts at length reached the ears of her uncle Abraham, and not a little astonished were those who knew the recluse to see him one morning, attired in a pourpoint of rich stuff, with a cloak like Almaviva's, yellow buskins with a fall of lace over the tops, a jaunty cap and feather on his head, a rapier on his thigh, and a steed between his legs, which curveted under his burden as though the fun of the thing had given it lightness. At Mary's supper, this cavalier was present on the night of his arrival in Edessa. He scattered his gold like a Crœsus, and Mary considered him worth all the more penniless knights put together. When these had gone, as being less welcome, Abraham declared his relationship, and acted on the right it gave him to rate a niece who was not only an ungrateful minx, but who was as mendacious as an ungrateful niece could well be. The old gentleman, however, had truth on his side, and finally so overwhelmed Mary with its terrible application, that she meekly followed him back to the desert, and passed fifteen years in a walled-up cell close to that of her uncle. The miracles the two performed are adduced as proofs of the genuineness of the personages and their story; matters which I would not dispute even if I had room for it.

The next knight whom I can call to mind as having been frightened by marriage into monkery, is St. Vandrille, Count of the Palace to King Dagobert. During the period of his knightship he was a very Don Juan for gallantry, and railed against matrimony as conclusively as a Malthusian. His friends pressed him to marry nevertheless; and introduced him to a lady with a hundred thousand golden qualities, and prospects as auriferous as those of Miss Kilmansegg. He took the lady's hand with a reluctance that might be called aversion, and which he did not affect to conceal. When the nuptial ceremony was concluded, Knight Vandrille, as eccentric as the cavaliers whose similar conduct I have already noticed, mildly intimated that it was not his intention to proceed further, and that for his part, he had renounced the vanities of this world for aye. Taking the lady apart, he appears to have produced upon *her* a conviction that the determination was one he could not well avoid; and we are not told that she even reproached him for a conduct which seems to me to have been a thousand times more selfish and inexcusable than that of the clever but despicable Abelard. The church, however, did not disapprove of the course adopted, and St. Vandrille, despite his worse than breach of promise, has been forgiven as knight, and canonized as saint.

Far more excusable was that little Count of Arian, Elzear, the boy-knight at the court of Charles II., King of Sicily, whom that monarch married at the age of thirteen years, to Delphina of Glandeves, a young lady of fifteen. When I say far more excusable, I do Elzear some injustice, for the boy was willing enough to be wed, and looked forward to making his lady proud of his own distinction as a knight. Delphina, however, it was who proposed that they should part at the altar, and never meet again. She despised the boy, and the little cavalier took it to heart — so much so, that he determined to renounce the career of arms and enter the church. Thereby chivalry lost a worthy cavalier, and the calendar gained a very active saint.

Elzear might well feel aggrieved. There have been knights even younger than he, who have carried spurs before they were thirteen. This reminds me of a paragraph in an article which I contributed to "Fraser's Magazine," in March, 1844, under the title of "A Walk across Bohemia," in which, speaking of the Imperial Zeughaus at Vienna, I noticed "the suit of armor of that little hero, the second Louis of Hungary, he who came into this breathing world some months before he was welcome, and who supported his character for precocity by marrying at twelve, and becoming the legitimate bearer of all the honors of paternity as soon as he entered his teens; who moreover maintained his consistency by turning a gray old man at sixteen, and finally terminated his ephemeral course on the field of battle before he became of age." Elzear then was not, perhaps, so poor a knight as his older lady seemed disposed to count him.

I must be briefer with noticing the remaining individuals who either flung up chivalry for the Church, or who preferred the latter to following a knightly career. First, there was St. Anscharius, who after he had made the change alluded to, was standing near the easy Olas, King of Sweden, when the latter cast lots to decide whether Christianity should be the religion of the state, or not. We are told that the prayers of St. Anscharius caused the king to throw double-sixes in favor of the better cause.

St. Andrew Cossini made an admirable saint after being the most riotous of cavaliers. So St. Amandus of Nantes won his saintship by resigning his lordship over men-at-arms. Like him was that St. Romuald of the family of the Dukes of Ravenna, who, whether fighting or hunting, loved to retire from the fray and the chase, to pray at peace, in shady places. St. John of Malta and St. Stephen of Grandmont were men of the like kidney. St. Benedict of Anian was that famous cup-bearer of Charlemagne, who left serving the Emperor in hall and field, to serve a greater master with less ostentation. He followed the example of that St. Auxentius, who threw up his commission in the equestrian guard of Theodosius the Younger, to take service in a body of monks.

Many of those who renounced arms, or would not assume military service when opportunity offered itself, profited personally by the adoption of such a course. Thus St. Porphyrius was a knight till he was twenty-five years of age, and he died Bishop of Gaza. The knight St. Wulfran became Bishop of Sens. St. Hugh won the bishopric of Grenoble, by not only renouncing knighthood himself, but by inducing his father to follow his example. St. Norbert became Archbishop of Magdeburg, after leading a jolly life, not only as a knight but as priest. A fall from his horse brought him to a sense of decency. A prophecy of a young maiden to St. Ulric gained him his saintship and the bishopric of Augsburg. Had she not foretold he would die a bishop, he would have been content to carry a banner. Examples like these are very numerous, but I have cited enough.

Few in a worldly sense made greater sacrifice than St. Casimir, son of Casimir III., King of Poland. He so loved his reverend tutor, Dugloss, that, tŏ be like him, he abandoned even his chance of the throne, and became a priest. St. Benedict of Umbria took a similar course, upon a smaller scale; and not all the persuasions of his nurse, who ran after him when he ran away from home, could induce him to be anything but a priest. St. Herman Joseph, of Cologne, showed how completely he had abandoned the knightly character, when, as monk, he begged the peasants whom he taught, to be good enough to buffet him well, and cuff him soundly, as it was impossible for him to have a sufficiency of kicks and contempt. St. Guthlac, the noble hermit of Croyland, evinced more dignity in his retirement, and the same may be said of St. Peter Regalati, and St. Ubaldus of Gabio. The latter was resolute neither to marry nor take arms. He liked no turmoil, however qualified. St. Vincent of Lerins *did* bear arms for years, but he confessed he did not like the attendant dangers—threatening him spiritually, not bodily, and he took the cowl and gained a place in the sacred calendar accordingly. St. Aloysius Gonzaga, whose father was a prince, was another of the young gentlemen for whom arms had little attraction. The humility of this young gentleman, however, had a very silly aspect, if it all resembled what is said of him by Father Caperius. "He never looked on women, kept his eye strictly guarded, and generally cast down; would never stay with his mother alone in her chamber, and if she sent in any message to him by some lady in her company, he received it, and gave his answer in a few words, with his eyes shut, and his chamber-door only half open; and when bantered on that score, he ascribed such behavior to his bashfulness. It was owing to his original modesty that he did not know by their face many ladies among his own relations, with whom he had frequently conversed; and that he was afraid and ashamed to let a footman see so much as his foot uncovered." Whatever the soft Aloysius may have been fit for, it is clear that he was *not* fit for chivalry. Something akin to him was St. Theobald of Champagne, who probably would never have been a saint, if his father had not ordered him to lead a body of troops to the succor of a beleaguered cousin. Theobald declined, and at once went into a monastery.

St. Walthen, one of the sons of the Earl of Huntingdon, and

Maud, daughter of Judith, which Judith was the niece of the Conqueror, only narrowly escaped being a gallant knight. As a boy, indeed, he used to build churches with his box of bricks, while his brothers built castles; but at least he gave promise of being a true knight, and, once, not only accepted the gift of a ring from a lady, but wore the sparkling diamond on his finger. "Ah! ah!" exclaimed the saucy courtiers, "Knight Walthen is beginning to have a tender heart for the ladies!" Poor Walthen! he called this a devil's chorus, tossed the ring into the fire, broke the lady's heart, and went into a monastery for the remainder of his days. He escaped better than St. Clarus, who had a deaf ear and stone-blind eyes for the allurements of a lady of quality, and who only barely escaped assassination, at the hands of two ruffians hired by the termagant to kill the man who was above allowing her holy face to win from him a grin of admiration. But though I could fill a formidable volume with names of *ci-devant* knights who have turned saints, I will spare my readers, and conclude with the great name of St. Bernard. He did not, indeed, take up arms, but when he adopted a religious profession, he enjoyed the great triumph of inducing his uncle, all his brothers, knights, and simple officers, to follow his example. The uncle Gualdri, a famous swordsman and seigneur of Touillon, was the first who was convinced that Bernard was right. The two younger brothers of the latter, Bartholomew and Andrew, next knocked off their spurs and took to their breviary. Guy, the eldest brother, a married man, of wealth, broke up his household, sold his armor, sent his lady to a convent and his daughters to a nunnery, put on the cowl, and followed St. Bernard. Others of his family and many of his friends followed his example, with which I conclude my record of saints who have had any connection with arms. As for St. Bernard, I *will* say of him, that had he assumed the sword and been as merciless to his enemies as he was, in his character of abbot, without bowels of compassion for an adversary whom he could crush by wordy argument, he would have been the most terrible cavalier that ever sat in saddle!

Perhaps the most perfect cavalier who ever changed that dignity for the cowl, was the Chevalier de Rancé. Of him and his Trappist followers I will here add a few words.

## THE CHEVALIER DE RANCE AND THE TRAPPISTS.

De Rancé was born in 1626. He was of a ducal house, and the great Cardinal de Richelieu was his godfather. In his youth he was very sickly and scholastic. He was intended for the Church, held half a score of livings before he could speak — and when he *could* express his will, resolved to live only by his sword. He remained for a while neither priest nor swordsman, but simply the gayest of libertines. He projected a plan of knight-errantry, in society with all the young cavaliers, and abandoned the project to study astrology. For a period of some duration, he was half-knight, half-priest. He then received full orders, dressed like the most frivolous of marquises, seduced the Duchess de Montbazon, and absolved in others the sins which he himself practised. "Where are you going?" said the Chevalier de Champvallon to him one day. "I have been preaching all the morning," said De Rancé, "like an angel, and I am going this afternoon to hunt like the very devil." He may be said to have been like those Mormons who describe their fervent selves as "Hell-bent on Heaven!"

Nobody could ever tell whether he was soldier or priest, till death slew the Duchess de Montbazon. De Rancé unexpectedly beheld the corpse disfigured by the ravages of small-pox or measles, and he was so shocked, that it drove him from the world to the cloister, where, as the reconstructor, rather than the founder, of the order of Trappists, he spent thirty-seven years — exactly as many as he had passed in the "world."

The companions and followers of the chivalrous De Rancé claim a few words for themselves. The account will show in what strong contrasts the two portions of their lives consisted. They had learned obedience in their career of arms, but they submitted to a far more oppressive rule in their career as monks. Some century and a half ago there was published in Paris a dreadfully dreary series of volumes, entitled "Relations de la Vie et de la Mort de quelques Religieux de l'Abbaye de la Trappe." They consist chiefly of tracts, partly biographical and partly theological, uninteresting in the main, but of interest as showing what noble soldiers or terrible freebooters asked for shelter in, and endured the austerities of, La Trappe. I have alluded to the unreserved submission required at the hands of the brothers. The latter, according to the volumes which I have just named, were sworn to impart even their *thoughts* to the Abbot. They who thus delivered themselves with least reserve appear to have been commanded in very bad Latin; but their act of obedience was so dear to Heaven, that their persons became surrounded with a glory, which their less communicative brethren, says the author naïvely, could not possibly gaze at for any length of time:—the which I implicitly believe.

The candidates for admission included, without doubt, many very pious persons, but with them were degraded priests, with whom we have little to do, and ex-officers, fugitive men-at-arms, robbers who had lived by the sword, and murderers, of knightly degree, who had used their swords to the unrighteous slaying of others, and who sought safety within the cloisters of La Trappe. All that was asked of them was obedience. Where this failed it was compelled. Where it abounded it was praised. Next to it was humility. One brother, an ex-soldier reeking with blood, is lauded because he lived on baked apples, when his throat was too sore to admit of his swallowing more substantial food. Another brother, who had changed arms for the gown, is most gravely compared with Moses, because he was never bold enough to enter the pantry with sandals on his feet. Still, obedience was the first virtue eulogized—so eulogized that I almost suspect it to have been rare. It was made of so much importance, that the community were informed that all their faith, and all their works, without blind obedience to the superior, would fail in securing their salvation. Practical blindness was as strongly enjoined. He who used his eyes to least purpose, was accounted the better man. One ex-military brother did this in so praiseworthy a way, that in eight years he had never seen a fault in any of his brethren.

It was not, however, this sort of blindness that De Rancé required, for he encouraged the brethren to bring accusations against each other. Much praise is awarded to a brother who never looked at the roof of his own cell. Laudation more unmeasured is poured upon another faithful knight of the new order of self-negation, who was so entirely unaccustomed to raise his eyes from the ground, that he was not aware of the erection of a new chapel in the garden, until he broke his head against the wall.

On one occasion the Duchess de Guiche and an eminent prelate visited the monastery together. After they had left, a monk entered the Abbot's apartment, threw himself at the feet of his superior, and begged permission to confess a great crime. He was told to proceed.

"When the lady and the bishop were here just now," said he, "I dared to raise my eyes, and they rested upon the face—"

"Not of the lady, thou reprobate!" exclaimed the Abbot.

"Oh no," calmly rejoined the monk, "but of the old bishop!" A course of bread and water was needed to work expiation for the crime.

Some of the brethren illustrated what they meant by obedience and humility, after a strange fashion. For example, there was one who having expressed an inclination to return to the world, was detained against his will. His place was in the kitchen, and the devastation he committed among the crockery was something stupendous — and probably not altogether unintentional. He was not only continually fracturing the delf earthenware dishes, but was incessantly running from the kitchen to the Abbot, from the Abbot to the Prior, from the Prior to the Sub-Prior, and from the Sub-Prior to the Master of the Novices to confess his fault. Thence he returned to the kitchen again, once more to smash whole crates of plates, following up the act with abundant confessions, and deriving evident enjoyment, alike in destroying the property, and assailing with noisy apologies the governing powers whom he was resolved to inspire with a desire of getting rid of him.

In spite of forced detention there was a mock appearance of liberty at monthly assemblies. The brethren were asked if there was anything in the arrangement of the institution and its rules which they desired to see changed. As an affirmative reply, however, would have brought "penance" and "discipline" on him who made it, the encouraging phrase that "They had only to speak," by no means rendered them loquacious, and every brother, by his silence, expressed his content.

If death was the suicidal object of many, the end appears to have been generally attained with a speedy certainty. The superiors and a few monks reached an advanced age; only a few of the brethren died old men. Consumption, inflammation of the lungs, and abscess (at memory of the minute description of which the very heart turns sick), carried off the victims with terrible rapidity. Men entered, voluntarily or otherwise, in good health. If they did so, determined to achieve suicide, or were driven in by the government with a view of putting them to death, the end soon came, and was, if we may believe what we read, welcomed with alacrity. After rapid, painful, and unresisted decay, the sufferer saw as his last hour approached, the cinders strewn on the ground in the shape of a cross; a thin scattering of straw was made upon the cinders, and that was the death-bed upon which every Trappist expired. The body was buried in the habit of the order, as some knights have been in panoply, without coffin or shroud, and was borne to the grave in a cloth upheld by a few brothers. If it fell into its last receptacle with huddled-up limbs, De Rancé would leap into the grave and dispose the unconscious members, so as to make them assume an attitude of repose.

A good deal of confusion appears to have distinguished the rules of nomenclature. In many instances, where the original names had impure or ridiculous significations, the change was advisable. But I can not see how a brother became more cognisable as a Christian, by assuming the names of Palemon, Achilles, Moses, or even Dorothy. Theodore, I can understand; but Dorothy, though it bears the same meaning, seems to me but an indifferent name for a monk, even in a century when the male Montmorencies delighted in the name of "Anne."

None of the monks were distinguished by superfluous flesh. Some of these ex-soldiers were so thin-skinned, that when sitting on hard chairs, their bones fairly rubbed through their very slight epidermis. They who so suffered, and joyfully, were held up as bright examples of godliness.

There is matter for many a sigh in these saffron-leaved and worm-eaten tomes, whose opened pages are now before me. I find a monk who has passed a sleepless night through excess of pain. To test his obedience, he is ordered to confess that he has slept well and suffered nothing. The submissive soldier obeys his general's command. Another confesses his readiness, as Dr. Newman has done, to surrender any of his own deliberately-made convictions at the bidding of his superior. "I am wax," he says, "for you to mould me as you will;" and his unreserved surrender of himself is commended with much windiness of phrase. A third, inadvertently remarking that his scalding broth is over-salted, bursts into tears at the enormity of the crime he has committed by thus complaining; whereupon praise falls upon him more thickly than the salt did into his broth: "Yes," says the once knight, now abbot, "it is not praying, nor watching, nor repentance, that is alone asked of you by God, but humility and obedience therewith; and *first* obedience."

To test the fidelity of those professing to have this humility and obedience, the most outrageous insults were inflicted on such as in the world had been reckoned the most high-spirited. It is averred that these never failed. The once testy soldier, now passionless monk, kissed the sandal raised to kick, and blessed the hand lifted to smite him. A proud young officer of mousquetaires, of whom I have strong suspicions that he had embezzled a good deal of his majesty's money, acknowledged that he was the greatest criminal that ever lived; but he stoutly denied the same when the officers of the law visited the monastery and accused him of fraudulent practices. This erst young warrior had no greater delight than in being permitted to clean the spittoons in the chapel, and provide them with fresh sawdust. Another, a young marquis and chevalier, performed with ecstacy servile offices of a more disgusting character. This monk was the flower of the fraternity. He was for ever accusing himself of the most heinous crimes, not one of which he had committed, or was capable of committing. "He represented matters so ingeniously," says De Rancé, who on this occasion is the biographer, "that without lying, he made himself pass for the vile wretch which in truth he was not." He must have been like that other clever individual who "lied like truth."

When I say that he was the flower of the fraternity, I probably do some wrong to the Chevalier de Santin, who under the name of Brother Palemon, was undoubtedly the chief pride of La Trappe. He had been an officer in the army; without love for God, regard for man, respect for woman, or reverence for law. In consequence of a rupture between Savoy and France, he lost an annuity on which he had hitherto lived. As his constitution was considerably shattered, he at the same time took to reading. He was partially converted by perusing the history of Joseph; and he was finally perfected by seeing the dead body of a very old and very ugly monk, assume the guise and beauty of that of a young man.

This was good ground for conversion; but the count—for the chevalier of various orders was of that degree by birth—the count had been so thorough a miscreant in the world, that they who lived in the latter declined to believe in the godliness of Brother Palemon. Thereupon he was exhibited to all comers, and he gave ready replies to all queries put to him by his numerous visiters. All France, grave and gay, noble and simple, flocked to the spectacle. At the head of them was that once sovereign head of the Order of the Garter, James II., with his illegitimate son, from whom is descended the French ducal family of Fitz-James. The answers of Palemon to his questioners edified countless crowds. He shared admiration with another ex-military brother, who guilelessly told the laughing ladies who flocked to behold him, that he had sought refuge in the monastery because his sire had wished him to marry a certain lady; but that his soul revolted at the idea of touching even the finger-tips of one of a sex by the first of whom the world was lost. The consequent laughter was immense.

From this it is clear that there were occasionally gay doings at the monastery, and that those at least who had borne arms, were not addicted to close their eyes in the presence of ladies. Among the most remarkable of the knightly members of the brotherhood, was a certain Robert Graham, whose father, Colonel Graham, was first cousin to Montrose. Robert was born, we are told, in the "Château de Rostourne," a short league (it is added by way of help, I suppose, to perplexed travellers), from Edinburgh. By his mother's side he was related to the Earl of Perth, of whom the Trappist biographer says, that he was even more illustrious for his piety, and for what he suffered for the sake of religion, than by his knighthood, his viceroyship, or his offices of High Chancellor of England, and "Governor of the Prince of Wales, now (1716) rightful king of Great Britain." The mother of Robert, a zealous protestant, is spoken of as having "as much piety as one *can* have in a false religion." In spite of her teaching, however, the young Robert early exhibited an inclination for the Romish religion; and at ten years of age, the precocious boy attended mass in the chapel of Holyrood, to the great displeasure of his mother. On his repeating his visit, she had him soundly whipped by his tutor; but the young gentleman declared that the process could not persuade him to embrace Presbyterianism. He accordingly rushed to the house of Lord Perth, " himself a recent convert from the Anglican Church," and claimed his protection. After some family arrangements had been concluded, the youthful protégé was formally surrendered to the keeping of Lord Perth, by his mother, and not without reluctance. His father gave him up with the unconcern of those Gallios who care little about questions of religion.

Circumstances compelled the earl to leave Scotland, when Robert sojourned with his mother at the house of her brother, a godly protestant minister. Here he showed the value of the instructions he had received at the hands of Lord Perth and his Romish chaplain, by a conduct which disgusted every honest man, and terrified every honest maiden, in all the country round. His worthy biographer is candid enough to say that Robert, in falling off from Popery, did not become a protestant, but an atheist. The uncle turned him out of his house. The prodigal repaired to London, where he rioted prodigally; thence he betook himself to France, and he startled even Paris with the bad renown of his evil doings. On his way thither through Flanders, he had had a moment or two of misgiving as to the wisdom of his career, and he hesitated while one might count twenty, between the counsel of some good priests, and the bad example of some Jacobite soldiers, with whom he took service. The latter prevailed, and when the chevalier Robert appeared at the court of St Germains, Lord Perth presented to the fugitive king and queen there, as accomplished a scoundrel as any in Christendom.

There was a show of decency at the exiled court, and respect for religion. Young Graham adapted himself to the consequent influences. He studied French, read the lives of the saints, entered the seminary at Meaux, and finally reprofessed the Romish religion. He was now seized with a desire to turn hermit, but accident having taken him to La Trappe, the blasé libertine felt himself reproved by the stern virtue exhibited there, and, in a moment of enthusiasm, he enrolled himself a postulant, bade farewell to the world, and devoted himself to silence, obedience, humility, and austerity, with a perfectness that surprised alike those who saw and those who heard of it. Lord Perth opposed the reception of Robert in the monastery. Thereon arose serious difficulty, and therewith the postulant relapsed into sin. He blasphemed, reviled his kinsmen, swore oaths that set the whole brotherhood in speechless terror, and finally wrote a letter to his old guardian, so crammed with fierce and unclean epithets, that the abbot refused permission to have it forwarded. The excitement which followed brought on illness; with the latter, came reflection and sorrow. At length all difficulties vanished, and ultimately, on the eve of All Saints, 1699, Robert Graham became a monk, and changed his name for that of Brother Alexis. King James visited him, and was much edified by the spiritual instruction vouchsafed him by the second cousin of the gallant Montrose. The new monk was so perfect in obedience that he would not in winter throw a crumb to a half-starved sparrow, without first applying for leave from his spiritual superior. "Indeed," says his biographer, "I could tell you a thousand veritable stories about him; but they are so extraordinary that I do not suppose the world would believe one of them." The biographer adds, that Alexis, after digging and cutting wood all day; eating little, drinking less, praying incessantly, and neither washing nor unclothing himself, lay down; but to pass the night without closing his eyes in sleep! He was truly a brother Vigilantius.

The renown of his conversion had many influences. The father of Alexis, Colonel Graham, embraced Romanism, and the colonel and an elder son, who was already a Capuchin friar, betook themselves to La Trappe, where the reception of the former into the church was marked by a double solemnity — De Rancé dying as the service was proceeding. The wife of Colonel Graham is said to have left Scotland on the receipt of the above intelligence, to have repaired to France, and there embrace the form of faith followed by her somewhat facile husband. There is, however, great doubt on this point.

The fate of young Robert Graham was similar to that of most of the Trappists. The deadly air, the hard work, the watchings, the scanty food, and the uncleanliness which prevailed, soon slew a man who was as useless to his fellow-men in a convent, as he had ever been in the world. His confinement was, in fact, a swift suicide. Consumption seized on the poor boy, for he was still but a boy, and his rigid adherence to the severe discipline of the place, only aided to develop what a little care might have easily checked. His serge gown clove to the carious bones which pierced through his diseased skin. The portions of his body on which he immovably lay, became gangrened, and nothing appears to have been done by way of remedy. He endured all with patience, and looked forward to death with a not unaccountable longing. The "infirmier" bade him be less eager in pressing forward to the grave.—"I will now pray God," said the nursing brother, "that he will be pleased to save you."—"And I," said Alexis, "will ask him not to heed you." Further detail is hardly necessary: suffice it to say that Robert Graham died on the 21st May, 1701, little more than six months after he had entered the monastery, and at the early age of twenty-two years. The father and brother also died in France, and so ended the chivalrous cousins of the chivalrous Montrose.

The great virtue inculcated at La Trappe, was one of the cherished virtues of old chivalry, obedience to certain rules. But there was no excitement in carrying it out. Bodily suffering was encountered by a knight, for mere glory's sake. At La Trappe it was accounted as the only means whereby to escape Satan. The knight of the cross purchased salvation by the sacrifice of his life; the monk of La Trappe, by an unprofitable suicide. With both there was doubtless the one great hope common to all Christians; but that great hope, so fortifying to the knight, seemed not to relieve the Trappist of the fear that Satan was more powerful than the Redeemer. When once treating this subject at greater length, I remarked that there was a good moral touching Satan in Cuvier's dream, and the application of which might have been profitable to men like these monks. The great philosopher just named, once saw, in his sleep, the popular representative of the great enemy of man. The fiend approached with a loudly-expressed determination to "eat him." "Eat me!" exclaimed Cuvier, examining him the while with the eye of a naturalist. "Eat me! Horns! Hoofs!" he added, scanning him over. "Horns? Hoofs? *Graminivorous!* needn't be afraid of you!"

And now let us get back from the religious orders of men to chivalrous orders of ladies. It is quite time to exclaim, *Place aux Dames!*

## FEMALE KNIGHTS AND JEANNE DARC.

Mein ist der Helm, und mir gehört er zu. — SCHILLER.

"ORDERS for ladies" have been favorite matters with both Kings and Queens, Emperors and Empresses. The Austrian Empress, Eleanora de Gonzague, founded two orders, which admitted only ladies as members. The first was in commemoration of the miraculous preservation of a particle of the true cross, which escaped the ravages of a fire which nearly destroyed the imperial residence, in 1668. Besides this Order of the Cross, the same Empress instituted the Order of the Slaves of Virtue. This was hardly a complimentary title, for a slave necessarily implies a compulsory and unwilling servant. The number of members were limited to thirty, and these were required to be noble, and of the Romish religion. The motto was, *Sole ubique triumphat;* which may have implied that she only who best served virtue, was likely to profit by it. This was not making a very exalted principle of virtue itself. It was rather placing it in the point of view wherein it was considered by Pamela, who was by far too calculating a young lady to deserve all the eulogy that has been showered upon her.

Another Empress of Germany, Elizabeth Christiana, founded, in the early part of the last century, at Vienna, an Order of Neighborly Love. It consisted of persons of both sexes; but nobody was accounted a neighbor who was not noble. With regard to numbers, it was unlimited. The motto of the order was *Amor Proximi;* a motto which exactly characterized the feelings of Queen Guinever for any handsome knight who happened to be her neighbor for the nonce. "Proximus" at the meetings of the order was, of course, of that convenient gender whereby all the members of the order could profit by its application. They might have had a particularly applicable song, if they had only possessed a Béranger to sing as the French lyrist has done.

There was also in Germany an order for ladies only, that was of a very sombre character. It was the Order of Death's Head; and was founded just two centuries ago, by a Duke of Wirtemburg, who decreed that a princess of that house should always be at the head of it. The rules bound ladies to an observance of conduct which they were not likely to observe, if the rule of Christianity was not strong enough to bind them; and probably many fair ladies who wore the double cross, with the death's head pending from the lower one, looked on the motto of "Memento Mori," as a reminder to daring lovers who dared to look on *them*.

France had given us, in ladies' orders, first, the Order of the Cordelière, founded by that Anne of Brittany who brought her independent duchy as a dower to Charles VIII. of France, and who did for the French court what Queen Charlotte effected for that of England, at a much later period. Another Anne, of Austria, wife of Louis XIII., and some say of Cardinal Mazarin also, founded, for ladies, the Order of the Celestial Collar of the Holy Rosary. The members consisted of fifty young ladies of the first families in France; and they all wore, appended to other and very charming insignia hanging from the neck, a portrait of St. Dominic, who found himself in the best possible position for instilling all sorts of good principles into a maiden's bosom.

The Order of the Bee was founded a century and a half ago by Louisa de Bourbon, Duchess of Maine. The ensign was a medal, with the portrait of the duchess on one side, and the figure of a bee, with the motto, *Je suis petite, mais mes piqueures sont profondes*, on the other.

In Russia, Peter the Great founded the Order of St. Catherine, in honor of his wife, and gave as its device, *Pour l'amour et la fidélité envers la patrie*. It was at first intended for men, but was ultimately made a female order exclusively. A similar change was found necessary in the Spanish Order of the Lady of Mercy, founded in the thirteenth century by James, King of Aragon. There were other female orders in Spain, and the whole of them had for their object the furtherance of religion, order, and virtue. In some cases, membership was conferred in acknowledgment of merit. Who forgets Miss Jane Porter in her costume and insignia of a lady of one of the orders of Polish female chivalry—and who is ignorant that Mrs. Otway has been recently decorated by the Queen of Spain with the Order of Maria Louisa?

The Order of St. Ulrica, in Sweden, was founded in 1734, in honor of a lady, the reigning Queen, and to commemorate the liberty which Sweden had acquired and enjoyed from the period of her accession. Two especial qualities were necessary in the candidates for knighthood in this order. It was necessary that a public tribunal should declare that they were men of pure public spirit; and it was further required of them to prove that in serving the country, they had never been swayed by motives of private interest. When the order was about to be founded, not less than five hundred candidates appeared to claim chivalric honor. Of these, only fifty were chosen, and decree was made that the number of knights should never exceed that amount. It was an unnecessary decree, if the qualifications required were to be stringently demanded. But, in the conferring of honors generally, there has often been little connection between cause and effect; as, for instance, after Major-General Simpson had failed to secure the victory which the gallantry of our troops had put in his power at the Redan, the home government was so delighted, that they made field-marshals of two very old gentlemen. The example was not lost on the King of the Belgians. He, too, commemorated the fall of Sebastopol by enlarging the number of his knights. He could not well scatter decorations among his army, for that has been merely a military police, but he made selection of an equally destructive body, and named eighteen doctors—Knights of St. Leopold.

These orders of later institution appear to have forgotten one of the leading principles of knighthood—love for the ladies—but perhaps this is quite as well. When Louis II., Duke of Bourbon, instituted the Order of the Golden Shield, he was by no means so forgetful. He enjoined his knights to honor the ladies above all, and never permit any one to slander them with impunity; "because," said the good duke, "after God, we owe everything to the labors of the ladies, and all the honor that man can acquire." One portion of which assertion may certainly defy contradiction.

The most illustrious of female knights, however, is, without dispute, the Maid of Orleans. Poor Jeanne Darc seems to me to have been an illustrious dupe and an innocent victim. Like Charlotte Corday, the calamities of her country weighed heavily upon her spirits, and her consequent eager desire to relieve them, caused her to be marked as a fitting instrument for a desired end. Poor Charlotte Corday commissioned herself for the execution of the heroic deed which embellishes her name—Jeanne Darc was evidently commissioned by others.

The first step taken by Jeanne to obtain access to the Dauphin, was to solicit the assistance of the proud De Baudricourt, who resided not far from the maid's native place, Domremy. However pious the young girl may have been, De Baudricourt was not the man to give her a public reception, had not some foregone conclusion accompanied it. She needed his help to enable her to proceed to Chinon. The answer of the great chief was that she should not be permitted to go there. The reply of the maid, who was always uncommonly "smart" in her answers, was that she *would* go to Chinon, although she were forced to crawl the whole way on her knees. She *did* go, and the circumstances of a mere young girl, who was in the habit of holding intercourse with angels and archangels, thus overcoming, as it were, the most powerful personage in the district, was proof enough to the common mind, as to whence she derived her strength and authority. The corps of priests by whom she was followed, as soon as her divine mission was acknowledged or invented by the court, lent her additional influence, and sanctified in her own mind, her doubtless honest enthusiasm. The young girl did all to which she pledged herself, and in return, was barbarously treated by both friend and foe, and was most hellishly betrayed by the Church, under whose benediction she had raised her banner. She engaged to relieve Orleans from the terrible English army which held it in close siege, and she nobly kept her engagement. It may be noticed that the first person slain in this siege, was a young lady named Belle, and the fair sex thus furnished the first victim, as well as the great conqueror, in this remarkable conflict.

I pass over general details, in order to have the more space to notice particular illustrative circumstances touching our female warrior. Jeanne, it must be allowed, was extremely bold of assertion as well as smart in reply. She would have delighted a Swedenborgian by the alacrity with which she protested that she held intercourse with spirits from Heaven and prophets of old. Nothing was so easy as to make her believe so; and she was quite as ready to deny the alleged fact when her clerical accusers, in the day of her adversity, declared that such belief was a suggestion of the devil. I think there was some humor and a little reproach in the reply by Jeanne, that she would maintain or deny nothing but as she was directed by the Church.

Meanwhile, during her short but glorious career, she manifested true chivalrous spirit. She feared no man, not even the brave Dunois. "Bastard, bastard!" said she to him on one occasion, "in the name of God, hear me; I command you to let me know of the arrival of Fastolf as soon as it takes place; for, hark ye, if he passes without my knowledge, I give you my word, you shall lose your head." And thereon she turned to her dinner of dry bread and wine-and-water—half a pint of the first to two pints of the last, with the quiet air of a person able and determined to realize every menace.

It is very clear that her brother knights, while they profited by her services, and obeyed (with some reluctance) her orders, neither thought nor spoke over-well of her. Their comments were not complimentary to a virgin reputation, which a jury of princesses, with a queen for a forewoman, had pronounced unblemished. She even risked her *prestige* over the common rank and file, but generally by measures which resulted in strengthening it. Thus, on taking the Fort of the Augustins from the English, she destroyed all the rich things and lusty wine she found there, lest the men should be corrupted by indulgence therein. It may be remembered that Gustavus Vasa highly disgusted his valiant Dalecarlians by a similar exhibition of healthy discipline.

The Maid undoubtedly placed the work of fighting before the pleasure of feasting. When she was about to issue from her lodgings, to head the attack against the bastion of the Tourelles, where she prophesied she would be wounded, her host politely begged of her to remain and partake of a dish of freshly-caught shad. It was the 7th of May, and shad was just in season; the Germans call it distinctively "the May-fish." Jeanne resisted the temptation for the moment. "Keep the fish till to-night," said she, "till I have come back from the fray; for I shall bring a Goden [a 'God d—n,' or Englishman] with me to partake of my supper."

She was not more ready of tongue than she was quick of eye. An instance of the latter may be found in an incident before Jargeau. She was reconnoitring the place at a considerable distance. The period was more than a century and a half before Hans Lippershey, the Middleburg spectacle-maker, had invented, and still more before Galileo had improved, the telescope. The Duke d'Alençon was with Jeanne, and she bade him step aside, as the enemy were pointing a gun at him. The Duke obeyed, for he knew her acuteness of vision; the gun was fired, and De Lude, a gentleman of Anjou, standing in a line with the spot which had been occupied by the Duke, was slain — which must have been very satisfactory to the Duke!

I have said that some of the knights had but a scanty respect for the gallant Maid. A few, no doubt, objected to the assumption of heavenly inspiration on her part. One, at least, was not so particular. I allude to the Baron De Richemond, who had been exiled from court for the little misdemeanor of having assassinated Cannes de Beaulieu. The Baron had recovered his good name by an actively religious exercise, manifested by his hunting after wizards and witches, and burning them alive, to the delight and edification of dull villagers. This pious personage paid a visit to Jeanne, hoping to obtain, by her intercession, the royal permission to have a share in the war. The disgraced knight, who brought with him a couple of thousand men, when these were most wanted, was not likely to meet with a refusal of service, and the permission sought for was speedily granted. Jeanne playfully alluded to her own supernatural inspiration and the Baron's vocation as "witch-finder." "Ah well," said De Richemond, "with regard to yourself, I have only this to say, that it is difficult to say anything; but if you are from Heaven, it is not I who shall be afraid of you; and if you come from the devil, I do not fear even him, who, in such case, sends you." Thereupon, they laughed merrily, and began to talk of the next day's battle.

That battle was fought upon the field of Patay, where the gallant Talbot was made prisoner by the equally gallant Saintrailles. When the great English commander was brought into the presence of Jeanne, he was good-humoredly asked if he had expected such a result the day before. "It is the fortune of war," philosophically exclaimed the inimitable John; and thereby he made a soldier's comment, which has often since been in the mouths of the valiant descendants of the French knights who heard it uttered, and which is frequently quoted as being of Gallic origin. But, again, I think that "fortuna belli" was not an uncommon phrase, perhaps, in old days before the French language was yet spoken.

And here, talking of origin, let me notice a circumstance of some interest. Jeanne Darc is commonly described as Jeanne D'Arc, as though she had been ennobled. This, indeed, she was, by the King, but not by that name. To the old family name was added that of *du Lys*, in allusion to the Lily of France, which that family had served so well. The brothers of Jeanne, now Darc du Lys, entered the army. When Guise sent a French force into Scotland, some gallant gentlemen of this name of Lys were among them. They probably settled in Caledonia, for the name is not an uncommon one there; and there is a gallant major in the 48th who bears it, and who, perhaps, may owe his descent to the ennobled brothers of "The Maid of Orleans."

Jeanne was not so affected as to believe that nobility was above the desert of her deeds. When her relatives, including her brothers, Peter and John, congratulated her and themselves on all that she had accomplished, her remark was: "My deeds are in truth those of a ministry; but in as great truth never were greater read of by cleric, however profound he may be in all clerical learning." The degree of nobility allowed to the deserving girl was that of a countess. Her household consisted of a steward, almoner, squire, pages, "hand, foot, and chamber men," independently of the noble maidens who tended her, and who seem to have been equally served by three "valets de main, de pied, et de chambre."

But short-lived was the glory; no, I will not say *that*, let me rather remark that short-lived was the worldly splendor of the chivalrous my-lady countess. She had rendered all the service she could, when she fell wounded before Paris, and was basely abandoned for a while by her own party. She was rescued, ultimately, by D'Alençon, but only to be more disgracefully abandoned on the one side, and evilly treated on the other. When as a bleeding captive she was rudely dragged from the field at Compiègne; church, court, and chivalry, ignobly abandoned the poor and brave girl who had served all three in turn. By all three she was now as fiercely persecuted; and it may safely be said, that if the English were glad to burn her as a witch, to account for the defeat of the English and their allies, the French were equally eager to furnish testimony against her.

Her indecision and vacillation after falling into the hands of her enemies, would seem to show that apart from the promptings of those who had guided her, she was but an ordinary personage. She, however, never lost heart, and her natural wit did not abandon her. "Was St. Michael naked when he appeared to you?" was a question asked by one of the examining commissioners. To which Jeanne replied, "Do you think heaven has not wherewith to dress him?" "Had he any hair on his head?" was the next sensible question. Jeanne answered it by another query, "Have the goodness to tell me," said she, "why Michael's head should have been shaved?" It was easy, of course, to convict a prejudged and predoomed person, of desertion of her parents, of leading a vagabond and disreputable life, of sorcery, and finally, of heresy. She was entrapped into answers which tended to prove her culpability; but disregarding at last the complicated web woven tightly around her, and aware that nothing could save her, the heart of the knightly maiden beat firmly again, and as a summary reply to all questions, she briefly and emphatically declared: "All that I have done, all that I do, I have done well, and do well to do it." In her own words, "Tout ce que j'ai fait, tout ce que je fais, j'ai bien fait, et fais bien de le faire;" and it was a simply-dignified *resume* in presence of high-born ecclesiastics, who did not scruple to give the lie to each other like common ploughmen.

She was sentenced to death, and suffered the penalty, as being guilty of infamy, socially, morally, religiously, and politically. Not a finger was stretched to save her who had saved so many. Her murder is an indelible stain on two nations and one church; not the less so that the two nations unite in honoring her memory, and that the church has pronounced her innocent. Never did gallant champion meet with such base ingratitude from the party raised by her means from abject slavery to triumph; never was noble enemy so ignobly treated by a foe with whom, to acknowledge and admire valor, is next to the practice of it; and never was staff selected by the church for its support, so readily broken and thrown into the fire when it had served its purpose. All the sorrow in the world can not wash out these terrible facts, but it is fitting that this sorrow should always accompany our admiration. And so, honored be the memory of the young girl of Orleans!

After all, it is a question whether our sympathies be not thrown away when we affect to feel for Jeanne Darc. M. Delepierre, the Belgian Secretary of Legation, has printed, for private circulation, his "Doute Historique." This work consists chiefly of official documents, showing that the "Maid" never suffered at all, but that some criminal having been executed in her place, she survived to be a pensioner of the government, a married lady, and the mother of a family! The work in which these documents are produced, is not to be easily procured, but they who have any curiosity in the matter will find the subject largely treated in the *Athenæum*. This "Historical Doubt" brings us so closely in connection with romance, that we, perhaps, can not do better in illustrating our subject, than turn to a purely romantic subject, and see of what metal the champions of Christendom were made, with respect to chivalry.

## THE CHAMPIONS OF CHRISTENDOM GENERALLY AND HE OF ENGLAND IN PARTICULAR.

> "Are these things true?
> Thousands are getting at them in the streets."
> *Sejanus His Fall.*

I can hardly express the delight I feel as a biographer in the present instance, in the very welcome fact that no one knows anything about the parentage of St. George. If there had been a genealogical tree of the great champion's race, the odds, are that I should have got bewildered among the branches. As there is only much conjecture with a liberal allowance of assertion, the task is doubly easy, particularly as the matter itself is of the very smallest importance.

The first proof that our national patron ever existed at all, according to Mr. Alban Butler, is that the Greeks reverenced him by the name of "the Great Martyr." Further proof of a somewhat similar quality, is adduced in the circumstance that in Greece and in various parts of the Levant, there are or were dozens of churches erected in honor of the chivalrous saint; that Georgia took the holy knight for its especial patron; and that St. George, in full panoply, won innumerable battles for the Christians, by leading forward the reserves when the vanguard had been repulsed by the infidels, and the Christian generals were of themselves too indolent, sick, or incompetent, to do what they expected St. George to do for them.

From the East, veneration for this name, and some imaginary person who once bore it, extended itself throughout the West. It is a curious fact, that long before England placed herself under the shield of this religious soldier, France had made selection of him, at least as a useful adjutant or aide-de-camp to St. Denis.

Indeed, our saint was at one time nearly monopolized by France. St. Clotilde, the wife of the first Christian king of France, raised many altars in his honor—a fact which has not been forgotten in the decorations and illustrative adornments of that splendid church which has just been completed in the Faubourg St. Germain, and which is at once the pride and glory of Paris. That city once possessed relics which were said to be those of St. George; but of their whereabouts, no man now knows anything. We do, however, know that the Normans brought over the name of the saint with them, as that of one in whose arm of power they trusted, whether in the lists or in battle. In this respect *we*, as Saxons, if we choose to consider ourselves as such, have no particular reason to be grateful to the saint, for his presence among us is a symbol of national defeat if not of national humiliation. Not above six centuries have, however, elapsed since the great council of Oxford appointed his feast to be kept as a holyday of lesser rank throughout England; and it is about five hundred years since Edward III. established the Order of the Garter, under the patronage of this saint. This order is far more ancient than that of St. Michael, instituted by Louis XI.; of the Golden Fleece, invented by that 'good' Duke Philip of Burgundy, who fleeced all who were luckless enough to come within reach of his ducal shears; and of the Scottish Order of St. Andrew, which is nearly two centuries younger than that of St. George. Venice, Genoa, and Germany, have also instituted orders of chivalry in honor of this unknown cavalier.

These honors, however, and a very general devotion prove nothing touching his birth, parentage, and education. Indeed, it is probably because nothing is known of either, that his more serious biographers begin with his decease, and write his history, which, like one of Zschokke's tales, might be inscribed " Alles Verkerht." They tell us that he suffered under Diocletian, in Nicomedia, and on the 23d of April. We are further informed that he was a Cappadocian—a descendant of those savagely servile people, who once told the Romans that they would neither accept liberty at the hands of Rome, nor tolerate it of their own accord. He was, it is said, of noble birth, and after the death of his father, resided with his mother in Palestine, on an estate which finally became his own. The young squire was a handsome and stalwart youth, and, like many of *that* profession, fond of a military life. His promotion must have been pretty rapid, for we find him, according to tradition, a tribune or colonel in the army at a very early age, and a man of much higher rank before he prematurely died. His ideas of discipline were good, for when the pagan emperor persecuted the Christians, George of Cappadocia resigned his commission and appointments, and not till then, when he was a private man, did he stoutly remonstrate with his imperial ex-commander-in-chief against that sovereign's bloody edicts and fiercer cruelty against the Christians. This righteous boldness was barbarously avenged; and on the day after the remonstrance the gallant soldier lost his head. Some authors add to this account that he was the "illustrious young man" who tore down the anti-Christian edicts, when they were first posted up in Nicomedia, a conjecture which, by the hagiographers is called "plausible," but which has no shadow of proof to give warrant for its substantiality.

The reason why all knights and soldiers generally have had confidence in St. George, is founded, we are told, on the *facts* of his reappearance on earth at various periods, and particularly at the great siege of Antioch, in the times of the crusades. The Christians had been well nigh as thoroughly beaten as the Russians at Silistria. They were at the utmost extremity, when a squadron was seen rushing down from a mountain defile, with three knights at its head, in brilliant panoply and snow-white scarfs. "Behold," cried Bishop Adhemar, "the heavenly succor which was promised to you! Heaven declares for the Christians. The holy martyrs, George, Demetrius, and Theodore, come to fight for you." The effect was electrical. The Christian army rushed to victory, with the shout, "It is the will of God!" and the effect of the opportune appearance of the three chiefs and their squadron, who laid right lustily on the Saracens, was decisive of one of the most glorious, yet only temporarily productive of triumphs.

When Richard I. was on his expedition against enemies of the same race, he too was relieved from great straits by a vision of St. George. The army, indeed, did not see the glorious and inspiring sight, but the king affirmed that *he* did, which, in those credulous times was quite as well. In these later days men are less credulous, or saints are more cautious. Thus the Muscovites assaulted Kars under the idea that St. Sergius was with them; at all events, Pacha Williams, a good cause, and sinewy arms, were stronger than the Muscovite idea and St. Sergius to boot.

Such, then, is the hagiography of our martial saint. Gibbon has sketched his life in another point of view — business-like, if not matter-of-fact. The terrible historian sets down our great patron as having been born in a fuller's shop in Cilicia, educated (perhaps) in Cappadocia, and as having so won promotion, when a young man, from his patrons, by the skilful exercise of his profession as a parasite, as to procure, through their influence, "a lucrative commission or contract to supply the army with bacon!" In this commissariat employment he is said to have exercised fraud and corruption, by which may be meant that he sent to the army bacon as rusty as an old cuirass, and charged a high price for a worthless article. In these times, when the name and character of St. George are established, it is to be hoped that Christian purveyors for Christian armies do not, in reverencing George the Saint, imitate the practices alleged against him as George the Contractor. It would be hard, indeed, if a modern contractor who sent foul hay to the cavalry, uneatable food to the army generally, or poisonous potted-meat to the navy, could shield himself under the name and example of St. George. Charges as heavy *are* alleged against him by Gibbon, who adds that the malversations of the pious rogue "were so notorious, that George was compelled to escape from the pursuit of justice." If he saved his fortune, it is allowed that he made shipwreck of his honor; and he certainly did not improve his reputation if, as is alleged, he turned Arian. The career of our patron saint, as described by Gibbon, is startling. That writer speaks of the splendid library subsequently collected by George, but he hints that the volumes on history, rhetoric, philosophy, and theology, were perhaps as much proof of ostentation as of love for learning. That George was raised by the intrigues of a faction to the pastoral throne of Athanasius, in Alexandria, does not surprise us. Bishops were very irregularly elected in those early days, when men were sometimes summarily made teachers who needed instruction themselves; as is the case in some enlightened districts at present. George displayed an imperial pomp in his archiepiscopal character, "but he still betrayed those vices of his base and servile extraction," yet was so impartial that he oppressed and plundered all parties alike. "The merchants of Alexandria,' says the historian of the "Decline and Fall," "were impoverished by the unjust and almost universal monopoly which he acquired of nitre, salt, paper, funerals, &c., and the spiritual father of a great people condescended to practise the vile and pernicious arts of an informer. He seems to have had as sharp an eye after the profit to be derived from burials, as a certain archdeacon, who thinks intramural burial of the dead a very sanitary measure for the living, and particularly profitable to the clergy. Thus the example of St. George would seem to influence very "venerable" as well as very "martial" gentlemen. The Cappadocian most especially disgusted the Alexandrians by levying a house tax, of his own motion, and as he pillaged the pagan temples as well, all parties rose at length against the common oppressor, and "under the reign of Constantine he was expelled by the fury and justice of the people." He was restored only again to fall. The accession of Julian brought destruction upon the archbishop and many of his friends, who, after an imprisonment of three weeks, were dragged from their dungeons by a wild and cruel populace, and murdered in the streets. The bodies were paraded in triumph upon camels (as that of Condé was by his Catholic opponents, after the battle of Jarnac, on an ass), and they were ultimately cast into the sea. This last measure was adopted in order that, if the sufferers were to be accounted as martyrs, there should at least be no relics of them for men to worship. Gibbon thus concludes: "The fears of the Pagans were just, and their precautions ineffectual. The meritorious death of the archbishop obliterated the memory of his life. The rival of Athanasius was dear and sacred to the Arians, and the seeming conversion of those sectaries introduced his worship into the bosom of the Catholic church. The odious stranger, disguising every circumstance of time and place, assumed the rank of a martyr, a saint, and a Christian hero; and the infamous George of Cappadocia has been transformed into the famous St. George of England, the patron of arms, of chivalry, and of the garter."

The romancers have treated St. George and his knightly confraternity after their own manner. As a sample of what reading our ancestors were delighted with, especially those who loved chivalric themes, I know nothing better than "The Famous History of the Seven Champions of Christendom, St. George of England, St. Denis of France, St. James of Spain, St. Anthony of Italy, St. Andrew of Scotland, St. Patrick of Ireland, and St. David of Wales. Shewing their honourable battles by sea and land. Their tilts, justs, tournaments for ladies; their combats with gyants, monsters, and dragons; their adventures in foreign nations; their enchantments in the Holy Land; their knighthoods, prowess, and chivalry, in Europe, Africa, and Asia; with their victories against the enemies of Christ; also the true manner and places of their deaths, being seven tragedies, and how they came to be called the Seven Saints of Christendom." The courteous author or publisher of the veracious details, prefaces them with a brief address "to all courteous readers," to whom " Richard Johnson wisheth increase of virtuous knowledge." " Be not," he says, " like the chattering cranes, nor Momus's mates that carp at everything. What the simple say, I care not. What the spiteful say, I pass not; only the censure of the conceited," by which good Richard means the learned, "I stand unto; that is the mark I aim at,"—an address, it may be observed, which smacks of the Malaprop school; but which seemed more natural to our ancestors than it does to us.

For these readers Richard Johnson presents a very highly-spiced fare. He brings our patron saint into the world by a Cæsarean operation performed by a witch, who stole him from his unconscious mother, and reared him up in a cave, whence the young knight ultimately escaped with the other champions whom the witch, now slain, had kept imprisoned. The champions, it may be observed, travel with a celerity that mocks the "Express," and rivals the despatch of the Electric Telegraph. They are scarcely departed from the seven paths which led from the brazen pillar, each in search of adventures, when they are all "in the thick of it," almost at the antipodes. A breath takes St. George from Coventry, his recovered home, after leaving the witch, to Egypt. At the latter place he slays that terrible dragon, which some think to imply the Arian overcoming the Athanasian, and rescues the Princess Sabra, in whose very liberal love we can hardly trace a symbol of the Church, although her antipathies are sufficiently strong to remind one of the *odium theologicum*. George goes on performing stupendous feats, and getting no thanks, until he undertakes to slay a couple of lions for the Soldan of Persia, and gets clapped into prison, during seven years, for his pains. The biographer I suspect, shut the knight up so long, in order to have an excuse to begin episodically with the life of St. Denis.

The mystic number seven enters into all the principal divisions of the story. Thus, St. Denis having wandered into Thessaly was reduced to such straits as to live upon mulberries; and these so disagreed with him that he became suddenly transformed into a hart; a very illogical sequence indeed. But the mulberry tree was, in fact, Eglantius the King's daughter, metamorphosed for her pride. Seven years he thus remained; at the end of which time, his horse, wise as any regularly-ordained physician, administered to him a decoction of roses which brought about the transformation of both his master and his master's mistress into their "humane shapes." That they went to court sworn lovers may be taken as a matter of course. There they are left, in order to afford the author an opportunity of showing how St. James, having most unorthodoxically fallen in love with a Jewish maiden, was seven years dumb, in consequence. St. James, however, is a patient and persevering lover. If I had an ill-will against any one I would counsel him to read this very long-winded history, but being at peace with all mankind, I advise my readers to be content with learning that the apostolic champion and the young Jewess are ultimately united, and fly to Seville, where they reside in furnished lodgings, and lead a happy life;—while the author tells of what befell to the doughty St. Anthony.

This notable Italian is a great hand at subduing giants and ladies. We have a surfeit of combats and destruction, and love-making and speechifying, in this champion's life; and when we are compelled to leave him travelling about with a Thracian lady, who accompanies him, in a theatrical male dress, and looks in it like the Duchess—at least, like Miss Farebrother, in the dashing white sergeant of the Forty Thieves—we shake our head at St. Anthony and think how very unlike he is to his namesake in the etching by Callot, where the fairest of sirens could not squeeze a sigh from the anchorite's wrinkled heart.

While they are travelling about in the rather disreputable fashion above alluded to, we come across St. Andrew of Scotland, who has greater variety of adventure than any other of the champions. With every hour there is a fresh incident. Now he is battling with spirits, now struggling with human foes, and anon mixed up, unfavorably, with beasts. At the end of all the frays, there is— we need hardly say it—a lady. The bonny Scot was not likely to be behind his fellow-champions in this respect. Nay, St. Andrew has six of them, who had been swans, and are now natural singing lasses. What sort of a blade St. Andrew was may be guessed by the "fact," that when he departed from the royal court, to which he had conducted the half dozen ladies, they all eloped in a body, after him. There never was so dashing a hero dreamed of by romance—though a rhymer *has* dashed off his equal in wooing, and Burns's "Finlay" is the only one that may stand the parallel.

When the six Thracian ladies fall into the power of "thirty bloody-minded satyrs," who so likely, or so happy to rescue them as jolly St. Patrick. How he flies to the rescue, slays one satyr, puts the rest to flight, and true as steel, in love or friendship, takes the half dozen damsels under his arm, and swings singingly along with them in search of the roving Scot! As for St. David, all this while, he had not been quite so triumphant, or so tried, as his fellows. He had fallen into bad company, and "four beautiful damsels wrapped the drousie champion in a sheet of fine Arabian silk, and conveyed him into a cave, placed in the middle of a garden, where they laid him on a bed, more softer than the down of Culvers." In this agreeable company the Welsh champion wiled away *his* seven years. It was pleasant but not proper. But if the author had not thus disposed of him, how do you think he would ever have got back to St. George of England? The author indeed exhibits considerable skill, for he brings St. George and St. David together, and the first rescues the second from ignoble thraldom, and what is worse, from the most prosy enchanter I ever met with in history, and who is really not enchanting at all. This done, George is off to Tripoli.

There, near there, or somewhere else, for the romances are dreadfully careless in their topography, he falls in with his old love

Sabra, married to a Moorish King. If George is perplexed at this, seeing that the lady had engaged to remain an unmarried maiden till he came to wed her, he is still more so when she informs him that she has, in all essentials, kept her word, "through the secret virtue of a golden chain steeped in tiger's blood, the which she wore seven times double about her ivory neck." St. George does not know what to make of it, but as on subsequently encountering two lions, Sabra, while he was despatching one, kept the other quietly with its head resting on her lap, the knight declared himself perfectly satisfied, and they set out upon their travels, lovingly together.

By the luckiest chance, all the wandering knights and their ladies met at the court of a King of Greece, who is not, certainly, to be heard of in Gillies' or Goldsmith's history. The scenery is now on a magnificent scale, for there is a regal wedding on foot, and tournaments, and the real war of Heathenism against all Christendom. As the Champions of Christendom have as yet done little to warrant them in assuming the appellation, one would suppose that the time had now arrived when they were to give the world a taste of their quality in that respect. But nothing of the sort occurs. The seven worthies separate, each to his own country, in order to prepare for great deeds; but none are done for the benefit of Christianity, unless indeed we are to conclude that when George and Sabra travelled together, and he overcame all antagonists, and she inspired with love all beholders;—he subdued nature itself and she ran continually into danger, from which he rescued her; —and that when, after being condemned to the stake, the young wife gave birth to three babes in the wood, and was at last crowned Queen of Egypt, something is meant by way of allegory, in reference to old church questions, and in not very clear elucidation as to how these questions were beneficially affected by the Champions of Christendom!

I may add that when Sabra was crowned Queen of Egypt, every one was ordered to be merry, on pain of death! It is further to be observed there is now much confusion, and that the confusion by no means grows less as the story thunders on. The Champions and the three sons of St. George are, by turns, East, West, North, and South, either pursuing each other, or suddenly and unexpectedly encountering, like the principal personges in a pantomime. Battles, love-making, and shutting up cruel and reprobate magicians from the "humane eye," are the chief events, but to every event there are dozens of episodes, and each episode is as confusing, dazzling, and bewildering as the trunk from which it hangs.

St. George, however, is like a greater champion than himself; and when he is idle and in Italy, he does precisely what Nelson did in the same place—fall in love with a lady, and cause endless mischief in consequence. By this time, however, Johnson begins to think, rightly, that his readers have had enough of it, and that it is time to dispose of his principal characters. These too, are so well disposed to help him, that when the author kills St. Patrick, the saint burys himself! In memory of his deeds, of which we have heard little or nothing, some are accustomed to honor him, says Mr. Johnson—"wearing upon their hats, each of them, a cross of red silk, in token of his many adventures under the Christian Cross." So that the shamrock appears to have been a device only of later times.

St. David is as quickly despatched. This champion enters Wales to crush the pagans there. He wears a leek in his helmet, and his followers adopt the same fashion, in order that friend may be distinguished from foe. The doughty saint, of course, comes conqueror out of the battle, but he is in a heated state, gets a chill and dies after all of a common cold. Bruce, returning safe from exploring the Nile, to break his neck by falling down his own stairs, hardly presents a more practical bathos than this. Why the leek became the badge of Welshmen need not be further explained.

It is singular that in recounting the manner of the death of the next champion, St. Denis, the romancer is less romantic than common tradition. He tells us how the knight repaired to then pagan France; how he was accused of being a Christian, by another knight of what we should fancy a Christian order, St. Michael, and how the pagan king orders St. Denis to be beheaded, in consequence. There are wonders in the heavens, at this execution, which convert the heathen sovereign to Christianity; but no mention is made of St. Denis having walked to a monastery, after his head was off, and *with* his head under his arm. Of this prodigy Voltaire remarked, " Ce n'est que le premier pas qui coute," but of that the romancer makes no mention. St. James suffers by being shut up in his chapel in Spain, and starved to death, by order of the Atheist king. Anthony dies quietly in a good old age, in Italy; St. Andrew is beheaded by the cruel pagan Scots whom, in his old age, he had visited, in order to bring them to conversion: and St. George, who goes on, riding down wild monsters and rescuing timid maidens, to the last—and his inclination, was always in the direction of the maidens—ultimately meets his death by the sting of a venomous dragon.

And now it would seem that two or three hundred years ago, authors were very much like the actors in the *Critic*, who when they *did* get hold of a good thing, could never give the public enough of it. Accordingly, the biography of the Seven Champions was followed by that of their sons. I will spare my readers the turbulent details: they will probably be satisfied with learning that the three sons of St. George became kings, "according as the fairy queen had prophesied to them," and that Sir Turpin, son of David, Sir Pedro, son of James, Sir Orlando, son of Anthony, Sir Ewen, son of Andrew, Sir Phelim, son of Patrick, and Sir Owen, son of David, like their sires, combated with giants, monsters, and dragons; tilted and tournamented in honor of the ladies, did battle in defence of Christianity, relieved the distressed, annihilated necromancers and table-turners, in short, accomplished all that could be expected from knights of such prowess and chivalry.

When Richard Johnson had reached this part of his history, he gave it to the world, awaiting the judgment of the critics, before he published his second portion: that portion wherein he was to unfold what nobody yet could guess at, namely, wherefore the Seven Champions were called *par excellence*, the Champions of Christendom. I am afraid that meanwhile those terrible, god-like, and inexorable critics, had not dealt altogether gently with him. The *Punch* they offered him was not made exclusively of sweets. His St. George had been attacked, and very small reverence been expressed for his ladies. But see how calmly and courteously— all the more admirable that there must have been some affectation in the matter—he turns from the censuring judges to that benevolent personage, the gentle reader. "Thy courtesy," he says, "must be my buckler against the carping malice of mocking jesters, that being worse able to do well, scoff commonly at that they can not mend; censuring all things, doing nothing, but (monkey-like) make apish jests at anything they do in print, and nothing pleaseth them, except it savor of a scoffing and invective spirit. Well, what they say of me I do not care; thy delight is my sole desire." Well said, bold Richard Johnson. He thought he had put down criticism as St. George had the dragon.

I can not say, however, that good Richard Johnson treats his gentle reader fairly. This second part of his Champions is to a reader worse than what all the labors of Hercules were to the lusty son of Alcmena. An historical drama at Astley's is not half so bewildering, and is almost as credible, and Mr. Ducrow himself when he was rehearsing his celebrated "spectacle drama" of "St. George and the Dragon" at old Drury—and who that ever saw him on those occasions can possibly forget him?—achieved greater feats, or was more utterly unlike any sane individual than St. George is, as put upon the literary stage by Master Johnson.

One comfort in tracing the tortuosities of this chivalric romance is that the action is rapid; but then there is so much of it, and it is so astounding! We are first introduced to the three sons of St. George, who are famous hunters in England, and whose mother, the lady Sabra, "catches her death," by going out attired like Diana, to witness their achievements. The chivalric widower thereupon sets out for Jerusalem, his fellow-champions accompany, and George's three sons, Guy, Alexander, and David, upon insinuation from their mother's spirit, start too in pursuit. The lads were knighted by the king of England before they commenced their journey, which they perform with the golden spur of chivalry attached to their heels. They meet with the usual adventures by the way: destroying giants, and rescuing virgins, who in these troublesome times seem to have been allowed to travel about too much by themselves. Meanwhile, their sire is enacting greater prodigies still, and is continually delivering his fellow-champions from difficulties, from which they are unable to extricate themselves. Indeed, in all circumstances, his figure is the most prominent; and although the other half-dozen *must* have rendered some service on each occasion, St. George makes no more mention of the same than Marshal St. Arnaud, in his letters on the victory at the Alma, does of the presence and services of the English.

It is said that Mrs. Radcliffe, whose horrors used to delight and distress our mothers and aunts, in their younger days, became herself affected by the terrors which she only paints to explain away natural circumstances. What then must have been the end of Richard Johnson? His scene of the enchantments of the Black Castle is quite enough to have killed the author with bewilderment. There is a flooring in the old palace of the Prince of Orange in Brussels, which is so inlaid with small pieces of wood, of a thousand varieties of patterns, as to be a triumph of its kind. I was not at all surprised, when standing on that floor, to hear that when the artist had completed his inconceivable labor, he gave one wild gaze over the *parquet* of the palace, and dropped dead of a fit of giddiness. I am sure that Richard Johnson must have met with some such calamity after revising this portion of his history. It is a portion in which it is impossible for the Champions or for the readers to go to sleep. The noise is terrific, the incidents fall like thunderbolts, the changes roll over each other in a succession made with electric rapidity, and when the end comes we are all the more rejoiced, because we have comprehended nothing; but we are especially glad to find that the knight of the Black Castle, who is the cause of all the mischief, is overcome, flies in a state of destitution to a neighboring wood, and being irretrievably "hard up," stabs himself with the first thing at hand, as ruthlessly as the lover of the "Ratcatcher's Daughter."

Time, place, propriety, and a respect for contemporary history, are amusingly violated throughout the veracious details. Nothing can equal the confusion, nothing can be more absurd than the errors. But great men have committed errors as grave. Shakespeare opened a seaport in Bohemia, and Mr. Macaulay wrote of one Penn what was only to be attributed to another. And now, have the dramatists treated St. George better than the romancers?

The national saint was, doubtless, often introduced in the Mysteries; but the first occasion of which I have any knowledge of his having been introduced on the stage, was by an author named John Kirke. John was so satisfied with his attempt that he never wrote a second play. He allowed his fame to rest on the one in question, which is thus described on his title-page: "The Seven Champions of Christendome. Acted at the *Cocke Pit*, and at the *Red Bull* in St. John's Streete, with a general liking, And never printed till this *yeare* 1638. Written by J. K.— London, printed by J. Okes, and are (*sic*) to be sold by James Becket, at his Shop in the Inner Temple Gate, 1638."

John Kirke treats his subject melodramatically. In the first scene, Calib the Witch, in a speech prefacing her declarations of a love for foul weather and deeds, tells the audience by way of prologue, how she had stolen the young St. George from his now defunct parent, with the intention of making a bath for her old bones out of his young warm blood. Love, however, had touched her, and she had brought up "the red-lipped boy," with some indefinite idea of making something of him when a man.

With this disposition the old lady has some fears as to the possible approaching term of her life; but, as she is assured by "Tarfax the Devill" that she can not die unless she love blindly, the witch, like a mere mortal, accounting that she loves wisely, reckons herself a daughter of immortality, and rejoices hugely. The colloquy of this couple is interrupted by their son Suckabud, who, out of a head just broken by St. George, makes complaint with that comic lack of fun, which was wont to make roar the entire inside of the Red Bull. The young clown retires with his sire, and then enters the great St. George, a lusty lad, with a world of inquiries touching his parentage. Calib explains that his lady mother was anything but an honest woman, and that his sire was just the partner to match. "Base or noble, pray?" asks St. George. To which the witch replies:—

> "Base and noble too;
> Both base by thee, but noble by descent;
> And thou born base, yet mayst thou write true gent:"

and it may be said, parenthetically, that many a "true gent" is by birth equal to St. George himself.

Overcome by her affection, the witch makes a present to St. George of the half-dozen champions of England whom she holds in chains within her dwelling. One of them is described as "the lively, brisk, cross-cap'ring Frenchman, Denis." With these for slaves, Calib yields her wand of power, and the giver is no sooner out of sight when George invokes the shades of his parents, who not only appear and furnish him with a corrected edition of his biography, but inform him that he is legitimate Earl of Coventry, with all the appurtenances that a young earl can desire.

Thereupon ensues a hubbub that must have shaken all the lamps in the cockpit. George turns the Witch's power against herself, and she descends to the infernal regions, where she is punningly declared to have gained the title of Duchess of Helvetia. The six champions are released, and the illustrious seven companions go forth in search of adventures, with Suckabus for a "Squire." The father of the latter gives him some counsel at parting, which is a parody on the advice of Polonius to Laertes. "Lie," says Torpax:—

> "Lie to great profit, borrow, pay no debts,
> Cheat and purloin, they are gaming dicers' bets."

"If Cottington outdo me," says the son, "he be-whipt." And so, after the election of St. George as the seventh champion of Christendom, ends one of the longest acts that Bull or Cockpit was ever asked to witness and applaud.

The next act is briefer but far more bustling. We are in that convenient empire of Trebizond, where everything happened which never took place, according to the romances. The whole city is in a state of consternation at the devastations of a detestable dragon, and a lion, his friend and co-partner. The nobles bewail the fact in hexameters, or at least in lines meant to do duty for them; and the common people bewail the fact epigrammatically, and describe the deaths of all who have attempted to slay the monsters, with a broadness of effect that doubtless was acknowledged by roars of laughter. Things grow worse daily, the fiends look down, and general gloom is settling thick upon the empire, when Andrew of Scotland and Anthony of Italy arrive, send in their cards, and announce their determination to slay both these monsters.

Such visitors are received with more than ordinary welcome. The emperor is regardless of expense in his liberality, and his daughter Violetta whispers to her maid Carinthia that she is already in love with one of them, but will not say which; a remark which is answered by the pert maid, that she is in love with both, and would willingly take either. All goes on joyously until in the course of conversation, and it is by no means remarkable for brilliancy, the two knights let fall that they are Christians. Now, you must know, that the established Church at Trebizond at this time, which is at any period, was heathen. The court appeared to principally affect Apollo and Diana, while the poorer people put up with Pan, and abused him for denouncing may-poles! Well, the Christians had never been emancipated; nay, they had never been tolerated in Trebizond, and it was contrary to law that the country should be saved, even in its dire extremity, by Christian help. The knights are doomed to die, unless they will turn heathens. This, of course, they decline with a dignified scorn; whereupon, in consideration of their nobility, they are permitted to choose their own executioners. They make choice of the ladies, but Violetta and Carinthia protest that they can not think of such a thing. Their high-church sire is disgusted with their want of orthodoxy, and he finally yields to the knights their swords, that they may do justice on themselves as the law requires. But Andrew and Anthony are no sooner armed again than they clear their way to liberty, and the drop scene falls upon the rout of the whole empire of Trebizond.

The third act is of gigantic length, and deals with giants. There is mourning in Tartary. David has killed the king's son in a tournament, and the king remarks, like a retired apothecary, that "Time's plaster must draw the sore before he can feel peace again." To punish David, he is compelled to undertake the destruction of the enchanter Ormandine, who lived in a cavern fortress with "some selected friends." The prize of success is the reversion of the kingdom of Tartary to the Welsh knight. The latter goes upon his mission, but he is so long about it that our old friend Chorus enters, to explain what he affirms they have not time to act — namely, the great deeds of St. George, who, as we learn, had slain the never-to-be-forgotten dragon, rescued Sabrina, been cheated of his reward, and held in prison seven years upon bread and water. His squire, Suckabus, alludes to giants whom he and his master had previously slain, and whose graves were as large as Tothill Fields. He also notices "Ploydon's law," and other matters, that could hardly have been contemporaneous with the palmy days of the kingdom of Tartary. Meanwhile, David boldly assaults Ormandine, but the enchanter surrounds him with some delicious-looking nymphs, all thinly clad and excessively seductive; and we are sorry to say that the Welsh champion, not being cavalierly mounted on proper principles, yields to seduction, and after various falls under various temptations, is carried to bed by the rollicking nymph Drunkenness.

But never did good, though fallen, men want for a friend at a pinch. St. George is in the neighborhood; and seedy as he is after seven years in the dark, with nothing more substantial by way of food than bread, and nothing more exhilarating for beverage than *aqua pura*, the champion of England does David's work, and with more generosity than justice, makes him a present of the enchanter's head. David presents the same to the King of Tartary, that, according to promise pledged in case of such a present being made, he may be proclaimed heir-apparent to the Tartarian throne. With this bit of cheating, the long third act comes to an end.

The fourth act is taken up with an only partially successful attack by James, David, and Patrick, on a cruel enchanter, Argalio, who at least is put to flight, and *that*, at all events, as the knights remark, is something to be thankful for. The fifth and grand act reveals to us the powerful magician, Brandron, in his castle. He holds in thrall the King of Macedon — a little circumstance not noted in history; and he has in his possession the seven daughters of his majesty transformed into swans. The swans contrive to make captives of six of the knights as they were taking a "gentle walk" upon his ramparts. They are impounded as trespassers, and Brandron, who has some low comedy business with Suckubus, will not release them but upon condition that they fight honestly in his defence against St. George. The six duels take place, and of course the champion of England overcomes all his friendly antagonists; whereupon Brandron, with his club, beats out his own brains, in presence of the audience.

At this crisis, the King of Macedon appears, restored to power, and inquires after his daughters. St. George and the rest, with a use of the double negatives that would have shocked Lindley Murray, declare

"We never knew, nor saw no ladies here."

The swans, however, soon take their pristine form, and the three daughters appear fresh from their plumes and their long bath upon the lake. Upon this follows the smart dialogue which we extract as a sample of how sharply the King of Macedon looked to his family interests, and how these champion knights were "taken in" before they well knew how the fact was accomplished.

*Mac.* Reverend knights, may we desire to know which of you are unmarried?
*Ant., Den., and Pat.* We are.
*Geo.* Then here's these ladies, take 'em to your beds.
*Mac.* George highly honors aged Macedon.
*The three Knights.* But can the ladies' love accord with us?
*The three Ladies.* Most willingly!
*The three Knights.* We thus then seal our contract.
*Geo.* Which thus we ratifie.
    Sit with the brides, most noble Macedon;
    And since kind fortune sent such happy chance,
    We'll grace your nuptials with a soldier's dance.

And, fore George, as our fathers used to say, they make a night of it. The piece ends with a double military reel, and the audiences at the Bull and the Cockpit probably whistled the tune as they wended their way homeward to crab-apple ale and spiced gingerbread.

Next to the Champions of Christendom, the King's Knight Champion of England is perhaps the most important personage — in the point of view of chivalry. I think it is some French author who has said, that revolutions resemble the game of chess, where the pawns or pieces (*les pions*) may cause the ruin of the king, save him, or take his place. Now the *champ pion*, as this French remark reminds me, is nothing more than the field *pion*, pawn, or piece, put forward to fight in the king's quarrel.

The family of the Champion of England bears, it may be observed, exactly the name which suits a calling so derived. The appellation "Dymoke" is derived from *De Umbrosâ Quercu;* I should rather say it is the translation of it; and Harry De Umbrosâ Quercu is only Harry of the Shady or Dim Oak, a very apt dwelling-place and name for one whose chief profession was that of field-pawn to the king.

This derivation or adaptation of names from original Latin surnames is common enough, and some amusing pages might be written on the matter, in addition to what has been so cleverly put together by Mr. Mark Anthony Lower, in his volume devoted especially to an elucidation of English surnames.

The royal champions came in with the Conquest. The Norman dukes had theirs in the family of Marmion — ancestors of that Marmion of Sir Walter Scott's, who commits forgery, like a common knave of more degenerate times. The Conqueror conferred sundry broad lands in England on his champions; among others, the lands adjacent to, as well as the castle of Tamworth. Near this place was the first nunnery established in this country. The occupants were the nuns of St. Edith, at Polesworth. Robert de Marmion used the ladies very "cavalierly," ejected them from their house, and deprived them of their property. But such victims had a wonderfully clever way of recovering their own.

My readers may possibly remember how a certain Eastern potentate injured the church, disgusted the Christians generally, and irritated especially that Simeon Stylites who sat on the summit of a pillar, night and day, and never moved from his abiding-place. The offender had a vision, in which he not only saw the indignant Simeon, but was cudgelled almost into pulp by the *simulacre* of that saint. I very much doubt if Simeon himself was in his airy dwelling-place at that particular hour of the night. I was reminded of this by what happened to the duke's champion, Robert de Marmion. He was roused from a deep sleep by the vision of a stout lady, who announced herself as the wronged St. Edith, and who proceeded to show her opinion of De Marmion's conduct toward her nuns, by pommelling his ribs with her crosier, until she had covered his side with bruises, and himself with repentance. What strong-armed young monk played St. Edith that night, it is impossible to say; but that he enacted the part successfully, is seen from the fact that Robert brought back the ladies to Polesworth, and made ample restitution of all of which they had been deprived. The nuns, in return, engaged with alacrity to inter all defunct Marmions within the chapter-house of their abbey, for nothing.

With the manor of Tamworth in Warwickshire, Marmion held that of Scrivelsby in Lincolnshire. The latter was held of the King by grand sergeantry, "to perform the office of champion at the King's coronation." At his death he was succeeded by a son of the same Christian name, who served the monks of Chester precisely as his sire had treated the nuns at Polesworth. This second Robert fortified his ill-acquired prize—the priory; but happening to fall into one of the newly-made ditches, when inspecting the fortifications, a soldier of the Earl of Chester killed him, without difficulty, as he lay with broken hip and thigh, at the bottom of the fosse. The next successor, a third Robert, was something of a judge, with a dash of the warrior, too, and he divided his estates between two sons, both Roberts, by different mothers. The eldest son and chief possessor, after a bustling and emphatically "battling" life, was succeeded by his son Philip, who fell into some trouble in the reign of Henry III. for presuming to act as a judge or justice of the peace, without being duly commissioned. This Philip was, nevertheless, one of the most faithful servants to a king who found so many faithless; and if honors were heaped upon him in consequence, he fairly merited them all. He was happy, too, in marriage, for he espoused a lady sole heiress to a large estate, and who brought him four daughters, co-heiresses to the paternal and maternal lands of the Marmions and the Kilpecs.

This, however, is wandering. Let us once more return to orderly illustration. In St. George I have shown how pure romance deals with a hero. In the next chapter I will endeavor to show in what spirit the lives and actions of real English heroes have been treated by native historians. In so doing, I will recount the story of Sir Guy of Warwick, after their fashion, with original illustrations and "modern instances."

# SIR GUY OF WARWICK,

## AND WHAT BEFELL HIM.

> "His desires
> Are higher than his state, and his deserts
> Not much short of the most he can desire."
> *Chapman's Byron's Conspiracy.*

THE Christian name of Guy was once an exceedingly popular name in the county of York. I have never heard a reason assigned for this, but I think it may have originated in admiration of the deeds and the man whose appellation and reputation have survived to our times. I do not allude to Guy Faux; *that* young gentleman was the Father of Perverts, but by no means the first of the Guys.

The "Master Guy" of whom I am treating here, or, rather, about to treat, was a youth whose family originally came from Northumberland. That family was, in one sense, more noble than the imperial family of Muscovy, for its members boasted not only of good principles, but of sound teeth.

The teeth and principles of the Romanoffs are known to be in a distressing state of dilapidation.

Well; these Northumbrian Guys having lived extremely fast, and being compelled to compound with their creditors, by plundering the latter, and paying them zero in the pound, migrated southward, and finally settled in Warwickshire. Now, the head of the house had a considerable share of common sense about him, and after much suffering in a state of shabby gentility, he not only sent his daughters out to earn their own livelihood, but, to the intense disgust of his spouse, hired himself as steward to that noble gentleman the Earl of Warwick. "My blood is as good as ever it was," said he to the fine lady his wife. "It is the blood of an upper servant," cried she, "and my father's daughter is the spouse of a flunkey.

The husband was not discouraged; and he not only opened his office in his patron's castle but he took his only son with him, and made him his first clerk. This son's name was Guy; and he was rather given to bird-catching, hare-snaring, and "gentism" generally. He had been a precocious youth from some months previous to his birth, and had given his lady-mother such horrid annoyance, that she was always dreaming of battles, fiery-cars, strong-smelling dragons, and the wrathful Mars. "Well," she used to remark to her female friends, while the gentlemen were over their wine, "I expect that this boy" (she had made up her mind to that) "will make a noise in the world, draw bills upon his father, and be the terror of maid-servants. Why, do you know——" and here she became confidential, and I do not feel authorized to repeat what she then communicated.

But Master Guy, the "little stranger" alluded to, proved better than was expected. He might have been considerably worse, and yet would not have been so bad as maternal prophecy had depicted him. At eight years . . . but I hear you say, "When did all this occur?" Well, it was in a November's "Morning Post," that announcement was made of the birth; and as to the year, Master Guy has given it himself in the old metrical romance,

> "Two hundred and twenty years and odd,
> After our Savior Christ his birth,
> When King Athelstan wore the crown,
> I livéd here upon the earth."

At eight years old, I was about to remark, young Guy was the most insufferable puppy of his district. He won all the prizes for athletic sports; and by the time he was sixteen there was not a man in all England who dared accept his challenge to wrestle with both arms, against *him* using only one.

It was at this time that he kept his father's books and a leash of hounds, with the latter of which he performed such extraordinary feats, that the Earl of Warwick invited him from the steward's room to his own table; where Guy's father changed his plate, and Master Guy twitched him by the beard as he did it.

At the head of the earl's table sat his daughter "Phillis the Fair," a lady who, like her namesake in the song, was "sometimes forward, sometimes coy," and altogether so sweetly smiling and so beguiling, that when the earl asked Guy if he would not come and hunt (the dinner was at 10 A. M.), Guy answered, as the Frenchman did who could not bear the sport, with a *Merci, j'ai été!* and affecting an iliac seizure, hinted at the necessity of staying at home.

The youth forthwith was carried to bed. Phillis sent him a posset, the earl sent him his own physician; and this learned gentleman, after much perplexity veiled beneath the most affable and confident humbug, wrote a prescription which, if it could do the patient no good would do him no harm. He was a most skilful man, and his patients almost invariably recovered under this treatment. He occasionally sacrificed one or two when a consultation was held, and he was called upon to prescribe *secundum artem;* but he compensated for this professional slaying by, in other cases, leaving matters to Nature, who was the active partner in his firm, and of whose success he was not in the least degree jealous. So, when he had written the prescription, Master Guy fell a discoursing of the passion of love, and *that* with a completeness and a variety of illustration as though he were the author of the chapter on that subject in Burton's "Anatomy of Melancholy." The doctor heard him to the end, gently rubbing one side of his nose the while with the index-finger of his right hand; and when his patient had concluded, the medical gentleman smiled, hummed "Phillis is my only joy," and left the room with his head nodding like a Chinese Mandarin's.

By this time the four o'clock sun was making green and gold pillars of the trees in the neighboring wood, and Guy got up, looked at the falling leaves, and thought of the autumn of his hopes. He whistled "Down, derry, down," with a marked emphasis on the *down;* but suddenly his hopes again sprang up, as he beheld Phillis among her flower-beds, engaged in the healthful occupation which a sublime poet has given to the heroine whom he names, and whose action he describes, when he tells us that

"Miss Dinah was a-walking in her garding one day."

Guy trussed his points, pulled up his hose, set his bonnet smartly on his head, clapped a bodkin on his thigh, and then walked into the garden with the air of the once young D'Egville in a ballet, looking after a nymph—which indeed was a pursuit he was much given to when he was *old* D'Egville, and could no longer bound throught his ballets, because he was stiff in the joints.

Guy, of course, went down on one knee, and at once plunged into the most fiery style of declaration, but Phillis had not read the Mrs. Chapone of that day for nothing. She brought him back to prose and propriety, and then the two started afresh, and they *did* talk! Guy felt a little "streaked" at first, but he soon recovered his self-possession, and it would have been edifying for the young mind to have heard how these two pretty things spoke to, and answered each other in moral maxims stolen from the top pages of their copy-books. They poured them out by the score, and the proverbial philosophy they enunciated was really the origin of the book so named by Martin Tupper. He took it all from Phillis and Guy, whose descendants, of the last name, were so famous for their school-books. This I expect Mr. Tupper will (not) mention in his next edition.

After much profitable interchange of this sort of article, the lady gently hinted that Master Guy was not indifferent to her, but that he was of inferior birth, yet of qualities that made him equal with her; adding, that hitherto he had done little but kill other people's game, whereas there were nobler deeds to be accomplished. And then she bade him go in search of perilous adventures, winding up with the toast and sentiment, "Master Guy, eagles do not care to catch flies."

Reader, if you have ever seen the prince of pantomimists, Mr. Payne, tear the hair of his theatrical wig in a fit of amorous despair, you may have some idea as to the intensity with which Master Guy illustrated his own desperation. He stamped the ground with such energy that all the hitherto quiet aspens fell a-shaking, and their descendants have ever since maintained the same fashion. Phillis fell a-crying at this demonstration, and softened considerably. After a lapse of five minutes, she had blushingly directed Master Guy to "speak to papa."

Now, of all horrible interviews, this perhaps is the most horrible. Nelson used to say that there was only one thing on earth which he dreaded, and that was dining with a mayor and corporation.

Doubtless it is dreadful, but *what* is it compared with looking a grave man in the face, who has no sentiment into him, and whose first remark is sure to be, " Well, sir, be good enough to tell me— what can you settle on my daughter? What can you do to secure her happiness?"

" Well," said Guy, in reply to this stereotyped remark, " I can kill the Dun cow on the heath. *She* has killed many herself who've tried the trick on her; and last night she devoured crops of clover, and twice as many fields of barley on your lordship's estate."

" First kill the cow, and then ———," said the earl with a smile; and Shakespeare had the echo of this speech in his ear, when he began the fifth act of his Othello. Now Guy was not easily daunted. If I cared to make a pun, I might easily have said " cowed," but in a grave and edifying narrative this loose method of writing would be extremely improper. Guy, then, was not a coward—nay, nothing is hidden under the epithet. He tossed a little in bed that night as he thought the matter over, and the next morning made sheets of paper as crumpled as the cow's horns, as he rejected the plans of assault he had designed upon them, and sat uncertain as to what he should do in behoof of his own fortune. He at length determined to go and visit the terrible animal " incognito." It is the very word used by one of the biographers of Guy, an anonymous Northumbrian, who published the life on a broad sheet, with a picture of Master Guy which might have frightened the cow, and which is infinitely more ugly. Neither the black-letter poem, the old play, nor the pamphlets or ballads, use the term *incognito*, but all declare that Guy proceeded with much caution, and a steel cuiras over his jerkin. I mention these things, because without correctiness my narrative would be worthless. I am not imaginative, and would not embroider a plain suit of fact upon any account.

Guy's carefulness is to be proved. Here was a cow that had been more destructive than ever Red Riding Hood's Wolf was— that Count Wolf, who used to snap up young maidens, and lived as careless of respectability as was to be expected of a man once attached to a " marching regiment," and who turned monk. The cow was twelve feet high, from the hoof to the shoulder, and eighteen feet long, from the neck to the root of the tail. All the dragons ever heard of had never been guilty of such devastation to life and property as this terrible cow. Guy looked at her and did not like her. The cow detected him and rushed at her prey. Guy was active, attacked her in front and rear, as the allies did the forts of Bomarsund; very considerably confused her by burying his battle-axe in her skull; hung on by her tail as she attempted to fly; and finally gave her the *coup de grace* by passing his rapier rapidly and repeatedly through her especially vulnerable point behind the ear. In proof of the fact, the scene of the conflict still bears the name of Dunsmore Heath, and that is a wider basis of proof than many "facts" stand upon, to which we are required by plodding teachers to give assent.

Besides, there is a rib of this very cow exhibited at Bristol. To be sure it is not a rib now of a cow, but out of reverence to the antiquity of the assertion which allegedly makes it so, I think we are bound to believe what is thus advanced. Not that I do myself, but that is of no consequence. . I have a strong idea that the cow was not a cow, but a countess (not a Countess Cowper), who made war in her own right, lived a disreputable life, was as destructive to wealthy young lords as a *Lorette*, and won whole estates by cheating at *écarté*. Guy took a hand, and beat her.

Poor Master Guy, he was as hardly used as ever Jacob was, and much he meditated thereupon in the fields at eventide. The stern earl would by no means give his consent to the marriage of his daughter with the young champion, until the latter had performed some doughtier deeds than this. The boy (he was still in his teens) took heart of grace, divided a crooked sixpence with Phillis, and straightway sailed for Normandy, where he arrived, after meeting as many thieves by the way as if he had walked about for a month in the streets of Dover. But Master Guy killed all *he* met; there is a foolish judicial, not to say social, prejudice against our doing the same with the bandits of Dover. I can not conjecture why; perhaps they have a privilege under some of the city companies, whereby they are constituted the legal skinners of all sojourners among them, carrying filthy lucre.

Guy met in Normandy with the last person he could have expected to fall in with — no other than the Emperor of Almayne, a marvellously ubiquitous person to be met with in legends, and frequently encountered in the seaports of inland towns. The historians are here a little at issue. One says that Master Guy having found a certain Dorinda tied to the stake, and awaiting a champion who would stake his own life for her rescue, inquired the "antecedents" of the position. Dorinda, it appears, had been as rudely used as young lady possibly could be, "by the Duke of Blois, his son," and the duke was so enraged at Dorinda's charge against his favorite Otto, that he condemned her to be burned alive, unless a champion appeared in time to rescue her by defeating the aforesaid Otto in single combat. Guy, of course, transacted the little business successfully; spoiled Otto's beauty by slashing his nose; and so enchanted Dorinda, that she never accused her champion of doing aught displeasing to her.

Anxious as I am touching the veracity of this narrative, I have recorded what biographers state, though not in their own words. But I must add, that in some of the histories this episode about Dorinda is altogether omitted, and we only hear of Master Guy appearing in panoply at a tournament given by the Emperor of Allemagne, in Normandy — which is much the same, gentle reader, as if I were, at your cost, to give a concert and ball, with a supper from Farrance's, and all, not in my house, but in yours. Nevertheless, in Normandy the tournament was held, and the paternal Emperor of Allemagne, having then a daughter, Blanche, of whom he wished to get rid, he set her up as the prize of the conquering knight in the tournament.

I think I hear you remark something as to the heathenness of the custom. But it is a custom sacred to these times; and our neighbors (for of course neither you nor I could condescend to such manners) get up evening tournaments of whist, quadrilles, and a variety of singing — of every variety but the good and intelligible, and at these modern tournaments given for the express purpose which that respectable old gentleman, the Emperor of Allemagne, had in view when he opened his lists; the "girls" are the prizes of the carpet-knights. So gentlemen, *faites votre jeu*, as the philosopher who presided at Frescati's used to say — *faites votre jeu, Messieurs;* and go in and win. Perhaps if you read Cowper, you may be the better armed against loss in such a conflict.

I need not say that Master Guy's good sword, which gleamed like lightning in the arena, and rained blows faster than ever Mr. Blanchard rained them, in terrific Coburg combats, upon the vulnerable crest of Mr. Bradley — won for him the peerless prize — to say nothing of a dog and a falcon thrown in. Master Guy rather ungallantly declined having the lady, though her father would have given him *carte blanche ;* he looked at her, muttered her name, and then murmured, " Blanche, as thou art, yet art thou black-a-moor, compared with my Phillis;"—and with this unchivalric avowal, for it was a part of chivalry to say a thing and think another, he returned to England, carrying with him the "Spaniel King's Charls," as French authors write it, and the falcon, with a ring and a perch, like a huge parroquet.

Master Guy entered Warwick in a "brougham," as we now might say, and sorely was he put to it with the uneasy bird. At every lurch of the vehicle, out flapped the wings, elongated was the neck, and Master Guy had to play at "dodge" with the falcon, who was intent upon darting his terrific beak into the cavalier's nose. At length, however, the castle was safely reached; the presents were deposited at the feet of Phillis the Fair, and Guy hoped, like the Peri, and also like that gentle spirit to be disappointed, that the gates of paradise were about to open. But not so. Phillis warmly praised his little regard for that pert minx, Blanche, or *Blanc d'Espagne*, as she wickedly added; and she patted the spaniel, and offered sugar to the falcon; and, after the dinner to which Guy *was* invited, she intimated in whispers, that they were both "too young as yet" (not that she believed so), and that more deeds must be done by Guy, ere the lawyers would be summoned by her papa to achieve some of their own.

The youthful Guy went forth "reluctant but resolved," and he *would* have sung as he went along,

"Elle a quinze ans, moi j'en ai seize,"

of Sedaine and Grétry, only neither poet nor composer, nor the opera of *Richard Cœur de Lion*, had yet appeared to gladden heart and ear. But the sentiment was there, and perhaps Sedaine knew of it when he penned the words. However this may be, Master Guy, though soft of heart, was not so of arm, for on this present cause of errantry he enacted such deeds that their very enumeration makes one breathless. His single sword cleared whole forests of hordes of brigands, through whose sides his trenchant blade passed as easily as the sabre, when held by Corporal Sutton, through a dead sheep. Our hero was by no means particular as to what he did, provided he was doing something; nor what cause he fought for, provided there were a cause and a fight. Thus we find him aiding the Duke of Louvain against his old friend the Emperor of Allemagne. He led the Duke's forces, slew thousands upon thousands of the enemy, and, as though he had the luck of a modern Muscovite army, did not lose more than "one man," with slight damage to the helmet of a second.

Master Guy, not yet twenty, surpassed the man whom Mr. Thiers calls "*ce pur Anglais*," Mr. Pitt, for he became a prime minister ere he had attained his majority. In that capacity he negotiated a peace for the Duke with the Emperor. The two potentates were so satisfied with the negotiator, that out of compliment they offered him the command of their united fleet against the Pagan Soldan of Byzantium. They did not at all expect that he would accept it; but then they were not aware that Master Guy had much of the spirit which Sidney Smith, in after-years, discerned in Lord John Russell—and the enterprising Guy accepted the command of the entire fleet, with quite an entire confidence.

He did therewith, if chroniclers are to be credited, more than we might reasonably expect from Lord John Russell, were that statesman to be in command of a Channel squadron. Having swept the sea, he rather prematurely, if dates are to be respected, nearly annihilated Mohammedanism—and he was as invincible and victorious against every kind of Pagan. It was in the East that he overthrew in single combat, the giants Colbron and his brother Mongadora. He was resting after this contest, and leaning like the well-breathed Hotspur, upon his sword, at the entrance to his tent, when the Turkish governor Esdalante, approaching him, politely begged that he might take his head, as he had promised the same to an Osmanlee lady, who was in a condition of health which might be imperilled by refusal. Master Guy as politely bade him take it if he could, and therewith, they went at it "like French falconers," and Guy took off the head of his opponent instead of losing his own. This little matter being settled, Guy challenged the infidel Soldan himself, putting Christianity against Islamism, on the issue, and thus professing to decide questions of faith as Galerius did when he left Olympus and Calvary to depend upon a vote of the Roman senate. Master Guy, being thrice armed by the justness of his quarrel, subdued the infidel Soldan, but the latter, to show, as we are told, his insuperable hatred for Christianity, took handfuls of his own blood, and cast it in the face of his conqueror—and no doubt here, the victor had in his mind the true story of Julian insulting "the Galilæan." We thus see how history is made to contribute to legend.

And now the appetite of the errant lover grew by what it fed upon. He mixed himself up in every quarrel, and could not see a lion and a dragon quietly settling their disputes in a wood, by dint of claws, without striking in for the lion, slaying his foe, and receiving with complacency the acknowledgments of the nobler beast.

He achieved something more useful when he met Lord Terry in a wood, looking for his wife who had been carried off by a score of ravishers. While the noble lord sat down on a mossy bank, like a gentleman in a melodrama, Guy rescued his wife in his presence, and slew all the ravishers, "in funeral order," the youngest first. He subsequently stood godfather to his friend Terry's child, and as I am fond of historical parallels, I may notice that Sir Walter Scott performed the same office for a Terry, who if he was not a lord, often represented them, to say nothing of monarchs and other characters.

Master Guy's return to England was a little retarded by another characteristic adventure. As he was passing through Louvain, he found Duke Otto besieging his father in his own castle— "governor" of the castle and the Duke. Now nothing shocked Master Guy so much as filial ingratitude, and despite all that Otto could urge about niggardly allowance, losses at play, debts of honor, and the parsimony of the "governor," our champion made common cause with the "indignant parent," and not only mortally wounded Otto, but, before the latter died, Guy brought him to a "sense of his situation," and Otto died in a happy frame of mind, leaving all his debts to his father. The legacy was by way of a "souvenir," and certainly the governor never forgot it. As for

Guy, he killed the famous boar of Louvain, before he departed for England, and as he drew his sword from the animal's flank, he remarked, there lies a greater boar, and not a less beast than Otto himself. However, he took the head and hams with him, for Phillis was fond of both; and as she was wont to say, if there was anything that could seduce her, it was brawn!

When Master Guy stepped ashore at Harwich, where that amphibious town now lies soaking, deputations from all quarters were awaiting him, to ask his succor against some terrible dragon in the north that was laying waste all the land, and laying hold of all the waists which the men there wished to enclose. King Athelstan was then at York hoping to terrify the indomitable beast by power of an army, which in combat with the noxious creature made as long a tail, in retreat, as the dragon itself.

Now whatever this nuisance was which so terribly plagued the good folks in the North, whether a dragon with a tongue thirty feet long, or anything else equally hard to imagine, it is matter of fact that our Master Guy assuredly got the better of it. On his return he met an ovation in York; Athelstan entertained him at a banquet, covered him with honor, endowed him with a good round sum, and *thus* all the newborn male children in the county became Guys. At least two thirds of them received the popular name, and for many centuries it remained in favor, until disgrace was brought upon it by the York proctor's son, whose effigy still glides through our streets on each recurring 5th of November.

I will not pause on this matter. I will only add that the Earl of Warwick, finding Guy a man whom the King delighted to honor, accepted him for a son-in-law; and then, ever wise, and civil, and proper, he discreetly died. The King made Guy Earl of Warwick, in his place, and our hero being now a married man, he of course ceased to be *Master* Guy.

And here I might end my legend, but that it has a moral in it. Guy did a foolish but a common thing, he launched out into extravagant expenses, and, suddenly, he found himself sick, sad, and insolvent. Whether, therewith, his wife was soured, creditors troublesome, and bailiffs presuming, it is hard to say. One thing, however, is certain, that to save himself from all three, Earl Guy did what nobles often do now, in the same predicament, " went abroad." Guy, however, travelled in primitive style. He went on foot, and made his inn o'nights in church-yards, where he colloquized with the skulls after the fashion of Hamlet with the skull of "poor Yorick." He had given out that he was going to Jerusalem, but hearing that the Danes were besieging Athelstan at Winchester, he went thither, and, in modest disguise, routed them with his own unaided hand. Among his opponents, he met with the giant Colbron whom he had previously slain in Orient lands, and the two fought their battles o'er again, and with such exactly similar results as to remind one of the peculiar philosophy of Mr. Boatswain Cheeks.

This appearance of Colbron in two places is a fine illustration of the "myth," and I mention it expressly for the benefit of the next edition of the Right Reverend Doctor Whateley's "Historical Fallacies." But to resume.

Guy, imparting a confidential statement of his identity and intentions to the King, left him, to take up his abode in a cave, in a cliff, near his residence; and at the gates of his own castle he received, in the guise of a mendicant, alms of money and bread, from the hands of his wife. I strongly suspect that the foundation of this section of our legend rests upon the probable fact that Phillis was of that quality which is said to belong to gray mares; and that she led Guy a life which made him a miserable Guy indeed; and that the poor henpecked man took to bad company abroad, and met with small allowance of everything but reproach at home And *so* he "died."

A dramatic author of Charles I.'s reign, has, however, resuscitated him in "A Tragical History of Guy, Earl of Warwick," enacted several times in presence of that monarch, and professedly written by a certain "B. J.," whom I do not at all suspect of being Ben Jonson. The low comedy portion of this tragic drama is of the filthiest sort, dealing in phrases and figures which I can hardly conceive would now be tolerated in the lowest den of St. Giles's, certainly not out of it. If Charles heard this given more than once, as the titlepage intimates, "more shame for him." If his Queen was present, she haply may not have understood the *verba ad summam caveam spectantia*, and if a daughter could have been at the royal entertainment, why then the very idea revolts one, and pity is almost lost in indignation. That the author himself thought well of the piece, which he printed in 1661, is proved by the defiant epigraph which says:—

"Carpere vel noli nostra vel ede tua."

I must not devote much space to a retrospective review of this piece, particularly as the action begins after Guy has ceased to be "Master," and when, on his announcement of going to Jerusalem (perhaps to the Jews to do a little business in bills), Phillis makes some matronly remarks in a prospective sense, and a liberty of illustration which would horrify a monthly nurse.

However, Guy goes forth and meets with a giant so huge, that his squire Sparrow says it required four-and-twenty men to throw mustard in his mouth when he dined. From such giants, Heaven protects the errant Guy, and with a troop of fairies, wafts him to Jerusalem. Here he finds Shamurath of Babylon assaulting the city, but Guy heaps miracle on miracle of valor, and produces such astounding results that Shamurath, who is a spectator of the deeds and the doer, inquires, with a suspicion of Connaught in the accent of the inquiry, "What divil or man is this?"

The infidel is more astonished than ever when Guy, after defeating him, takes him into controversy, and laying hold of him as Dr. Cumming does of Romanism, so buffets his belief that the soldier, fairly out of breath and argument, gives in, and declares himself a Christian, on conviction.

During one-and-twenty years, Guy has a restless life through the five acts of this edifying tragedy, and when he is seen again in England, overcoming the Danes, he intimates to Athelstan that he has six years more to pass in disguise, ere a vow, of which we have before heard nothing, will be fulfilled. Athelstan receives all that is said, in confidence; and promises affably, "upon my word," not to betray the secret. Guy is glad to hear that Phillis is "pretty well;" and then he takes up his residence as I have before told, according to the legend. He and an Angel occasionally have a little abstruse disquisition; but the most telling scene is doubtless where the bread is distributed to the beggars, by Phillis. Guy is here disguised as a palmer, and Phillis inquires if he knew the great Earl, to which Guy answers, with a wink of the eye, that he and the Earl had often drank at the same crystal spring. But Phillis is too dull, or too melancholy to trace her way through so sorry a joke.

And now, just as the hour of completion of the vowed time of his disguise, Guy takes to dying, and in that state he is found by Rainhorn, the son who knows him not. He sends a token by the young fellow to Phillis, who begins to suspect that the palmer who used to be so particular in asking for "brown bread" at her gate, must be the "Master Guy" of the days of sunny youth, short kirtles, and long love-making. Mother and son haste to the spot, but the vital spark has fled. Phillis exclaims, with much composed thought, not unnatural in a woman whose husband has been seven-and-twenty years away from home, and whose memory is good: "If it be he, he has a mould-wart underneath his ear;" to which the son as composedly remarks, "View him, good mother, satisfy your mind." Thereupon the proper identification of the "party" is established; and the widow is preparing to administer, without will annexed, when Rainhorn bids her banish sorrow, as the King is coming. The son evidently thinks the honor of a living king should drown sorrow for a deceased parent; just as a Roman family that can boast of a Pope in it, does not put on mourning even when that Pope dies; the *having had him*, being considered a joy that no grief should diminish.

Athelstan is evidently a King of Cockayne, for he affably expresses surprise at the old traveller's death, seeing, says his Majesty, that "I had appointed *for* to meet Sir Guy;" to which the son, who has now succeeded to the estate, replies, in the spirit of an heir who has been waiting long for an inheritance:—that the death has happened, and can not now be helped.

But the most remarkable matter in this tragedy is that uttered by Time, who plays prologue, epilogue, and interlude between the acts. Whatever Charles may have thought of the piece, he was doubtless well-pleased with Time, who addresses the audience in verse, giving a political turn to the lesson on the stage. I dare say the following lines were loudly applauded, if not by the king, by the gallants, courtiers, and cavaliers generally:—

> "In Holy Land abroad Guy's spirits roam,
> And not in deans and chapters' lands at home.

> His sacred fury menaceth that nation,
> Which held Judea under sequestration.
> *He* doth not strike at surplices and tippets,
> To bring an olio in of sects and sippets;
> But deals his warlike and death-doing blows
> Against his Saviour's and his sov'reign's foes."

How the Royalist throats must have roared applause, and warrantably too, at these genial lines; and how must the churchmen in the pit have stamped with delight when Time subsequently assured them that Guy took all his Babylonian prisoners to Jerusalem, and had them probably christened by episcopally-ordained ministers! If the house did not ring with the cheers of the Church-and-King audience there, why they were unworthy of the instruction filtered through legend and tragedy.

Such is the story of "Master Guy;" a story whose incidents have doubtless meaning in them, but which were never turned to more practical purpose than when they were employed to support a tottering altar and a fallen throne. Reader, let us drink to the immortal memory of MASTER GUY; and having seen what sort of man he was whom the king delighted to honor, let us see what honors were instituted by kings for other deserving men.

## GARTERIANA.

> "Honor! Your own worth before
> Hath been sufficient preparation."— *The Maid's Revenge.*

A BRIEF sketch of the history of the foundation of the Order of the Garter will be found in another page. Confining myself here to anecdotical detail, I will commence by observing, that in former times, no Knight could be absent from two consecutive feasts of the order, without being fined in a jewel, which he was to offer at St. George's altar. The fine was to be doubled every year, until he had made atonement. Further, every knight was bound to wear the Garter in public, wherever he might be, on pain of a mulct of half a mark. Equally obligatory was it on the knight, in whatever part of the world he was residing, or however he was engaged, to wear the sanguine mantle of the order from the eve of St. George till vesper-time on the morrow of the festival. Some of the chevaliers who were in distant lands must have caused as much surprise by their costume, as a Blue-coat boy does, wandering in his strangely-colored garb, in the streets of Paris. I need not allude to the absurd consequence which would attend the enforcing of this arrangement in our own days. Hunting is generally over before the eve of St. George's day, and therefore a robed Knight of the Garter could never be seen taking a double fence, ditch and rail, at the tail of the "Melton Mowbray." But even the sight of half a dozen of them riding down Parliament street at the period in question, would hardly be a stranger spectacle. A slight money offering of a penny exempted any rather loose-principled knight from attending divine service at St. George's Chapel when he was in or near Windsor. When a knight died, all his surviving comrades were put to the expense of causing a certain number of masses to be said for his soul. The sovereign-lord of the order had one thousand masses chanted in furtherance of his rescue from purgatory. There was a graduated scale through the various ranks till the knight-bachelor was come to. For him, only one hundred masses were put up. This proves either that the knight's soul was not so difficult of deliverance from what Prince Gorschakoff would call the "feu d'enfer," or that the King's was so heavily pressed to the lowest depths of purgatory by its crimes, that it required a decupled effort before it could be rescued.

"Companionship," it may be observed, profited a knight in some degree if, being knave as well as knight, he fell under the usual sentence of being "drawn, hanged, and beheaded." In such case, a Knight of the Garter only suffered decapitation, as Sir Simon Burley in 1388. The amount of favor shown to the offending knight did not admit of his being conscious of much gratitude to him at whose hands it was received. It may be mentioned, that it did not always follow that a nobleman elected to be knight willingly accepted the proffered Garter. The first who refused it, after due election, in 1424, was the Duke of Burgundy. He declined it with as much scorn as Uhland did the star of merit offered to the poet by the present King of Bavaria.

In treating of stage knights, I shall be found to have placed at their head Sir John Falstaff. The original of that character according to some namely, Sir John Fastolf, claims some notice here, as a Knight of the Garter who was no more the coward which he was said to be, than Falstaff is the bloated buffoon which some commentators take him for. Sir John Fastolf was elected Knight of the Garter in 1426. Monstrelet says he was removed from the order for running away, without striking a blow, at the battle of Patay. Shakespeare's popular Sir John has nothing in common with this other Sir John, but we have Falstolf himself in Henry VI. act iv. sc. 1, with Talbot, alluding to his vow, that

> "When I did meet thee next,
> To tear the Garter from thy craven's leg,
> The which I have done, because unworthily
> Thou wast installed in that high degree."

This sort of suspension or personal deprivation was never allowed by the rules of the order, which enjoined the forms for degrading a knight who was proved to have acted cowardly. The battle of

Patay was fought in 1429; and as there is abundant testimony of Sir John having been in possession of the Garter and all its honors long after that period; and, further, that his tomb in Pulham Mary, Norfolk, represented him in gilt armor, with his crest and two escutcheons, with the cross of St. George within the order, we may fairly conclude that if the charge was ever made, of which there is no trace, it assuredly never was proven.

If there were some individuals who refused to accept the honor at all, there were others who were afraid to do so without curious inquiry. Thus, in the reign of Henry VI. we hear of the embassador from Frederick III. Emperor of Germany (one Sir Hertook von Clux), stating that his master wishes to know "what it would stand him in, if he were to be admitted into the honorable order!" Cautious Austria!

There are examples both of courtesy and sarcasm among the Knights of the Garter. I may cite, for instance, the case of the Duke of York, in the reign of Henry VI. A. D. 1453. The King was too ill to preside at the Chapter; the Duke of Buckingham was his representative; and the Duke of York, so little scrupulous in most matters, excused himself from attending on this occasion, because, as he said, "the sovereign having for some time been angry with him, he durst not attend, lest he should incur his further displeasure, and thereby aggravate the illness under which the King was suffering." When the same Duke came into power, he gave the Garter to the most useful men of the York party, beheading a few Lancastrian knights in order to make way for them. At the Chapter held for the purpose of electing the York aspirants, honest John de Foix, Earl of Kendal, declined to vote at all. He alleged that he was unable to discern whether the candidates were "without reproach" or not, and he left the decision to clearsighted people. The Earl was a Lancastrian, and he thus evaded the disagreeable act of voting for personal and political enemies.

But whatever the intensity of dislike one knight may have had against another, there were occasions on which they went, hand in hand, during the celebration of mass, to kiss that esteemable relic, the heart of St. George. This relic had been brought to England by the Emperor Sigismund. Anstis remarks, after alluding to the obstinacy of those who will not believe all that St. Ambrose says touching the facts of St. George, his slaying of the dragon, and his rescue of a royal virgin, that "whosoever is so refractory as obstinately to condemn every part of this story, is not to be bore with." He then adds: "this true martyr and excellent and valued soldier of Christ, after many unspeakable torments inflicted on him by an impious tyrant, when he had bent his head, and was just ready to give up the ghost, earnestly entreated Almighty God, that whoever, in remembrance of him, and his name, should devoutly ask anything, might be heard, a voice instantly came from Heaven, signifying that that was granted which he had requested. . . . While living, by prayer he obtained that whoever should fly to him for his intercession, should not pray nor cry out in vain. He ordered the trunk of his body, which had origin from among infidels, to be sent to them, that they whom he had not been able to serve, when living, might receive benefit from him, when dead; that those infidels who by any misfortune had lost their senses, by coming to him or his chapel, might be restored to soundness of mind and judgment. His head and other members were to be carried, some one way and some another. But his heart, the emblem of lively love, was bequeathed wholly to Christians, for whom he had the most fervent affection. Not to all them in general, though Christians, but to Englishmen alone; and not to every part of England, but only to his own Windsor, which on this account must have been more pleasing to the sovereigns and all other the knights of this most illustrious order. Thus his heart, together with a large portion of his skull, is there kept with due honor and veneration. Sigismund, Emperor of Alemain, always august, being chosen in this honorable order, presented this heart to the invincible Henry V., who gave orders to have it preserved in that convenient place, where he had already instituted for himself solemn exequies for ever, that the regard he had for all others might be past dispute." This is very far, indeed, from being logical, but the fact remains that during the reign of Henry VI., the heart seems to have been regarded with more than usual reverence by the knights of the two factions which were rending England. Each hoped to win St. George for a confederate.

The chapters were not invariably held at Windsor, nor in such solemn localities as a chapel. In 1445, Henry VI., held a chapter at the Lion Inn in Brentford. In this hostelrie the King created Sir Thomas Hastings and Sir Alonzo d'Almade, Knights of the Garter. To the latter, who was also made Earl of Avranches, in the best room of a Brentford inn, the monarch also presented a gold cup. The whole party seems to have made a night of it in the pleasant locality, and the new chevaliers were installed the next morning—after which, probably, mulled sack went round in the golden cup.

Shakespeare makes Richard III. swear by his George, his Garter, and his Crown; but the George and Collar were novelties introduced by Henry VII. The latter King held one of the most splendid chapters which ever assembled, at York, prefacing the work there by riding with all the knights, in their robes, to the morning mass of requiem, and following it up by similarly riding to even-sung. This was more decent than Henry VI.'s tavern chapter of the (Red) Lion, in Brentford. Henry VII. was fond of the solemn splendor of installations, at which he changed his costume like a versatile actor, was surrounded by ladies as well as knights, and had Skelton, the poet, near to take notes for songs and sonnets, descriptive of the occasion. A sovereign of the order, like Henry VII., so zealous to maintain its splendor and efficiency, merited the gift which was conferred upon him by the Cardinal of Rouen—of the bones of one of the legs of St. George. The saint had many legs, but it is not said where these bones were procured, and they who beheld them, at the chapter held in St. Paul's Cathedral in 1505, probably little troubled themselves as to whence the precious relics were derived. Henry, in return, left an image of St. George, of one hundred and forty ounces, adorned with masses of precious stones, to the College of Windsor, " there to remain *while the world shall endure,* to be set upon the high altar at all solemn feasts." Leg bones and costly image would now be sought for in vain. The world has outlived them, and suffers nothing by their loss.

It was the successor of Richmond, namely Henry VIII. who granted to these knights what may be termed a sumptuary privilege, that of being permitted to wear woollen cloth made out of the realm. None but a knight, save the peers, dared don a coat or mantle made of foreign cloth. In love of splendor, Henry was equal to his predecessor, and perhaps never was a more brilliant spectacle seen than on the 27th of May, 1519, when the King and a glittering cortège rode from Richmond to Windsor, and changed steeds and drank a cup at the " Catherine's Wheel," in Colnbrook, by the way. The Queen and a galaxy of ladies met them in Eton, and the usual solemnities were followed by a gorgeous banquet, at which there were such meat and music as had scarcely ever been so highly enjoyed at a festival before. The middle of the hall was crowded with spectators, but at the close of the repast, these were turned out, when " the King was served of his void, the knights also, standing all along"—which must have been a remarkably edifying exhibition.

Henry re-modelled the order, and framed the statutes by which it is now chiefly governed. Among them was the one directing that no person of mean birth should be elected, and this the King himself very speedily broke, by electing Thomas Cromwell. The latter returned thanks for the honor in the very humblest strain, and while he seemed conscious that he was entirely unworthy of the distinction, he appeared desirous to assure the sneering knights' companions who had been compelled to give him their suffrages, that ignoble as he was, he would imitate nobility as closely as possible. But there were men, from the period of the institution of the order downward to Henry's time, who, if of higher birth than Cromwell, were not of higher worth. Very many had forfeited their dignity as knights by treasonable practices; and Henry decreed that wherever these names occurred in the records, the words " Vœ Proditor !"—Out upon the traitor—should be written against them in the margin. The text had thus a truly Tudor comment.

Under the succeeding sovereign, Edward VI., a great portion of the splendor of the religious ceremonies at the installation was abolished. It was in this reign that Northumberland procured the ejection of Lord Paget from the order, on the ground that the meanness of his birth had always disqualified him, or as Edward VI. says in his journal, " for divers his offences, and *chiefly* because he was no gentleman of blood, neither of father-side nor mother-side." Lord Paget, however, was restored under Mary, and the record of his degradation was removed from the register.

Under Mary, if there was some court servility there was also some public spirit. When the Queen created her husband Philip a knight, an obsequious herald, out of compliment to the "joint-sovereigns," took down the arms of England in the chapel at Windsor, and was about to set up those of Spain. This, however, was forbidden "by certain lords," and brave men they were, for in such a display of English spirit there was peril of incurring the ill-will of Mary, who was never weary of heaping favors on the foreign King-consort, whom she would have made generalissimo of her forces if she had dared. It is a curious fact that Philip was not ejected from the order, even when he had despatched the Spanish Armada to devastate the dominions of the sovereign.

In illustration of the fact that the Garter never left the leg of a knight of the order, there are some lines by the Elizabethan poet Peele, which are very apt to the occasion. Speaking of the Earl of Bedford, Peele says—

>—"Dead is Bedford! virtuous and renowned
>For arms, for honor, and religious love;
>And yet alive his name in Fame's records,
>That held his Garter dear, and wore it well.
>Some worthy wight but blazon his deserts:
>Only a tale I thought on by the way,
>As I observed his honorable name.
>I heard it was his chance, o'erta'en with sleep,
>To take a nap near to a farmer's lodge.
>Trusted a little with himself belike,
>This aged earl in his apparel plain,
>Wrapt in his russet gown, lay down to rest,
>His badge of honor buckled to his leg.
>Bare and naked. There came a pilfering swad
>And would have preyed upon this ornament
>Essayed t' unbuckle it, thinking him asleep.
>The noble gentleman, feeling what he meant—
>'Hold, foolish lad,' quoth he, 'a better prey:
>'This Garter is not fit for ev'ry leg,
>'And I account it better than my purse.
>The varlet ran away, the earl awaked.
>And told his friends, and smiling said withal,

> "'A would not, had 'a understood the French
> 'Writ on my Garter, dared t' have stol'n the same.'
> This tale I thought upon, told me for truth,
> The rather for it praiséd the Posy,
> Right grave and honorable, that importeth much—
> 'Evil be to him,' it saith, 'that evil thinks.'"

Elizabeth was distinguished for loving to hold newly-chosen knights in suspense, before she ratified their election by her approval. The anniversary banquets too fell into disuse during her reign, and she introduced the most unworthy knight that had ever stood upon the record of the order. This was Charles IX. of France. On the other hand she sent the Garter to Henri Quatre. He was the last French monarch who was a companion of the order, till the reign of Louis XVIII. On the day the latter came up from Hartwell to Stanmore, on his way to France, at the period of the first restoration, the Prince Regent invested him with the brilliant insignia at Carlton House. It was on this occasion Louis XVIII. observed that he was the first King of France who had worn the garter since the period of Henri Quatre. Louis had erased his own name from the Golden Book of Nobility of Venice, when he heard that the name of Bonaparte had been inserted therein. He, perhaps, would have declined receiving the Garter, if he could have foreseen that the royal niece of the Prince Regent would, in after years, confer the order on the imperial nephew of Napoleon.

The period of James is marked by some pretty quarrels among the officials. Thus at the installation of Prince Henry, there was a feast which was well nigh turned into a fray. At the very beginning of it, the prebends and heralds fell to loggerheads on the delicate question of precedency. The alms-knights mingled in the quarrel by siding with the prebends, and claiming the next degree of precedency before the heralds. Reference was made to the Earls of Nottingham and Worcester. The referees adjudged the heralds to have right of precedency before the prebends. Thereupon the proud prebends, oblivious of Christian humility, refused to go to church at the tail of the heralds. The latter went in exultingly without them, and the prebends would not enter until a long time had elapsed, so that it could not be said they followed the gentlemen of the tabard. The delicate question was again angrily discussed, and at length referred to the whole body of knights. The noble fraternity, after grave deliberation, finally determined that on the next day of St. George, being Sunday, in the procession to the church, the alms-knights should go first, then the pursuivants of arms, then the prebends (many of whom were doctors of divinity), and finally the heralds. The latter were cunning rogues, and no inconsiderable authority in matters of precedency; and they immediately declared that the knights had decreed to them the better place, inasmuch as that in most processions the principal personages did not walk first.

Of the knights of this reign, Grave Maurice, Prince of Orange, and Frederick the (Goody) Palsgrave of the Rhine, were among the most celebrated. They were installed in 1613, the Prince by proxy, and the Palsgrave in person. A young and graceful Count Ludovic of Nassau, was chosen at the last moment, to represent the Prince, whose appointed representative, Count Henry, was detained in Holland by adverse winds. "The feast," says an eye-witness, "was in the Great Hall, where the king dined at the upper table alone, served in state by the Lord Gerard as Sewer, the Lord Morris as Cupbearer, the Lord Compton as Carver; all that were of the order, at a long cross table across the hall. The Prince by himself alone, and the Palatine a little distance from him. But the Count Nassau was ranged over-against my Lord Admiral, and so took place of all after the Sovereign Princes, not without a little muttering of our Lords, who would have had him ranged according to seniority, if the king had not overruled it by prerogative."

Wilson, in his history of James I., narrates a curious anecdote respecting this Grave Maurice and the ribbon of the order. "Prince Maurice took it as a great honor to be admitted into the Fraternity of that Order, and wore it constantly; till afterward, some villains at the Hague, that met the reward of their demerit (one of them, a Frenchman, being groom of the Prince's chamber) robbed a jeweller of Amsterdam that brought jewels to the Prince. This groom, tempting him into his chamber, to see some jewels, there, with his confederates, strangled the man with one of the Prince's Blue Ribbons; which being afterward discovered, the Prince would never suffer so fatal an instrument to come about his neck."

James, by raising his favorite Buckingham, then only Sir George Villiers, to the degree of Knight of the Garter, was considered to have as much outraged the order as Henry VIII. had done by investing Cromwell with the insignia. Chamberlain, in a letter to Sir Dudley Carleton, says, "The King went away the next day after St. George's Feast, toward Newmarket and Thetford, the Earl of Rutland and Sir George Villiers being that morning elected into the order of the Garter, which seemed at first a strange choice, in regard that the wife of the former is an open and known recusant, and *he* is said to have many dangerous people about him; and the latter is so lately come into the sight of the world, and withal it is doubted that he had not sufficient likelihood to maintain the dignity of the place, according to express articles of the order. But to take away that scruple, the King hath bestowed upon him the Lord Gray's lands, and means, they say, to mend his grant with much more, not far distant, in the present possession of the Earl of Somerset, if he do *cadere causâ* and sink in the business now in hand." The last passage alludes to the murder of Overbury.

The going down to Windsor was at this time a pompous spectacle. The riding thither of the Knights Elect is thus spoken of by a contemporary: "On Monday," (St. George's day, 1615), "our Knights of the Garter, Lord Fenton and Lord Knollys, ride to Windsor, with great preparation to re-vie one with another who shall make the best show. Though I am of opinion the latter will carry it by many degrees, by reason of the alliance with the houses of the Howards, Somerset, Salisbury, and Dorset, with many other great families that will bring him their friends, and most part of the pensioners. Yet most are persuaded the other will bear away the bell, as having the best part of the court, all the bed-chamber, all the prince's servants and followers, with a hundred of the Guard, that have new rich coats made on purpose, besides Sir George Villiers (the favorite), and Mr. Secretary—whose presence had been better forborne, in my judgment, for many reasons—but that every man abound in his own sense." James endeavored to suppress, in some measure, the expensive ride of the Knights Elect to Windsor, but only with partial success. His attempted reform, too, had a selfish aspect; he tried to make it profitable to himself. He prohibited the giving of livery coats, "for saving charge and avoiding emulation," and at the same time ordered that all existing as well as future companions should present a piece of plate of the value of twenty pounds sterling at least for the use of the altar in St. George's Chapel.

Charles I. held chapters in more places in England than any other king — now at York, now at Nottingham, now at Oxford, and in other localities. These chapters were sometimes attended by as few as four knights, and for the most part they were shorn of much of the ancient ceremony. He held some brilliant chapters at Windsor, nevertheless. At one of them, the election of the Earl of Northumberland inspired a bard, whose song I subjoin because it is illustrative of several incidents which are far from lacking interest.

"A brief description of the triumphant show made by the Right Honorable Aulgernon Percie Earl of Northumberland, at his installation and initiation into the princely fraternity of the Garter, on the 13th of May, 1635."

*To the tune of " Quell the Pride."*

"You noble buds of Britain,
 That spring from honor's tree,
Who love to hear of high designs,
 Attend awhile to me.
And I'll (in brief) discover what
 Fame bids me take in hand —
  To blaze
  The praise
 Of great Northumberland.

"The order of the Garter,
 Ere since third Edward reigned
Unto the realm of England hath
 A matchless honor gained.
The world hath no society,
 Like to this princely band,
  To raise
  The praise
 Of great Northumberland.

"The honor of his pedigree
  Doth claim a high regard,
And many of his ancestors
  For fame thought nothing hard.
And he, through noble qualities,
  Which are exactly scanned,
      Doth raise
      The praise
  Of great Northumberland.

"Against the day appointed,
  His lordship did prepare;
To publish his magnificence
  No charges he did spare.
The like within man's memory
  Was never twice in hand
      To raise
      The praise
  Of great Northumberland.

"Upon that day it seemed
  All Brittany did strive,
And did their best to honor him
  With all they could contrive.
For all our high nobility
  Joined in a mutual land
      To blaze
      The praise
  Of great Northumberland.

'The common eyes were dazzled
  With wonder to behold
The lustre of apparel rich,
  All silver, pearl, and gold,
Which on brave coursers mounted,
  Did glisten through the Strand,
      To blaze
      The praise
  Of great Northumberland.

"But ere that I proceed
  This progress to report,
I should have mentioned the feast
  Made at Salisbury Court.
Almost five hundred dishes

Did on the table stand,
To raise
The praise
Of great Northumberland."

*The Second Part, to the same tune.*

"The mightiest prince or monarch
That in the world doth reign,
At such a sumptuous banquet might
Have dined without disdain,
Where sack, like conduit water,
Was free ever at command,
To blaze
The praise
Of great Northumberland.

"The famous Fleet-street conduit,
Renowned so long ago,
Did not neglect to express what love
She to my lord did owe.
For like an old proud woman
The painted face doth stand
To blaze
The praise
Of great Northumberland.

"A number of brave gallants,
Some knights and some esquires,
Attended at this triumph great,
Clad in complete attires.
The silver half-moon gloriously
Upon their sleeves doth stand,
To blaze
The praise
Of great Northumberland.

"All these on stately horses,
That ill endured the bit,
Were mounted in magnific cost,
As to the time was fit.
Their feathers white and red did show,
Like to a martial band,
To blaze
The praise
Of great Northumberland.

"The noble earls and viscounts,
  And barons, rode in state:
This great and high solemnity
  All did congratulate.
To honor brave Earl Percy
  Each put a helping hand
      To blaze
      The praise
  Of great Northumberland.

"King Charles, our royal sovereign,
  And his renownéd Mary,
With Britain's hope, their progeny,
  All lovingly did tarry
At noble Viscount Wimbleton's,
  I' the fairest part o' th' Strand,
      To blaze
      The praise
  Of great Northumberland.

"To famous Windsor Castle,
  With all his gallant train,
Earl *Pearcy* went that afternoon
  His honor to obtain.
And there he was installed
  One of St. George's band,
      To blaze
      The praise
  Of great Northumberland.

"Long may he live in honor,
  In plenty and in peace;
For him, and all his noble friends,
  To pray I'll never cease.
This ditty (which I now will end)
  Was only ta'en in hand
      To blaze
      The praise
  Of great Northumberland."

This illustrative ballad bears the initials "M. P." These, probably, do not imply either a member of Parliament, or of the house of Percy. Beneath the initials we have the legend, "Printed at London, for Francis Coules, and are" (verses *subaudiuntur*) "to be sold at his shop in the Old Bayley." There are three woodcuts to illustrate the text. The first represents the Earl on horseback; both peer and charger are very heavily caparisoned, and the steed looks as intelligent as the peer. In front of this stately, solid, and leisurely pacing couple, is a mounted serving-man, armed with a stick, and riding full gallop at nobody. The illustration to the second part represents the Earl returning from Windsor in a carriage, which looks very much like the Araba in the Turkish Exhibition. The new Knight wears his hat, cloak, collar and star; his figure, broad-set to the doorway, bears no distant resemblance to the knave of clubs, and his aristocratic self-possession and serenity are remarkable, considering the bumping he is getting, as implied by the wheels of his chariot being several inches off the ground. The pace of the steeds, two and twohalves of whom are visible, is not, however, very great. They are hardly out of a walk. But perhaps the bareheaded coachman and the as bareheaded groom have just pulled them up, to allow the running footmen to reach the carriage. Two of these are seen near the rear of the vehicle, running like the brace of mythological personages in Ovid, who ran the celebrated match in which the apples figured so largely. The tardy footmen have just come in sight of their lord, who does not allow his serenity to be disturbed by chiding them. The Percy wears as stupid an air as his servants, and the only sign of intelligence anywhere in the group is to be found in the off-side wheeler, whose head is turned back, with a sneering cast in the face, as if he were ridiculing the idea of the whole show, and was possessed with the conviction that he was drawing as foolish a beast as himself.

The Earl appears to have ridden eastward, in the direction pointed by his own lion's tale, before he drove down to Windsor. The show seems to have interested all ranks between the Crown and the Conduit in Fleet street. Where Viscount Wimbledon's house was, "in the fairest part of the Strand," I can not conjecture, and as I can not find information on this point in Mr. Peter Cunningham's "Hand-Book of London," I conclude that the site is not known.

In connection with Charles I. and his Garter, I will here cite a passage from the third volume of Mr. Macaulay's "History of England," page 165. "Louvois hated Lauzun. Lauzun was a favorite at St. Germains. He wore the Garter, a badge of honor which has very seldom been conferred on aliens who were not sovereign princes. It was believed, indeed, in the French court, that in order to distinguish him from the other knights of the most illustrious of European orders, he had been decorated with that very George which Charles I. had, on the scaffold, put into the hands of Juxon." Lauzun, I shall have to notice under the head of foreign knights. I revert here to the George won by Charles and given to Lauzun. It was a very extraordinary jewel, curiously cut in an onyx, set about with twenty-one large table diamonds, in the fashion of a garter. On the under side of the George was the portrait of Henrietta Maria, "rarely well limned," says Ashmole, "and set in a case of gold, the lid neatly enamelled with goldsmith's work, and surrounded with another Garter, adorned with a like number of equal-sized diamonds, as was the foresaid." The onyx George of Charles I. was in the possession of the late Duke of Wellington, and is the property of the present Duke.

There is something quite as curious touching the history of the Garter worn by Charles I., as what Mr. Macaulay tells concerning the George. The diamonds upon it, forming the motto, were upward of four hundred in number. On the day of the execution, this valuable ornament fell into the hands of one of Cromwell's captains of cavalry, named Pearson. After one exchange of hands, it was sold to John Ireton, sometime Lord-Mayor of London, for two hundred and five pounds. At the Restoration, a commission was appointed to look after the scattered royal property generally; and the commissioners not only recovered some pictures belonging to Charles, from Mrs. Cromwell, who had placed them in charge of a tradesman in Thames street, but they discovered that Ireton held the Garter, and they summoned him to deliver it up accordingly. It has been said that the commissioners offered him the value of the jewel if he would surrender it. This is not the case. The report had been founded on a misapprehension of terms. Ireton did not deny that he possessed the Garter by purchase, whereupon "composition was offered him, according to the direction of the Commission, as in all other like cases where anything could not be had in kind." That is, he was ordered to surrender the jewel, or if this had been destroyed, its value, or some compensation in lieu thereof. Ireton refused the terms altogether. The King, Charles II., thereupon sued him in the Court of King's Bench, where the royal plaintiff obtained a verdict for two hundred and five pounds, and ten pounds costs of suit.

In February, 1652, the Parliament abolished all titles and honors conferred by Charles I. since the 4th of January, two years previously. This was done on the ground that the late King had conferred such titles and honors, in order to promote his wicked and treacherous designs against the parliament and people of England. A fine of one hundred pounds was decreed against every offender, whenever he employed the abolished title, with the exception of a knight, who was let off at the cheaper rate of forty pounds. Any one convicted of addressing a person by any of the titles thus done away with, was liable to a fine of ten shillings. The Parliament treated with silent contempt the titles and orders of knighthood conferred by Charles I. As monarchy was defunct, these adjuncts of monarchy were considered as defunct also. The Protector did not create a single Knight of the Garter, nor of the Bath. "*These* orders," says Nicolas, "were never formally abolished, but they were probably considered so inseparably united to the person, name, and office of a king, as to render it impossible for any other authority to create them." Cromwell, however, made one peer, Howard, Viscount Howard of Morpeth, ten baronets and knights, and conferred certain degrees of precedency. It was seldom that he named an unworthy person, considering the latter in the Protector's own point of view, but the Restoration was no sooner an accomplished fact, when to ridicule one of Oliver's knights was a matter of course with the hilarious dramatic poets. On this subject something will be found under the head of "Stage Knights." Meanwhile, although there is nothing to record touching Knights of the Garter, under the Commonwealth, we may notice an incident showing that Garter King-at-arms was not altogether idle. This incident will be sufficiently explained by the following extract from the third volume of Mr. Macaulay's "History of England." The author is speaking of the regicide Ludlow, who, since the Restoration, had been living in exile at Geneva. "The Revolution opened a new prospect to him. The right of the people to resist oppression, a right which, during many years, no man could assert without exposing himself to ecclesiastical anathemas and to civil penalties, had been solemnly recognised by the Estates of the realm, and had been proclaimed by Garter King-at-arms, on the very spot where the memorable scaffold had been set up."

Charles II. did not wait for the Restoration in order to make or unmake knights. He did not indeed hold chapters, but at St. Germains, in Jersey, and other localities, he unknighted knights who had forgotten their allegiance in the "late *horrid* rebellion," as he emphatically calls the Parliamentary and Cromwellian periods, and authorized other individuals to wear the insignia, while he exhorted them to wait patiently and hopefully for their installations at Windsor. At St. Germains, he gave the Garter to his favorite Buckingham; and from Jersey he sent it to two far better men — Montrose, and Stanley, Earl of Derby. The worst enemies of these men could not deny their chivalrous qualities. Montrose on the scaffold, when they hung (in derision) from his neck the book in which were recorded his many brave deeds, very aptly said that he wore the record of his courage with as much pride as he ever wore the Garter. Stanley's chivalry was never more remarkable than in the skirmish previous to Worcester, when in the hot affray, he received seven shots in his breast-plate, thirteen cuts on his beaver, five or six wounds on his arms and shoulders, and had two horses killed under him. When he was about to die, he returned the Garter, by the hands of a faithful servant, to the king, "in all humility and gratitude," as he remarked, "spotless and free from any stain, as he received it, according to the honorable example of my ancestors."

Charles made knights of the Garter of General Monk and Admiral Montague. The chapter for election was held in the Abbey of St. Augustine's at Canterbury. It was the first convenient place which the king could find for such a purpose after landing. "They were the only two," says Pepys, "for many years who had the Garter given them before they had honor of earldom, or the like, excepting only the Duke of Buckingham, who was only Sir George Villiers when he was made a knight of the Garter." The honor was offered to Clarendon, but declined as above his deserts, and likely to create him enemies. James, Duke of York, however, angrily attributed Clarendon's objection to being elected to the

Garter to the fact that James himself had asked it for him, and that the Chancellor was foolishly unwilling to accept any honer that was to be gained by the Duke's mediation.

Before proceeding to the next reign, let me remark that the George and Garter of Charles II. had as many adventures or misadventures as those of his father. In the fight at Worcester his collar and garter became the booty of Cromwell, who despatched a messenger with them to the Parliament, as a sign and trophy of victory. The king's lesser George, set with diamonds, was preserved by Colonel Blague. It passed through several hands with much risk. It at length fell again into the hands of the Colonel when he was a prisoner in the Tower. Blague, "considering it had already passed so many dangers, was persuaded it could yet secure one hazardous attempt of his own." The enthusiastic royalist looked upon it as a talisman that would rescue him from captivity. Right or wrong in his sentiment, the result was favorable. He succeeded in making his escape, and had the gratification of restoring the George to his sovereign.

The short reign of James II. offers nothing worthy of the notice of the general reader with respect to this decoration; and the same may be said of the longer reign of William III. The little interest in the history of the order under Queen Anne, is in connection with her foreign nominations, of which due notice will be found in the succeeding section. Small, too, is the interest connected with these matters in the reign of George I., saving, indeed, that under *him* we find the last instance of the degradation of a knight of the garter, in the person of James, Duke of Ormund, who had been attainted of high treason. His degradation took place on the 12th July, 1716. The elections were numerous during this reign. The only one that seems to demand particular notice is that of Sir Robert Walpole, First Lord of the Treasury. He gave up the Bath on receiving the Garter in 1726, and he was the only commoner who had received the distinction since Sir George Monk and Sir Edward Montague were created, sixty-six years previously.

The first circumstance worthy of record under George II. is, that the color of the garter and ribbon was changed from light blue to dark, or "Garter-blue," as it is called. This was done in order to distinguish the companions made by Brunswick from those assumed to be fraudulently created by the Pretender Stuart. Another change was effected, but much less felicitously. What with religious, social, and political revolution, it was found that the knights were swearing to statutes which they could not observe. Their consciences were disturbed thereat—at least they said so; but their sovereign set them at ease by enacting that in future all knights should promise to break no statutes, except on dispensation from the sovereign! This left the matter exactly where it had been previously.

The first circumstance worthy of attention in the reign of George III., was that of the election of Earl Gower, president of the council, in 1771. The sharp eye of Junius discovered that the election was a farce, for in place of the sovereign and at least six knights being present, as the statutes required, there were only four knights present, the Dukes of Gloucester, Newcastle, Northumberland, and the Earl of Hertford. The first duke too was there against his will. He had, says Junius, " entreated, begged, and implored," to be excused from attending that chapter—but all in vain. The new knight seems to have been illegally elected, and as illegally installed. The only disagreeable result was to the poor knights of Windsor. People interested in the subject had made remarks, and while the illegal election of the president of the council was most properly put before the King, representation was made to him that the poor knights had been wickedly contravening their statutes, for a very long period. They had for years been permitted to reside with their families wherever they chose to fix their residence. This was pronounced irregular, and George III., so lax with regard to Lord Gower, was very strict with respect to these poor knights. They were all commanded to reside in their apartments attached to Windsor Castle, and there keep up the poor dignity of their noble order, by going to church twice every day in full uniform. There were some of them at that period who would as soon have gone out twice a day to meet the dragon.

The order of the Garter was certainly ill-used by this sovereign. In order to admit all his sons, he abolished the statute of Edward (who had as many sons as George had when he made the absurd innovation, but who did not care to make knights of them *because* they were his sons), confining the number of companions to twenty-five. Henceforward, the sovereign's sons were to reckon only as over and above that number. As if this was not sufficiently absurd, the king subsequently decreed eligibility of election to an indefinite number of persons, provided only that they could trace their descent from King George II.!

No Companion so well deserved the honor conferred upon him as he who was the most illustrious of the English knights created during the sway of the successor of George III., as Regent; namely, the late Duke of Wellington. Mr. Macaulay, when detailing the services and honors conferred on Schomberg, has a passage in which he brings the names of these two warriors, dukes, and knights of the Garter, together. "The House of Commons had, with general approbation, compensated the losses of Schomberg, and rewarded his services by a grant of a hundred thousand pounds. Before he set out for Ireland, he requested permission to express his gratitude for this magnificent present. A chair was set for him within the bar. He took his seat there with the mace at his right hand, rose, and in a few graceful words returned his thanks and took his leave. The Speaker replied that the Commons could never forget the obligation under which they already lay to his Grace, that they saw him with pleasure at the head of an English army, that they felt entire confidence in his zeal and ability, and that at whatever distance he might be he would always be, in a peculiar manner, an object of their care. The precedent set on this interesting occasion was followed with the utmost minuteness, a hundred and twenty-five years later, on an occasion more interesting still. Exactly on the same spot, on which, in July, 1689, Schomberg had acknowledged the liberality of the nation, a chair was set in July, 1814, for a still more illustrious warrior, who came to return thanks for a still more splendid mark of public gratitude."

There is nothing calling for particular notice in the history of the Order since the election of the last-named knight. Not one on whose shoulders has been placed "the robe of heavenly color," earned so hardly and so well the honor of companionship. This honor, however, costs every knight who submits to the demand, not less than one hundred and eight pounds sterling, in fees. It is, in itself, a heavy fine inflicted on those who render extraordinary service to the country, and to whom are presented the order of the Garter, and an order from the Garter King-at-arms to pay something more than a hundred guineas in return. The fine, however, is generally paid with alacrity; for, though the non-payment does not unmake a knight, it has the effect of keeping his name from the register.

I have already observed that Mr. Macaulay, in his recently-published History, has asserted that very few foreigners, except they were sovereign princes, were ever admitted into the companionship of the Garter. Let us, then, look over the roll of illustrious aliens, and see how far this assertion is correct.

## FOREIGN KNIGHTS OF THE GARTER.

There is some error in Mr. Macaulay's statement, which, as a matter of history, may be worth correcting. So far from there having been few aliens, except sovereign princes, admitted into the order, the fact, save in recent times, is exactly the reverse. The order contemplated the admission of foreigners, from the very day of its foundation. On that day, three foreigners were admitted, none of whom was a sovereign prince. Not one of the foreign sovereigns with whom Edward was in alliance, nor any of the royal relatives of the Queen, were among the original companions. The aliens, who were not sovereign princes, were the Captal de Buch, a distinguished Gascon nobleman, and two bannerets or knights, who with the other original companions had served in the expeditions sent by Edward against France.

Again, under Richard II., among the most famous alien gentlemen created knights of the Garter, were the Gascon soldier Du Preissne; Soldan de la Tour, Lord of much land in Xaintonge; the Dutch Count William of Ostervant, who made a favor of accepting the honorable badge; the Duke of Bavaria (not yet Emperor), and Albert, Duke of Holland, who was hardly a sovereign prince, but who, nevertheless, may be accounted as such, seeing that, in a small way indeed, more like a baron than a monarch, he exercised some sovereign rights. The Duke of Britanny may, with more justice, be included in the list of sovereign dukes who were members of the order. Under Henry IV., neither alien noble nor foreign prince appears to have been elected, but under his successor, fifth of the name, Eric X., King of Denmark, and John I., King of Portugal, were created companions. They were the first kings regnant admitted to the order. Some doubt exists as to the date of their admission, but none as to their having been knights' companions. Dabrichecourt is the name of a gentleman lucky enough to have been also elected during this reign, but I do not know if he were of foreign birth or foreign only by descent. The number of the fraternity became complete in this reign, by the election of the Emperor Sigismund. Under Henry V., the foreign sovereign princes, members of the order, were unquestionably more numerous than the mere alien gentlemen; but reckoning from the foundation, there had been a greater number of foreign knights not of sovereign quality than of those who were. The sovereign princes did not seem to care so much for the honor as private gentlemen in foreign lands. Thus the German, Sir Hartook von Clux, accepted the honor with alacrity, but the King of Denmark allowed five years to pass before he intimated that he cheerfully or resignedly tendered his acceptance. At the first anniversary festival of the Order, held under Henry VI., as many robes of the order were made for alien knights not sovereign princes, as for gartered monarchs of foreign birth. The foreign princes had so little appreciated the honor of election, that when the Sovereign Duke of Burgundy was proposed, under Henry VI., the knights would not go to election until that potentate had declared whether he would accept the honor. His potentiality declared very distinctly that he would not; and he is the first sovereign prince who positively refused to become a knight of the Garter! In the same reign Edward, King of Portugal, was elected in the place of his father, John:—this is one of the few instances in which the honor has passed from father to son. The Duke of Coimbra, also elected in this reign, was of a foreign princely house, but he was not a sovereign prince. He may reckon with the alien knights generally. The Duke of Austria too, Albert, was elected before he came to a kingly and to an imperial throne; and against these princes I may place the name of Gaston de Foix, whom Henry V. had made Earl of Longueville, as that of a simple alien knight of good estate and knightly privileges. One or two scions of royal houses were elected, as was Alphonso, King of Aragon. But there is strong reason for believing that Alphonso declined the honor. There is some uncertainty as to the period of the election of Frederick III., that economical Emperor of Austria, who begged to know what the expenses would amount to, before he would "accept the order." All the garters not home-distributed, did not go to deck the legs of foreign sovereign princes. Toward the close of the reign we find the Vicomte de Chastillion elected, and also D'Almada, the Portuguese knight of whose jolly installation at the Lion in Brentford, I have already spoken. An Aragonese gentleman, Francis de Surienne, was another alien knight of simply noble quality; he was elected in the King's bed-chamber at Westminster; and the alien knights would more than balance the foreign sovereign princes, even if we throw in Casimir, King of Poland, who was added to the confraternity under the royal Lancastrian.

The first foreigner whom Edward IV. raised to companionship in the order, was not a prince, but a private gentleman named Gaillard Duras or Durefort. The honor was conferred in ac-knowledgment of services rendered to the King, in France; and the new knight was very speedily deprived of it, for traitorously transferring his services to the King of France. Of the foreign monarchs who are said to have been *elected* companions, during this reign—namely, the Kings of Spain and Portugal—there is much doubt whether the favor was conferred at all. The Dukes of Ferrara and Milan were created knights, and these may be reckoned among ducal sovereigns, although less than kings; and let me add that, if the Kings of Spain and Portugal *were* elected, the elections became void, because these monarchs failed to send proxies to take possession of their stalls. Young Edward V. presided at no election, and his uncle and successor, Richard III., received no foreign prince into the order. At the installation, however, of the short-lived son of Richard, that sovereign created Geoffrey de Sasiola, ambassador from the Queen of Spain, a knight, by giving him three blows on the shoulders with a sword, and by investing him with a gold collar.

Henry VII. was not liberal toward foreigners with the many garters which fell at his disposal, after Bosworth, and during his reign. He appears to have exchanged with Maximilian, the Gar-ter for the Golden Fleece, and to have conferred the same decora-tion on one or two heirs to foreign thrones, who were not sover-eign princes when elected. It was not often that these princes were installed in person. Such installation, however, did occasionally happen; and never was one more singular in its origin and circumstances, than that of Philip, Archduke of Austria. Philip had resolved to lay claim to the throne of Spain by right of his wife Joan, daughter of Ferdinand of Castile and Aragon. He was on his way to Spain, when foul winds and a tempestuous sea drove him into Weymouth. Henry invited him to Windsor, treated him with great hospitality, and installed him Knight of the Garter. Philip "took the oath to observe the statutes, without any other qualification than that he might not be obliged to attend personally at the chapters, or to wear the collar, except at his own pleasure. In placing the collar round his neck, and in conducting him to his stall, Henry addressed him as 'Mon fils,' while Philip, in return, called the King 'Mon père,' and these affectionate appellations are repeated in the treaty of peace and unity between the two countries, which was signed by Henry and Philip, while sitting in their respective stalls, and to the maintenance of which they were both then solemnly sworn. Previously to the offering, Philip wished to stand before his stall, like the other knights, and to follow the King to the altar, requesting to be allowed to do his duty as a knight and brother of the order ought to do to the sovereign; but Henry declined, and taking him by the left hand, the two Kings offered together. After the ceremony, Philip invested Henry, Prince of Wales, with the collar of the Golden Fleece, into which order he had, it is said, been elected at Middleburgh in the preceding year," 1506.

Under Henry VIII. we find the first Scottish monarch who ever wore the Garter, namely James V. He accepted the insignia "with princely heart and will," but, in a formal instrument, he set down the statutes which he would swear to observe, and he rejected all others. Francis, King of France, Charles V., Emperor of Germany, and Ferdinand, King of Hungary, were also members of the order. But the *sovereign* princes elected during this reign did not outnumber the alien knights of less degree. When Henry was at Calais, he held a chapter, at which Marshal Montmorency, Count de Beaumont, and Philip de Chabot, Count de Neublanc, were elected into the order. This occasion was the first and only time that the Kings of England and France attended together and voted as companions in the chapters of their respective orders. Like the other knights, Francis nominated for election into the Garter, three earls or persons of higher degree, three barons, and three knights-bachelors, and the names present an interesting fact, which has not been generally noticed. Henry was then enamored of Anne Boleyn, whom he had recently created Marchioness of Pembroke, and who accompanied him to Calais. With a solitary exception, the French King gave all his suffrages for his own countrymen, and as the exception was in favor of her brother, George, Lord Rochford, it was evidently intended as a compliment to the future Queen of England.

It was the intention of Edward VI. to have created Lewis, Marquis of Gonzaga, a knight of the order, but there is no evidence that he was elected. It is difficult to ascertain the exact course of things during this reign; for Mary, subsequently, abrogated all the changes made by Edward, in order to adopt the statutes to the exigencies of the reformed religion. She did even more than this; she caused the register to be defaced, by erasing every insertion which was not in accordance with the Romish faith. It is known, however, that Henri II. of France was elected. His investiture took place in a bed-room of the Louvre in Paris. He rewarded the Garter King-at-arms with a gold chain worth two hundred pounds, and his own royal robe, ornmented with "aglets," and worth twenty-five pounds. Against this one sovereign prince we have to set the person of an alien knight—the Constable of France. The foreign royal names on the list were, however, on the accession of Mary, three against one of foreign knights of lower degree. That of Philip of Spain soon made the foreign royal majority still greater; and this majority may be said to have been further increased by the election of the sovereign Duke of Savoy. Mary elected no foreign knight beneath the degree of sovereign ruler—whether king or duke.

Elizabeth very closely followed the same principle. Her foreign knights were sovereigns, or about to become so. The first was Adolphus, Duke of Holstein, son of the King of Denmark, and heir of Norway. The second was Charles IX. of France, and the third, Frederick, King of Denmark; the Emperor Rudolf was, perhaps, a fourth; and the fifth, Henri Quatre, the last king of France who wore the Garter till the accession of Louis XVIII.

As for the Spanish widower of Mary, Sir Harris Nicholas observes, " Philip, king of Spain, is said to have returned the Garter by the hands of the Queen's ambassador, Viscount Montague, who had been sent to induce him to renew the alliance between England and Burgundy. Philip did not conceal his regret at the change which had taken place in the religion and policy of his country ; but he displayed no sectarian bitterness, expresses himself still desirous of opposing the designs of the French, who sought to have Elizabeth excommunicated, and stated that he had taken measures to prevent this in the eyes of a son of the Church of Rome, the greatest of all calamities, from befalling her, without her own consent. It appears, however, that Elizabeth did not accept of Philip's resignation of the Garter, for he continued a companion until his decease, notwithstanding the war between England and Spain, and the attempt to invade this country by the Spanish Armada in 1588."

When I say Elizabeth closely followed the example of Mary I should add as an instance wherein she departed therefrom—the election of Francis Duke of Montmorency, envoy from the French King. The Queen bestowed this honor on the Duke, "in grateful commemoration," says Camden, "of the love which Anne, constable of France, his father, bore unto her." At the accession of James I., however, Henri IV. of France was the only foreigner, sovereign or otherwise, who wore the order of the Garter. Those added by James were the King of Denmark, the Prince of Orange, and the Prince Palatine. Of the latter I have spoken in another place ; I will only notice further here, that under James, all precedence of stalls was taken away from princes below a certain rank; that is to say, the last knights elected, even the King's own son, must take the last stall. It was also then declared "that all princes, not absolute, should be installed, henceforth, in the puisne place."

There was *one* foreign knight, however, whose installation deserves a word apart, for it was marked by unusual splendor, considering how very small a potentate was the recipient of the honor. This was Christian, Duke of Brunswick-Wolfenbüttel. On the last day of the year 1624, James, with his own hands, placed the riband and George round the neck of the Duke. The latter was then twenty-four years of age. "The Duke of Brunswick," says Chamberlain, in a letter to Sir Dudley Carleton, January 8, 1625, "can not complain of his entertainment, which was every way complete, very good and gracious-words from the King, with the honor of the Garter, and a pension of two thousand pounds a year. The Prince lodged him in his own lodgings, and at parting, gave him three thousand pounds in gold, besides other presents." James conferred the Garter on no less than seven of his Scottish subjects. If these may be reckoned now, what they were considered then, as mere foreigners, the alien knights will again outnumber the foreign sovereign princes, wearers of the Garter.

The first knight invested by Charles I. was an alien chevalier, of only noble degree. This was the Duke de Chevreuse, who was Charles's proxy at his nuptials with Henrietta Maria, and who thus easily won the honors of chivalry among the Companions of St. George. It seems, however, that the honor in question was generally won by foreigners, because of their being engaged in furthering royal marriages. Thus, when the King's agent in Switzerland, Mr. Fleming, in the year 1633, suggested to the government that the Duke of Rohan should be elected a knight of the Garter, Mr. Secretary Coke made reply that "The proposition hath this inconvenience, that the rites of that ancient order comport not with innovation, and no precedent can be found of any foreign subject ever admitted into it, if he were not employed in an intermarriage with this crown, as the Duke of Chevreuse lately was." There certainly was not a word of truth in what the Secretary Coke thus deliberately stated. Not only had the Garter frequently been conferred on foreign subjects who had had nothing to do as matrimonial agents between sovereign lovers, but only twelve years after Coke thus wrote, Charles conferred the order upon the Duke d'Espernon, who had no claim to it founded upon such service as is noticed by the learned secretary.

At the death of Charles I. there was not, strictly speaking, a single foreign sovereign prince belonging to the order. The three foreign princes, Rupert, William of Orange, and the Elector Palatine, can not justly be called so. The other foreign knights were the Dukes of Chevreuse and Espernon.

The foreign knights of the order created by Charles II. were

Prince Edward, son of " Elizabeth of Bohemia;" Prince Maurice, his elder brother; Henry, eldest son of the Duke de Thouas, William of Nassau, then three years of age, and subsequently our William III.; Frederick, Elector of Brandenburg; Gaspar, Count de Morchin; Christian, Prince Royal of Denmark; Charles XI., King of Sweden; George, Elector of Saxony; and Prince George of Denmark, husband of the Princess Anne. It will be seen that those who could be strictly called "sovereign princes," claiming allegiance and owing none, do not outnumber alien knights who were expected to render obedience, and could not sovereignly exert it. Denmark and Sweden, it may be observed, quarrelled about precedency of stalls with as much bitterness as if they had been burghers of the "Krähwinkel" of Kotzebue.

The short reign of James II. presents us with only one alien Knight of the Garter, namely, Louis de Duras, created also Earl of Feversham. "Il était le second de son nom," says the Biographie Universelle, "qui eut été honoré de cette decoration, remarque particulière dans la noblesse Française."

The great Duke of Schomberg, that admirable warrior given to England by the tyranny of Louis XIV., was the first person invested with the Garter by William III. The other foreign knights invested by him were the first King of Prussia, William Duke of Zell, the Elector of Saxony, William Bentinck (Earl of Portland), Von Keppel (Earl of Albemarle), and George of Hanover (our George I.) Here the alien knights, not of sovereign degree, again outnumbered those who *were* of that degree. The Elector of Saxony refused to join William against France, unless the Garter were first conferred on him.

Anne conferred the Garter on Meinhardt Schomberg, Duke of Leinster, son of the great Schomberg; and also on George Augustus of Hanover (subsequently George II. of England). Anne intimated to George Louis, the father of George Augustus, that, being a Knight of the Garter, he might very appropriately invest his own son. George Louis, however, hated that son, and would have nothing to do with conferring any dignity upon him. He left it with the commissioners, Halifax and Vanbrugh, to act as they pleased. They performed their vicarious office as they best could, and that was only with "maimed rights." George Louis, with his ordinary spiteful meanness, ordered the ceremony to be cut short of all display. He would not even permit his son to be invested with the habit, under a canopy as was usual, and as had been done in his own case; all that he would grant was an ordinary arm-chair, whereon the electoral prince might sit in state, if he chose, or was able to do so! These were the only foreigners upon whom Anne conferred the Garter; an order which she granted willingly to very few persons indeed.

"It is remarkable," says Nicolas, "that the order was not conferred by Queen Anne upon the Emperor, nor upon any of the other sovereigns with whom she was for many years confederated against France. Nor did her Majesty bestow it upon King Charles III. of Spain, who arrived in England in September, 1703, nor upon Prince Eugene (though, when she presented him with a sword worth five thousand pounds sterling on taking his leave in March, 1712 (there were seven vacant ribands), nor any other of the great commanders of the allied armies who, under the Duke of Marlborough, gained those splendid victories that rendered her reign one of the most glorious in the annals of this country."

George I. had more regard for his grandson than for his son; and he made Frederick (subsequently father of George III.) a Companion of the Order, when he was not more than nine years of age. He raised to the same honor his own brother, Prince Ernest Augustus, and invested both knights at a Chapter held in Hanover in 1711. With this family exception, the Order of the Garter was not conferred upon any foreign prince in the reign of George I.

George II. gave the Garter to that deformed Prince of Orange who married his excitable daughter Anne. The same honor was conferred on Prince Frederick of Hesse Cassel, who espoused George's amiable daughter Mary; Prince Frederick of Saxe Gotha, the Duke of Saxe Weisenfels, the Margrave of Anspach, the fatherless son of the Prince of Orange last named, and, worthiest of all, that Prince Ferdinand of Brunswick who won the honor by gaining the battle of Minden. He was invested with cap, habit, and decorations, in front of his tent and in the face of his whole army. His gallant enemy, De Broglie, to do honor to the new knight, proclaimed a suspension of arms for the day, drew up his own troops where they could witness the spectacle of courage and skill receiving their reward, and with his principal officers dining with the Prince in the evening. "Each party," says Miss Banks, "returned at night to his army, in order to recommence the hostilities they were engaged in, by order of their respective nations, against each other, on the next rising of the sun." I do not know what this anecdote most proves — the cruel absurdity of war, or the true chivalry of warriors.

The era of George III. was indeed that in which foreign princes, sovereign and something less than that, abounded in the order. The first who received the Garter was the brother of Queen Charlotte, the reigning Duke of Mecklenburg Strelitz. Then came the Duke of Brunswick-Wolfenbüttel, who married Augusta, the sister of George III. Caroline of Brunswick was the issue of this marriage. Of the kings, *roitelets*, and petty princes of Germany who were added to the Garter, or rather, had the Garter added to them, it is not worth while speaking; but there is an incident connected with the foreign knights which *does* merit to be preserved. When Bonaparte founded the Legion of Honor, he prevailed on the King of Prussia (willing to take anything for his own, and reluctant to sacrifice anything for the public good) to accept the cross of the Legion for himself, and several others assigned to him for distribution. The king rendered himself justly abhorred for this disgraceful act; but he found small German princes quite as eager as he was to wear the badge of the then enemy of Europe. A noble exception presented itself in the person of the Duke of Brunswick, a Knight of the Garter, to whom the wretched king sent the insignia of the French order in 1805. The duke, in a letter to the king, refused to accept such honor, "because, in his quality of Knight of the most noble Order of the Garter, he was prevented from receiving any badge of chivalry instituted by a person at war with the sovereign of that order." The Prussian king found an easier conscience in the Prince of Hesse Cassel, who was also a Knight of the Garter. This individual, mean and double-faced as the king, wore the cross of the Legion of Honor with the Garter. At *that* troubled period, it was exactly as if some nervous lairds, in the days of Highland feuds, had worn, at the same time, the plaids of the Macdonalds and Campbells, in order to save their skins and estates by thus pretending to be members of two hostile parties.

Under the Regency of George IV., the foreign sovereign princes were admitted into the order without any regard whatever to the regulations by statute. Within one year, or very little more than that period, two emperors, three kings, and an heir to a throne, who soon after came to his inheritance, were enrolled Companions of the order. But it was the era of victories and rejoicings, and no one thought of objecting to a prodigality which would have astounded the royal founder. Long after the period of victory, however, the same liberality continued to be evinced toward foreign princes of sovereign degree. Thus at the accession of Charles X., the England monarch despatched the Duke of Northumberland as Embassador Extraordinary to attend at the coronation of the French monarch, and to invest him, subsequently, with the Order of the Garter. I remember seeing the English procession pass from the duke's residence in the Rue du Bac, over the Pont Royal to the Tuileries. It puzzled the French people extremely. It took place on Tuesday, June 7, 1825. At noon, "four of the royal carriages," says the Galignani of the period, "drawn by eight horses, in which were the Baron de Lalivre and M. de Viviers, were sent to the Hotel Galifet for the Duke of Northumberland." The two envoys who thus contrived to ride in four carriages and eight horses—a more wonderful feat than was ever accomplished by Mr. Ducrow—having reached the ducal hotel, were received by the duke, Lord Granville, our ordinary embassador, and Sir George Naylor, his Britannic Majesty's Commissioners charged to invest the King of France with the insignia of the Garter. The procession then set out; and, as I have said, it perplexed the French spectators extremely. They could not imagine that so much ceremony was necessary in order to put a garter round a leg, and hang a collar from a royal neck. Besides the four French carriages-and-eight, there were three of the duke's carriages drawn by six horses; one carriage of similar state, and two others more modestly drawn by pairs, belonging to Lord Granville. The carriage of "Garter" himself, behind a couple of ordinary steeds; and eight other carriages, containing the suites of the embassadors, or privileged persons who passed for such in order to share in the spectacle, closed the procession. The duke had a very noble gathering around him, namely, the Hon. Algernon Percy, his secretary, the Marquis of Caermarthen, the Earl of Hopetoun, Lords Prudhoe (the present duke), Strathaven, Pelham, and Hervey, the Hon. Charles Percy, and the goodhumored-looking Archdeacon Singleton. Such was the *entourage* of the embassador extraordinary. The ordinary embassador, Lord Granville, was somewhat less nobly surrounded. He had with him the Hon. Mr. Bligh, and Messrs. Mandeville, Gore, Abercrombie, and Jones. Sir George Naylor, in his Tabard, was accompanied by a cloud of heralds, some of whom have since become kings-of-arms — namely, Messrs. Woods, Young, and Wollaston, and his secretary, Mr. Howard. More noticeable men followed in the train. There were Earl Gower and Lord Burghersh, the "Honorables" Mr. Townshend, Howard, and Clive, Captain Buller, and two men more remarkable than all the rest — the two embassadors included — namely, Sir John Malcolm and Sir Sidney Smith. Between admiring spectators, who were profoundly amazed at the sight of the duke in his robes, the procession arrived at the palace, where, after a pause and a reorganizing in the Hall of Embassadors, the party proceeded in great state into the Gallery of Diana. Here a throne had been especially erected for the investiture, and the show was undoubtedly most splendid. Charles X. looked in possession of admirable health and spirits — of everything, indeed, but bright intellect. He was magnificently surrounded. The duke wore with his robes that famous diamond-hilted sword which had been presented to him by George IV., and which cost, I forget how many thousand pounds. His heron's plume alone was said to be worth five hundred guineas. His superb mantle of blue velvet, embroidered with gold, was supported by his youthful nephew, George Murray (the present Duke of Athol), dressed in a Hussar uniform, and the Hon. James Drummond, in a Highland suit. Seven gentlemen had the responsible mission of carrying the insignia on cushions, and Sir George preceded them, bearing a truncheon, as "Garter Principal King-at-arms." The duke recited an appropriate address, giving a concise history of the order, and congratulating himself on having been employed on the present honorable mission. The investiture took place with the usual ceremonies; but I remember that there was no salute of artillery, as was enjoined in the book of instructions drawn up by Garter. The latter official performed his office most gracefully, and attached to the person of the King of France, that day, pearls worth a million of francs. The royal knight made a very pleasant speech when all was concluded, and the usual hospitality followed the magnificent labors of an hour and a half's continuance.

On the following evening, the Duke gave a splendid *fête* at his hotel, in honor of the coronation of Charles X., and of his admission into the Order of the Garter. The King and Queen of Wurtemburg were present, with some fifteen hundred persons of less rank, but many of whom were of greater importance in society. Perhaps not the least remarkable feature of the evening was the presence together, in one group, of the Dauphin and that Duchess of Angoulême who was popularly known as the "orphan girl of the Temple," with the Duchess of Berri, the Duke of Orleans (Louis Philippe), and Talleyrand. The last-named still wore the long bolster-cravat, of the time of the Revolution, and looked as cunning as though he knew the destiny that awaited the entire group, three of whom have since died in exile — he alone breathing his last sigh, in calm tranquillity, in his own land.

Charles X. conferred on the ducal bearer of the insignia of the Garter a splendid gift — one of the finest and most costly vases ever produced at the royal manufacture of Porcelain at Sèvres. The painting on it, representing the Tribunal of Diana, is the work of M. Leguai, and it occupied that distinguished artist full three years before it was completed. Considering its vast dimensions, the nature of the painting, and its having passed twice through the fire without the slightest alteration, it is unique of its kind. This colossal vase now stands in the centre of the ball-room in Northumberland House.

The last monarch to whom a commission has carried the insignia of the Garter, was the Czar Nicholas. It was characteristic of the man that, courteous as he was to the commissioners, he would not, as was customary in such cases, dine with them. They were entertained, however, according to his orders, by other members of his family. It is since the reign of George III. that Mr. Macaulay's remark touching the fact of the Garter being rarely conferred on aliens, except sovereign princes, may be said to be well-founded. No alien, under princely rank, now wears the Garter. The most illustrious of the foreign knights are the two who were last created by patent, namely, the Emperor Louis Napoleon and the King of Sardinia. The King of Prussia is also a knight of the order, and, as such, he is bound by his oath never to act against the sovereign of that order; but in our struggle with felonious Russia, the Prussian government, affecting to be neutral, imprisons an English consul on pretence that the latter has sought to enlist natives of Prussia into the English service, while, on the other hand, it passes over to Russia the material for making war, and sanctions the raising of a Russian loan in Berlin, to be devoted, as far as possible, to the injury of England. The King is but a poor knight!— and, by the way, that reminds me that the once so-called poor knights of Windsor can not be more appropriately introduced than here.

# THE POOR KNIGHTS OF WINDSOR,
## AND THEIR DOINGS.

THE founder of the Order of the Garter did well when he thought of the "Milites pauperes," and having created a fraternity for wealthy and noble cavaliers, created one also for the same number of "poor knights, infirm of body, indigent and decayed," who should be maintained for the honor of God and St. George, continually serve God in their devotions, and have no further heavy duty, after the days of bustle and battle, than to pray for the prosperity of all living knights of the Garter, and for the repose of the souls of all those who were dead. It was resolved that none but really poor knights should belong to the fraternity, whether named, as was their privilege, by a companion of the noble order, or by the sovereign, as came at last to be exclusively the case. If a poor knight had the misfortune to become the possessor of property of any sort realizing twenty pounds per annum, he became at once disqualified for companionship. Even in very early times, his position, with house, board, and various aids, spiritual and bodily, was worth more than this.

To be an alms knight, as Ashmole calls each member, implied no degradation whatever; quite the contrary. Each poor but worthy gentleman was placed on a level with the residentiary canons of Windsor. Like these, they received twelvepence each, every day that they attended service in the chapel, or abode in the College, with a honorarium of forty shillings annually for small necessaries. Their daily presence at chapel was compulsory, except good and lawful reason could be shown for the contrary. The old knights were not only required to be at service, but at high mass, the masses of the Virgin Mary, as also at Vespers and Complins—from the beginning to the end. They earned their twelvepence honestly, but nevertheless the ecclesiastical corporation charged with the payment, often did what such corporations, of course, have never tried to do since the Reformation — namely, cheat those who ought to have been recipients of their due. Dire were the discussions between the poor (and pertinacious) knights, and the dean, canons, and treasurers of the College. It required a mitred Archbishop of York and Lord Chancellor of England to settle the dispute, and a very high opinion does it afford us of the good practical sense of Church and Chancery in the days of Henry VI., when we find that the eminent individual with the double office not only came to a happy conclusion rapidly, and ordered all arrears to be paid to the poor knights, but decreed that the income of the treasurer should be altogether stopped, until full satisfaction was rendered to the "milites pauper." For the sake of such Chancery practice one would almost consent to take the Church with it.

But not only did the lesser officials of that Church cheat the veteran knights of their pay, but their itching palm inflicted other wrong. It was the fitting custom to divide the fines, levied upon absentees from public worship, among the more habitually devout brethren. Gradually, however, the dean and canons appropriated these moneys to themselves, so that the less godly the knights were, the richer were the dean and canons. Further, many dying noblemen had bequeathed very valuable legacies to the College and poor fraternity of veterans. These the business-like ecclesiastics had devoted to their own entire profit; and it required stringent command from king and bishop, in the reign of Richard II., before they would admit the military legatees even to a share in the bequest.

Not, indeed, that the stout old veterans were always blameless. Good living and few cares made "fast men" of some of them. There were especially two in the reign last named, who created very considerable scandal. These were a certain Sir Thomas Tawne and Sir John Breton. They were married men, but the foolish old fellows performed homage to vessels of iniquity, placed by them on the domestic altar. In other words, they were by far too civil to a couple of hussies with red faces and short kirtles, and *that* — not that such circumstance rendered the matter worse—

before the eyes of their faithful and legitimate wives. The bishop was horror-stricken, no doubt, and the exemplary ecclesiastics of the College were enjoined to remonstrate, reprove, and, if amendment did not follow, to expel the offenders.

Sir Thomas, I presume, heeded the remonstrance and submitted to live more decorously, for nothing more is said of him. Jolly Sir John was more difficult to deal with. He too may have dismissed Cicely and made his peace with poor Lady Breton, but the rollicking old knight kept the College in an uproar, nevertheless. He resumed attendance at chapel, indeed, but he did this after a fashion of his own. He would walk slowly in the procession of red-mantled brethren on their way to service, so as to obstruct those who were in the rear, or he would walk in a ridiculous manner, so as to rouse unseemly laughter. I am afraid that old Sir John was a very sad dog, and, however the other old gentleman may have behaved, he was really a godless fellow. Witness the fact that, on getting into chapel, when he retired to pray, he forthwith fell asleep, and could, or would, hardly keep his eyes open, even at the sacrament at the altar.

After all, there was a gayer old fellow than Sir John Breton among the poor knights. One Sir Emanuel Cloue is spoken of who appears to have been a very Don Giovanni among the silly maids and merry wives of Windsor. He was for ever with his eye on a petticoat and his hand on a tankard; and what with love and spiced canary, he could never sit still at mass, but was addicted to running about among the congregation. It would puzzle St. George himself to tell all the nonsense he talked on these occasions.

When we read how the bishop suggested that the King and Council should discover a remedy to check the rollicking career of Sir Edmund, we are at first perplexed to make out why the cure was not assigned to the religious officials. The fact, however, is that they were as bad as, or worse than, the knights. They too were as often to be detected with their lips on the brim of a goblet, or on the cheek of a damsel. There was Canon Lorying. He was addicted to hawking, hunting, and jollification; and the threat of dismissal, without chance of reinstalment, was had recourse to, before the canon ceased to make breaches in decorum. The vicars were as bad as the canons. The qualifications ascribed to them of being "inflated and wanton," sufficiently describe by what sins these very reverend gentlemen were beset. They showed no reverence for the frolicsome canons, as might have been expected; and if both parties united in exhibiting as little veneration for the dean, the reason, doubtless, lay in the circumstance that the dean, as the bishop remarked, was remiss, simple, and negligent, himself. He was worse than this. He not only allowed the documents connected with the Order to go to decay, or be lost, but he would not pay the vicars their salaries till he was compelled to do so by high authority. The dean, in short, was a sorry knave; he even embezzled the fees paid when a vicar occupied a new stall, and which were intended to be appropriated to the general profit of the chapter, and pocketed the entire proceeds for his own personal profit and enjoyment. The canons again made short work of prayers and masses, devoting only an hour each day for the whole. This arrangement may not have displeased the more devout among the knights; and the canons defied the bishop to point out anything in the statutes by which they were prevented from effecting this abbreviation of their service, and earning their shilling easily. Of this ecclesiastical irregularity the bishop, curiously enough, solicited the state to pronounce its condemnation; and an order from King and Council was deemed a good remedy for priests of loose thoughts and practices. A matter of more moment was submitted to the jurisdiction of meaner authority. Thus, when one of the vicars, John Chichester, was "scandalized respecting the wife of Thomas Swift" (which is a very pretty way of putting his offence), the matter was left to the correction of the dean, who was himself censurable, if not under censure — for remissness, negligence, stupidity, and fraud. The dean's frauds were carried on to that extent that a legacy of £200 made to the brotherhood of poor knights, having come to the decanal hands, and the dean not having accounted for the same, compulsion was put on him to render such account; and *that* appears to be all the penalty he ever paid for his knavery. Where the priests were of such kidney, we need not wonder that the knights observed in the dirty and much-encumbered cloisters, the licentiousness which was once common to men in the camp.

Churchmen and knights went on in their old courses, notwithstanding the interference of inquisitors. Alterations were made in the statutes, to meet the evil; some knights solicited incorporation among themselves, separate from the Church authorities; but this and other remedies were vainly applied.

In the reign of Henry VIII. the resident knights were not all military men. Some of them were eminent persons, who, it is thought, withdrew from the world and joined the brotherhood, out of devotion. Thus there was Sir Robert Champlayne, who had been a right lusty knight, indeed, and who proved himself so again, after he returned once more to active life. Among the laymen, admitted to be poor knights, were Hulme, formerly Clarencieux King-at-arms; Carly, the King's physician: Mewtes, the King's secretary for the French language; and Westley, who was made second baron of the Exchequer in 1509.

The order appears to have fallen into hopeless confusion, but Henry VIII., who performed many good acts, notwithstanding his evil deeds and propensities, bequeathed lands, the profits whereof (£600) were to be employed in the maintenance of "Thirteen Poor Knights." Each was to have a shilling a day, and their governor, three pounds, six and eightpence, additional yearly. Houses were built for these knights on the south side of the lower ward of the castle, where they are still situated, at a cost of nearly £3000. A white cloth-gown and a red cloth-mantle, appropriately decorated, were also assigned to each knight. King James doubled the pecuniary allowance, and made it payable in the Exchequer, quarterly.

Charles I. intended to increase the number of knights to their original complement. He did not proceed beyond the intention. Two of his subjects, however, themselves knights, Sir Peter La Maire and Sir Francis Crane, left lands which supplied funds for the support of five additional knights.

Cromwell took especial care that no knight should reside at Windsor, who was hostile to his government; and he was as careful that no preacher should hold forth there, who was not more friendly to the commonwealth than to monarchy.

At this period, and for a hundred years before this, there was not a man of real knight's degree belonging to the order, nor has there since been down to the present time. In 1724 the benevolent Mr. Travers bequeathed property to be applied to the maintenance of Seven Naval Knights. It is scarcely credible, but it is the fact, that seventy years elapsed before our law, which then hung a poor wretch for robbing to the amount of forty shillings, let loose the funds to be appropriated according to the will of the testator, and under sanction of the sovereign. What counsellors and attorneys fattened upon the costs, meantime, it is not now of importance to inquire. In 1796, thirteen superannuated or disabled lieutenants of men-of-war, officers of that rank being alone eligible under Mr. Travers's will, were duly provided for. The naval knights, all unmarried, have residences and sixty pounds per annum each, in addition to their half-pay. The sum of ten shillings, weekly, is deducted from the "several allowances, to keep a constant table."

The Military and Naval Knights—for the term "Poor" was dropped, by order of William IV.—no longer wear the mantle, as in former times; but costumes significant of their profession and their rank therein. There are twenty-five of them, one less than their original number, and they live in harmony with each other and the Church. The ecclesiastical corporation has nothing to do with their funds, and these unmarried naval knights do not disturb the slumbers of a single Mr. Brook within the liberty of Windsor.

In concluding this division, let me add a word touching the

### KNIGHTS OF THE BATH.

There was no more gallant cavalier in his day than Geoffrey, Earl of Anjou. He was as meek as he was gallant. In testimony of his humility he assumed a sprig of the broom plant (planta genista) for his device, and thereby he gave the name of Plantagenet to the long and illustrious line.

If his bravery raised him in the esteem of women, his softness of spirit earned for him some ridicule. Matilda, the "imperially perverse," laughed outright when her sire proposed she should accept the hand of Geoffrey of Anjou. "He is so like a girl," said

Matilda. "There is not a more lion-hearted knight in all Christendom," replied the king. "There is none certainly so sheep-faced," retorted the arrogant heiress; she then reluctlantly consented to descend to be mate of the wearer of the broom.

Matilda threw as many obstacles as she could in the way of the completion of the nuptial ceremony. At last this solemn matter was definitively settled to come off at Rouen, on the 26th of August, 1127. Geoffrey must have been a knight before his marriage with Matilda. However this may be, he is said to have been created an English knight in honor of the occasion. To show how he esteemed the double dignity of knight and husband, he prepared himself for both, by first taking a bath, and afterward putting on a clean linen shirt. Chroniclers assure us that this is the first instance, since the Normans came into England, in which bathing is mentioned in connection with knighthood. Over his linen shirt Geoffrey wore a gold-embroidered garment, and above all a purple mantle. We are told too that he wore silk stockings, an article which is supposed to have been unknown in England until a much later period. His feet were thrust into a gay pair of slippers, on the outside of each of which was worked a golden lion. In this guise he was wedded to Matilda, and never had household lord a greater virago for a lady.

From this circumstance the Knights of the Bath are said to have had their origin. For a considerable period, this order of chivalry ranked as the highest military order in Europe. All the members were companions. There was but one chief, and no knight ranked higher, nor lower, than any other brother of the society. The order, nevertheless, gradually became obsolete. Vacancies had not been filled up; that Garter had superseded the Bath, and it was not till the reign of George II. that the almost extinct fraternity was renewed.

Its revival took place for political reasons, and these are well detailed by Horace Walpole, in his "Reminiscences of the Courts of George the First and Second." "It was the measure," he says, "of Sir Robert Walpole, and was an artful bunch of thirty-six ribands, to supply a fund of favors, in lieu of places. He meant, too, to stave off the demand for garters, and intended that the red should have been a stage to the blue; and accordingly took one of the former himself. He offered the new order to old Sarah, Duchess of Marlborough, for her grandson the Duke, and for the Duke of Bedford, who had married one of her granddaughters. She haughtily replied, that they should take nothing but the Garter. 'Madam,' said Sir Robert, coolly, 'they who take the Bath will the sooner have the Garter.' The next year he took the latter himself, with the Duke of Richmond, both having been previously installed knights of the revived institution."

Sir Robert respected the forms and laws of the old institution, and these continued to be observed down to the period following the battle of Waterloo. Instead of their creating a new order for the purpose of rewarding the claimants for distinction, it was resolved to enlarge that of the Bath, which was, therefore, divided into three classes.

First, there was the Grand Cross of the Bath (G. C. B.), the reward of military and diplomatic services.

The second class, of Knights Commanders (C. B.), was open to those meritorious persons who had the good luck to hold commissions not below the rank of Lieutenant-Colonel or Post-Captain. The members of this class rank above the ordinary knights-bachelors.

The third class, of Knights Companions, was instituted for officers holding inferior commissions to those named above, and whose services in their country's cause rendered them eligible for admission.

These arrangements have been somewhat modified subsequently, and not without reason. Henry VIIth's Chapel in Westminster Abbey is the locality in which the installation of the different knights takes place. The statutes of the order authorize the degradation of a knight "convicted of heresy against the Articles of the Christian religion;" or who has been "attainted of high treason," or of "cowardly flying from some field of battle." It is rather curious that felony is not made a ground of degradation. The Duke of Ormond was the last Knight of the Garter who was degraded, for treason against George I. Addison, after the degradation, invariably speaks of him as "the late Duke." A more grievous offender than he was that Earl of Somerset, who had been a reckless page, and who was an unworthy Knight of the

Garter, under James I. He was convicted of murder, but he was not executed, and to the day of his death he continued to wear the Garter, of which he had been pronounced unworthy. The last instances of degradation from the Order of the Bath were those of Lord Cochrane (in 1814), for an alleged misdemeanor, and Sir Eyre Coote, two years subsequently. In these cases the popular judgment did not sanction the harsh measures adopted by those in authority.[*]

In olden times, the new Knights of the Bath made as gallant display in public as the Knights of the Garter. In reference to this matter, Mr. Mackenzie Walcott, in his "Westminster," cites a passage from an author whom he does not name. The reverend gentleman says: "On Sunday, July 24th, 1603, was performed the solemnity of Knights of the Bath riding honorably from St. James's to the Court, and made show with their squires and pages about the Tilt-yard, and after went into the park of St. James, and there lighted from their horses and went up into the King's Majesty's presence, in the gallery, where they received the order of Knighthood of the Bath."

The present "Horse-Guards" occupies a portion of the old Tilt-yard; but for the knightly doings there, and also in Smithfield, I must refer all curious readers to Mr. Charles Knight's "Pictorial History of London."

THE ORDER OF THE THISTLE, if Scottish antiquaries may be credited, is almost as ancient as the times in which the first thistle was nibbled at by the primitive wild-ass. Very little, however, is known upon the subject, and that little is not worth repeating. The earliest certain knowledge dates from Robert II., whose coins bore the impress of St. Andrew and his cross. James III. is the first monarch who is known to have worn the thistle, as his badge. There is no evidence of these emblems being connected with knighthood until the reign of James V. The Reformers, subsequently, suppressed the chivalric order, as popish, and it was not till the reign of James II. of England that the thistle and chivalry again bloomed together. The order is accessible only to peers.

[*] Subsequently, the Prince Regent ordered the name of Captain Hanchett to be erased from the roll of the Bath, he having been struck off the list of Captains in the Royal Navy.

A commoner may have conferred more honor and service on his country than all the Scottish peers put together, but no amount of merit could procure him admission into the Order of the Thistle. Nevertheless three commoners *did* once belong to it; but their peculiar merit was that they were heirs presumptive to dukedoms.

Ireland was left without an order until the year 1783, when George III. good-naturedly established that of St. Patrick, to the great delight of many who desired to be knights, and to the infinite disgust of all who were disappointed. Except in name and local circumstances there is nothing that distinguishes it from other orders.

I must not conclude this section without remarking, that shortly after the sovereignty of Malta and the Ionian Isles was ceded to Great Britain, the Order of St. Michael was instituted in 1818, for the Purpose of having what Walpole calls " a fund of ribands," to reward those native gentlemen who had deserved or desired favors, if not places.

The Order of the Guelphs was founded by the Prince Regent in 1815. George III. had designed such an order for the most distinguished of his Hanoverian subjects. Down to the period of the accession of Queen Victoria, however, the order was conferred on a greater number of Englishmen than of natives of Hanover. Since the latter Kingdom has passed under the rule of the male heir of the line of Brunswick, the order of Guelph has become a foreign order. Licenses to accept this or any other foreign order does not authorize the assumption of any style, appellation, rank, precedence, or privilege appertaining unto a knight-bachelor of these realms. Such is the law as laid down by a decision of Lord Ellenborough, and which does not agree with the judgment of Coke.

The history of foreign orders would occupy too much of my space; but there is something so amusing in the history of an order of knights called " Knights of the Holy Ampoule," that a few words on the subject may not be unacceptable to such readers as are unacquainted with the ephemeral cavaliers in question.

## THE KNIGHTS OF THE "SAINTE AMPOULE."

"*Mais ce sont des chevaliers pour rire.*" —*Le Sage.*

THERE have been knights who, like "special constables," have been created merely "for the nonce;" and who have been as ephemeral as the shortlived flies so called. This was especially the case with the Knights of the Holy "Ampoule," or anointing oil, used at the coronation of the kings of France.

This oil was said to have been brought to St. Remy (Remigius) by a dove, from Heaven, and to have been placed by the great converter of Clovis, in his own tomb, where it was found, by a miraculous process. St. Remy himself never alluded either to the oil or the story connected with it. Four centuries after the saint's death the matter was first spoken — nay, the oil was boldly distilled, by Hinckmar, Archbishop of Rheims. This archi-episcopal biographer of St. Remy has inserted wonders in the saint's life, which staggered, while they amused, the readers who were able to peruse his work by fireside, in castle-hall, or convent refectory. I can only allude to one of these wonders — namely, the "Sainte Ampoule." Hinckmar actually asserted that when St. Remy was about to consecrate with oil, the humble King Clovis, at his coronation, a dove descended from Heaven, and placed in his hands a small vial of holy oil. Hinckmar defied any man to prove the contrary. As he further declared that the vial of oil was still to be found in the saint's sepulchre, and as it was so found, accordingly, Hinckmar was allowed to have proved his case. Thenceforward, the chevaliers of the St. Ampoule were created, for a day — that of the crowning of the sovereign. They had charge of the vial, delivered it to the archbishop, and saw it restored to its repository; and therewith, the coronation and their knightly character concluded together. From that time, down to the period of Louis XVI., the knights and the vial formed the most distinguished portion of the coronation procession and doings at the crowning of the kings of France.

Then ensued the Revolution; and as that mighty engine never touched anything without smashing it, you may be sure that the vial of St. Remy hardly escaped destruction.

On the 6th of October, 1793, Citizen Rhull entered the modest apartment of Philippe Hourelle, chief *marguillier* of the Cathedral of Rheims, and without ceremony demanded that surrender should be made to him of the old glass-bottle of the *ci-devant* Remy. Philippe's wig raised itself with horror; but as Citizen Rhull told him that it would be as easy to lift his head from his shoulders as his wig from his head, if he did not obey, the *marguillier* stammered out an assertion that the reliquary was in the keeping of the curé, M. Seraine, to whom he would make instant application.

"Bring pomatum and all," said Citizen Rhull, who thus profanely misnamed the sacred balm or thickened oil, which had anointed the head and loins of so many kings from Charles the Bald, downward.

"May I ask," said Philippe, timidly, "what you will do therewith?"

"Grease *your* neck, that the knife may slip the easier through it, unless you bring it within a decade of minutes."

"Too much honor by half," exclaimed Philippe. "I will slip to the curé as rapidly as if I slid the whole way on the precious ointment itself. Meanwhile, here is a bottle of Burgundy—"

"Which I shall have finished within the time specified. So, despatch; and let us have t'other bottle, too!"

When Philippe Hourelle had communicated the request to the curé, Monsieur Seraine, with a quickness of thought that did justice to his imagination, exclaimed, "We will take the rogues in, and give them a false article for the real one." But the time was so short; there was no second ancient-looking vial at hand; there was not a pinch of pomatum, nor a spoonful of oil in the house, and the curé confessed, with a sigh, that the genuine relic must needs be surrendered. "But we can save some of it!" cried M. Seraine; "here is the vial, give me the consecrating spoon."

And with the handle of the spoon, having extracted some small portions, which the curé subsequently wrapped up carefully, and rather illegibly labelled, the vial was delivered to Philippe, who surrendered it to Citizen Rhull, who carried the same to the front of the finest cathedral in France, and at the foot of the statue of Louis XV. Citizen Rhull solemnly hammered the vial into powder, and, in the name of the Republic, trod the precious ointment underfoot till it was not to be distinguished from the mud with which it was mingled.

"And so do we put an end to princes and pomatum," cried he.

Philippe coughed evasively; smiled as if he was of the same way of thinking with the republican, and exclaimed, very mentally indeed, "Vivent les princes et la pommade." Neither, he felt assured, was irrevocably destroyed.

The time, indeed, did come round again for princes, and Napoleon was to be crowned at Notre Dame. He cared little as to what had become of the Heaven-descended ointment, and he might have anointed, as well as crowned, himself. There were some dozen gentlemen who hoped that excuse might be discovered for creating the usual order of the Knights of the Ampoule; but the Emperor did not care a fig for knights or ointment, and, to the horror of all who hoped to be chevaliers, the imperial coronation was celebrated without either. But then Napoleon was discrowned, as was to be expected from such profanity; and therewith returned the Bourbons, who, having forgotten nothing, bethought themselves of the Saint Ampoule. Monsieur de Chevrières, magistrate at Rheims, set about the double work of discovery and recovery. For some time he was unsuccessful. At length, early in 1819, the three sons of the late Philippe Hourelle waited on him. They made oath that not only were they aware of a portion of the sacred ointment having been in the keeping of their late father, but that his widow succeeded the inheritance, and that she reckoned it as among her choicest treasures.

"She has nothing to do but to make it over to me," said Monsieur Chevrières; "she will be accounted of in history as the mother of the knights of the Ampoule of the Restoration."

"It is vexatious," said the eldest son, "but the treasure has been lost. At the time of the invasion, our house was plundered, and the relic was the first thing the enemy laid his hands on."

The disappointment that ensued was only temporary. A judge named Lecomte soon appeared, who made oath that he had in his keeping a certain portion of what had at first been consigned to the widow Hourelle. The portion was so small that it required an eye of faith, very acute and ready indeed, to discern it. The authorities looked upon the relic, and thought if Louis XVIII. could not be crowned till a sufficient quantity of the holy ointment was recovered wherewith to anoint him, the coronation was not likely to be celebrated yet awhile.

Then arose a crowd of priests, monks, and ex-monks, all of whom declared that the curé, M. Seraine, had imparted to them the secret of his having preserved a portion of the dried anointing oil, but they were unable to say where he had deposited it. Some months of hesitation ensued, when, in summer, M. Bouré, a priest of Berry-au-Bac, came forward and proclaimed that he was the depositary of the long-lost relic, and that he had preserved it in a portion of the winding-sheet of St. Remy himself. A week later M. Champagne Provotian appeared, and made deposition to the following effect: He was standing near Rhull when the latter, in October, 1793, destroyed the vial which had been brought from Heaven by a dove, at the foot of the statue of Louis XV. When the republican struck the vial, some fragments of the glass flew on to the coat-sleeve of the said M. Champagne. These he dexterously preserved, took home with him, and now produced in court.

A commission examined the various relics, and the fragments of glass. The whole was pronounced genuine, and the chairman thought that by process of putting "that and that together," there was enough of legend, vial, and ointment to legitimately anoint and satisfy any Christian king.

"There is nothing now to obstruct your majesty's coronation," said his varlet to him one morning, after having spent three hours in a service for which he hoped to be appointed one of the knights of the Sainte Ampoule; "there is now absolutely nothing to prevent that august ceremony."

"Allons donc!" said Louis XVIII. with that laugh of incredulity, that shrug of the shoulders, and that good-humored impatience at legends and absurdities, which made the priests speak of him as an infidel.

"What shall be done with the ointment?" said the knight-expectant.

"Lock it up in the vestry cupboard, and say no more about it." And this was done with some ceremony and a feeling of disappointment. The gathered relics, placed in a silver reliquary lined with white silk, and enclosed in a metal case under three locks, were deposited within the tomb of St. Remy. There it remained till Charles X. was solemnly crowned in 1825. In that year, positively for the last time, the knights of the Sainte Ampoule were solemnly created, and did their office. As soon as Charles entered the choir, he knelt in the front of the altar. On rising, he was led into the centre of the sanctuary, where a throned chair received his august person. A splendid group half-encircled him; and then approached the knights of tho Sainte Ampoule in grand procession, bearing all that was left of what the sacred dove did or did not bring to St. Remy, for the anointing of Clovis. Not less than three prelates, an archbishop and two bishops, received the ointment from the hands of the knights, and carried it to the high altar. Their excellencies and eminences may be said to have performed their office with unction, but the people laughed alike at the knights, the pomatum, and the ceremony, all of which combined could not endow Charles X. with sense enough to keep his place. The knights of the Sainte Ampoule may be said now to have lost their occupation for ever.

Of all the memorabilia of Rheims, the good people there dwelt upon none more strongly than the old and splendid procession of these knights of the Sainte Ampoule. The coronation cortège seemed only a subordinate point of the proceedings; and the magnificent canopy, upheld by the knights over the vial, on its way from the abbey of St. Remy to the cathedral, excited as much attention as the king's crown.

The proceedings, however, were not always of a peaceable character. The Grand Prior of St. Remy was always the bearer of the vial, in its case or shrine. It hung from his neck by a golden chain, and he himself was mounted on a white horse. On placing the vial in the hands of the archbishop, the latter pledged himself by solemn oath to restore it at the conclusion of the ceremony; and some half-dozen barons were given as hostages by way of security. The procession back to the abbey, through the gayly tapestried streets, was of equal splendor with that to the cathedral.

The horse on which the Grand Prior was mounted was furnished by the government, but the Prior claimed it as the property of the abbey as soon as he returned thither. This claim was disputed by the inhabitants of Chêne la Populeux, or as it is vulgarly called, " Chêne la Pouilleux." They founded their claim upon a privilege granted to their ancestors. It appeared that in the olden time, the English had taken Rheims, plundered the city, and rifled the tomb of St. Remy, from which they carried off the Sainte Ampoule. The inhabitants of Chêne, however, had fallen upon the invaders and recovered the inestimable treasure. From that time, and in memory and acknowledgment of the deed, they had enjoyed, as they said, the right to walk in the procession with the knights of the Sainte Ampoule, and had been permitted to claim the horse ridden by the Grand Prior. The Prior and his people called these claimants scurvy knaves, and would by no means attach any credit to the story. At the coronation of Louis XIII. they did not scruple to support their claim by violence. They pulled the Prior from his horse, terribly thrashed the monks who came to his assistance, tore the canopy to pieces, thwacked the knights right lustily, and carried off the steed in triumph. The respective parties immediately went to law, and spent the value of a dozen steeds, in disputes about the possession of a single horse. The contest was decided in favor of the religious community; and the turbulent people of Chêne were compelled to lead the quadruped back to the abbey stables. They renewed their old claim subsequently, and again threatened violence, much to the delight of the attorneys, who thought to make money by the dissension. At the coronations of Louis XV. and Louis XVI. these sovereigns issued special decrees, whereby the people of Chêne were prohibited from pretending to any property in the horse, and from supporting any such pretensions by acts of violence.

The history of foreign orders would require a volume as large as Anstis's; but though I can not include such a history among my gossiping details, I may mention a few curious incidents connected with

## THE ORDER OF THE HOLY GHOST.

There is a singular circumstance connected with this order. It was founded by the last of the Valois, and went out with the last of the Bourbons. Louis Philippe had a particular aversion for the orders which were most cherished by the dynasty he so cleverly supplanted. The Citizen King may be said to have put down both "St. Louis" and the "Holy Ghost" cavaliers. He did not abolish the orders by decree; but it was clearly understood that no one wearing the insignia would be welcome at the Tuileries.

The Order of the Holy Ghost was instituted by Henri, out of gratitude for two events, for which no other individual had cause to be grateful. He was (when Duke of Anjou) elected King of Poland, on the day of Pentecost, 1573, and on the same day in the following year he succeeded to the crown of France. Hence the Order with its hundred members, and the king as grand master.

St. Foix, in his voluminous history of the order, furnishes the villanous royal founder with a tolerably good character. This is more than any other historian has done; and it is not very satisfactorily executed by this historian himself. He rests upon the principle that the character of a king, or his disposition rather, may be judged by his favorites. He then points to La Marck, Mangiron, Joyeuse, D'Epernon, and others. Their reputations are not of the best, rather of the very worst; but then St. Foix says that they were all admirable swordsmen, and carried scars about them, in front, in proof of their valor: he evidently thinks that the *bellica virtus* is the same thing as the other virtues.

On the original roll of knights there are names now more worthy of being remembered. Louis de Gonzague, Duke de Nevers, was one of these. On one occasion, he unhorsed the Huguenot Captain de Beaumont, who, as he lay on the ground, fired a pistol and broke the ducal kneepan. The Duke's squire bent forward with his knife to despatch the Captain; the Duke, however, told the latter to rise. "I wish," said he, "that you may have a tale to tell that is worth narrating. When you recount, at your fireside, how you wounded the Duke de Nevers, be kind enough to add that he gave you your life." The Duke was a noble fellow. Would that his generosity could have restored his kneepan! but he limped to the end of his days.

But there was a nobler than he, in the person of the Baron d'Assier, subsequently Count de Crussol and Duke d'Uzes. He was a Huguenot, and I confess that I can not account for the fact of his being, at any time of his life, a Knight of the Order of the Holy Ghost. Henri III. was not likely to have conferred the insignia even on a pervert. His name, however, is on the roll. He was brave, merciful, pious, and scrupulously honest. When he captured Bergerai, he spared all who had no arms in their hands, and finding the women locked up in the churches, he induced them to return home, on promise of being protected from all molestation. These poor creatures must have been marvellously fair; and the baron's eulogy on them reminds me of the expression of the soldiers when they led Judith through the camp of Holofernes: "Who could despise this people that have among them such women."

The baron was not a little proud of his feat, and he thought that if all the world talked of the continence of Scipio, he had a right to claim some praise as the protector of female virtue. Accordingly, in forwarding an account of the whole affair to the Duc de Montpensier, he forwarded also a few samples of the ladies. "I have *only* chosen twenty of the handsomest of them," he writes, "whom I have sent you that you may judge if they were not very likely to tempt us to reprisals; they will inform you that they have suffered not the least dishonor." By sending them to Montpensier's quarters the ladies were in great danger of incurring that from which the Baron had saved them. But he winds up with a small lecture. He writes to the Duke: "You are a devotee [!]; you have a ghostly father; your table is always filled with monks; your hear two or three masses every day; and you go frequently to confession. *I* confess myself only to God. I hear no masses. I have none but soldiers at my table. Honor is the sole director of my conscience. It will never advise me to order violence against woman, to put to death a defenceless enemy, or to break a promise once given." In this lecture, there was, in fact, a double-handed blow. Two birds were killed with one stone. The Baron censured, by implication, both the Duke and his religion. I was reminded of him by reading a review in the "Guardian," where the same skilful method is applied to criticism. The reviewer's subject was Canon Wordsworth's volume on Chevalier Bunsen's "Hippolytus." "The canon's book," said the reviewer (I am quoting from memory), "reminds us—and it must be a humiliation and degradation to an intelligent, educated, and thoughtful man—of one of Dr. Cumming's Exeter Hall lectures." Here the ultra high church critic stunned, with one blow, the merely high-church priest and the no-church presbyterian.

There was generosity, at least, in another knight of this order, Francis Goaffier, Lord of Crèvecœur. Catherine of Medicis announced to him the appointment of his son to the command of a regiment of foot. "Madame," said the Knight of the Holy Ghost, "my son was beset, a night or two ago, by five assassins; a Captain La Vergne drew in his defence, and slew two of the assailants. The rest fled, disabled. If your majesty will confer the regiment on one who deserves it, you will give it to La Vergne."—"Be it so," said Catherine, "and your son shall not be the less well provided for."

One, at least, of the original knights of this order was famous for his misfortunes; this was Charles de Hallewin, Lord of Piennes. He had been in six-and-twenty sieges and battles, and never came out of one unscathed. His domestic wounds were greater still. He had five sons, and one daughter who was married. The whole of them, with his son-in-law, were assassinated, or died accidentally, by violent deaths. The old chevalier went down to his tomb heart-broken and heirless.

Le Roi, Lord of Chavigny, and who must not be mistaken for an ancestor of that Le Roi who died at the Alma under the title of Marshal St. Arnaud, is a good illustration of the blunt, honest knight. Charles IX. once remarked to him that his mother, Catherine de Medicis, boasted that there was not a man in France, with ten thousand livres a year, at whose hearth she had not a spy in her pay. "I do not know," said Le Roi, "whether tyrants make spies, or spies tyrants. For my own part, I see no use in them, except in war."

For honesty of a still higher sort, commend me to Scipio de

Fierques, Lord of Lavagne. Catherine de Medicis offered to make this, her distant relative, a marshal of France. "Good Heavens, Madame!" he exclaimed, "the world would laugh at both of us. I am simply a brave gentleman, and deserve *that* reputation; but I should perhaps lose it, were you to make a marshal of me." The dignity is taken with less reluctance in our days. It was this honest knight who was asked to procure the appointment of queen's chaplain for a person who, by way of bribe, presented the gallant Scipio with two documents which would enable him to win a lawsuit he was then carrying on against an obstinate adversary. Scipio perused the documents, saw that they proved his antagonist to be in the right, and immediately withdrew his opposition. He left the candidate for the queen's chaplaincy to accomplish the object he had in view, in the best way he might.

There was wit, too, as might be expected, among these knights. John Blosset, Baron de Torci, affords us an illustration. He had been accused of holding correspondence with the enemy in Spain, and report said that he was unworthy of the Order of the Holy Ghost. He proved his innocence before a chapter of the order. At the end of the investigation, he wittily applied two passages from the prayer-book of the knights, by turning to the king, and saying, " Domine ne projicias me a facie tuâ, et *spiritum sanctum tuum* ne auferas a me." "Lord, cast me out from thy presence, and take not thy 'Holy Spirit' from me." And the king bade him keep it, while he laughed at the rather profane wit of John Blosset.

There was wit, too, of a more practical nature, among these knights of the Holy Spirit. The royal founder used occasionally to retire with the knights to Vincennes. There they shut themselves up, as they said, to fast and repent; but, as the world said, to indulge in pleasures of a very monster-like quality. The royal dukes of a later period in France used to atone for inordinate vice by making their mistresses fast; the royal duchesses settled their little balance with Heaven, by making their servants fast. It appears that there was nothing of this vicarious penance in the case of Henri III. and his knights. Not that all the knights willingly submitted to penance which mortified their appetites. Charles de la Marck, Count of Braine, was one of those impatient penitents.

On a day on which rigid abstinence had been enjoined, the king was passing by the count's apartment, when he was struck by a savory smell. King as he was, he immediately applied his eye to the keyhole of the count's door, and beheld the knight blowing lustily at a little fire under a chafing-dish, in which there were two superb soles frying in savory sauce. "Brother knight, brother knight," exclaimed Henri, "I see all and smell much. Art thou not ashamed thus to transgress the holy rule?"—"I should be much more so," said the count, opening the door, "if I made an enemy of my stomach. I can bear this sort of abstinence no longer. Here am I, knight and gentleman, doubly famished in that double character, and I have been, in my own proper person, to buy these soles, and purchase what was necessary for the most delicious of sauces: I am cooking them myself, and they are now done to a turn. Cooked *aux gratins*, your majesty yourself cannot surely resist tasting. Allow me"—and he pushed forward a chair, in which Henri seated himself, and to the "soles *aux gratins*," such as Vefour and Very never dished up, the monarch sat down, and with the hungry count, discussed the merits of fasting, while they enjoyed the fish. It was but meagre fare after all; and probably the repast did not conclude there.

Charity is illustrated in the valiant William Pot (a very ancient name of a very ancient family, of which the late archdeacon of Middlesex and vicar of Kensington was probably a descendant). He applied a legacy of sixty thousand livres to the support of wounded soldiers. Henri III., who was always intending to accomplish some good deed, resolved to erect an asylum for infirm military men; but, of course, he forgot it. Henri IV., who has received a great deal more praise than he deserves, also expressed his intention to do something for his old soldiers; but he was too much taken up with the fair Gabrielle, and she was not like Nell Gwynne, who turned her intimacy with a king to the profit of the men who poured out their blood for him. The old soldiers were again neglected; and it was not till the reign of Louis XIV. that Pot's example was again recalled to mind, and profitable action adopted in consequence. When I think of the gallant Pot's legacy, what he did therewith, and how French soldiers benefited thereby, I am inclined to believe that the German troops, less well cared for, may thence have derived their once favorite oath, and that *Potz tausend!* may have some reference to the sixty thousand livres which the compassionate knight of Rhodes and the Holy Ghost devoted to the comfort and solace of the brave men who had been illustriously maimed in war.

The kings of France were accustomed to create a batch of knights of the Holy Ghost, on the day following that of the coronation, when the monarchs became sovereign heads of the order. The entire body subsequently repaired from the Cathedral to the Church of St. Remi, in grand equestrian procession, known as the "cavalcade." Nothing could well exceed the splendor of this procession, when kings were despotic in France, and funds easily provided. Cavalry and infantry in state uniforms, saucy pages in a flutter of feathers and ribands, and groups of gorgeous officials preceded the marshals of France, who were followed by the knights of the Holy Ghost, after whom rode their royal Grand Master, glittering like an Eastern king, and nodding, as he rode, like a Mandarin.

The king and the knights performed their devotions before the shrine of Saint Marcoul, which was brought expressly from the church of Corbeni, six leagues distance from Rheims. This particular ceremony was in honor of the celebrated old abbot of Nantua, who, in his lifetime, had been eminently famous for his success in curing the scrofulous disorder called "the king's evil." After this devotional service, the sovereign master of the order of the Holy Ghost was deemed qualified to cure the evil himself. Accordingly, decked with the mantle and collar of the order, and half encircled by the knights, he repaired to the Abbey Park to touch and cure those who were afflicted with the disease in question. It was no little labor. When Louis XVI. performed the ceremony, he touched two thousand four hundred persons. The form of proceeding was singular enough. The king's first physician placed his hand on the head of the patient; upon which a captain of the guard immediately seized and held the patient's hands closely joined together. The king then advanced, head uncovered, with his knights, and touched the sufferers. He passed his right hand from the forehead to the chin, and from one cheek to the other; thus making the sign of the cross, and at the same time pronouncing the words, "May God cure thee; the king touches thee!"

In connection with this subject, I may add here that Evelyn, in his diary, records that Charles II. "began first to touch for the evil, according to custom," on the 6th of July, 1660, and after this fashion. "His Majesty sitting under his state in the Banqueting House, the chirurgeons caused the sick to be brought, and led up to the throne, where they kneeling, the king strokes their faces or cheeks with both his hands at once, at which instant a chaplain, in his formalities, says, 'He put his hands upon them, and He healed them.' This is said to every one in particular. When they have been all touched, they come up again in the same order, and the other chaplain kneeling, and having angel-gold strung on white riband on his arm, delivers them one by one to his Majesty, who puts them about the necks of the touched as they pass, while the first chaplain repeats, 'That is the true light who came into the world.'" The French ceremonial seems to me to have been the less pretentious; for the words uttered by the royal head of the order of the Holy Ghost, simply formed a prayer, and an assertion of a fact: "May God heal thee; the king touches thee!" And yet who can doubt the efficacy of the royal hand of Charles II., seeing that, at a single touch, he not only cured a scrofulous Quaker, but converted him into a good churchman?

The history of the last individual knight given in these imperfect pages (Guy of Warwick), showed how history and romance wove themselves together in biography. Coming down to a later period, we may find another individual history, that may serve to illustrate the object I have in view. The Chevalier de Bayard stands prominently forward. But there was before *his* time, a knight who was saluted by nearly the same distinctive titles which were awarded to Bayard. I allude to Jacques de Lelaing, known as "the knight without fear and without doubt." His history is less familiar to us, and will, therefore, the better bear telling. Besides, Bayard was but a butcher. If he is not to be so accounted, then tell us, gentle shade of Don Alonzo di Sotomayor, why thy painful spirit perambulates the groves of Elysium, with a scented handkerchief alternately applied to the hole in thy throat and the gash in thy face? Is it not that, with cruel subtlety of fence

Bayard run his rapier into thy neck "four good finger-breadths," and when thou wast past resistance, did he not thrust his dagger into thy nostrils, crying the while, "Yield thee, Signor Alonzo, or thou diest!" The shade of the slashed Spaniard bows its head in mournful acquiescence, and a faint sound seems to float to us upon the air, out of which we distinguish an echo of "*The field of Monervyne.*"

## JACQUES DE LELAING,

### THE GOOD KNIGHT WITHOUT FEAR AND WITHOUT DOUBT.

"Faites silence; je vais parler de *lui!*"—*Boileau.*

BETWEEN the city of Namur and the quaint old town of Dinant there is as much matter of interest for the historian as of beauty for the traveller and artist. War has been the most terrible scourge of the two localities on the Meuse which I have just named. Namur has a present reputation for cutlery, and an old one for "slashing blades" of another description. Don John, the great victor at Lepanto, lies entombed in the city, victim of the poison and the jealousy of his brother Philip. There the great Louis proved himself a better soldier than Boileau did a poet, when he attempted to put the royal soldier's deeds into rhyme. Who, too, can stand at St. Nicholas's gate, without thinking of "my uncle Toby," and the Frenchmen, for whose dying he cared so little, on the glacis of Namur? At present the place, it is true, has but a dull and dreamy aspect. Indeed, it may be said of the inhabitants, as of Molly Carew's lovers, that "It's dhrames and not sleep that comes into their heads." Such, at least, would seem to be the case, if I may draw a conclusion from what I saw during the last summer, at the bookseller's stall at the Namur station, where I found more copies of a work professing to interpret dreams than of any other production, whether grave or *gaillard*.

Dinant, a curious old town, the high limestone-rocks behind which seems to be pushing it from off its narrow standing-ground into the Meuse, has even bloodier reminiscences than Namur; but of these I will not now speak. Between the two cities, at the most picturesque part of the stream, and on the loftiest cliff which rises above the stream, is the vast ruin of the old *titanic* castle of Poilvache, the once rather noisy home of the turbulent household of those terrible brothers, known in chivalrous history as the "Four Sons of Aymon." During one of the few fine evenings of the last summer, I was looking up at this height, from the opposite bank, while around me stood in groups a number of those brilliant-eyed, soft-voiced, ready-witted Walloons, who are said to be the descendants of a Roman legion, whose members colonized the country and married the ladies in it! A Walloon priest, or one at least who spoke the dialect perfectly, but who had a strong Flemish accent when addressing to me an observation in French, remained during the period of my observation close at my side. "Are these people," said I to him, "a contented people?" He beckoned to a cheerful-looking old man, and assuming that he was contented with the dispensation that had appointed him to be a laborer, inquired of him which part of his labor he loved best? After pausing for a minute, the old peasant replied in very fair French, "I think the sweetest task I have is when I mow that meadow up at Bloquemont yonder, for the wild thyme in it embalms the very air." "But your winter-time," said I, "must be a dark and dreary time." "Neither dark nor dreary," was the remark of a tidy woman, his wife, who was, at the moment, on her knees, sewing up the ragged rents in the gaberdine of a Walloon beggar—"Neither dark nor dreary. In winter-time, at home, we don't want light to get the children about us to teach them their catechism." The priest smiled. "And as for spring-time," said her husband, "you should be here to enjoy it; for the fields are then all flower, and the sky is one song." "There is poetry in their expressions," said I to the priest. "There is better than that," said he, "there is love in their hearts;" and, turning to the woman who was mending the raiment of the passive mendicant, he asked her if she were not afraid of infection. "Why should I fear?" was her remark. "I am doing but little; Christ did more; He washed the feet of beggars; and we must risk something, if we would gain Paradise." The particular beggar to whom she was thus extending most practical charity was by no means a picturesque bedesman; but, not to be behind-hand in χάρις toward him, I expressed compassion for his lot. "My lot is not so deplorable," said he, uncovering his head; "I have God for my hope, and the charity of humane people for my succor."

As he said this, my eye turned from him to a shepherd who had just joined our group, and who was waiting to be ferried over to the little village of Houx. I knew him by name, and knew something of the solitariness of his life, and I observed to him, "Jacques, you, at least, have a dull life of it; and you even now look weary with the long hours you have been spending alone." "Alone!" he exclaimed, in a joyful tone, "I am never alone, and never weary. How should I be either, when my days are passed in the company of innocent animals, and time is given me to think of God!" The priest smiled even more approvingly than before; and I remarked to him, "We are here in Arcadia." "But not without human sin," said he, and pointing to a woman at a distance, who was in the employ of the farmer's wife, he asked the latter how she could still have anything to do with a well-known thief. "Eh, father," was the comment of a woman whom John Howard would have kissed, "starving her in idleness would not cure her of pilfering; and between working and being well-watched, she will soon leave her evil habits." "You are a good Christian," I said to her, "be you of what community you may." "She *is* a good Catholic," added the priest. "I am what the good God has made me," was the simple reply of the Walloon wife; "and my religion is this to go on my knees when all the house is asleep, and then pray for the whole world." "Ay, ay," was the chorus of those around her, "that is true religion." "It is a part of true religion," interposed the priest; but I could not help thinking that he would have done as well had he left Marie Justine's text without his comment. We walked together down to the bank of the river opposite the Chateau of the young Count de Levignon the proprietor and burgomaster of Houx. I looked up from the modern chateau to the ruins of the vast castle where the sons of Aymon once held barbaric state, maintained continual war, and affected a reverence for the mother of Him who was the Prince of Peace. The good priest seemed to guess my thoughts, for he remarked, "We live now in better times; the church is less splendid, and chivalry less 'glorious,' if not 'extinct; but there is a closer brotherhood of all men — at least," he added hesitatingly— "at least I hope so." "I can not remember," said I, "a single virtue possessed by either Aymon or his sons, except brute courage,

and a rude sort of generosity, not based on principle, but born of
impulse. It is a pity that Belgium can not boast of more perfect
chevaliers than the old proprietors of Poilvache, and that you
have not a hero to match with Bayard." "Belgium," was his
answer, "can make such boast, and had a hero who had finished
his heroic career long before Bayard was born. Have you never
heard of 'the Good Knight without fear and without doubt'?"
"I have heard of one without fear and without reproach." "That
title," he remarked, "was but a plagiarism from that conferred on
Jacques de Lelaing, by his contemporaries." And then he sketched
the outline of the good knight's career, and directed me to sources
where I might gather more detailed intelligence. I was interested
in what I learned, and it is because I hope also to interest readers
at home, that I venture to place before them, however imperfectly
rendered, a sketch of the career of a brave man before the time
of Bayard; one who illustrates the old saying that—

"Vixere fortes ante Agamemnona."

Jaques de Lelaing, the good knight, without fear and without
doubt, was born in the château of Lelaing, in the first quarter of
the fifteenth century. The precise year is not known, but it was
full half a century before the birth of Bayard. He came of a
noble race; that is, of a race, the male portion of which saw more
honor in slaughter than in science. His mother was celebrated
for her beauty as well as nobility. She was wise, courteous, and
*débonnaire;* well-mannered, and full of all good virtues. So, at
least, in nearly similar terms, wrote George Chastellan of her, just
two centuries ago.

Jacques de Lelaing was as precocious a boy as the Duke of
Wharton in his youth. At the age of seven, a priestly tutor had
perfected him in French and Latin, and the good man had so im-
bued him with literary tastes that, in after life, the good knight
found time to cultivate the acquaintance of Captain Pen, as well
as of Captain Sword; and specimens of his handiwork are yet
said to exist in the libraries of Flanders and Brabant.

Jacques, however, was never a mere student, "sicklied o'er with
the pale cast of thought." He loved manly sports; and he was
yet but a blooming youth when the "demoiseau of Clèves," nephew

of that great Duke whom men, for no earthly reason, called Philip *the Good*, carried off his young friend from the castle of Lelaing, and made of him a squire, not of dames, but of knights, in the turbulent court of the ducál Philip, with the benevolent qualification to his name.

The youth entered upon his career with a paternal provision which bespoke at once the liberality and the wisdom of his father, stout William de Lelaing. The sire bestowed upon his son four splendid horses, a well-skilled groom, and a "*gentleman of service*," which, in common phrase, means a valet, or "gentleman's gentleman." But the young soldier had more than this in his brain; namely, a well-lettered cleric, commissioned to be for ever expounding and instructing, with a special object, to boot, that Jacques should not forget his Latin! Excellent sire thus to care for his son! If modern fathers only might send into barracks with their sons, when the latter first join their regiments, reverend clerks, whose office it should be to keep their pupils well up in their catechism, the Eton grammar, and English orthography, what a blessing it would be to the young gentlemen and to all acquainted with them! As it is, we have officers worse instructed and less intelligent than the sons of the artists who make their uniforms.

When Jacques went forth into the world, his sire gave him as good advice as Polonius threw away on his son Laertes. The sum of it was according to the old French maxim, "Noblesse oblige"— "Inasmuch," said the old man, "as you are more noble than others by birth, so," said he, "should you be more noble than they by virtues." The hearty old father added an assurance, that "few great men gained renown for prowess and virtue who did not entertain love for some dame or damoislle." This last, however, was but an equivocal assurance, for by counselling Jacques to fall in love with " some dame or damoiselle," he simply advised him to do so with any man's wife or daughter. But it was advice commonly given to young gentlemen in arms, and is, to this day, commonly followed by them. Jacques bettered the paternal instruction, by falling in love with two ladies at the same time. As ambitious youths are wont to do, he passed by the white and pink young ladies whom he met, and paid his addresses, with remarkable success, to two married duchesses. Neither of these suspected that the smooth-chinned young "squire" was swearing eternal fidelity to the other, or that this light-mailed Macheath wooed his madiæval Polly with his pockets full of "favors," just bestowed on him by an unsuspecting Lucy. Thus has love ever been made by officers and highwaymen.

But if Jacques loved two, there was not a lady at the Court of Burgundy who did not love *him*. The most virtuous of them sighingly expressed a wish that their husbands, *or their lovers*, were only like him. The men hated him, while they affected to admire his grace, his bearing, and his irresistible bravery. Jacques very complacently accepted the love of the women and the envy of the men; and feeling that he had something to be thankful for, he repaired to the shrine of the Virgin at Hal, and thanked "Our Lady," accordingly.

Now Philip the Good was good only just as Nicholas the Czar was "good." He had a fair face and a black heart. Philip, like Nicholas, joined an outward display of conjugal decency with some private but very crapulous indecency; and the Duke, like the Czar, was *the* appalling liar of his day. Philip had increased the ducal territory of Burgundy by such means as secured Finland to Muscovy, by treachery of the most fiendish quality; and in 1442, affecting to think that Luxembourg was in the sick condition which Nicholas described as the condition of Turkey — when the imperial felon thought he was making a confederate of Sir Hamilton Seymour, the Duke resolved to seize on the territory in question, and young Jacques de Lelaing was in an ecstacy of delight at being permitted to join in this most rascally of expeditions.

Within a year, desolation was spread throughout a wide district. Fire and sword did their devastating work, and the earth was swept of the crops, dwellings, and human beings, which lay between the invaders and Luxembourg. The city was ultimately taken by surprise, and the good Philip delivered it up to pillage; then ensued a scene which hell itself could not equal; and the Duke and his followers having enacted horrors from which devils would have recoiled, they returned to Brussels, where they were received with ten times more delight than if they had come back from an expedition which had been undertaken for the benefit of humanity.

What was called *peace* now followed, and Jacques de Lelaing, having fleshed his maiden sword, and gained the praise of brave men, and the love of fair women, resolved to commence a series of provincial excursions for his own especial benefit. As, in modern times, professors without scholars, and actors without engagements, wander from town to town, and give lectures at "the King's Arms," so Jacques de Lelaing went forth upon his way, offering to fight all comers, in presence of kings themselves.

His first appearance on this provincial tour was at Nancy, in 1445, where a brilliant French Court was holding joyous festival while awaiting the coming of Suffolk, who was commissioned to escort to England a royal bride, in the person of Margaret of Anjou. The French knights made light of the soldier of Burgundy; but Jacques, when announcing that he was the holder of the tournament, added that no French knight should unhorse him, unless God and his good lady decreed otherwise.

The latter was not likely, and he felt himself secure, doubly so, for he rode into the lists decorated with favors, gold embroidery, and rich jewels, the gifts of the Duchesses of Orleans and Calabria, each of whom fondly believed that she was the sole fair one by whose bright eyes Jacques de Lelaing swore his prettiest oath. Accordingly, there was not a cavalier who rode against him in that passage of arms, who left the field otherwise than with broken or bruised bones. "What manner of man will this be?" cried they, "if, even as a lad, he lays on so lustily?"

The lad, at the subsequent banquet, to which he was borne in triumph, again proved that he had the capacity of a man. He was fresh as a rose just blown; gay as a lark in early spring. The queens of France and Sicily conversed with him by the half hour, while ladies of lower degree gazed at him till they sighed; and sighed, knowing full well *why*, and caring very much, wherefore. Charles VII. too, treated him with especial distinction, and conferred on him the rich prizes he had won as victor in the rough tourney of the day. But there were other guerdons awarded him that night, which he more highly prized. Jacques visited the Duchess of Orleans in her bower, and carried away with him, on leaving, the richest diamond she had to bestow.  He then passed to the pavilion of the Duchess of Calabria, a lady who, among other gifts willingly made by her, placed upon his finger a brilliant ruby set in a gorgeous gold ring.  He went to his own bed that night as impudently happy as a modern Lifeguardsman who is successfully fooling two ladies' maids.  His *cleric* had left him, and Jacques had ceased to care for the keeping-up of his Latin, except, perhaps, the conjugation of the imperative mood of *amo*. "Amemus," *let us love*, was the favorite part of the mood, and the most frequently repeated by him and his brace of duchesses.

Sometime after this very successful first appearance, and toward the end of 1445, our doughty squire was traversing the cathedral of Notre Dame of Antwerp, and was on the point of cursing the singers for their bad voices, just as one might be almost justified in doing now, so execrable are they; he was there and thus engaged, when a Sicilian knight, named Bonifazio, came jingling his spurs along the transept, and looking jauntingly and impertinently as he passed by.  Jacques looked boldly at this "pretty fellow" of the time, and remarked that he wore a golden fetter ring on his left leg, held up by a chain of the same metal fastened to a circlet above his knee.  His shield bore the device, "Who has fair lady, let him look to her well!"  "It's an impertinent device," said Jacques, touching the shield, by way of token that he would fight the bearer for carrying it.  "Thou art but a poor squire, albeit a bold man," said the Sicilian, with the air of one who was half inclined to chastise the Hainaulter for his insolence.  Toison d'Or, the herald, whispered in the ear of the Hainaulter; thereupon, Jacques exclaimed, "If my master, Duke Philip, will give me permission to fight, thou darest not deny me, on his Grace's territory."  Bonifazio bowed by way of assent.  The permission was gained, and the encounter came off at Ghent.  The first day's combat was a species of preliminary struggle on horseback, in which Jacques showed himself so worthy of the spurs he did not yet wear, that Philip fastened them to his heels the next day, and dubbed him Knight in solemn form.  As the combatants strode into the lists, on the second day, the Duke of Orleans remarked to his Duchess, that Jacques was not so "gent as the Sicilian."  The Duchess smiled, as Guinever smiled when she looked on Sir

Launcelot, while her husband, King Arthur, commented upon him; and she said, in phrase known to all who read Spenser, "he loves a lady gent;" and she added, with more of the smile and less of the blush, "he is a better man than the Sicilian, and, to my thinking, he will this day prove it."

"We shall see," remarked the Duke carelessly.

"We shall see," re-echoed the Duchess, with the sunniest of smiles.

Jacques, like the chivalric "gent" that he was, did honor to the testimony of the Duchess. The combatants went at it, like stout men. Jacques belabored his antagonist with a staff, the Sicilian answered by thrusting a javelin at his adversary's uncovered face. They then flung away their arms and their shields, and hewed at each other with their battle-axes. Having spoiled the edges of these, and loosened them from their handles, by battering at each other's skulls, they finally drew their lusty and well-tempered swords, and fought so fiercely that the gleaming of their swiftly manœuvred blades made them seem as if they were smiting each other with lightning. Jacques had well-nigh dealt a mortal thrust at the Sicilian, when, at the intervention of the Duke of Orleans, Philip the Good flung his truncheon into the lists, and so saved the foreign knight, by ending the fray. The Duchess reproved her consort for being over-intrusive, but she smiled more gleesomely than before. "Whither away, Sir Jacques?" asked she, as the latter modestly bowed on passing her—the multitude the while rending the welkin with their approving shout. "To the chapel in the wood," replied Jacques, "to render thanks for the aid vouchsafed to me by our Lady." "Marry," murmured the Duchess, "we will be there too." She thought it not less edifying to see knight at his devotions than at beholding him in the duello. "I am grateful to the Lady of Good Succor," said Jacques. "And thou doest right loyally," was the comment of the Duchess.

The victory of the Belgian cavalier over the Sicilian gained for him the distinctive name which he never lost, that of "the Good Knight." To maintain it, he proceeded to travel from court to court, as pugilists itinerate it from fair to fair, to exhibit prowess and to gather praise. The minor pugilist looks to pence as well as praise, and the ancient knight had an eye to profit also—he invariably carried off the horse, armor, and jewels of the vanquished. As Sir Jacques deemed himself invincible, he looked to the realization of a lucrative tour. "Go on thy way, with God's blessing," exclaimed his sire. "Go on thy way, Jacques," murmured his mother through her tears; "thou wilt find ointment in thy valise, to cure all bruises. Heaven send thee a surgeon, and thou break thy bones."

Across the French frontier merrily rode Sir Jacques, followed by his squire, and attended by his page. From his left arm hung a splendidly-wrought helmet, by a chain of gold—the prize offered by him to any one who could overcome him in single combat. Jacques announced that, in addition, he would give a diamond to any lady or demoiselle indicated to him by his conqueror. He stipulated that whichever combatant first dropped his axe, he should bestow a bracelet upon his adversary; and Jacques would only fight upon the condition that neither knight should be fastened in his saddle—a regulation which I should never think of seeing insisted upon anywhere, except by equestrian aldermen when they amble on Mr. Batty's horses, to meet the Sovereign at Temple Bar. For the rest Jacques put his trust in God, and relied upon the strength given him in the love of "the fair lady who had more power over him than aught besides throughout the entire world." A hundred ladies fair, matrons and maids, who heard of this well-advertised confidence, did not hesitate to exclaim, "Delicious fellow! He means *me!*"

It was the proud boast of Jacques, that he traversed the capital, and the provincial cities of France, without meeting with a knight who would accept his defiance. It would be more correct to say —a knight who *could* take up his challenge. Charles VII. forbade his chivalry from encountering the fierce Hainaulter anywhere but at the festive board. In the South of France, then held by the English, he met with the same civility; and he rode fairly into Spain, his lance in rest, before his onward career was checked by the presence of an adversary. That adversary was Don Diego de Guzman, Grand-master of Calatrava, and, although he knew it not, ancestor to a future Empress of the French. The Don met the Belgian on the borders of Castile, and accepted his published challenge out of mere love, as the one silly fellow said of the other, out of mere love for his "*très aimée dame.*" The "*dames*" of those days enjoyed nothing so much as seeing the gentlemen thwack each other; and considering what a worthless set these latter, for the most part, were, the ladies had logically comic reasons to support their argument.

It was necessary, however, for Don Diego to obtain the consent of his sovereign to encounter in mortal combat a knight of the household of Burgundy, then in alliance with Spain. The Sovereign was absent from the country, and while an answer was being expected from him to the application duly made, Jacques, at the head of a most splendid retinue, trotted leisurely into Portugal, to tempt the Lusitanian knights to set their lances against him. He rode forward to the capital, and was greeted by the way, as if he had been as illustrious a monarch as his ducal master. It was one ovation, from the frontier to Lisbon, where he was welcomed by the most crowded of royal balls, at which the King (Alphonso XV.) invited him to foot it with the Queen. The King, however, was but an indifferent master of the ceremonies. The late Mr. Simpson of Vauxhall, or the illustrious Baron Nathan of Rosherville, would never have dreamed of taking the lady to introduce her to the gentleman. This uncourteous process was, however, the one followed by Alphonso, who taking his consort by the hand, led her to Sire Jacques, and bad him tread a measure with her. Messire Jacques consented, and there was more than enough of dancing, and feasting, and pleasure-seeking, but no fighting. Lisbon was as dull to the Belgian as Donnybrook Fair without a skrimmage used to be to all its lively *habitués*. "I have had a turn with the Queen," said Jacques, "let me now have a tourney with your captains." "Burgundy is my good friend," answered the King—and he was right in a double sense, for Burgundy was as dear to him as Champagne is to the Czar's valet, Frederick William, who resides at Berlin. "Burgundy is our good friend," answered Alphonso, "and Heaven forbid that a knight from such a court should be roughly treated by any knights at mine." "By St. George! I defy them!" exclaimed Jacques. "And even so let it rest," said the monarch; "ride back to Castile, and do thy worst upon the hard ribs of the Guzman." Jacques adopted the suggestion; and on the 3d of February, 1447, there was not a bed in Valladolid to be had "for love or money;" so crowded was that strong-smelling city with stronger-smelling Spaniards, whose curiosity was even stronger than the odors they distilled, to witness the "set-to" between the Belgian Chicken and the Castile Shaver!

I will not detail the preliminary ceremonies, the processions to the field, the entry of the sovereigns, the fluttering of the ladies, the excitement of the knights, and the eagerness of the countless multitude. Jacques was on the ground by ten o'clock, where Guzman kept him waiting till three; and then the latter came with an axe so much longer than that wielded by the Belgian, that even the Spanish umpires forbade its being employed. Don Diego's own "godfather" for the occasion was almost minded to thump him with the handle; and there was all the trouble in the world to induce him to select another. This being effected, each knight was conducted to his tent, with the understanding that he was not to issue therefrom until the clarions had thrice sounded by way of signal. At the very first blast, however, out rushed the Guzman, looking as ferocious as a stage Richard who has killed five false Richmonds, and is anxiously inquiring for the real one wherewith to finish the half-dozen. The too volatile Don was beckoned back by the chief herald as haughtily as when the sempiternal Widdicombe points out with his whip some obvious duty to be performed by Mr. Merryman. Diego retired muttering, but he again appeared in front of his tent at the second note of summons from the trumpet, and only withdrew after the king had assailed him "with an ugly word." At the third "flourish," the two champions flew at each other, battle-axe in hand. With this weapon they hammered at each other's head, until there was little sense left in either of them. At length, Diego was disarmed; then ensued a contest made up partly of wrestling and partly of boxing; finally, they had recourse to their swords, when the king, perceiving that murder was likely to ensue, to one or both, threw his bâton into the lists, put an end to the combat, and refused permission to the adversaries to continue the struggle on horseback. The antagonists shook hands, and the people shouted. The Spanish knight is deemed, by Belgian chroniclers, as having come off "second best" in the struggle; but it is also clear that Diego de

Guzman was by far the "toughest customer" that ever confronted Jacques de Lelaing. There was some jealousy on the part of the Iberian, but his behavior was, altogether, marked by generosity. He praised the prowess of Jacques, and presented him with an Andalusian horse covered with the richest trappings; and de Lelaing, as unwilling to be outdone in liberality as in fight, sent to Guzman, by a herald, a magnificent charger, with coverings of blue velvet embroidered in gold, and a saddle of violet velvet, to be seated in which, was of itself a luxury. Much dancing at court followed; and finally, the "good knight" left Valladolid loaded with gifts from the king, praises from men, and love from the ladies, who made surrender of more hearts than he had time to accept.

In Navarre and in Aragon he challenged all comers, but in vain. Swords slept in scabbards, and battle-axes hung quietly from saddle-bows, and there was more feasting than fighting. At length Jacques, after passing through Perpignan and Narbonne, arrived at Montpelier, where he became the guest of the famous Jacques Cœur, the silversmith and banker of Charles VII. Old Cœur was a hearty old host, for he offered the knight any amount of money he would honor him by accepting; and he intimated that if De Lelaing, in the course of his travels had found it necessary to pawn any of his plate or jewelry, *he* (Jacques Cœur) would redeem it free of expense. "My good master, the Duke of Burgundy," replied the errant chevalier, "provides all that is necessary for me, and allows me to want for nothing;" and thereupon he went on his way to the court of Burgundy, where he was received with more honor than if he had been executing a mission for the especial benefit of humanity.

But these honors were little, compared with the rejoicings which took place when the "good knight" revisited his native château, and the parents who therein resided. His sire hugged him till his armor was warm again; and his lady mother walked about the halls in a state of ecstacy and thanksgiving. Finally, the rafters shook at the efforts of the joyous dancers, and many a judicious matron instructed her daughter how Jacques, who subdued the stoutest knights, might be himself subdued by the very gentlest of ladies. The instruction was given in vain. The good chevalier made love alike to young widows, wives, and daughters, and having broken more hearts than he ever broke lances, he suddenly left home in search of new adventures.

Great was the astonishment, and *that* altogether of a pleasurable sort, when the herald Charolais appeared at the Scottish court in July, 1449, and delivered a challenge from Jacques to the whole of the Douglases. It was accepted in their name by James Douglas, the brother of the lieutenant-general of the kingdom; and in December of the year last named, Jacques, with a retinue of fighting uncles, cousins, and friends, embarked at Ecluse and set sail for Caledonia. The party were more battered about by the sea than ever they had been by enemy on land; and when they arrived at Leith, they looked so "shaky," were so pale and haggard, and had so little of a "slashing" look, wrapped up as they were in surcoats and comforters, that the Scottish cavaliers, observing the draggled condition of the strangers and of the plumes which seemed to be moulting from their helmets, fairly asked them what motive induced them to come so far in so sorry a plight, for the mere sake of getting bruised by knights ashore after having been tossed about, sick and sorry, during whole nights at sea. When the northern cavaliers heard that honor and not profit had moved the Belgian company, they marvelled much thereat, but prepared themselves, nevertheless, to meet the new-comers in dread encounter at Stirling.

James II. presided at the bloody fray, in which three fought against three. What the Scottish chroniclers say of the struggle, I can not learn, but the Belgian historians describe their champions as having been eminently victorious with every arm; and, according to them, the Douglases were not only soundly drubbed, but took their beating with considerable sulkiness. But there is much poetry in Belgian history, and probably the doughty Douglas party may not have been so thoroughly worsted as the pleasant chroniclers in question describe them to have been. No doubt the conquerors behaved well, as we know "les braves Belges" have never failed to do, if history may be credited. However this may be, Jacques and his friends hurried from Scotland, appeared at London before the meek Lancastrian king, Henry VI.; and as the latter would not license his knights to meet the Burgundians in the lists, the foreign fighting gentlemen had their passports *visé*, and taking passage in the fast sailer "Flower of Hainault," duly arrived at home, where they were hailed with enthusiasm.

Jacques had short space wherein to breathe. An English knight, named Thomas Karr, speedily appeared at the court of Philip the Duke, and challenged De Lelaing, for the honor of old England. This affair caused a great sensation, and the lists were dressed in a field near Bruges. The English knight was the heavier man in flesh and armor, but Jacques, of course, was the favorite. Dire was the conflict. The adversaries strove to fell each other with their axes, as butchers do oxen. Karr paralyzed, if he did not break, the arm of Jacques; but the Belgian, dropping his axe, closed with his foe, and after a struggle, fell with and upon him. Karr was required, as a defeated man, to carry the gauntlet of the victor to the lady pointed out by him. But obstinate Tom Karr protested against this, as he had only fallen on his elbow. The umpires declared that he had had a full fall, "head, belly, arms, and legs;" Jacques, however, was generous and would not insist. On the contrary, adverting to the fact that he had himself been the first to drop his own axe, he presented Karr with a rich diamond, as the forfeit due by him who first lost a weapon in the combat.

Karr had terribly wounded Jacques, and the wound of the latter took long to cure. The Duke Philip hastened his convalescence by naming him counsellor and chamberlain; and as soon as the man so honored by his master, had recovered from his wounds, he repaired to Chalons on Saone, where he opened a "tourney," which was talked of in the country for many a long year afterward. Jacques had vowed that he would appear in the closed lists thirty times before he had attained his thirtieth year; and this tourney at Chalons was held by him against all comers, in order the better to enable him to fulfil his vow. The detail would be tedious; suffice it to say that the affair was of barbarian magnificence, and that knights smashed one another's limbs, for personal honor, ladies' love, and the glory of Our Lady in Tears! Rich prizes were awarded to the victors, as rich forfeits were exacted from the vanquished, and there was not only a sea of good blood spilt in this splendidly atrocious fray, but as much bad blood made as there was good blood shed. But then there was empty honor acquired, a frail sort of affection gained, and an impalpable glory added to the non-existent crown of an imaginary Venus Victrix, decorated with the name of Our Lady of Tears! What more could true knights desire? Chivalry was satisfied; and commonplace men, with only common sense to direct them, had to look on in admiring silence, at risk of being cudgelled if they dared to speak out.

Jacques was now at the height of his renown. He was "the good knight without fear and without doubt;" and Duke Philip placed the last rose in his chaplet of honor, by creating him a knight of the illustrious order of the Golden Fleece. Thus distinguished, he rode about Europe, inviting adversaries to measure swords with him, and meeting with none willing to accept the invitation. In 1451 he was the embassador of Burgundy at Rome, charged to negotiate a project of crusade against the Turks. M. Alexander Henne, the author of the best compendium, gathered from the chronicles, of the deeds of Jacques de Lelaing—says that after the knight's mission to Rome, he appeared at a passage of arms held in the park at Brussels, in honor of the Duke of Burgundy's son, the Count of Charolais, then eighteen years of age, and about to make his first appearance in the lists. The Duchess, tender of her son as the Dowager Czarina who kept her boys at home, and had not a tear for other mothers, whose children have been bloodily sacrificed to the savage ambition of Nicholas—the Duchess careful of the young Count, was desirous that he should make essay before he appeared in the lists. Jacques de Lelaing was accordingly selected to run a lance with him. "Three days before the fête, the Duke, the Duchess, and the Court repaired to the park of Brussels, where the trial was to be made. In the first onset, the Count de Charolais shattered his lance against the shield of Jacques, who raised his own weapon, and passed without touching his adversary. The Duke perceived that the good knight had spared his young adversary; he was displeased thereat, and sent Jacques word that if he intended to continue the same course, he would do well to meddle no further in the matter. Other lances were then brought, and Jacques, running straight against the Count, both lances flew into splinters.

At this incident, the Duchess, in her turn, gave expression to her discontent; but the Duke only laughed; and thus mother and father were of different opinions; the one desiring a fair trial, the other security for her son." On the day of the great tourney, there were assembled, with the multitude, on the great square at Brussels, not less then two hundred and twenty-five princes, barons, knights, and squires. Some of the noblest of these broke a lance with, and perhaps the limbs of, their adversaries. The Count de Charolais broke eighteen lances on that day, and he carried off the the prize, which was conferred upon him by the ladies.

This was the last of the show-fights in which Jacques de Lelaing exhibited himself. The bloodier conflicts in which he was subsequently engaged, were far less to his credit. They formed a part of the savage war which the despotic Duke and the nobles carried on against the free and opulent cities, whose spirit of liberty was an object of hatred, and whose wealth was an object of covetous desire, to the Duke and his body of gentleman-like assassins. Many a fair town was devastated by the Duke and his followers, who affected to be inspired by religious feelings, a desire for peace, and a disinclination to make conquests. Whereby it may be seen that the late Czar was only a Burgundian duke enlarged, impelled by much the same principle, and addicted to a similar sort of veracity. It was a time of unmitigated horrors, when crimes enough were committed by the nobles to render the name of aristocracy for ever execrable throughout Belgium; and atrocities were practised by the enraged commons, sufficient to insure, for the plebeians, the undying hatred of their patrician oppressors. There was no respect on either side for age, sex, or condition. The people, of every degree, were transformed into the worst of fiends—slaying, burning, violating, and plundering; and turning from their accursed work to kneel at the shrine of that Mary whose blessed Son was the Prince of Peace. Each side slaughtered, hung, or drowned its prisoners; but the nobles gave the provocation by first setting the example, and the commons were not cruel till the nobility showed itself alike destitute of honor and of mercy. The arms of the popular party were nerved by the infamy of their adversaries, but many an innocent man on either side was condemned to suffer, undeservedly, for the sins of others. The greatest efforts were made against the people of the district and city of Ghent, but all Flanders sympathized with them in a war which was considered national. In the struggle, the Duke won no victory over the people for which the latter did not compel him to pay a frightful price; he was heartily sick of the war before it was half concluded — even when his banner was being most successfully upheld by the strong arm and slender scruples of Jacques de Lelaing.

The good knight was however, it must be confessed, among the few — if he were not the only one — of the betterminded nobles. He had been commissioned by the Duke to set fire to the Abbey of Eenaeme, and he obeyed without hesitation, and yet with reluctance. He destroyed the religious edifice with all which it contained, and which could be made to burn; but having thus performed his duty as a soldier, he forthwith accomplished his equally bounden duty, as a Christian — and, after paying for three masses, at which he devoutly assisted, he confessed himself to a predicant friar, "making a case of conscience," says one of his biographers, "of having, out of respect for discipline, committed an act which the uprightness of his heart compelled him to condemn as criminal." Never was there a better illustration of that so-called diverse condition of things which is said to represent a distinction without a difference.

The repentance of Jacques de Lelaing came, it is hoped, in time. He did well, at all events, not to defer it any longer, for he was soon on the threshold of that world where faith ceases and belief begins. He was engaged, although badly wounded, in inspecting the siege-works in the front of the Château de Pouckes, that Flemish cradle of the Pooks settled in England. It was on a June afternoon of the year 1453, that Jacques, with a crowd of nobles half-encircling him, rode out, in pite of the protest of his doctors (because, as he said, if he were to remain doing nothing he should certainly die), in order that he might have *something* to do. There was a famous piece of artillery on the Burgundian side, which was sorely troublesome to the stout little band that was defending Pouckes. It was called the "Shepherdess," but never did shepherdess speak with so thundering-unlovely a voice, or fling her favors about her with such dire destruction to those upon whom they were showered. Jacques drew up behind the *manteau* of this cannon, to watch (like our gallant seamen at Sebastopol) the effects of the shot discharged from it. At the same moment a stone projectile, discharged from a culverin by the hand of a young artilleryman of Ghent, who was known as the son of Henry the Blindman, struck Jacques on the forehead, carrying away the upper part of his head, and stretched him dead upon the field. A Carmelite brother rushed up to him to offer the succor and consolation of religion, but it was too late. Jacques had sighed out his last breath, and the friar decently folded the dead warrior's arms over his breast. A mournful troop carried the body back to the camp.

The hero of his day died in harness. He had virtues that fitted him for a more refined, a more honest, in short, a more Christian, period. These he exercised whenever he could find opportunity, but such opportunity was rare. He lived at a period when, as M. de Sismondi has remarked, " Knights thought of nothing but equalling the Rolands and Olivers of the days of Charlemagne, by the destruction of the vile canaille"—a sort of pastime which has been recently recommended in our senate, although the days of chivalry be gone. The noble comrades of Jacques, as M. Henne observes, acknowledged but one species of supreme pleasure and glory, which consisted in making flow abundantly the blood of villains—or, as they are now called, the lower orders. But in truth the modern "villain" or the low-class man is not exclusively to be found in the ranks which have had such names applied to them. As Bosquier-Gavaudan used so joyously to sing, some thirty years ago, in the *Ermite de St. Avelle* :—

> " Les gens de bien
> Sont souvent des gens de rien ;
> Et les gens de rien
> Sont souvent des gens de bien !"

For a knight, Jacques was really a respectable man, and so disgusted with his butcher-like occupation, that, just before his death, he had resolved to surrender his estate to a younger brother, and, since fate had made of him a licensed murderer, to henceforth murder none but eastern infidels—to slay whom was held to be more of a virtue than a sin. Let us add of him, that he was too honest to earn a reputation by being compassionate to half-a-dozen helpless foes, after directing his men to slaughter a score of the mutilated and defenceless enemy. Jacques de Lelaing would sooner have sent his dagger up to the hilt in his own heart, than have violated the safeguard of a flag of truce. *Such* days and such doings of chivalry are not those most agreeable to Russian chivalry. Witness Odessa, where the pious governor directed the fire on a flag of truce which he swore he could not see; and witness the massacre of Hango, the assassins concerned in which exploit were defended by their worthy superior De Berg.

Jacques de Lelaing, however, it must not be forgotten, fell in a most unworthy cause — that of a despot armed against free people. His excellent master swore to avenge him; and he kept his word. When the Château de Pouckes was compelled to surrender, Philip the Good ordered every one found alive in it to be hung from the walls. He made exception only of a priest or two, one soldier afflicted with what was called *leprosy*, but which has now another name in the catalogue of avenging maladies, and a couple of boys. It was precisely one of these lads who had, by his well-laid shot, slain "the good knight without fear and without doubt;" but Philip was not aware of this till the lad was far beyond his reach, and in safety at Ghent.

Those who may be curious to know the course taken by the war until it was terminated by the treaty of Lille, are recommended to study the Chronicles of De Lettenhooe, of Olivier de la Marche, of Chastellain, and Du Clery. I had no intention, at setting out, to paint a battle-piece, but simply to sketch a single figure. My task is done, however imperfectly, and, as old chroniclers were wont to say, May Heaven bless the gentle reader, and send pistoles and abounding grace to the unworthy author.

Such is the history of an individual; let us now trace the fortunes of a knightly house. The story of the Guises belongs entirely to chivalry and statesmanship.

## THE FORTUNES OF A KNIGHTLY FAMILY.

> "This deals with nobler knights and monarchs,
> Full of great fears, great hopes, great enterprises."
> *Antony Brewer, "Lingua."*

In the pleasant spring-time of the year 1506, a little boy, mounted on a mule, and accompanied by a serving man on foot, crossed over the frontier from Lorraine into France. The boy was a pretty child, some ten years old. He was soberly clad, but a merry heart beat under his gray jerkin; and his spirits were as light as the feather in his bonnet. The servant who walked at his side was a simple yet faithful follower of his house; but there was no more speculation in his face than there was in that of the mule. Nothing could have looked more harmless and innocent than the trio in question; and yet the whole — joyous child, plodding servitor, and the mule whose bells rang music as he trod — formed one of the most remarkable invasions of which the kingdom of France has ever been the victim.

The boy was the fifth child of René and Philippa de Gueldres, the ducal sovereigns of Lorraine. This duchy, a portion of the old kingdom of Lotharingia — in disputes for the possession of which the children of Charlemagne had shed rivers of blood — had maintained its independence, despite the repeated attempts of Germany and France to reduce it to subjection. At the opening of the sixteenth century, it had seen a legal succession of sovereign and independent masters during seven centuries. The reigning duke was René, the second of that name. He had acquired estates in France, and he had inherited the hatred of Lorraine to the Capetian race which had dethroned the heirs of Charlemagne. It was for this double reason that he unostentatiously sent into the kingdom of France one of his sons, a boy of fair promise. The mission of the yet unconscious child was to increase the territorial possessions of his family within the French dominions, and ultimately to rule both Church and State—if not from the throne, why then from behind it.

The merry boy proved himself in course of time to be no unfitting instrument for this especial purpose. He was brought up at the French court, studied chivalry, and practised passages of arms with French knights; was the first up at *réveillée*, the last at a feast, the most devout at mass, and the most winning in ladies' bower. The princes of the blood loved him, and so did the princesses. The army hailed him with delight; and the church beheld in him and his brother, Cardinal John, two of those champions whom it records with gladness, and canonizes with alacrity.

Such was Claude of Lorraine, who won the heart and lands of Antoinette de Bourbon, and who received from Francis I. not only letters of naturalization, but the title of Duke of Guise. The locality so named is in Picardy. It had fallen to the house of Lorraine by marriage, and the dignity of Count which accompanied it was now changed for that of Duke. It was not long before Claude made the title famous. The sword of Guise was never from his grasp, and its point was unceasingly directed against the enemies of his new country. He shed his own blood, and spilled that of others, with a ferocious joy. Francis saw in him the warmest of his friends and the bravest of his soldiers. His bravery helped to the glory that was reaped at Marignan, at Fontarabia, and in Picardy. Against internal revolt or foreign invasion he was equally irresistible. *His* sword drove back the Imperialists of Germany within their own frontier; and when on the night of Pavia the warriors of France sat weeping like girls amid the wide ruin around them, *his* heart alone throbbed with hopeful impulses, and *his* mind only was filled with bright visions of victories to come.

These came indeed, but they were sometimes triumphs that earned for him an immortality of infamy. The crest of his house was a double cross, and this device, though it was no emblem of the intensity of religion felt by those who bore it, *was* significant of the double sanguinary zeal of the family—a zeal employed solely for selfish ends. The apostolic reformers of France were, at this period, in a position of some power. Their preachers were in the pulpit, and their people in the field. They heard the gospel leaning on their swords; and, the discourse done, they rushed bravely into battle to defend what they had heard.

Against these pious but strong-limbed confederates the wrath of Guise was something terrible. It did not, like that of Francis I.—who banqueted one day the unorthodox friends whom he burned the next—alternate with fits of mercy. It raged without intermission, and before it the Reformers of Alsatia were swept as before a blast in whose hot breath was death. He spared neither sex nor age; and he justified his bloody deeds by blasphemously asserting that he was guided to them by the light of a cross which blazed before him in the heavens. The church honored him with the name of "good and faithful servant;" but there are Christian hearths in Alsatia where he is still whisperingly spoken of as "the accursed butcher."

When his own fingers began to hold less firmly the handle of his sword, he also began to look among his children for those who were most likely to carry out the mission of his house. His eye marked, approvingly, the bearing of his eldest son Francis, Count D'Aumale; and had no less satisfaction in the brothers of Francis, who, whether as soldiers or priests, were equally ready to further the interests of Lorraine, and call them those of Heaven. His daughter Mary he gave to James V. of Scotland; and the bride brought destruction for her dowry. Upon himself and his children, Francis I., and subsequently Henry II., looked at last with mingled admiration and dread. Honors and wealth were lavished upon them with a prodigal and even treasonable liberality. The generous king gave to the insatiate Guise the property of the people; and when these complained somewhat menacingly, Guise achieved some new exploit, the public roar of applause for which sanctioned a quiet enjoyment of his ill-gotten treasures.

For the purpose of such enjoyment he retired to his castle at Joinville. The residence was less a palace than a monastery. It was inhabited by sunless gloom and a deserted wife. The neglected garden was trimmed at the coming of the duke, but not for his sake nor for that of the faithful Antoinette. Before the eyes of that faithful wife he built a bower for a mistress who daily degraded with blows the hero of a hundred stricken fields. He deprecated the rough usage of the courtesan with tears and gold; and yet he had no better homage for the virtuous mother of his children, than a cold civility. His almost sudden death in 1550 was accounted for as being the effect of poison, administered at the suggestion of those to whom his growing greatness was offensive. The accusation was boldly graven on his monument; and it is probably true. No one however, profited by the crime.

The throne found in his children more dangerous supporters than he had ever been himself; and the people paid for their popular admiration with loss of life and liberty. The church, however, exulted; for Claude of Lorraine, first Duke of Guise, gave to it the legitimate son, Cardinal Charles, who devised the massacre of the day of St. Bartholomew; and the illegitimate son, the Abbé de Cluny, who, on that terrible day, made his dagger drink the blood of the Huguenots, till the wielder of it became as drunk with frenzy as he was wont to be with the fiery wine which was his peculiar and intense delight.

The first Duke of Guise only laid a foundation, upon which he left his heirs and successors to build at their discretion. He had, nevertheless, effected much. He had gained for his family considerable wealth; and if he had not also obtained a crown, he had acquired possession of rich crown-lands. The bestowing upon him of these earned popular execration for the king; the people, at the same time, confessed that the services of Guise were worthy of no meaner reward. When King Francis saw that he was blamed for bestowing what the recipient was deemed worthy of having granted to him, we can hardly wonder that Francis, while acknowledging the merits of the aspiring family, bade the members of his own to be on their guard against the designs of every child of the house of Lorraine.

But *he* was no child who now succeeded to the honors of his father, the first duke. Francis of Guise, at his elevation to the ducal title, saw before him two obstacles to further greatness. One was a weak king, Henry II.; and the other, a powerful favorite, the Constable de Montmorency, from whose family, it was popularly said, had sprung the first Christian within the realm of France. Francis speedily disposed of the favorite, and almost as speedily raised himself to the vacant office, which he exercised so as to further his remote purposes. In the meantime the king was taught to believe that his crown and happiness were dependent on his Lorraine cousins, who, on their side, were not only aiming at the throne of France for one member of the house, but were aspiring to the tiara for a second; the crown of Naples for a third—to influence in Flanders and in Spain, and even to the diadem of Elizabeth of England, succession to which was recognised as existing in them, by Mary Stuart, in case of her own decease without direct heirs. It is said that the British Romanists looked forward with unctuous complacency to the period when the sceptre of this island should fall into the blood-stained grasp of a "Catholic Guise."

It was not only the fortune of Francis to repair the ill luck encountered in the field by Montmorency, but to gain advantages in fight, such as France had not yet seen. The Emperor Charles V. had well-nigh got possession of beleaguered Metz, when Guise threw himself into the place, rescued it from the Emperor, and swept the Imperialists out of France. His fiery wrath cooled only in presence of the wounded, to whom he behaved with gentle and helping courtesy. His gigantic labors here brought on an attack of fever; and when he was compelled to seek rest in his house at Marchez, a host of priests and cardinals of his family gathered round his court, and excited him to laughter by rough games that suited but sorrily with their calling.

The second duke inherited his father's hatred for "heretics." The great Colligny had been his bosom friend; but when that renowned Reformer gave evidence of his new opinions upon religious subjects, then ensued, first a coldness, then fits of angry quarrelling, and at last a duel, in which, though neither combatant was even scratched, friendship was slain for ever. Duke Francis was prodigal like his father, but then his brother, Cardinal Charles, was minister of the finances: and the king and his mistress, Diana de Poictiers, cared not how the revenue was managed, so that money was forthcoming when necessity pressed. The consequence was, that the king's exchequer was robbed to supply the extravagances of Guise. But then men began to associate with the name the idea of deliverance from oppression; and they did not count the cost. And yet victory did not invariably select for her throne the glittering helm of the aspiring duke. The pope had selected him as commander of the papal army acting against Naples, but intrigue paralyzed the arm which had never before been conquered, and the pontiff showered epigrams upon him instead of laurels.

In this momentary eclipse of the sun of his glory, the duke placed his own neck under the papal heel. He served in the pope's chapel as an Acolyte, meekly bore the mantle of obese and sneering cardinals, and exhibited a humility which was not without success. When at a banquet given by a cardinal, Guise humbly sat down at the lower end of the table, he asked a French officer who was endeavoring to thrust in below him, "Why comest thou here, friend?" "That it might not be said," answered the soldier, "that the representative of the King of France took the very lowest place at a priest's table!"

From such reproaches Guise gladly fled, to buckle on his armor and drive back an invasion of France by the Hispano-Flemings on the north. The services he now rendered his country made the people almost forget the infamy of their king, who was wasting life in his capital, and the oppressive imposts of the financial cardinal, whom the sufferers punningly designated as Cardinal *La Ruine*. The ruin he achieved was forgiven in consideration of the glory accomplished by his brother, who had defeated and destroyed the armies which threatened the capital from the north; and who had effected much greater glory by suddenly falling on Calais with a force of ten to one, and tearing from the English the last of the conquests till then held by them in France. Old Lord Wentworth, the governor, plied his artillery with a roar that was heard on the English coast: but the roar was all in vain. There was a proverb among our neighbors, and applied by them to every individual of mediocre qualifications, that "he was not the sort of man to drive the English out of France." That man was found in Guise; and the capital began naturally to contrast him with the heartless king, who sat at the feet of a concubine, and recked little of the national honor or disgrace. And yet, the medals struck to commemorate the recovery of Calais bear the names only of Henri and Diana. They omit all mention of the great liberator, Guise!

The faults of Henri, however, are not to be entirely attributed to himself. He had some feelings of compassion for the wretched but stout-hearted Huguenots, with whom, in the absence of Guise, he entered into treaties, which, Guise present, he was constrained to violate! In pursuit of the visions of dominion in France, and of the tiara at Rome, the ambitious house sought only to gain the suffrages of the church and the faithful. To win smiles from them, the public scaffolds were deluged with the blood of heretics; and all were deemed so who refused to doff their caps to the images of the virgin, raised in the highways at the suggestion of the duke and the cardinal. This terrific persecution begat remonstrance; but when remonstrance was treated as if it were rebellion, rebellion followed thereupon; as, perhaps, was hoped for; and the swords of the Guisards went flashing over every district in France, dealing death wherever dwelt the alleged enemies of God, who dared to commune with Him according to conscience, rather than according to Rome. Congregations, as at Vassi, were set upon and slaughtered in cold blood, without resistance. In the Huguenot "temple" of this last place was found a Bible. It was brought to the duke. This noble gentleman could spell no better than the great Duke of Marlborough; and Guise was, moreover, worse instructed in the faith which he professed. He looked into the Book of Life, unconscious of what he held, and with a wondering exclamation as to what it might be all about, he flung it aside, and turned to the further slaughter of those who believed therein.

In such action he saw his peculiar mission for the moment, but he was not allowed to pursue it unopposed. His intrigues and his cruelties made rebels even of the princes of the blood; and Condé took the field to revenge their wrongs, as well as those of the Reformers. The issue was tried on the bloody day at Dreux, when the setting sun went down on a Protestant army routed, and on Condé a captive; but sharing the bed, as was the custom of the time, of his proved victor Guise. Never did two more deadly enemies lie on the same couch, sleepless, and full of mutual suspicion. But the hatred of Condé was a loyal hatred; that of Guise was marked by treacherous malignity. The Protestant party, in presence of that hot fury, seemed to melt away like a snow-wraith in the sun. He and his Guisards were the terror of the so-called enemies of the Faith. Those whom he could not reach by the sword, he struck down by wielding against them the helpless hand of the king, who obeyed with the passiveness of a *Marionette*, and raised stakes, and fired the pile, and gave the victim thereto, simply because Guise would so have it.

The duke received one portion at least of his coveted reward. At every massacre of inoffensive Protestants, the Catholic pulpits resounded with biblical names, showered down upon him by the exulting preachers. When his banner had swept triumphantly over successive fields, whose after-crops were made rich by heretical blood, then did the church pronounce him to be a soldier divinely armed, who had at length "consecrated his hands, and avenged the quarrel of the Lord."

Guise lived, it is true, at a period when nothing was held so cheap as life. Acts of cruelty were but too common in all factions. If he delivered whole towns to pillage and its attendant horrors, compared with which death were merciful, he would himself exhibit compassion, based on impulse or caprice. He was heroic, according to the thinking of his age, which considered heroism as being constituted solely of unflinching courage. In all other respects, the duke, great as he was, was as mean as the veriest knave who trailed a pike in his own bands. Scarcely a letter addressed to his officers reached them without having been previously read to their right worshipful master. There was scarcely a mansion in the kingdom, whose lord was a man of influence, but that at that table and the hearth there sat a guest who was the paid spy of Francis of Guise.

It is hardly necessary to add that his morality generally was on a par with the particular specimens we have given of it. Crowds of courtesans accompanied him to the camp, while he deliberately exposed his own wife, Anne of Este, the sister of Tasso's Leonora, to the insulting homage of a worthless king. Emphatically may it be said that the truth was not in him. He gloried in mendacity. No other personage that I can call to mind ever equalled him in lying—except, perhaps, those very highly professing heroes who swagger in Greek tragedy. He procured, by a lie, the capital conviction of Condé. The latter escaped the penalty, and taxed the duke with his falsehood. Guise swore by his sword, his life, his honor, his very soul, that he was innocent of the charge. Condé looked on the ducal liar with a withering contempt, and turned from him with a sarcasm that should have pierced him like a sword. Pointed as it was, it could not find way through his corslet to his heart. He met it with a jest, and deemed the sin unregistered.

There was a watchful public, nevertheless, observing the progress made toward greatness by the chivalric duke, and his brother the cardinal. Henry II. had just received the mortal blow dealt him at a tournament by the lance of Montgomery. Francis II., his brother, the husband of Mary Stuart, and therewith nephew to Guise, succeeded to the uneasy throne and painful privileges of Henri. On the night of this monarch's decease, two courtiers were traversing a gallery of the Louvre. "This night," said one, "is the eve of the Festival of the Three Kings." "How mean you by that?" asked the other with a smile. "I mean," rejoined the first, "that to-morrow we shall have three monarchs in Paris —one of them, King of France; the others Kings *in* France— from Lorraine."

Under the latter two, Duke and Cardinal, was played out the second act of the great political drama of Lorraine. It was altogether a melo-drama, in which there was abundance of light and shadow. At times, we find the hero exhibiting exemplary candor; anon, he is the dark plotter, or the fierce and open slayer of his kind. There are stirring scenes of fights, wherein his adversaries draw their swords against him, at the instigation of a disgusted King, who no sooner saw Guise triumphant, than he devoted to death the survivors whom he had clandestinely urged into the fray.

The battles were fought, on one side, for liberty of conscience; on the other, for the sake of universal despotism. The bad side triumphed during a long season; and field after field saw waving over it the green banner of Lorraine. Catherine de Medicis, and her son Charles IX., accompanied the Duke in more than one struggle, after the short-lived reign of Francis II. had come to an end. They passed, side by side, through the breach at Rouen; but accident divided them at Orleans, where had assembled the gallant few who refused to despair for the Protestant cause.

Guise beleaguered the city, and was menacingly furious at its obstinacy in holding out. One evening he had ridden with his staff to gaze more nearly at the walls, from behind which defiance was flung at him. "You will never be able to get in," remarked roughly a too presuming official. "Mark me!" roared the chafed Duke, "yon setting sun will know to-morrow how to get behind that rampart; and by Heaven, so will I!" He turned his horse, and galloped back alone to his quarters. He was encountered on his way by a Huguenot officer, Poltrot de la Mer, who brought him down by a pistol-shot. The eyes of the dying Duke, as he lay upon the ground, met for the last time the faint rays of that departing sun, with which he had sworn to be up and doing on the morrow. He died in his hut. His condition was one of extreme "comfortableness." He had robbed the King's exchequer to gratify his own passions;—and he thanked Heaven that he had been a faithful subject to his sovereign! He had been notoriously unfaithful to a noble and virtuous wife; and he impressed upon her with his faltering lips, the assurance that "generally speaking" his infidelity as a husband did not amount to much worth mentioning! He confessed to, and was shriven by his two brothers, Cardinals John and Charles. The former was a greater man than the Duke. The latter was known in his own times and all succeeding, as "the bottle cardinal," a name of which he was only not ashamed, but his title to which he was ever ostentatiously desirous to vindicate and establish.

The first Duke had acquired possession of crown-lands; the second had at his disposal the public treasure; and the third hoped to add to the acquisitions of his family the much-coveted sceptre of the Kings of France.

Henri, surnamed *Le Balafré*, or "the scarred," succeeded his father in the year 1560. During the greater portion of his subsequent life, his two principal objects were the destruction of Protestantism, and the possession of the King's person. He therewith flattered the national vanity by declaring that the natural limits of France, on two sides, were the Rhine and the Danube—an extension of frontier which was never effected, except temporarily, in the latter days of Napoleon. But the declaration entailed a popularity on the Duke which was only increased by his victory at Jarnac, when the French Protestants not only suffered defeat, but lost their leader, the brave and unfortunate Condé. This gallant chief had surrendered, but he was basely murdered by a pistol-shot, and his dead body, flung across an ass, was paraded through the ranks of the victors, as a trophy. How far the Duke was an accomplice in the crime, is not determined. That such incidents were deemed lightly of by him, is sufficiently clear by his own proclamation in seven languages, wherein he accused Coligny as the instigator of the murder of the late Duke of Guise, and set a price upon that noble head, to be won by any assassin.

For that so-called murder, Guise had his revenge on the day of St. Bartholomew, when he vainly hoped that the enemies of his house had perished for ever. On the head of more than one member of the house of Guise rests the responsibility of that terrible day. During the slaughter, Guise gained his revenge, but lost his love. The cries of the victims were the nuptial songs chanted at the marriage-ceremony of Henri of Navarre and Margaret, the King's sister. The latter had looked, nothing loath, upon the suit offered to her by Guise, who was an ardent wooer. But the wooing had been roughly broken in upon by the lady's brother, the Duc d'Anjou, who declared aloud in the Louvre, that if Guise dared look with lover's eyes upon "Margot," he would run his knife into the lover's throat! The threat had its influence, and the unfaithful wooer, who had been all the while solemnly affianced to a Princess Catherine of Cleves, married that remarkable brunette, and showed his respect for her, by speaking and writing of her as "that amiable lady, the negress." It may be noticed in passing, that the objection of D'Anjou to Guise as a brother-in-law, was not personal; it had a political foundation. The two dukes became, indeed, brothers-in-law; not by Guise marrying the sister of D'Anjou, but by D'Anjou marrying the sister of Guise, and by sharing with her the throne which he, subsequently, occupied rather than enjoyed, as Henri III.

When summoned to the throne by the unedifying death of Charles IX., Henry of Anjou was king of Poland. He escaped from that country with difficulty, in order to wear a more brilliant but a more fatal crown in France. He had no sooner assumed it, when he beheld the Guises encircling him, and leaving him neither liberty nor will. The Protestants were driven into rebellion. They found a leader in Henry of Navarre, and Guise and his friends made war against them, irrespective of the King's consent, and cut in pieces, with their swords, the treaties entered into between the two Henrys, without the consent of the third Henri — of Guise and Lorraine. The latter so completely enslaved the weak and unhappy sovereign, as to wring from him, against his remonstrance and conviction, the famous articles of Nemours, wherein it was solemnly decreed in the name of the King, and confirmed by the signature of Guise, that, thenceforward, it was the will of God that there should be but one faith in France, and that the opposers thereof would find that opposition incurred death.

There is a tradition that when Henri III. was told of this decree, he was seated in deep meditation, his head resting upon his hand; and that when he leaped to his feet with emotion, at the impiety of the declaration, it was observed that the part of his moustache which had been covered by his hand, had suddenly turned gray.

The misery that followed on the publication of these infamous articles was widely spread, and extended to other hearths besides those of the Huguenots. Sword, pestilence, and famine, made a desert of a smiling country; and the universal people, in their common sorrow, cursed all parties alike—"King and Queen, Pope and Calvin," and only asked from Heaven release from all, and peace for those who suffered by the national divisions. The King, indeed, was neither ill-intentioned nor intolerant; but Guise so intrigued as to persuade the "Catholic" part of the nation that Henri was incapable. Faction then began to look upon the powerful subject as *the* man best qualified to meet the great emergency. He fairly cajoled them into rebellion. They were, indeed, willing to be so cajoled by a leader so liberal of promises, and yet he was known to be as cruel as he engaged himself to be liberal. He often kept his own soldiers at a point barely above starvation; and the slightest insubordination in a regiment entailed the penalty of death. To his foes he was more terrible still. As he stood in the centre of a conquered town that had been held by the Huguenots, it was sport to him to see the latter tossed into the flames. On one occasion he ordered a Huguenot officer to be torn asunder by young horses for no greater crime than mutilating a wooden idol in a church. The officer had placed the mutilated figure on a bastion of the city, with a pike across its breast, as a satire on the guardianship which such a protector was popularly believed to afford.

He could, however, be humane when the humor and good reason for it came together. Thus he parted with a pet lioness, which he kept at his quarters, on the very sufficient ground that the royal beast had, on a certain morning, slain and swallowed one of his *favorite* footmen! A commonplace lacquey he might have spared without complaining; but he could not, without some irritation, hear of a *valet* being devoured who, though a valet, had a profound belief that his master was a hero.

The "Bartholomew" had not destroyed all the foes of the name of Guise. What was not accomplished on that day was sought to be achieved by the "League." The object of this society was to raise the Duke to the throne of Henri, either before or after the death of the latter. The King was childless, and the presumptive heir to the throne, Henri of Navarre, was a Protestant. The Lorrainers had double reason, then, for looking to themselves. The reigning sovereign was the last of three brothers who had inherited the crown, and there was then a superstitious idea that when three brothers had reigned in France, a change of dynasty was inevitable.

Guise fired his followers with the assurance that the invasion of England, and the establishment of Popery there, should be an enterprise which they should be called upon to accomplish. The King was in great alarm at the "League," but he wisely constituted himself a member. The confederates kept him in the dark as to the chief of their objects. The suspicious monarch, on the other hand, encouraged his minions to annoy his good cousin of Lorraine. One of these unworthy favorites, St. Megrim, did more: he slandered the wife of Guise, who took, thereon, a singular course of trial and revenge. He aroused his Duchess from her solitary couch, in the middle of the night, hissed in her alarmed ear the damning rumor that was abroad, and bade her take at once from his hands the dagger or the poison-cup, which he offered her:—adding that she had better die, having so greatly sinned. The offended and innocent wife cared not for life, since she was suspected, and drank off the contents of the cup, after protestation of her innocence. The draught was of harmless preparation, for the Duke was well assured of the spotless character of a consort whom he himself daily dishonored by his infidelities. He kissed her hand and took his leave; but he sent a score of his trusty-men into the courtyard of the Louvre, who fell on St. Megrim, and butchered him almost on the threshold of the King's apartments.

The monarch made no complaint at the outrage; but he raised a tomb over the mangled remains of his favorite minion, above which a triad of Cupids represented the royal grief, by holding their stony knuckles to their tearless eyes, affecting the passion which they could not feel.

In the meantime, while the people were being pushed to rebellion at home, the ducal family were intriguing in nearly every court in Europe. Between the intrigues of Guise and the recklessness of the King, the public welfare suffered shipwreck. So nearly complete was the ruin, that it was popularly said, "The Minions crave all: the King gives all; the Queen-mother manages all; Guise opposes all; the Red Ass (the Cardinal) embroils all, and would that the Devil had all!"

But the opposition of Guise was made to some purpose. By exercising it he exacted from the King a surrender of several strong cities. They were immediately garrisoned by Guisards, though held nominally by the sovereign. From the latter the Duke wrung nearly all that it was in the power of the monarch to yield; but when Guise, who had a design against the life of the Protestant Henri of Navarre, asked for a royal decree prohibiting the granting of "quarter" to a Huguenot in the field, the King indignantly banished him from the capital. Guise feigned to obey; but his celebrated sister, the Duchess of Montpensier, refused to share in even a temporary exile. This bold woman went about in public, with a pair of scissors at her girdle, which, as she intimated, would serve for the *tonsure* of brother Henri of Valois, when weariness should drive him from a palace into a monastery.

The King, somewhat alarmed, called around him his old Swiss

body guard, and as the majority of these men professed the reformed faith, Guise made use of the circumstance to obtain greater ends than any he had yet obtained. The people were persuaded that their religion was in peril; and when the Duke, breaking his ban, entered Paris and, gallantly attired, walked by the side of the sedan of Catherine of Medicis, on their way to the Louvre, to remonstrate with the unorthodox king, the church-bells gave their joyous greeting, and the excited populace hung upon the steps of the Duke, showering upon him blessings and blasphemous appellations. "Hosanna to our new son of David!" shouted those who affected to be the most pious; and aged women, kissing his garment as he passed, rose from their knees, exclaiming, "Lord, now lettest thou thy servant depart in peace, for mine eyes have seen thy salvation!"

The less blasphemous or the more sincere sufficiently expressed their satisfaction by hailing him, as he went on his way, smiling, "King of Paris!"

The sound of this title reached the ears of Henri. Coupling it with the unauthorized return of Guise to court, he passed into alternate fits of ungovernable wrath and profound melancholy. He was under the influence of the latter when there fell on his ear, words which make him start from his seat—"*Percutiam pastorem, et dispergentur oves;*" and when the Monarch looked round for the speaker, he beheld the Abbé d'Elbene, who had thus calmly quoted Scripture, in order to recommend murder. The King, though startled, was not displeased. On the contrary, he smiled; and the smile was yet around his lips, and in his eyes, when Guise entered the presence, and mistook the expression of the royal face for one of welcome. The Duke, emboldened by what he saw, hurried through a long list of grievances, especially dwelling on the lenity, not to say favor, with which Henri treated the heretics generally. The sovereign made a few excuses, which Guise heeded not; on the contrary, he hastened to denounce the body of minions who polluted the palace. "Love me, love my dog," said Henri, in a hoarse voice. "Yes," answered Guise, peering into the royal and unnaturally sparkling eyes, "provided he does n't bite!" The two men stood revealed before each other; and from that hour the struggle was deadly. Henri would not give away, with reference to his Swiss guard; and Guise, passing through Paris, with his sword unsheathed, awoke the eager spirit of revolt, and looked complacently on while the barricades were raised to impede the march of the execrable Calvinistic Archers of the Guard. The "King of Paris" earned a decisive victory; but before it was achieved, the King of France hurried, in an agony of cowardly affright, from his capital. He gazed for a moment on the city, as he departed, venting curses on its ingratitude; for, said the fugitive Monarch, "I loved you better than I did my own wife;"—which was indisputably true.

Guise might now have ascended the throne, had he not been too circumspect. He deemed the royal cause lost, but he was satisfied for the moment with ruling in the capital, as generalissimo. He stopped the King's couriers, and opened his letters. He confiscated the property of Huguenots, and sold the same for his own benefit, while he professed to care only for that of the Commonwealth. Finally, he declared that the disturbed condition of affairs should be regulated by a States-General, which he commanded rather than prayed Henri to summon to a meeting at Blois. The King consented; and the 18th of October, 1588, was appointed for the opening. Guise entered the old town with his family, and a host of retainers, cased in armor, and bristling with steel. Henri had his mother Catherine at his side; but there were also a few faithful and unscrupulous followers with him in the palace at Blois; and as he looked on any of those who might happen to salute him in passing, the King smiled darkly, and *Percutiam pastorem* fell in murmured satisfaction from his lips. The saturnine monarch became, all at once, cheerful in his outward bearing, even when Guise was so ruling the States as to make their proceedings turn to the detriment of the monarchy. The Guise faction became anxious for the safety of their leader, whose quarters were in the palace; but when the King, in token of reconciliation, begged the Duke to participate with him in the celebration of the Holy Sacrament, there was scarcely a man capable of interpreting the manner of the times, who did not feel assured that under such a solemn pledge of security, there lay concealed the very basest treachery. Guise, over-confident, scorned alike open warning and dark inuendoes. He was so strong, and his royal antagonist so weak, that he despised the idea of violence being used against him — especially as the keys of the palatial castle were in his keeping, as "Grand-Master" of the Court.

The 23d of December had arrived. The King intimated that he should proceed early in the morning, soon after daybreak (but subsequently to holding a council, to which he summoned the Duke and Cardinal), to the shrine of Our Lady of Clery, some two miles distant; and the keys of the gates were demanded, in order to let Henri have issue at his pleasure, but in reality to keep the Guises within, isolated from their friends without. Larchant, one of the Archers of the Guard, also waited upon the Duke, to pray him to intercede for himself and comrades with the King, in order to obtain for them an increase of pay. "We will do ourselves the honor," said Larchant, "to prefer our petition to your Highness, in the morning, in a body." This was a contrivance to prevent Guise from being surprised at seeing so many armed men together in the King's antechamber, before the council was sitting. Henri passed a sleepless night. His namesake of Guise, who had just sent his Duchess homeward, her approaching confinement being expected, spent the whole of the same night in the apartments of the Countess de Noirmoutier.

He was seen coming thence, before dawn, gayly dressed, and proceeding to the Chapel of the Virgin, to perform his morning devotions. Long before this, the King was a-foot, visiting the select archers who had accepted the bloody mission of ridding the perplexed monarch of his importunate adversary. He posted them, altered the arrangements, reposted them, addressed them again and again on the lawfulness of their office, and had some trouble to suppress an enthusiasm which threatened to wake the Queen-mother, who slept below, and to excite the suspicion of the Guards in the vicinity. Staircase and hall, closet and arras, no coign of vantage but had its assassin ready to act, should his fellows have failed.

Precisely at seven o'clock, Guise, attired in a light suit of gray satin, and followed by Pericart, his secretary, entered the council-chamber, where he found several members assembled; among others, his younger brother, the "Bottle-Cardinal" de Guise. An hour passed without the appearance of any message from the

King, who was in an inner apartment, now half-frightened at the pale faces of his own confidants, and anon endeavoring to excite his own resolution, by attempts to encourage theirs. It was a long and weary hour for all parties. As it slowly passed away, Guise, he knew not wherefore, grew anxious. He complained of the cold, and heaped billets of wood upon the fire. He spoke of feeling sick, faint, and unnerved; and from his silver sweetmeat-case he took a few bonbons, by way of breakfast. He subsequently asked for some Damascus raisins, and conserve of roses; but these, when supplied to him did not relieve him of an unaccountable nervousness, which was suddenly increased, when the eye next to the scar from which he derived his appellation of *Le Balafré*, began to be suffused with tears. He indignantly wiped away the unwelcome suffusion, and had quite recovered as Rivol, Secretary of State, entered, and requested him to attend on the King, who awaited him in his own chamber.

Guise gayly flung his *bonbonnière* across the council-table, and laughingly bade the grave counsellors scramble for the scattered sweets. He started up, overturned his chair in so doing, drew his thin mantle around him, and with cap and gloves in hand, waved a farewell to the statesmen present. He passed through two rooms, and closely followed by various of the archers, reached the tapestried entrance to the King's cabinet. No one offered to raise the arras for him. Guise lifted his own right arm to help himself at the same time looking half-round at the archers who were near him. At that moment, a dagger was buried in his breast, up to the very hilt. The blow was delivered by Montsery, from behind. The Duke let fall his hand to the pommel of his sword, when one assassin clung to his legs, a second, also from behind, stabbed him in the neck; while a third passed his weapon through the Duke's ribs.

Guise's first cry was, "Ho, friends!" His second, as Sarine ran him through the lower part of the back, was, "Mercy, Jesus!" He struggled faintly across the chamber, bleeding from a dozen wounds, in every one of which sat death. The murderers hacked at him as he staggered, and wildly yet feebly fought. All paused for a moment, when he had reached the extreme end of the room, where he again attempted to raise his sword; but in the act he rolled over, stone dead, at the foot of the bed of Henri III.

At that moment the tapestry was raised, and the king, whispering "Is it done?" approached the body, moodily remarking as he gazed upon it, "He looks greater than he did when living." Upon the person of the duke was found a manuscript memorandum, in these words:—"To maintain a war in France, I should require 700,000 livres per month." This memorandum served in the king's mind as a justification of the murder just committed by his orders. The body was then unceremoniously rolled up in the Turkey carpet on which it had fallen, was covered with quick lime, and flung into the Loire. Some maimed rites were previously performed over it by Dourgin the royal chaplain, who could not mutter the *De Profundis* without a running and terrified commentary of "Christ!—the awful sight!" Guise's second cardinal-brother and the Archbishop of Lyons were murdered on the following day; but the lesser victims were forgotten in the fate which had fallen upon the more illustrious, yet certainly more guilty personages.

The widow of Guise, soon after the dread event, gave birth to a son, subsequently the Chevalier Louis de Guise. "The boy," said the bereaved lady, "came into the world with his hands clasped, as if praying for vengeance on the assassins of his father." Every male member of the family whom the king could reach was now subjected to arrest. The young heir of *Balafré*, Charles, now fourth Duke of Guise, was now placed in close restriction in the Castle of Tours, where, sleeping or waking, four living eyes unceasingly watched him—*voire même allant à la garderobe*—but which eyes he managed to elude nevertheless.

In the meantime Rome excommunicated the murderer of her champion. Paris put on mourning; officials were placed in the street to strip and scourge even ladies who ventured to appear without some sign of sorrow. Wax effigies of the king were brought into the churches, and frantically stabbed by the priests at the altar. The priests then solemnly paraded the streets, chanting as they went, "May God extinguish the Valois!"

The whole city broke into insurrection, and the brother of Guise, the Duke de Mayenne, placed himself at the head of the "league," whose object was the deposing of the king, and the transferring of the crown to a child of Lorraine. In the contest which ensued, Valois and Navarre united against the Guisards, and carried victory with them wherever they raised their banners. The exultation of Henri III. was only mitigated by the repeated Papal summonses received by him to repair to Rome, and there answer for his crime.

Henri of Navarre induced him to rather think of gaining Paris than of mollifying the Pope; and he was so occupied when the double vengeance of the church and the house of Guise overtook him in the very moment of victory.

The Duchess de Montpensier, sister of the slaughtered duke, had made no secret of her intentions to have public revenge for the deed privately committed, whereby she had lost a brother. There was precaution enough taken that she should not approach the royal army or the king's quarters; but a woman and a priest rendered all precautions futile. The somewhat gay duchess was on unusually intimate terms with a young monk, named Jacques Clement. This good Brother was a fanatic zealot for his church, and a rather too ardent admirer of the duchess, who turned both sentiments to her own especial purpose. She whispered in his ears a promise, to secure the fulfilment of which, he received with furious haste, the knife which was placed in his hands by the handsomest woman in France. It is said that knife is still preserved, a precious treasure, at Rome.

However this may be, on the 1st of August, 1589, the young Brother, with a weapon hid in the folds of his monkish gaberdine, and with a letter in his hand, sought and obtained access to the king. He went straightforward to his butcher's work, and had scarcely passed beneath the roof of the royal tent before he had buried the steel deep in the monarch's bosom. He turned to fly with hot haste to the lady from whom he had received his commission; but a dozen swords and pikes thrust life out of him ere he had made three steps in the direction of his promised recompence.

She who had engaged herself to pay for the crime cared for neither victim. She screamed indeed, but it was with a hysteric joy that threatened to slay her, and which was only allayed by the thought that the last King of the Valois race did not know that he had died by a dagger directed by a sister of Guise.

In testimony of her exultation she distributed green scarfs, the color of Lorraine, to the people of Paris. She brought up from the provinces the mother of Clement, to whom was accorded the distinction of a triumphal entry. Priests and people worshipped the mother of the assassin as she passed wonderingly on her way; and they blasphemously saluted her with the chanted words, " Blessed be the womb that bare him, and the paps that gave him suck." She was led to the seat of honor at the table of Guise, and Rome sheltered the infamy of the assassin, and revealed its own, by pronouncing his work to be a god-like act. By authority of the Vatican, medals were struck in memory and honor of the dead; but the Huguenots who read thereon the murderer's profession and name — *Frère Jacques Clement* — ingeniously discovered therein the anagrammatic interpretation " *C'est l'enfer qui m'a crée*"— " It is hell that created me."

The last Valois, with his last breath, had named the Protestant Henri of Navarre as his legal successor to the throne; but between Henri and his inheritance there stood Rome and the Guise faction. Then ensued the successive wars of the League, during which the heavy Mayenne suffered successive defeats at the hands of Henri of the snowy plume. While the contest was raging, the people trusted to the pulpits for their intelligence from the scene of action. From those pulpits was daily uttered more mendacity in one hour than finds expression in all the horse-fairs of the United Kingdom in a year. When famine decimated those who lived within the walls, the people were reduced to live upon a paste made from human bones, and which they called " Madame de Montpensier's cake."

Henri of Navarre, their deliverer, did not arrive before the gates of Paris without trouble. In 1521, Charles of Guise, the young Duke, had escaped most gallantly, in open day, from the Castle of Tours, by sliding from the ramparts, down a rope, which simply blistered his hands and made a rent in his hose. He was speedily accoutred and in the field, with Spain in his rear to help him. Now, he was making a dash at Henri's person; and, anon, leaping from his camp-bed to escape him. At other times he was idle, while his uncle Mayenne pursued the cherished object of their house — that crown which was receding from them more swiftly than ever. For the alert Bourbon, the slow and hard-drinking Mayenne was no match. The latter thought once to catch the former in his lady's bower, but the wakeful lover was gayly galloping back to his quarters before the trumpets of Mayenne had sounded to "boot and saddle." "Mayenne," said the Pope, "sits longer at table than Henri lies in bed."

The gates of Paris were open to Henri on the 21st of March, 1591. Old Cardinal Pellevi died of disgust and indignation, on hearing of the fact. The Duchess of Montpensier, after tearing her hair, and threatening to swoon, prudently concluded, with Henry IV., not only her own peace, but that of her family. The chief members of the house of Guise were admitted into places of great trust, to the injury of more deserving individuals. The young Duke de Guise affected a superabundant loyalty. In return, the King not only gave him the government of several chief towns, but out of compliment to him forbade the exercise of Protestant worship within the limits of the Duke's government! Such conduct was natural to a King, who to secure his throne had abandoned his faith; who lightly said that he had no cannon so powerful as the canon of the mass, and who was destitute of most virtues save courage and good-nature. The latter was abused by those on whom it was lavished; and the various assaults upon his life were supposed to be directed by those very Guises, on whom he had showered places, pensions, and pardons, which they were constantly needing and continually deriding.

The young Duke of Guise enjoyed, among other appointments, that of Governor of Marseilles. He was light-hearted, selfish, vain, and cruel. He hanged his own old partisans in the city, as enemies to the king; and he made his name for ever infamous by the seduction of the beautiful and noble orphan-girl, Marcelle de Castellane, whom he afterward basely abandoned, and left to die of hunger. He sent her a few broad pieces by the hands of a lacquey; but the tardy charity was spurned, and the poor victim died. He had little time to think of her at the brilliant court of the first Bourbon, where he and those of his house struggled to maintain a reputation which had now little to support it, but the memories of the past — and many of those were hardly worth appealing to. He was a mere fine gentleman, bold withal, and therewith intriguing; ever hoping that the fortunes of his house might once more turn and bring it near a throne, and in the meantime, making himself remarkable for his vanity, his airs of greatness, and his affectation. Brave as he was, he left his brothers, the cardinal and chevalier, to draw their swords and settle the quarrels which were constantly raging on disputed questions touching the assumed Majesty of the House of Guise.

The streets of Paris formed the stage on which these bloody tragedies were played, but they, and all other pretensions, were suppressed by that irresistible putter-down of such nuisances — the Cardinal de Richelieu. He used the sword of Guise as long as it was needed, but when Charles became troublesome the Cardinal not only banished him, but wounded the pride of his family by placing garrisons in the hitherto sovereign duchy of Lorraine. When Cardinal Fleury subsequently annexed Lorraine itself to the territory of France, the Guises thought the world was at an end. The universe, however, survived the shock.

Duke Charles died in exile at Cune, near Sienne, in the year 1640. Of his ten children by the Duchess de Joyeuse, he left five surviving. He was succeeded by Henri, the eldest, who was bishop and cardinal. He had been raised to the episcopate while yet in the arms of his wet-nurse; and he was in frocks when on his long curls was placed the scarlet hat of a cardinal. He was twenty years of age when he became Duke of Guise. He at once flung away all he possessed of his religious profession — its dress and titles, and walked abroad, spurs on his heels, a plume in his cap, and a long sword and a bad heart between!

The whole life of this chivalrous scoundrel was a romance, no portion of which reflects any credit on the hero. He had scarcely reached the age of manhood, when he entered into a contract of marriage with the beautiful Anne of Gonzaga. He signed the compact, not in ink, but with his own blood, calling Heaven to witness, the while, that he would never address a vow to any other lady. The breath of perjury had scarcely passed his lips when he married the Countess of Bossu, and he immediately abandoned *her* to sun himself in the eyes of Mademoiselle de Pons — an imperious mistress, who squandered the property he lavished on her, and boxed the ex-cardinal's ears, when he attempted, with degrading humility, to remonstrate with her for bringing down ruin upon his estate.

He was as disloyal to his King as to his "lady;" he tampered with rebellion, was sentenced to death, and was pardoned. But a state of decent tranquillity agreed ill with his constitution. To keep that and his nerves from rusting, he one day drew his sword in the street, upon the son of Coligny, whose presence seemed a reproach to him, and whom he slew on the spot. He wiped his bloody rapier on his mantle, and betook himself for a season to Rome, where he intrigued skilfully, but fruitlessly, in order to obtain the tiara for the brother of Mazarin. Apathy would now have descended upon him, but for a voice from the city of Naples, which made his swelling heart beat with a violence that almost threatened to kill.

Masaniello had just concluded his brief and mad career. The Neapolitans were not, on that account, disposed to submit again to Spain. They were casting about for a King, when Guise presented himself. This was in the year 1647. He left France in a frail felucca, with a score of bold adventurers wearing the colors of Lorraine, intertwined with "buff," in compliment to the Duke's mistress. The Church blessed the enterprise. The skiff sped unharmed through howling storms and thundering Spanish fleets; and when the Duke stepped ashore at Naples, and mounted a charger, the shouting populace who preceded him, burnt incense before the new-comer, as if he had been a coming god.

For love and bravery, this Guise was unequalled. He conquered all his foes, and made vows to all the ladies. In love he lost, however, all the fruits of bravery. Naples was but a mock Sardanapalian court, when the Spaniards at length mustered strongly enough to attack the new, bold, but enervated King. They took him captive, and held him, during four years, a prisoner in Spain. He gained liberty by a double lie, the common coin of Guise. He promised to reveal to the Court of Madrid the secrets of the Court of Paris; and bound himself by bond and oath never to renew his attempt on Naples. His double knavery, however, brought him no profit. At length, fortune seeming to disregard the greatness of his once highly-favored house, this restless reprobate gradually sunk into a mere court beau, passing his time in powdering his peruke, defaming reputations, and paying profane praise to the patched and painted ladies of the palace. He died before old age, like most of the princes of his house: and in his fiftieth year this childless man left his dignity and an evil name to his nephew, Louis Joseph.

The sixth Duke bore his greatness meekly and briefly. He was a kind-hearted gentleman, whose career of unobtrusive usefulness was cut short by small-pox in 1671. When he died, there lay in the next chamber an infant in the cradle. This was his little son Joseph, not yet twelve months old, and all unconscious of his loss, in a father; or of his gain, in a somewhat dilapidated coronet. On his young brow that symbol of his earthly rank rested during only four years. The little Noble then fell a victim to the disease which had carried off his sire, and made of himself a Duke — the last, the youngest, the most innocent, and the happiest of the race.

During a greater portion of the career of the Dukes, priest and swordsman in the family had stood side by side, each menacing to the throne; the one in knightly armor, the other in the dread panoply of the Church. Of the seven ducal chieftains of the house, there is only one who can be said to have left behind him a reputation for harmlessness; and perhaps that was because he lived at a time when he had not the power to be offensive. The boy on the mule, in 1506, and the child in the cradle, in 1676, are two pleasant extremes of a line where all between is, indeed, fearfully attractive, but of that quality also which might make not only men but angels weep.

It must be confessed that the Dukes of Guise played for a high prize; and lost it. More than once, however, they were on the very point of grasping the attractive but delusive prize. If they were so near triumph, it was chiefly through the co-operation of their respective brothers, the proud and able Cardinals. The Dukes were representatives of brute force; the Cardinals, of that which is far stronger, power of intellect. The former often spoiled their cause by being demonstrative. The latter never trusted to words when silver served their purpose equally well. When they *did* speak, it was with effective brevity. We read of a Lacedemonian who was fined for employing three words to express what might have been as effectually stated in two. No churchman of the house of Guise ever committed the fault of the Lacedemonian.

Cardinal John of Lorraine was the brother of the first Duke Claude. When the latter was a boy, riding his mule into France, John was the young Bishop-coadjutor of Metz. He was little more than two years old when he was first appointed to this responsible office. He was a Cardinal before he was out of his teens; and in his own person was possessed of twelve bishoprics and archbishoprics. Of these, however, he modestly retained but three, namely, Toul, Narbonne, and Alby — as they alone happened to return revenues worth acceptance. Not that he was selfish, seeing that he subsequently applied for, and received the Archbishopric of Rheims, which he kindly held for his nephew Charles, who was titular thereof, at the experienced age of ten. His revenues were enormous, and he was for ever in debt. He was one of the most skilful negotiators of his time; but whether deputed to emperor or pope, he was seldom able to commence his journey until he had put in pledge three or four towns, in order to raise money to defray his expenses. His zeal for what he understood as religion was manifested during the short but bloody campaign against the Protestants of Alsatia, where he accompanied his brother. At the side of the Cardinal, on the field of battle, stood the Apostolic Commissary, and a staff of priestly aides-de-camp. While some of these encouraged the orthodox troops to charge the Huguenots, the principal personages kept their hands raised to Heaven; and when the pennons of the army of Reformers had all gone down before the double cross of Lorraine, the Cardinal and his ecclesiastical staff rode to the church of St. Nicholas and sang *Te Deum laudamus*.

The chivalrous Cardinal was another man in his residence of the Hotel de Cluny. Of this monastery he made a mansion, in which a Sybarite might have dwelt without complaining. It was embellished, decorated, and furnished with a gorgeousness that had its source at once in his blind prodigality, his taste for the arts, and his familiar patronage of artists. The only thing not to be found in this celebrated mansion was the example of a good life. But how *could* this example be found in a prelate who assumed and executed the office of instructing the maids of honor in their delicate duties. Do Thou says it was an occupation for which he was pre-eminently fitted; and Brantome pauses, in his gay illustrations of the truth of this assertion, to remark with indignation, that if the daughters of noble houses arrived at court, endowed with every maiden virtue, Cardinal John was the man to despoil them of their dowry.

He was, nevertheless, not deficient in tastes and pursuits of a refined nature. He was learned himself, and he loved learning in others. His purse, when there was anything in it, was at the service of poor scholars and of sages with great purposes in view. He who deemed the slaughter of Protestant peasants a thing to thank God for, had something like a heart for *clever* sneerers at Papistry and also for Protestants of talent. Thus he pleaded the cause of the amphibious Erasmus, extended his protection to the evangelical Clement Marot, and laughed and drank with Rabelais, the caustic curé of Meudon. He was, moreover, the boon companion of Francis I., a man far less worthy of his intimacy than the equivocating Erasmus, the gentle Marot, or roystering Rabelais, who painted the manners of the court and church of his day, in his compound characters of Gargantua and Panurge.

He was a liberal giver, but he gave with an ostentation for which there is no warrant in the gospel. At one period of his life he walked abroad with a game-bag full of crowns slung from his neck. On passing beggars he bestowed, without counting, a rich alms, requesting prayers in return. He was known as the "game-bag Cardinal." On one occasion, when giving largesse to a blind mendicant in Rome, the latter was so astonished at the amount of the gift, that, pointing to the giver, he exclaimed, "If thou art not Jesus Christ, thou art John of Lorraine."

He was bold in his gallantry. When sent by Francis I. to negotiate some political business with the pope, he passed through Piedmont, where he was for a while the guest of the Duke and Duchess of Savoy. The duchess, on the cardinal being presented, gravely offered her hand (she was a Portuguese princess) to be kissed. John of Lorraine, however, would not stoop so low, and made for her lips. A struggle ensued, which was maintained with rude persistance on one side, and with haughty and offended vigor on the other, until her highness's head, being firmly grasped within his eminence's arm, the cardinal kissed the ruffled princess two or three times on the mouth, and then, with an exultant laugh, released her.

The second cardinal of this branch, Charles of Lorraine, was brother of the second duke. He was the greatest man of his family, and the most powerful of his age. His ambition was to administer the finances of France, and he did so during three reigns, with an annual excess of expenditure over income, of two millions and a half. He was rather dishonest than incapable. His enemies threatened to make him account; he silenced them with the sound of the tocsin of St. Bartholomew, and when the slaughter was over he merrily asked for the presence of the accusers who had intended to make him refund.

He was an accomplished hypocrite, and at heart a religious reformer. At last he acknowledged to the leaders of the reformatory movement, whom he admitted to his familiarity, that the Reformation was necessary and warrantable; and yet policy made of him the most savage enemy that Protestantism ever had in France. He urged on the king to burn noble heretics rather than the common people; and when Henri was touched with compassion, in his dying moments, for some Protestant prisoners capitally condemned, the cardinal told him that the feeling came of the devil, and that it was better they should perish. And they perished.

He introduced the Inquisition into France, and was made Grand Inquisitor at the moment the country was rejoicing for the recovery of Calais from the English. And this was the man who, at the Council of Trent, advocated the celebration of divine worship in the vernacular tongue. He was the friend of liberty to the Gallican church, but he took the other side on finding that liberal advocacy periled his chances of being pope. The living pope used and abused him. "I am scandalized," said his holiness, "at finding you still in the enjoyment of the revenues of so many sees." "I would resign them all," said the cardinal, "for a single bishopric." "Which bishopric?" asked the pope. "Marry!" exclaimed Cardinal Charles, "the bishopric of Rome."

He was as haughty as he was aspiring. The Guise had induced the weak Anthony of Navarre to turn Romanist; but the cardinal did not treat that king with more courtesy on that account. One frosty morning, not only did the princely priest keep the mountain king tarrying at his garden gate for an audience, but when he went down to his majesty, he listened, all befurred as he was, to the shivering monarch who humbly preferred his suit, cap in hand.

He was covetous and haughty, but he sometimes found his match. His niece, Mary Stuart, had quarreled with Catherine de Medicis, whose especial wrath had been excited by Mary's phrase applied to Catherine, of "The Florentine tradeswoman." The Scottish Queen resolved, after this quarrel, to repair to the North. The cardinal was at her side when she was examining her jewels, previously to their being packed up. He tenderly remarked that the sea was dangerous, the jewels costly, and that his niece could not do better than leave them in his keeping. "Good uncle," said the vivacious Mary, "I and my jewels travel together. If I trust one to the sea, I may the other; and therewith, *adieu!*" The cardinal bit his lips and blessed her.

Ranke is puzzled where to find the principal author of the massacre of St. Bartholomew. There is no difficulty in the matter. The Guises had appealed to the chances of battle to overcome their chief adversaries in the kingdom. But for every Huguenot father slain, there arose as many filial avengers as he had sons. The causes of quarrel were individual as well as general. A Huguenot had slain the second Duke, and his widow was determined to be avenged. The Cardinal was wroth with the King for retaining Protestant archers in his body-guard. The archers took an unclean vengeance, and defiled the pulpit in the Chapel Royal, wherefrom the Cardinal was accustomed to denounce the doctrine of their teachers. His Eminence formed the confederacy by which it was resolved to destroy the enemy at a blow. To the general causes, I need not allude. The plot itself was formed in Oliver Clisson's house, in Paris, known as "the Hotel of Mercy." But the representatives of Rome and Spain, united with those of France, met upon the frontier, and there made the final arrangements which were followed by such terrible consequences. When the stupendous deed was being done, the Cardinal was absent from France; but he fairly took upon himself the guilt, when he conferred the hand of his illegitimate daughter Anne d'Arne on the officer Besme whose dagger had given the *first* mortal stab to Coligny, the chief of the immolated victims of that dreadful day — and Rome approved.

As a public controversialist he shone in his dispute with Beza. Of his pride, we have an illustration in what is recorded of him in the Council of Trent. The Spanish embassador had taken a place, at mass, above that of the embassador from France. Thereupon, the reverend Cardinal raised such a commotion in the cathedral, and dwelt so loudly and strongly in expletives, that divine worship was suspended, and the congregation broke up in most admired disorder.

So at the coronation, in the Abbey of St. Dennis, of the Queen of Charles IX. The poor, frail, Austrian Princess Elizabeth, after being for hours on her knees, declared her incapacity for remaining any longer without some material support from food or wine. The Cardinal declared that such an irreligious innovation was not to be thought of. He stoutly opposed, well-fed man that he was, the supplying of any refreshment to the sinking Queen; and it was only when he reflected that her life might be imperiled that he consented to "the smallest quantity of something very light," being administered to her.

He was the only man of his family who was not possessed of the knightly virtue of bravery. He was greatly afraid of being assassinated. In council, he was uncourteous. Thus, he once accused the famous Chancellor le Hospital of wishing to be "the cock of the assembly," and when the grave chancellor protested against such language, the Cardinal qualified him as "an old ram." It may be added that, if he feared the dagger directed by private vengeance, he believed himself protected by the guardianship of Heaven, which more than once, as he averred, carried him off in clouds and thunder, when assassins were seeking him. He was wily enough to have said this, in order to deter all attempts at violence directed against himself.

He died edifyingly, kissed Catherine de Medicis, and was believed by the latter, to mysteriously haunt her, long after his death. The real footing on which these two personages stood has yet to be discovered by curious inquiries.

The Cardinal-brother of the third Duke, Louis of Lorraine,

loved good living, and was enabled at an early age to indulge his propensities, out of the rich revenues which he derived from his numerous ecclesiastical preferments. He held half a dozen abbeys while he was yet in his cradle; and he was a bishop at the mature age of eighteen. Just before his death, in 1598, when he was about fifty years of age, he resigned his magnificent chuich appointments, in favor of his nephew and namesake, who was to be a future Cardinal at the side of the fourth Duke. Louis was a man of ability and of wit. He chose a device for his own shield of arms. It consisted of nine zeros, with this apt motto: " Hoc per se nihil est; sed si minimum addideris, maximum erit," intending, it is said, to imply that man was nothing till grace was given him. He was kindly-dispositioned, loved his ease, was proud of his church, and had a passion for the bottle. That was his religion. His private life was not marked by worse traits than those that characterized his kinsmen in the priesthood. He showed his affection for his mother after a truly filial fashion, bequeathing to her all his estates, in trust, to pay his debts.

The third duke had a second cardinal-brother, known as the Cardinal de Guise, who was murdered by Henri III. He was an intriguer; but as brave as any knight of his family. It was long before the king could find men willing to strike a priest; and when they *were* found, they approached him again and again, before they could summon nerve wherewith to smite him. After all, this second murder at Blois was effected by stratagem. The cardinal was requested to accompany a messenger to the royal presence. He complied with some misgiving, but when he found himself in a dark corridor with four frowning soldiers, he understood his doom; requested a few moments respite to collect his thoughts; and then, enveloping his head in his outer robe, bade them execute their bloody commission. He was instantly slain, without offering resistance, or uttering a word.

This cardinal was father of five illegitimate sons, of whom the most celebrated was the Baron of Ancerville, or, as he proudly designated himself, "Bastard of Guise."

By the side of the son of Balafré, Charles, the fourth duke, there stood the last cardinal-brother who was able to serve his house, and whose character presents any circumstance of note. This cardinal, if he loved anything more than the bottle, was fondest of a battle. He characteristically lost his life by both. He was present at the siege of St. Jean d'Angely, held by the Protestants in the year 1621. It was on the 20th of May; and the sun was shining with a power not known to our severe springs. The cardinal fought like a fiend, and swore with more than fiendish capacity. The time was high noon, and he himself was in the noontide of his wondrous vigor, some thirty years of age. He was laying about him in the bloody *mêlée* which occurred in the suburb, when he paused for awhile, panting for breath and streaming with perspiration. He called for a flask of red wine, which he had scarcely quaffed when he was seized with raging fever, which carried him off within a fortnight. He was so much more addicted to knightly than to priestly pursuits, that, at the time of his death, a negotiation was being carried on to procure from the pope permission for the cardinal to give up to his lay-brother, the Duc de Chevreuse, all his benefices, and to receive in return the duke's governorship of Auvergne. He was for ever in the saddle, and never more happy than when he saw another before him with a resolute foe firmly seated therein. He lived the life of a soldier of fortune, or knight-errant; and when peace temporarily reigned, he rode over the country with a band of followers, in search of adventures, and always found them at the point of their swords. He left the altar to draw on his boots, gird his sword to his hip, and provoke his cousin De Nevers to a duel, by striking him in the face. The indignant young noble regretted that the profession of his insulter covered the latter with impunity, and recommended him, at the same time, to abandon it, and to give De Nevers satisfaction. "To the devil I have sent it already!" said the exemplary cardinal, "when I flung off my frock, and belted on my sword:" and the two kinsmen would have had their weapons in each other's throat, but for the royal officers, who checked their Christian amusement.

This roystering cardinal, who was interred with more pomp than if he had been a great saint, or a merely honest man, left five children. Their mother was Charlotte des Escar. They were recognised as legitimate, on allegation that their parents had been duly married, on papal dispensation. He was the last of the cardinals, and was as good a soldier as any of the knights.

Neither the pride nor the pretensions of the house expired with either Dukes or Cardinals. There were members of the family whose arrogance was all the greater because they were not of the direct line of succession. Their great ambition in little things was satisfied with the privilege granted to the ladies of Guise, namely, the one which they held in common with royal princesses, at being presented at court previous to their marriage. This ambition gained for them, however, the hatred of the nobles and the princes of the Church, and at length caused a miniature insurrection in the palace at Versailles.

The occasion was the grand ball given in honor of the nuptials of Marie Antoinette and the Dauphin. Louis XV. had announced that he would open the brilliant scene by dancing a *minuet* with Mlle. de Lorraine, sister of the Prince de Lambesc. The uproar that ensued was terrific. The entire body of nobility protested against such marked precedence being allowed to the lady in question. The Archbishop of Rheims placed himself at the head of the opposing movement; and, assembling the indignant peerage, this successor of the Apostles, in company with his episcopal brother from Noyon, came to the solemnly important resolution, that between the princes of the blood-royal and *haute noblesse* there could be no intermediate rank; and that Mlle. de Lorraine, consequently, could not take precedence of the female members of the aristocracy, who had been presented. A memorial was drawn up. The entire nobility, old and new, signed it eagerly; and the King was informed that if he did not rescind his determination, no lady would dance at the ball after the *minuet* in question had been performed. The King exerted himself to overcome the opposition: but neither bishops nor baronesses would give way. The latter, on the evening of the ball, walked about the grand apartments in undress, expressed loudly their resolution not to dance, and received archiepiscopal benison for their pious obstinacy. The matter was finally arranged by compromise, whereby the Dauphin and the Count d'Artois were to select partners among the nobility, and not, as was *de rigueur*, according to the law of *minuets*, among princesses of their own rank. The hour for opening the famous ball was retarded in order to give the female insurrectionists time to dress, and ultimately all went off *à merveille!*

With the Prince de Lambesc above-named, the race of Guise disappeared altogether from the soil of France. He was colonel of the cavalry regiment, *Royal Allemand*, which in 1789 came into collision with the people. The Prince was engaged, with his men, in dispersing a seditious mob. He struck one of the most conspicuous of the rioters with the flat of his sword. This blow, dealt by a Guise, was the first given in the great Revolution, and it helped to deprive Louis XVI. of his crown. The Prince de Lambesc was compelled to fly from the country, to escape the indignation of the people. Nearly three centuries before, his great ancestor, the boy of the mule, had entered the kingdom, and founded a family which increased in numbers and power against the throne, and against civil and religious liberty. And now, the sole survivor of the many who had sprung from this branch of Lorraine, as proud, too, as the greatest of his house, having raised his finger against the freedom of the mob, was driven into exile, to seek refuge for a time, and a grave for age, on the banks of the distant Danube.

When Cardinal Fleury annexed the Duchy of Lorraine to France, it was by arrangement with Austria; according to which, Francis, Duke of Lorraine, received in exchange for his Duchy, the Grand Duchy of Tuscany and the hand of Maria Theresa. Their heirs form the imperial house of Hapsburgh-Lorraine. Such of my readers as have visited Nancy, the capital of old Lorraine, will remember there the round chapel near what is left of the old palace of the old Dukes. This chapel contains the tombs of the principal of the twenty-nine Dukes who ruled sovereignly in Lorraine. The expense of supporting the service and fabric, altar and priests, connected with this chapel, is sustained entirely by Austria. It is the only remnant preserved of the Lorraine sovereignty of the olden time. The priests and *employes* in the edifice speak of Hapsburgh-Lorraine as *their* house, to which they owe exclusive homage. When I heard expression given to this sentiment, I was standing in front of the tomb of that famous etcher, old Jean Callot. The latter was a native of Nancy; and

I could almost fancy that his merry-looking lip curled with scorn at the display of this rag of pride in behalf of the house of Lorraine.

With the story of part of that house I fear I may have detained the reader too long. I will tell more briefly the shifting fortunes of a material house, the knightly edifice of Rambouillet.

## THE RECORD OF RAMBOUILLET.

"Imagine that this castle were your court,
And that you lay, for pleasure, here a space,
Not of compulsion or necessity."—KIT MARLOWE.

RAMBOUILLET is an old château where feudal knights once lived like little kings. In its gardens Euphuism reigned supreme. It is a palace, in whose chambers monarchs have feasted, and at whose gates they have asked, when fugitives, for water and a crust of bread. It commenced its career as a cradle of knights; it is finishing it as an asylum for the orphan children of warriors. The commencement and finale are not unworthy of one another; but, between the two, there have been some less appropriate disposals of this old chevalier's residence. For a short period it was something between Hampton Court and Rosherville. In the very place where the canons of the Sainte Chapelle were privileged to kiss the cheeks of the Duchess of Burgundy, the denizens of the Faubourg St. Antoine could revel, if they could only pay for their sport. Where the knightly D'Amaurys held their feudal state, where King Francis followed the chase, and the Chevalier Florian sang, and Penthièvre earned immortality by the practice of heavenly virtues; where Louis enthroned Du Barry, and Napoleon presided over councils, holding the destiny of thrones in the balance of his will, there the sorriest mechanic had, with a few francs in his hand, the right of entrance. The gayest *lorettes* of the capital smoked their *cigarettes* where Julia D'Angennes fenced with love; and the bower of queens and the refuge of an empress rang with echoes, born of light-heartedness and lighter wine. Louis Napoleon has, however, established a better order of things.

To a Norman chief, of knightly character, if not of knightly title, and to the Norman tongue, *Rabouillet*, as it used to be written, or the "Rabbit warren," owes the name given to the palace, about thirteen leagues from Paris, and to the village which clusters around it. The former is now a quaint and confused pile, the chief tower of which alone is now older than the days of Hugues Capet. Some authors describe the range of buildings as taking the form of a horseshoe; but the hoof would be indescribable to which a shoe so shaped could be fittingly applied. The changes and additions have been as much without end as without taste. In its present architectural entirety it wears as motley an aspect as Cœur de Lion might, were he to walk down Pall Mall with a modern *paletôt* over his suit of complete steel.

The early masters of Rambouillet were a knightly, powerful but uninteresting race. It is sufficient to record of the chivalric D'Amaurys that they held it, to the satisfaction of few people but themselves, from 1003 to 1317. Further record these sainted proprietors require not. We will let them sleep on undisturbedly, their arms crossed on their breast, in the peace of a well-merited oblivion. *Requiescat!*

One relic of the knightly days, however, survived to the period of the first French Revolution. In the domain of Rambouillet was the fief of Montorgueil. It was held by the prior of St. Thomas d'Epernon, on the following service: the good prior was bound to present himself yearly at the gate of Rambouillet, bareheaded, with a garland on his brow, and mounted on a piebald horse, touching whom it was bad service if the animal had not four white feet.

The prior, fully armed like a knight, save that his white gloves were of a delicate texture, carried a flask of wine at his saddlebow. In one hand he held a cake, to the making of which had gone a bushel of flour—an equal measure of wheat was also the fee of the lord. The officers of the latter examined narrowly into the completeness of the service. If they pronounced it imperfect the prior of Epernon was mulcted of the revenues of his fief for the year ensuing.

In later days the ceremony lost much of its meaning; but down to the period of its extinction, the wine, the cake, and the garland, were never wanting; and the maidens of Rambouillet were said to be more exacting than the baronial knights themselves, from whom many of them were descended. The festival was ever a joyous one, as became a feudal lord, whose kitchen fireplace was of such dimensions that a horseman might ride into it, and skim the pot as he stood in his stirrups.

It is a singular thing that scarcely a monarch has had anything to do with the knightly residence of Rambouillet, but mischance has befallen him. The kings were unjust to the knights, and the latter found for the former a Nemesis. Francis I. was hunting in the woods of Rambouillet when he received the news of the death of Henry VIII. that knight-sovereign, with whom he had struggled on the Field of the Cloth of Gold. With the news, he received a shock, which the decay sprung from various excesses could not resist. He entered the chateau as the guest of the Chevalier d'Angennes, in whose family the proprietorship then resided. The chamber is still shown wherein he died, roaring in agony, and leaving proof of its power over him, in the pillow, which, in mingled rage and pain, he tore into strips with his teeth.

The French author, Leon Gozlau, has given a full account of the extraordinary ceremonies which took place in honor of Francis after his death. In front of the bed on which lay the body of the king, says M. Gozlau, "was erected an altar covered with embroidered cloth; on this stood two gold candlesticks, bearing two lights from candles of the whitest wax. The cardinals, prelates, knights, gentlemen, and officers, whose duty it was to keep watch, were stationed around the *catafalque*, seated on chairs of cloth of gold. During the eleven days that the ceremony lasted, the strictest etiquette of service was observed about the king, as if he had been a living monarch in presence of his court. His table was regularly laid out for dinner, by the side of his bed. A cardinal blessed the food. A gentleman in waiting presented the ewer to the figure of the dead king. A knight offered him the cup mantling with wine: and another wiped his lips and fingers. These functions, with many others, took place by the solemn and subdued light of the funeral torches."

The after ceremonies were quite as curious and extraordinarily magnificent; but it is unnecessary to rest upon them. A king, in not much better circumstances than Francis, just before his death, slept in the castle for one night in the year 1588. It was a night in May, and the knight proprietor Jean d'Angennes, was celebrating the marriage of his daughter. The ceremony was interrupted by a loud knocking at the castle gates. The wary Jean looked first at the clamorous visitors through the wicket, whence he descried Henri III. flurried, yet laughing, seated in an old carriage, around which mustered dusty horsemen, grave cavaliers, and courtiers scantily attired. Some had their points untrussed, and many a knight was without his boots. An illustrious company, in fact; but there were not two nobles in their united purses. Jean threw open his portals to a king and his knights flying from De Guise. The latter had got possession of Paris, and Henri and his friends had escaped in order to establish the regal authority at Chartres. The two great adversaries met at Blois: and after the assassination of Guise, the king, with his knights and courtiers, gallopped gayly past Rambouillet on his return to Paris, to profit by his own wickedness, and the folly of his trusty and well-beloved cousin, the duke.

Not long before this murder was committed, in 1588, the Hotel Pisani in Paris was made jubilant by the birth of that Catherine de Vivonnes, who was at once both lovely and learned. She lived to found that school of lingual purists whose doings are so pleasantly caricatured in the *Precieuses Ridicules* of Molière. Catherine espoused that noble chevalier, Charles d'Angennes, Lord of Rambouillet, who was made a marquis for her sake. The chevalier's lady looked upon marriage rather as a closing act of life than otherwise; but then *hers* had been a busy youth. In her second lustre she knew as many languages as a *lustrum* has years. Ere her fourth had expired, her refined spirit and her active intellect were disgusted and weary with the continual sameness and the golden emptiness of the court. She cared little to render homage to a most Christian king who disregarded the precepts of Christianity; or to be sullied by homage from a monarch, which could not be rendered without insult to a virtuous woman. Young Catherine preferred, in the summer eve, to lie under the shadow of her father's trees, which once reared a world of leafy splendor on the spot now occupied by the Palais Royal. There she read works coined by great minds. During the long winter evenings she lay in stately ceremony upon her bed, an unseemly custom of the period, and there, surrounded by chevaliers, wits, and philosophers, enjoyed and encouraged the "cudgelling of brains." At her suggestion the old hotel was destroyed, and after her designs a new one built; and when, in place of the old dark panelling, obscurely seen by casements that kept out the light, she covered the walls of her reception-rooms with sky-blue velvet, and welcomed the sun to shine upon them, universal France admiringly pronounced her mad, incontinently caught the infection, and broke out into an incurable disease of fancy and good taste.

The fruit of the union above spoken of was abundant, but the very jewel in that crown of children, the goodliest arrow in the family quiver, was that Julie d'Angennes who shattered the hearts of all the amorous chevaliers of France, and whose fame has, perhaps, eclipsed that of her mother. Her childhood was passed at the feet of the most eminent men in France; not merely aristocratic knights, but as eminent wits and philosophers. By the side of her cradle, Balzac enunciated his polished periods, and Marot his tuneful rhymes, Voiture his conceits, and Vaugelas his learning. She lay in the arms of Armand Duplessis, *then* almost as innocent as the little angel who unconsciously smiled on that future ruthless Cardinal de Richelieu; and her young ear heard the elevated measure of Corneille's "Melite." To enumerate the circles which was wont to assemble within the Hôtel Rambouillet in Paris, or to loiter in the gardens and hills of the country château, whose history I am sketching, would occupy more space than can be devoted to such purpose. The circle comprised parties who were hitherto respectively exclusive. Knights met citizen wits, to the great edification of the former; and Rambouillet afforded an asylum to the persecuted of all parties. They who resisted Henry IV. found refuge within its hospitable walls, and many nobles and chevaliers who survived the bloody oppression of Richelieu, sought therein solace, and balm for their lacerated souls.

Above all, Madame de Rambouillet effected the social congregation of the two sexes. Women were brought to encounter male wits, sometimes to conquer, always to improve them. The title to enter was, worth joined with ability. The etiquette was pedantically strict, as may be imagined by the case of Voiture, who, on one occasion, after conducting Julie through a suite of rooms, kissed her hand on parting from her, and was very near being expelled for ever from Rambouillet, as the reward of his temerity. Voiture subsequently went to Africa. On his return, he was not admitted to the illustrious circle, but on condition that he narrated his adventures, and to these the delighted assembly listened, all attired as gods and goddesses, and gravely addressing each other as such. Madame de Rambouillet presided over all as Diana, and the company did her abundant homage. This, it is true, was for the nonce; but there was a permanent travesty notwithstanding. It was the weak point of this assembly that not only was every member of it called by a feigned, generally a Greek, name, but the same rule was applied to most men and things beyond it; nay, the very oaths, for there were little expletives occasionally fired off in ecstatic moments, were all by the heathen gods. Thus, as a sample, France was *Greece.* Paris was *Athens;* and the Place Royale was only known at Rambouillet as the *Place Dorique.* The name of Madame de Rambouillet was *Arthemise;* that of Mademoiselle de Scudery was *Aganippe;* and *Thessalonica* was the purified cognomen of the Duchess de Tremouille. But out of such childishness resulted great good, notwithstanding that Molière laughed, and that the Academie derided Corneille and all others of the innovating coterie. The times were coarse; things, whatever they might be, were called by their names; ears polite experienced offence, and at Rambouillet periphrasis was called upon to express what the language otherwise conveyed offensively by the medium of a single word. The idea was good, although it was abused. Of its quality some conjecture may be formed by one or two brief examples; and I may add, by the way, that the French Academy ended by adopting many of the terms which it at first refused to acknowledge. Popularity had been given to much of the remainder, and thus a great portion of the vocabulary of Rambouillet has become idiomatic French. "Modeste," "friponne," and "secrète," were names given to the under-garments of ladies, which we now should not be afraid to specify. The sun was the "amiable illuminator;" to "fulfil the desire which the chair had to embrace you," was simply to "sit down." Horses were "plushed coursers;" a carriage was "four cornices," and chairmen were "baptized mules." A bed was the "old dreamer;" a hat, the "buckler against weather;" to laugh was to "lose your gravity;" dinner was the "meridional necessity;" the ear was the "organ, or the gate of hearing;" and the "throne of modesty" was the polished phrase for a fair young cheek. There is nothing very edifying in all this, it is true; but the fashion set people thinking, and good ensued. Old indelicacies disappeared, and the general, spoken language was refined. If any greater mental purity ensued from the change, I can scarcely give the credit of it to the party at Rambouillet, for, with all their proclaimed refinement, their nicety was of the kind described in the well-known maxim of the Dean of St. Patrick.

One of the most remarkable men in the circle of Rambouillet, was the Marquis de Salles, Knight of St. Louis. He was the second son of the Duke de Montausier, and subsequently inherited the title. At the period of his father's death, his mother found herself with little dower but her title. She exerted herself, however, courageously. She instructed her children herself, brought them up in strict Huguenot principles, and afterward sent them to the Calvinistic college at Sedan, where the young students were famous for the arguments which they maintained against all comers —and they were many—who sought to convert them to popery. At an early age he acquired the profession of arms, the only vocation for a young and portionless noble; and he shed his blood liberally for a king who had no thanks to offer to a protestant. His wit, refinement, and gallant bearing, made him a welcome guest at Rambouillet, where his famous attachment to Julie, who was three years his senior, gave matter for conversation to the whole of France. Courageous himself, he loved courage in others, and his love for Julie d'Angennes, was fired by the rare bravery exhibited by her in tending a dying brother, the infectious nature of whose disorder had made even his hired nurses desert him. In the season of mourning, the whole court, led by royalty, went and did homage to this pearl of sisters. But no admiration fell so sweetly upon her ear as that whispered to her by the young Montausier. One evidence of his chivalrous gallantry is yet extant. It is in that renowned volume called the "Guirlande de Julie," of which he was the projector, and in the accomplishing of which, knights, artists, and poets, lent their willing aid. It is superb vellum tome. The frontispiece is the garland or wreath, from which the volume takes its name. Each subsequent page presents one single flower from this wreath (there are eighteen of them) with verses in honor of Julie, composed by a dozen and a half of very insipid poets. This volume was sold some years ago to Madame D'Uzes, a descendant of the family, when its cost amounted to nearly one thousand francs per page.

As everything was singular at Rambouillet, so of course was the wooing of Julie and her knight. It was very " long a-doing," and we doubt if in the years of restrained ardor, of fabulous constancy, of reserve, and sad yet pleasing anguish, the lover ever dared to kiss the hand of his mistress, or even to speak of marriage, but by a diplomatic paraphrase.

The goddesses of Rambouillet entertained an eloquent horror of the gross indelicacy of such unions, for which Molière has whipped them with a light but cutting scourge. The lover, moreover, was a Huguenot. What was he to do? Like a true knight he rushed to the field, was the hero of two brilliant campaigns, and then wooed her as knight of half-a-dozen new orders, marechal-du-camp, and Governor of Alsatia. The nymph was still coy. The knight again buckled on his armor, and in the mêlée at Dettingen was captured by the foe. After a two months' detention, he was ransomed by his mother, for two thousand crowns. He re-entered Rambouillet lieutenant-general of the armies of France, and he asked for the recompense of his fourteen years of constancy and patience. Julie was shocked, for she only thought how brief had been the period of their acquaintance. At length the marquis made profession of Romanism, and thereby purchased the double aid of the church and the throne. The king, the queen, Cardinal Mazarin, and a host of less influential members, besought her to relent, and the shy beauty at length reluctantly surrendered. The marriage took place in 1645, and Julie was then within sight of forty years of age. The young chevaliers and wits had, you may be sure, much to say thereupon. The elder *beaux esprit* looked admiringly; but a world of whispered wickedness went on among them, nevertheless.

Montausier, for he now was duke and knight of the Holy Ghost, became the reigning sovereign over the literary circle at Rambouillet, during the declining years of Julie's mother. Catherine died in 1665, after a long retirement, and almost forgotten by the sons of those whom she once delighted to honor. The most delicate and the most difficult public employment ever held by the duke, was that of governor to the dauphin. This office he filled with singular ability. He selected Bossuet and Huet to instruct the young prince in the theoretical wisdom of books, but the practical teaching was imparted by himself. Many a morning saw the governor and his pupil issue from the gilded gates of Versailles to take a course of popular study among the cottages and peasantry of the environs.

The heart of the true knight was shattered by the death of Julie in 1671, at the age of sixty-four. He survived her nineteen years. They were passed in sorrow, but also in continual active usefulness; and when, at length, in 1690, the grave of his beloved wife opened to receive him, Flechier pronounced a fitting funeral oration over both.

The daughter and only surviving child of this distinguished pair gave, with her hand, the lordship of Rambouillet to the Duc d'Uzes, "Chevalier de l'ordre du Saint Esprit." The knightly family of D'Angennes had held it for three centuries. It was in 1706 destined to become royal. Louis XIV. then purchased it for the Count of Toulouse, legitimatized son of himself and Madame de Montespan. This count was knight and Grand Admiral of France, at the age of five years. In 1704, he had just completed his twenty-fifth year. He is famous for having encountered the fleet commanded by Rook and Shovel, after the capture of Gibraltar, and for having what the cautious Russian generals call, "withdrawn out of range," when he found himself on the point of being utterly beaten. He behaved himself as bravely as any knight could have done; but the government was not satisfied with him. Pontchartrain, the Minister of Marine, recalled him, sent him to Rambouillet, and left him there to shoot rabbits, and like Diocletian, raise cabbages.

His son and successor, who was the great Duke de Penthièvre, commenced his knighthood early. He was even made Grand

Admiral of France before he knew salt water from fresh. He studied naval tactics as Uncle Toby and the corporal fought their old battles — namely, with toy batteries. In the duke's case, it was, moreover, with little vessels and small sailors all afloat in a miniature fish-pond, made to represent, for the nonce, the mighty and boundless deep. This grand admiral never ventured on the ocean, but he bore himself chivalrously on the bloody field of Dettingen, and he won imperishable laurels by his valor at Fontenoy. For such scenes and their glories, however, the *preux chevalier* cared but little. Ere the French *Te Deum* was sung upon the last-named field, he hastened back to his happy hearth at home. Rambouillet was then the abiding-place of all the virtues. There the home-loving knight read the Scriptures while the duchess sat at his side making garments for the poor. There, the Chevalier Florian, his secretary and friend, meditated those graceful rhymes and that harmonious prose, in which human nature is in pretty masquerade, walking about like Watteau's figures, in vizors, brocades, high heels, and farthingales. When the duchess died in child-birth, of her sixth child, her husband withdrew to La Trappe where, among other ex-soldiers, he for weeks prayed and slept upon the bare ground. Five out of his children died early. Among them was the chivalrous but intemperate Prince de Lamballe, who died soon after his union with the unhappy princess who fell a victim to those fierce French revolutionists — who were ordinarily so amiable, according to M. Louis Blanc, that they were never so delighted as when they could rescue a human being from death.

It was by permission of the duke, who refused to sell his house, that Louis XV. built in the adjacent forest the hunting-lodge of St. Hubert. An assemblage of kings, courtiers, knights and ladies there met, at whose doings the good saint would have blushed, could he have witnessed them. One night the glittering crowd had galloped there for a carouse, when discovery was made that the materials for supper had been forgotten, or left behind at Versailles. "Let us go to Penthièvre!" was the universal cry; but the king looked grave at the proposition. Hunger and the universal opposition, however, overcame him. Forth the famished revellers issued, and played a *reveillée* on the gates of Rambouillet loud enough to have startled the seven sleepers. "Penthièvre is in bed!" said one. "He is conning his breviary!" sneered another. "Gentlemen, he *is*, probably, at prayers," said the king, who, like an Athenian, could applaud the virtue which he failed to practise. "Let us withdraw," added the exemplary royal head of the order of the Holy Ghost. "If we do," remarked Madame du Barry, "I shall die of hunger; let us knock again." To the storm which now beset the gates, the latter yielded; and as they swung open, they disclosed the duke, who, girt in a white apron, and with a ladle in his hand, received his visiters with the announcement that he was engaged in helping to make soup for the poor. The monarch and his followers declared that no poor could be more in need of soup than they were. They accordingly seized the welcome supply, devoured it with the appetite of those for whom it was intended, and paid the grave knight who was their host, in the false coin of pointless jokes. How that host contrasted with his royal guest, may be seen in the fact told of him, when a poor woman kissed his hand, and asked a favor as he was passing in a religious procession. "In order of religion before God," said he, "I am your brother. In all other cases, for ever your friend." The Order of the Holy Ghost never had a more enlightened member than he.

In 1785 Louis XVI. in some sort compelled him to part with Rambouillet for sixteen million of francs. He retired to Eu, taking with him the bodies of the dead he had loved when living. There were nine of that silent company; and as the Duke passed with them on his sad and silent way, the clouds wept over them, and the people crowded the long line of road, paying their homage in honest tears.

Then came that revolutionary deluge which swept from Rambouillet the head of the order of the Holy Ghost, and the entire chapter with him; and which dragged from the mead and the dairy the queen and princesses, whose pastime it was to milk the cows in fancy dresses. The Duke de Penthièvre died of the Revolution, yet not through personal violence offered to himself. The murder of his daughter-in-law, the Princess de Lamballe, was the last fatal stroke; and he died forgiving her assassins and his own.

During the first Republic there was nothing more warlike at Rambouillet than the merino flocks which had been introduced by Louis XVI. for the great benefit of his successors. A scene of some interest occurred there in the last days of the empire.

On the 27th of March, 1814, the empress Maria Louisa with the King of Rome in her arms, his silver-gray jacket bearing those ribboned emblems of chivalry which may still be seen upon it at the Louvre, sought shelter there, while she awaited the issue of the bloody struggle which her own father was maintaining against her husband. The empress passed three days at Rambouillet, solacing her majestic anguish by angling for carp. Ultimately, the Emperor of Austria entered the hall where his imperial son-in-law had made so many Knights of the Legion of Honor, to carry off his daughter and the disinherited heir. As the three sat that night together before the wood-fire, the Arch-Duchess Maria-Louisa talked about the teeth of the ex-king of Rome, while two thousand Austrian soldiers kept watch about the palace.

The gates had again to be open to a fugitive. On the last of the "three glorious days" of July a poor, pale, palsied fugitive rushed into the château, obtained, not easily, a glass of water and a crust, and forthwith hurried on to meet captivity at last. This was the Prince de Polignac. Two hours after he had left came the old monarch Charles X., covered with dust, dropping tears like rain, bewildered with past memories and present realities, and loudly begging for food for the two "children of France," the offspring of his favorite son, the Duke de Berri. In his own palace a king of France was compelled to surrender his own service of plate, before the village would sell him bread in return. When refreshed therewith, he had strength to abdicate in favor of his son, the Duke d'Angoulême, who at once resigned in favor of his nephew the Duke de Bordeaux; and this done, the whole party passed by easy stages into an inglorious exile. With them was extinguished the Order of the Holy Ghost; and never since that day have the emblematic dove and star been seen on the breast of any knight in France.

Louis Philippe would fain have appropriated Rambouillet to himself; but the government assigned it to the nation, and let it to a phlegmatic German, who had an ambition to sleep on the bed of kings, and could afford to pay for the gratification of his fancy. It was on the expiration of his lease that the house and grounds were made over to a company of speculators, who sadly desecrated fair Julie's throne. The present sovereign of France has given it a worthy occupation. It is now an asylum and a school for the children of the brave. It began as the cradle of knights; and the orphans of those who were as brave as any of the chevaliers of old now find a refuge at the old hearth of the Knights of Amaury.

I can well conclude, that, by this time, my readers may be weary of foreign scenes and incidents, as we are of real personages. May I venture then, for the sake of variety, to ask them to accompany me "to the well-trod stage, anon?" There I will treat, to the best of my poor ability, of Stage Knights generally; and first, of the greatest of them all—Sir John Falstaff.

## SIR JOHN FALSTAFF.

"I accept that heart
Which courts my love in most familiar phrase."—HEYWOOD.

HENRY, Earl of Richmond, always creates a favorable impression on young people who see him, for the first time, without knowing much about him, previously, at the end of Shakespeare's tragedy of Richard the Third. This is a far higher degree of favor than he merited, for Henry was a very indifferent personage indeed. On the other hand Sir John Falstaff has had injustice done him by the actors; and of Shakespeare's jolly old *gentleman* they have made what, down to Macklin's times, they made of Shylock, a mere mountebank.

In the very first scene, in the first part of Henry IV., when the Prince and Sir John appear in company, the knight is, by far, a more accomplished gentleman than the heir-apparent, for he speaks more refinedly of phrase, and indeed seldom indulges in scurrilous epithets, until provoked. Strong language is the result of his infirmity of nature, not of vicious inclination. Lord Castlereagh was not accounted the less a gentleman for using, as he *could* do, very unsavory phrases occasionally.

The Prince is the first to rail, while Sir John shows his breeding and, I will add, his reading, by quoting poetry. But, if he is poetical, still more is he philosophical. How gravely does he beseech Hal to trouble him no more with vanity! And what a censure does the heavy philosopher fling at the King's son, when he tells the latter that he was hurt to hear the wise remarks of a lord of the council touching that son's conduct! The fault of the knight is, that he is easily led away into evil; a common weakness with good-natured people. It is only since he held fellowship with the Prince, that the fat follower of the latter had become knowing in evil, and Heaven help him, little better, as he says, than one of the wicked. Nay, he has enough of orthodoxy left to elicit praise, even from the editor of the *Record.* "O, if a man were to be saved by merit," he exclaims, "what hole in hell were hot enough to hold him!"

He robs on the highway, it will be said. Well, let us not be too ready to doubt his gentility on that account. There was many a noble cut-purse in the grand gallery at Versailles, when it was most crowded; and George Prince of Wales once nearly lost the diamond-hilt of his sword, at one of his royal mother's "drawing-rooms." The offenders here were but petty-larceny rascals, compared with Falstaff on the highway. That he defrauded the King's exchequer is, certainly, not to be denied. But again, let us not be too hasty to condemn good men with little foibles. Recollect that St. Francis de Sales very often cheated at cards.

Robbery on the highway was, after all, only, as I may call it, a rag of knighthood. Falstaff robbed in good company. It was his vocation. It was the fashion. It was an aristocratic pastime. Young blood would have it so; and Sir John was a boy with the boys. In more recent times, your young noble, of small wit and too ample leisure, flings stale eggs at unsuspecting citizens, makes a hell of his quarters, if he be military, and breaks the necks of stage-managers.

Sir John was, doubtless, one of those of whom Gadshill speaks as doing the robbing profession some grace for mere sport's sake. "I am joined," says Gadshill, "with no foot land-rakers, no long-staff sixpenny strikers, none of those mad mustachio, purple-hued, malt-worms, but with nobility, and sanguinity; burgomasters, and great mongers." Indeed, it is matter of fact that, there were graver, if not greater men than these among the noble thieves, "who would, if matters were looked into, for their own credit-sake, make all whole." There was one at least who, for being a highway robber, made none the worse justice, charged to administer halters to poorer thieves.

But let us return to our old friend. Poor Sir John, I doubt if he would have gone robbing, even in the Prince's company, only that he was bewitched by his Royal Highness's social qualities.

But even then, while patiently enduring all sorts of hard jokes, he is really the Mentor of the party, and does not go to rob the travellers without first seriously reminding the gentlemen of the road, that it was a hanging matter. He would keep them from wrong, but as they are resolved on evil commission he accompanies them. He has explained the law, and he is not too proud to share the profits.

He is brave, too, despite all his detractors! When the Prince and Poins, in disguise, set upon the gentle robbers, as they are sharing their booty, Falstaff is the only one who is described as giving "a blow or two," before he imitates "the rest," and runs away. When he attacked the travellers he was content to fight his man; there were four to four. And as to the imaginative description of the assault given by Falstaff, I believe it to have been uttered in joke and gayety of heart. I have implicit faith in the assertion, that he knew the disguised parties as well as their mothers did. See how readily he detects the Prince and Poins, when they are disguised as "drawers" at the inn in Eastcheap. If Falstaff was right in the latter case, when he told the Prince that he, Falstaff, was a gentleman, I think, too, he had as sufficient authority for saying to Hal, "Thou *knowest* I am as valiant as Hercules." I can not believe otherwise of a man whose taste was so little vitiated that he could at once detect when there was "lime" in his sack, and who no sooner hears that the state is in danger, than he suggests to the young Prince that he *must* to court. His obesity may be suspected as not being the fruit of much temperance, but there is a Cardinal Archbishop in England who is the fattest man in the fifty-two counties, and why may we not conclude in both cases, that it is as Falstaff says, and that sighing and grief blow up a man like a bladder?

Then, only consider the reproof which Falstaff addresses to the Prince, speaking in the character of King to that illustrious scapegrace. Wisdom more austere, or graver condemnation of excess, could hardly be uttered by the whole college of cardinals, at any time. The prince is a mere plagiarist from the knight, and when he accuses the latter of being given to licentious ways, with what respectful humility does the old man plead guilty to his years, but "saving your reverence," not to the vices which are said to accompany them?

Not that he is perfect, or would boast of being so. "He *has had*," he says touchingly, "a true faith and a good conscience, but their date is out." How ill is he requited by the Prince, in whose service he has lost these jewels, when his Highness remarks, before setting out to the field, "I'll procure this fat rogue a charge of foot, and I know his death will be a charge of fourscore." And this is said of one who has forgotten what the inside of a church is like through keeping this Prince's villanous company; till when, he had been "as virtuously given as a gentleman need be." What he considers as the requisite practice of a gentleman, is explained by Falstaff in his low estate, and not in the spirit which moved him when he "lived well and in good compass."

But there is a Nemesis at every man's shoulder, and if Falstaff was cavalierly careless enough to run up a score at the Boar's Head, and to accept even a present of Holland shirts, which he ungratefully designates as "filthy dowlas," the way in which he was *dunned* must have been harsh to the feelings of a knight and a gentleman. In reviewing his gallantries and his extravagances, we must not, in justice to him, forget that he was a bachelor. If he degraded himself, he inflicted misery on no Lady Falstaff at home. Heroes have been buried, with whole nations for mourners, whose offences in this worse respect have been forgotten. Not that I would apologise for the knight's familiarity with either the Hostess or that remarkably nice young lady, Miss Dorothea Tearsheet. I do not know what the private life of that Lord Chief Justice may have been who was so very merciless in his censure upon the knight; but I do know that there have been luminaries as brilliant who have hidden their lights in very noisome places and who had not Falstaff's excuse.

I am as little embarrassed touching Sir John's character as a soldier, as I am about his morals. I do not indeed like to hear him acknowledge that he has "misused the King's press most damnably," or that he has pocketed "three hundred and odd pounds" by illegally releasing a hundred and fifty men. But at this very day practices much worse than this are of constant observance in the Russian service, where officers and officials, whose high-sounding names "exeunt in off," rob the Czar daily, and are decorated with the Order of St. Catherine.

In the field, I maintain that Falstaff is a hero. As for his catechism on honor, so far from detracting from his reputation, it seems to me to place him on an equality with that modern English hero who said that his body trembled at the thought of the perils into which his spirited soul was about to plunge him. Falstaff did not *court* death. "God keep lead out of me," is his reasonable remark; "I need no more weight than mine own bowels!" But the man who makes this prayer and comment was not afraid to encounter death. "*I have led* my ragamuffins where they are peppered." He went then at their head. That there was hot work in front of him is proved by what follows. "There's but three of my hundred and fifty left alive; and they are for the town's end, to beg during life!" A hundred and forty-seven men killed out of a hundred and fifty-one; of the four who survived, three are illustriously mutilated; while the bold soul who led them on is alone unscathed! Why, it reminds us of Windham and the Redan. It is Thermopylæ, with Leonidas surviving to tell his own story.

His discretion is not to be taken as disproving his valor. He fought Douglas, remember, and did not run away from him. He found the Scot too much for him, it is true; and quietly dropped down, as if dead. What then? When the Muscovite general fell back so hurriedly from Eupatoria, how did he describe the movement? "Having accomplished," he said, "all that was expected, the Russians *withdrew out of range.*" So, Sir John, with respect to Douglas.

Nor would *some* Muscovite officers and gentlemen object to another action of Falstaff's. The knight it will be remembered with regret, stabs the body of Hotspur, as the gallant Northumbrian lies dead, or wounded, upon the field. Now, by this we may see that Russia is not only some four centuries behind us in civilization. The barbarous act of Falstaff was committed a score of times over on the field of Inkerman. Many a gallant, breathing, but helpless English soldier, received the mortal thrust which they could not parry, from the hands of the Chevalier Ivan Falstaff, who fought under the doubtful inspiration of St. Sergius. And, moreover, there were men in authority there who virtually remarked to these heroes what Prince Henry does to Sir John,

> "If a lie may do thee grace,
> I'll gild it with the happiest terms I have."

That *our* Falstaff bore himself with credit on the field, is made clear in spite of the incident of Hotspur. I do not pause to point out the bearing of Morton's answer, when Northumberland asks him, "Didst thou come from Shrewsbury?"—"I *ran* from Shrewsbury, my noble lord," is the reply; confessing that he ran from a foe, among whom Falstaff was a leader: I am more content to rest on the verdict of so dignified yet unwilling a witness as the Lord Chief Justice. It is quite conclusive. "Your day's service at Shrewsbury," says my lord, "hath a little gilded over your night's exploit at Gadshill." Nothing can be more satisfactory. The bravery of Falstaff was the talk of the town.

When peace has come, or that Sir John has received permission to return home, on urgent private affairs, he enters a little into dissipation, it is true. He is not, however, guilty of such excess as to materially injure his health; otherwise his page would not have brought him so satisfactory a message from his doctor. He may, perhaps, be also open to the charge of being too easily taken by such white bait as he might find in the muslin of Eastcheap. Heroes, however, have usually very inflammable hearts. When Nelson was ashore, he immediately fell in love.

In spite of a trifle of rioting, the overflowing of animal spirits, Falstaff is governed by the laws of good society. Jokes are fired at him incessantly, but he takes them with good-humor, and repays them with interest. "I am not only witty in myself," he says, "but the cause that wit is in other men." Gregoire and La Bruyere expressly define the great rule of conversation to be that, while you exhibit your own powers, you should endeavor to elicit and encourage those of your companions. What they put down as a canon, Sir John had already, and long before, put in excellent practice. He had wit enough to foil the Chief Justice, but he left to his lordship ample opportunity to exhibit his own ability; and then the compliment to the great judicial dignitary, that he was not yet clean past his youth, although he had in him some relish of the saltness of time—this, combined with the benevolent recommendation that his lordship would have a reverend care of his health, robs the latter personage of any prejudice he might have entertained against the knight. Indeed, it would be difficult to conceive how the religiously-minded Lord Chief Justice could have entertained prejudice against a gallant old gentleman who had lost his voice with "hollaing" (his men to the charge), "and singing of anthems."

Brave! there can be no question touching his bravery. And if he does really rust a little at home, and impose a little upon the weakness of the Hostess and other ladies, whom he weekly woos to marry, and who find his gallantry and saucy promises irresistible; he is ever ready for service. He does not look for unlimited absence from scenes of danger. If he led his company of three hundred and a half to death, and comes out scot-free himself, he is by no means prepared to hang about town, inactive for the remainder of the campaign. When he is appointed on perilous enterprise with Prince John of Lancaster, he simply remarks, with a complacency which is doubtless warranted by truth, "There is not a dangerous action can peep out his head, but I am thrust upon it. Well, I can not last for ever;" and, with this remark buckled on to some satirical wit which he points at the Lord Chief Justice, he sets forth cheerily on his mission, the gout in his toe, and in his purse not more than seven groats and twopence. He has a rouse and a riot at the Boar's Head before he starts; but nothing more disreputable seems to have occurred than one might hear of at a modern club, before some old naval lion is hiccupped on to deeds of daring. Besides, the knight is no hypocrite; and he will not be accounted virtuous, like many of his contemporaries, by "making courtesy and saying nothing." Not, on the other hand, that even in his moments of jolly relaxation, he would be unseemly noisy. He can troll a merry catch, but, as he says to a vulgarly roystering blade, "Pistol, I would be quiet." It has been thought unseemly that he should quarrel with and even roughly chastise the "ancient" with whom he had been on such very intimate terms. But such things happen in the best society. At the famous Reform Club dinner, Sir James gave permission to Sir Charles to go and make war; but, since that time, Sir Charles, with words, instead of rapiers, has been poking his iron into the ribs of Sir James, after the fashion of Falstaff and Pistol.

And so, as I have said, Sir John girds him for the battle. If he did in his youth, hear the chimes at midnight, in company with

Master Shallow, the lean, but light-living barrister of Clement's Inn, he did not waste his vigor. So great indeed is his renown for this, and for the bravery which accompanies it, that no sooner does the doughty Sir John Colville of the Dale meet him in single combat, than Colville at once surrenders. The very idea of such a hero being face to face with him impels him to give up his sword at once. "I think you are Sir John Falstaff, and in that thought yield me." Was ever greater compliment paid to mortal hero?

Of this achievement Prince John most ungenerously says, that it was more the effect of Colville's courtesy than Falstaff's deserving. But, as the latter remarks, the young sober-blooded boy of a prince does not love the knight; and "that's no marvel," exclaims Falstaff, "he drinks no wine." The teetotaler of those days disparaged the deeds of a man who increased the sum of his country's glory. He was like a sour Anglo-Quaker, sneering down the merit of a Crimean soldier. We do not, however, go so far as Falstaff in his enthusiasm, when he exclaims that skill in the weapon is nothing without sack. There is something in the remark, nevertheless, as there is when Sir John subsequently says in reference to his wits suffering by coming in dull contact with obtuse Shallow. "It is certain," says he, "that either wise bearing or ignorant carriage is caught, as men take diseases, one of another; *therefore* let men take care of their company." Victor Hugo has manifestly condescended to plagiarize this sentiment, and has said in one of his most remarkable works, that "On devient vieux à force de regarder les vieux."

And, to come to a conclusion, how unworthily is this gallant soldier, merry companion, and profound philosopher, treated at last by an old associate, Prince Hal, when king. Counting on the sacredness of friendship, Sir John had borrowed from Master Shallow a thousand pounds. He depended upon being able to repay it out of the new monarch's liberality, but when he salutes the sovereign — very imopportunely, I confess — the latter, with a cold-hearted and shameless ingratitude, declares that he does not know the never-to-be-forgotten speaker. King Henry V. does indeed promise —

"For competence of life, I will allow you;
That lack of means enforce you not to evil;"

and departs, after intimating that the knight must not reside within ten miles of court, and that royal favor will be restored to the banished man, if merit authorize it.

"Be it your charge, my lord, to see performed the tenor of our word," says the King to the Chief Justice; and Falstaff, though sorely wounded in feelings, is still not without hope. But see what a royal word, or what *this* royal word is! The Monarch has no sooner passed on his way, than the Chief Justice fulfils its meaning, by ordering Sir John Falstaff and all his company to be close-confined in the Fleet! The great dignitary does this with as much hurried glee as we may conjecture Lord Campbell would have had, in rendering the same service to Miss Agnes Strickland, when the latter accused the judge of stealing her story of Queen Eleanor of Provence.

However this may be, the royal ingratitude broke the proud heart in the bosom of Sir John. He took to his bed, and never smiled again. "The King has killed his heart," is the bold assertion of Dame Quickly, at a time when such an assertion might have cost her her liberty, if not her life. How edifying too was his end! He did not "babble o' green fields." Mr. Collier has proved this, to the satisfaction of all Exeter Hall, who would deem such light talk trifling. But he died arguing against "the whore of Babylon," which should make him find favor even with Dr. Cumming, for it is a proof of the knight's Protestantism — and "Would I were with him," exclaims honest lieutenant Bardolph, with more earnestness than reverence — "Would I were with him, wheresome'er he is; either in heaven or in hell." If this has a profane ring in it, let us think of the small education and the hard life of him who uttered it. There was more profanity and terrible blasphemy to boot, in the assertion of Prince Menschikoff, after the death of the Czar Nicholas, namely, "that his late august master might be seen in the skies blessing his armies on their way to victory!" Decidedly, I prefer Bardolph to Menschikoff, and Falstaff to both.

I am sorry that Queen Elizabeth had the bad taste to request Shakespeare to represent "Falstaff in love." The result is only an Adelphi farce in five acts; in which the author, after all, has made the knight far more respectable than that sorry fool, Ford.

The "Wives" themselves are not much stronger in virtue than
Dorothea of Eastcheap, unless Sir John himself was mistaken in
them. Of Mrs. Ford, who holds her husband's purse-strings, he
says, "I can construe the action of her familiar style," and he tells
us what that manner was, pretty distinctly. When he writes to
Mrs. Page, he notices a common liking which exists in both, in
the words, "You love sack, and so do I." The "Wives," for mere
mischief's sake, we will say, tempted the gallant old soldier. In
their presence he had left off swearing, praised woman's modesty,
and gave such orderly and well-behaved reproof to all uncomeli-
ness, that Mrs. Page thought, perhaps, that drinking sack, and, in
company with Mrs. Ford, talking familiarly with him, would not
tempt him to turn gallant toward them. This consequence *did*
follow; and then the sprightly Wives, in place of bidding their ridiculous husbands cudgel him, come to the conclusion that "the
best way was to entertain him with hope," till his wickedly raised
fire should have "melted him in his own grease." A dangerous
process, ladies, depend upon it!

Then, what a sorry cur is that Master Ford who puts Falstaff
upon the way to seduce his own wife! Had other end come of it
than what did result, is there a jury even in Gotham, that would
have awarded Ford a farthing's-worth of separation. Falstaff is
infinitely more refined than Ford or Page. Neither of these
noodles could have paid such sparkling compliments as the knight
pays to the lady. "Let the court of France show me such another! I see how thine eyes would emulate the diamond; thou hast
the right-arched bent of the brow, that becomes the ship-tire, the
tire-valiant, or any tire of Venetian admittance!" Why this is a
prose Anacreontic! And if the speaker of it could offend once,
he did not merit to be allured again by hope to a greater punishment than he had endured for his first offence.

For one of the great characteristics of Falstaff is his own sense
of seemliness. When he was nearly drowned by being tossed
from the buck-basket into the river, his prevalent and uneasy idea
was, how disgusting he should look if he were to swell—a mountain of mummy! The Mantelini of Mr. Dickens borrowed from
Falstaff this aversion to a "demmed damp body." It is *not*
pleasant!

Once again, Sir John, though he could err, yet he was ashamed of his offence. Otherwise, would he have confessed, as he did, when recounting how the mock fairies had tormented him, "I was three or four times in the thought they were not fairies, but the *guiltiness of my mind,* the sudden surprise of my powers drove the grossness of the foppery into a received belief." How exquisitely is this said! How does it raise the knight above the broad farce of most of the other characters! How infinitely superior is he to the two dolts of husbands who, after hearing the confession of guilty intention against the honor of their wives, invite him to spend a jolly evening in company with themselves and the ladies. And so they —

> "Every one go home,
> And laugh this sport o'er by a wintry fire,
> Sir John and all."

This may be accounted too gross for probability; but worse than this is in the memory of our yet surviving fathers. There was, within such a memory, a case tried before Sir Elijah Impey, in which Talleyrand was the defendant, against whom a husband brought an action, the great statesman having robbed him of his wife. The action was brought to the ordinary issue; and a few weeks subsequently, plaintiff, defendant, judge, and lady, dined together in the Prince's residence at Paris.

Of Stage Falstaffs, Quin, according to all accounts, must have been the best, provided only that he had a sufficiency of claret in him, and the house an overflowing audience. Charles Kemble, I verily believe, must have been the worst of stage Falstaffs. At least, having seen him in the character, I can conscientiously assert that I can not imagine a poorer Sir John. He dressed the character well; but as for its "flavor," it was as if you had the two oyster-shells, *minus* the fat and juicy oyster. What a galaxy of actors have shined or essayed to shine in this joyous but difficult part! In Charles the Second's days, Cartwright and Lacy, by their acting in the first part of Henry IV., made Shakespeare popular, when the fashion at Court was against him. Betterton acted the same part in 1700, at Lincoln's Inn Fields and the Haymarket. Four years later, he played the Knight in the "Merry Wives;" and in 1730, at Drury Lane, he and Mills took the part alternately, and set dire dissension among the play-goers, as to their respective merits.

Popular as Betterton was in this character, after he had grown too stout for younger heroes, his manner of playing it was not original; and his imitation was at second-hand. Ben Jonson had seen it played in Dublin by Baker, a stone-mason. He was so pleased with the representation, that he described the manner of it, on his return to London, to Betterton, who, docile and modest as usual, acknowledged that the mason's conception was better than his own, and adopted the Irish actor's manner, accordingly.

Chetwood does not tell us how Baker played, but he shows us how he studied, namely in the streets, while overlooking the men who worked under him. "One day, two of his men who were newly come to him, and were strangers to his habits, observing his countenance, motion, gesture, and his talking to himself, imagined their master was mad. Baker, seeing them neglect their work to stare at him, bid them, in a hasty manner, mind their business. The fellows went to work again, but still with an eye to their master. The part Baker was rehearsing was Falstaff; and when he came to the scene where Sir Walter Blunt was supposed to be lying dead on the stage, gave a look at one of his new paviors, and with his eye fixed upon him, muttered loud enough to be heard, 'Who have we here? Sir Walter Blunt! There's honor for you.' The fellow who was stooping, rose on the instant, and with the help of his companion, bound poor Baker hand and foot, and assisted by other people no wiser than themselves, they carried him home in that condition, with a great mob at their heels."

Estcourt's Falstaff was flat and trifling, yet with a certain waggishness. That of Harper was droll, but low and coarse. The Falstaff of Evans seems to have been in the amorous scenes, as offensive as Dowton in Major Sturgeon; and the humor was misplaced. Accordingly, when we read in old Anthony Aston, that " Betterton wanted the waggery of Estcourt, the drollery of Harper, and the lasciviousness of Jack Evans," we are disposed to imagine that his Falstaff was none the worse for this trial of wants.

Throughout the eighteenth century, the character did not lack brilliant actors. In the first part of Henry IV., Mills played the character, at Drury, in 1716. Booth had previously played it for one night, in presence of Queen Anne. Bullock filled Lincoln's Inn Fields Theatre, with it, in 1721. Quin, in 1738, used to play the character in the two parts of Henry IV. on successive nights, and eight years later his Falstaff attracted crowds to "the Garden." Barry played it against him at Drury, in 1743 and 1747; but Barry was dull and void of impulse as a school-boy repeating his task. In 1762, the part, at Drury, fell to Yates, for whom the piece was brought out, with the character of Hotspur omitted! To give more prominence to our knight, a scene was left out. The public did not approve of the plan, for in the same year Love, celebrated by Churchill for his humor, made his first appearance at Drury, as Sir John, when Holland, the baker of Chiswick, played Hotspur, with well-bred warmth. I will add, that though Quin drew immense houses, yet when Harper, some years previously, played the same part at Drury, with Booth in Hotspur, Wilks as the Prince, and Cibber as Glendower, the combined excellence drew as great houses for a much longer period. So that Harper's Falstaff, although inferior to Quin's, was, as was remarked, more seen, yet less admired by the town. Shuter played it almost too "jollily" at the Garden, in 1774. But all other Falstaffs were extinguished for a time, when Henderson, although not physically qualified for the part, astonished the town with his "old boy of the castle," in 1777 at the Haymarket, and delighted them two years later, at Covent Garden. At the latter house, eight years subsequently, Ryder played it respectably, to Lewis's Prince of Wales; and in 1791, when the Drury Lane company were playing at the Haymarket, Palmer represented Falstaff, and John Kemble mis-represented Hotspur. King tried the knight at the same "little house," in 1792, but King, clever as he was, was physically incapable of representing Falstaff, and he soon ceased to pretend to do so. The next representative was the worst the world had yet seen—namely, Fawcett, who first attempted it at the Garden, in 1795. Blisset appeared in it in 1808, and disappeared also. From this time no new actor tried the Sir John, in the first part of Henry IV., till 1824, when Charles Kemble made the Ghost of Shakespeare very uneasy, by executing a part for which he was totally unfit. He persevered, however, but the success of Elliston in the part, two years later, settled the respective merits of two performers, to the advantage of Robert William, as effectually as Grisi showed the town that there was but one Norma, by playing it the night after the fatal attempt made on the Druidess, by Jenny Lind.

The succession of actors who represented Falstaff, in the second part of Henry IV., was as brilliant as that of the line of representatives above noticed. Ten years after Betterton and Mills, in 1720, we have Harper, and it is somewhat singular that when Mills resigned Falstaff to Harper, he took the part of the King. Hulett, two years subsequently played it at Covent Garden; and, after another two years, Quin made Drury ecstatic with his fun. He held the part without a real rival, and fifteen years later, in 1749, he was as attractive as ever in this portion of the knight's character, at Covent Garden. Shuter succeeded him in the part at this theatre, in 1755; but in 1758, all London, that is the playgoers of London, might be seen hurrying once more to Drury, to witness lively Woodward's *very* old Falstaff played to Garrick's King. The Garden can not be said to have found a superior means of attraction, when Shuter again represented Sir John, at the Garden, in 1761, on which occasion the parts of Shallow and Silence were omitted! The object, however, was to shorten the piece, and the main attraction was in the coronation pageant, at the conclusion, in honor of the then young King and Queen, who were well worthy of the honor thus paid to them.

Love and Holland, who played Falstaff and Hotspur, at Drury Lane, in 1762, played the Knight and the Prince of Wales, at the same house, two years subsequently. Nine years after this, the Garden found a Prince in Mrs. Lessingham, Shuter played Falstaff to her, but the travesty of the former character was only in a slight degree less incongruous than that made by Mrs. Glover, in the present century, who once, if not twice, played the fat knight, for her own benefit. For the next eight or nine years, the best Falstaff possessed by London was Henderson. He played the part first at Drury, and afterward at Covent Garden. Since Quin, there had been no better representative of Sir John; and even Palmer, in 1788, could not bring the town from its allegiance to " admirable Henderson."

The Falstaffs of the present century, in the second part of this historical play, have not achieved a greater triumph than Henderson. Cooke, who played the obese cavalier, in 1804, was not equal to the part; and Fawcett, in 1821, when the play was revived, with another coronation pageant in honor of George IV., was farther from success than Cooke. The managers at this period were wiser than those who "got up" the play at the period of the accession of George III., for they retained Shallow and Silence, and never were the illustrious two so inimitably represented as, on this occasion, by Farren and Emery.

The chief Falstaffs of the "Merry Wives of Windsor" are Betterton (1704), Hulett (1732), Quin (1734), Delane, the young Irish actor (1743), of whom Garrick was foolish enough to be jealous; Shuter (1758), Henderson, who first played it at the Haymarket in 1777, and Lee Lewis in 1784. Bartley, Phelps, and a clever provincial actor, now in London, named Bartlett, have also played this character with great effect. The Falstaff of the last-named actor is particularly good.

I have said that Quin was the greatest of Falstaffs, but the *greatest* in the physical acceptation of the term, was undoubtedly Stephen Kemble. This actor was born almost upon the boards. His clever, but not very gentle-tempered mother, had just concluded her performance of Anne Bullen, in a barn, or something like it, at Kingstown, Herefordshire (1758), when Stephen was born, about the period when, according to the action of the play, the Princess Elizabeth is supposed to first see the light. Stephen when he had grown to manhood, weighed as much as all his sisters and brothers put together; and on the 7th of October, 1802, he made his appearance at Drury, in the character of Falstaff. This was nearly twenty years after he had made his *début* in London, at Covent Garden, in Othello. Bannister junior prefaced his performance of the companion of Prince Hal, by some humorous lines, joking on the heaviness of the actor. As Pope played Hotspur, I should fancy, if Pope then was anything like what he was some fifteen or sixteen years later, that Hotspur was even heavier than Sir John. The lines alluded to were accounted witty; and I will conclude my record of the principal actors who have represented the knight, by reproducing them.

> A Falstaff here to-night, by nature made,
> Lends to your fav'rite bard his pond'rous aid;
> No man in buckram, he! no stuffing gear,
> No feather-bed, nor e'en a pillow here!
> But all good honest flesh and blood, and bone,
> And weighing, more or less, some thirty stone.
> Upon the northern coast by chance we caught him,
> And hither, in a broad-wheeled wagon, brought him:
> For in a chaise the varlet ne'er could enter,
> And no mail-coach on such a fare would venture.
> Blessed with unwieldiness, at least his size
> Will favor find in every critic's eyes.
> And should his humor and his mimic art
> Bear due proportion to his outward part,
> As once was said of Macklin in the Jew,
> "This is the very Falstaff Shakespeare drew."
> To you, with diffidence, he bids me say,
> Should you approve, you may command his stay,
> To lie and swagger here another day.
> If not, to better men he'll leave his sack,
> And go, as ballast, in a collier back.

In concluding this section of my gossiping record, I will add that the supposition of Shakespeare having intended to represent Sir John Oldcastle under the title of Sir John Falstaff, is *merely* a supposition. It has never been satisfactorily made out. Far otherwise is the case with that gallant Welsh man-at-arms, *Fluellin*. The original of this character was a David Gam of Brecknock, who having killed a cousin with an unpronounceable name, in the High Street of Brecknock, avoided the possibly unpleasant consequences by joining the Lancastrian party. *Gam* was merely a nickname, having reference to an obliquity of vision in the doughty and disputative David. The real name was Llewellyn; and if Shakespeare disguised the appellation, it was from notions of delicacy, probably, as the descendants of the hero were well known and respected at the English court in Shakespeare's time. Jones, in his "History of Brecknockshire," identifies the personage in question in this way: "I have called Fluellin a burlesque character, because his pribbles and prabbles, which were generally out-heroded, sound ludicrously to an English as well as a Welsh ear; yet, after all, Llewellyn is a brave soldier and an honest fellow. He is admitted into a considerable degree of intimacy with the King, and stands high in his good opinion, which is a strong presumptive proof, notwithstanding Shakespeare, the better to conceal his object, describes the death of Sir David Gam, that he intended David Llewellyn by his portrait of the testy Welshman, for there was no other person of that country in the English army, who could have been supposed to be upon such terms of familiarity with the King." It is singular that the descendants of the Welsh knight subsequently dropped the proud old name with more l's in it than syllables, and adopted the monosyllabic *soubriquet*. Squinting David, who fought so well at Agincourt, would have knocked down any man who would have dared to address him personally as " Gam," that is, " game," or " cock-eyed." His posterity proved less susceptible; and Mr. Jones says of them, in a burst of melancholy over fallen greatness: " At different periods between the years 1550 and 1700, I have seen the descendants of the hero of Agincourt (who lived like a wolf and died like a lion) in the possession of every acre of ground in the county of Brecon; at the commencement of the eighteenth century, I find one of them common bellman of the town of Brecknock, and before the conclusion, two others, supported by the inhabitants of the parish where they reside; and even the name of Gam is, in the legitimate line, extinct." Mr. Jones might have comforted himself by remembering that as the Gams went out, the Kembles cames in, and that the illustrious Sarah dignified by her birth the garret of that " Shoulder of Mutton" public-house, which stood in the street where chivalrous but squinting Davy had slain his cousin with the unpronounceable name.

John Kemble occasionally took some unwarrantable liberties with Shakespeare. When he produced the "Merry Wives of Windsor" at Covent Garden, in April, 1804 (in which he played Ford to Cooke's Falstaff), he deprived Sir Hugh Evans of his knightly title, out of sheer ignorance, or culpable carelessness. Blanchard was announced for " Hugh Evans," without the *Sir*. Hawkins, quoting Fuller, says that " anciently in England, there were more Sirs than Knights;" and as I have noticed in another page, the monosyllabic Sir was common to both clergymen and knights. To the first, however, only by courtesy, when they had attained their degree of B. A. In a " New Trick to cheat the

Devil," Anne says to her sire, "Nay, sir;" to which the father replies—

"Sir me no sirs! I am no knight nor churchman."

But John Kemble was complimentary to Shakespeare, compared with poor Frederick Reynolds, who turned the "Merry Wives of Windsor into an opera, in 1824; and although Dowton did not sing Falstaff, as Lablache subsequently did, the two wives, represented by Miss Stephens and Miss Cubitt, warbled, instead of being merry in prose, and gave popularity to "I know a bank." At the best, Fenton is but an indifferent part, but Braham was made to render it one marked especially by nonsense. Greenwood had painted a scene representing Windsor under *a glowing summer sky*, under which *Fenton* (Braham) entered, and remarked, very like Shakespeare: "How I love this spot where dear Anne Page has often met me and confessed her love! Ha! I think the *sky is overcast*—the wind, too, blows like an approaching storm. Well, let it blow on! I am prepared to brave its fury." Whereupon the orchestra commenced the symphony, and Mr. Braham took a turn up the stage, according to the then approved plan, before he commenced his famous air of "Blow, blow, thou *winter* wind!" And the fun-anent Falstaff and the Fords was kept waiting for nonsense like this!

While on the subject of the chivalrous originals of the mock knights of the Stage, I may be permitted to mention here, that Jonson's Bobadil was popularly said to have been named after, if not founded upon, a knight in the army of the Duke of Alva, engaged in subduing the Netherlands beneath the despotism of Philip II. According to Strada, after the victory at Giesen, near Mons, in 1570, Alva sent Captain Bobadilla to Spain, to inform Philip of the triumph to his arms. "The ostentation of the message, and still more of the person who bore it, was the origin of the name being applied to any vain-glorious boaster." The Bobadilla family was an illustrious one, and can hardly be supposed to have furnished a member who, in any wise, resembles Jonson's swashbuckler. On the other hand, there was Boabdil, the last sultan of Granada, who had indeed borne himself lustily, in his early days, in the field, but who at last cried like a child at losing that Granada which he was not man enough to defend. But it would be injustice even to the son of Muley Abel Hassan, to imagine that Jonson only took his name to distinguish therewith the knight of huge words and weapons who lodged with Oliver Cob the Waterbearer.

The few other Stage Knights whom I have to name, I will introduce them to the reader in the next chapter.

## STAGE KNIGHTS.

> "The stage and actors are not so contemptful
> As every innovating puritan,
> And ignorant swearer, out of jealous envy,
> Would have the world imagine."— GEORGE CHAPMAN.

THE Commonwealth had no admiration for the stage, and no toleration for actors. When theatricals looked up again, the stage took its revenge, and seldom represented a puritan who was not a knave. There is an instance of this in the old play, entitled "The Puritan, or the Widow of Watling Street." "Wilt steal me thy master's chain?" quoth Captain Idle to Nicholas St. Antlings, the puritan serving-man. "Steal my master's chain!" quoth Nicholas; "no, it shall ne'er be said that Nicholas St. Antlings committed bird-lime. Anything else that I can do," adds the casuist in a serge jerkin, "had it been to rob, I would ha' done it; but I must not steal, that's the word, the literal, *Thou shalt not steal;* and would you wish me to steal then?" "No, faith," answers Pyeboard, the scholar; "that were too much;—but wilt thou nim it from him?" To which honest St. Nicholas, so anxious to observe the letter of the law, so careless about its spirit, remarks, with alacrity, "*That,* I will!"

I have said in another page, that ridicule was especially showered down upon some of those whom Oliver delighted to honor. As late as the era of Sir George Etherege, we find "one of Oliver's knights" figuring as the buffoon of that delicate gentleman's comedy, "The Comical Revenge." It is hardly creditable to the times, or to the prevailing taste, that the theatre in Lincoln's-inn Fields cleared one thousand pounds, in less than a month, by this comedy; and that the company gained more reputation by it, than by any preceding piece represented on the same stage. The plot is soon told. Two very fine and not very profligate gentlemen, Lord Beaufort and Colonel Bruce, are in love with a tolerably-refined lady, Graciana. The lord wins the lady, and the philosophical soldier accepts a certain Aurelia, who has the singular merit of being in love with the Colonel. The under-plot has "Oliver's knight" for its hero. The latter is a Sir Nicholas Cully who is cheated out of a promissory note for one thousand pounds, by two gentlemen-sharpers, Wheadle and Palmer. Sir Nicholas is partly saved by the gay, rather than moral, Sir Frederick Frolick. The latter recovers the note, but he passes off his mistress on Sir Nicholas as his sister, and induces him to marry her. The only difference between the sharpers and the "Knight baronet," Sir Frederick, is this:— Wheadle had dressed up *his* mistress, Grace, as as Widow Rich; and Sir Nicholas had engaged to marry her, under certain penalties, forced on him by Wheadle and his friend. Sir Frederick, at the conclusion, marries the Widow, to oblige a lady who is fond of him, and the curtain falls upon the customary indecent jokes, and the following uneasy and metrical maxim :—

> "On what small accidents depends our Fate,
>   While Chance, not Prudence, makes us fortunate."

What the two Bettertons made of Lord Beaufort and Graciana, I do not pretend to say, but Nokes is said to have been "screamingly farcical," to adopt an equivalent modern phrase, in Sir Nichlas Cully. His successor, Norris, fell short of the great original in broad humor, but Nokes himself was surpassed by Dogget, who played "Oliver's Knight" with all the comic effect which he imparted to the then low comedy part of Shylock. It is inexplicable to me how any actor would ever have extracted a laugh from the audience at anything he had to say, or chose to do, when enacting the "Cavalier of the Commonwealth." There is not a humorous speech, nor a witty remark, nor a comic situation for the knight to profit by. In 1664, however, people could laugh heartily at seeing one of the Protector's knights swindled, and beaten on the stage. The knight is represented as a thirsty drunkard, "all the drier for the last night's wetting," with a more eager desire to attack the ladies of cavaliers than cavaliers themselves, and no reluctance to cheat any man who will undertake to throw a main with him at dice. He has, however, great reluctance to pay his losses, when he unconsciously falls into the hands of a greater knave than himself, and bodily declares—

> "I had been a madman to play at such a rate,
> If I had ever intended to pay."

He had less boldness in accepting the results of such a declaration, and in meeting his antagonist at the end of a rapier. He is brought to the sticking-point, just as Acres is, by an assurance that his adversary is an arrant coward. The scene of "the Field" is worth quoting in part, inasmuch as it is not only an illustration of the spirit of chivalry, as imputed to Oliver's knights by cavalier-poets, but also as it will, perhaps, serve to show that when Sheridan sat down at his table in Orchard Street, Portman Square, to bring Acres and Beverley together in mortal combat, he probably had a copy of Etherege's play before—or the memory of it strong within—him.

Wheadle and Cully are on the stage:—

*W.* What makes you so serious?

*C.* I am sorry I did not provide for both our safeties.

*W.* How so?

*C.* Colonel Hanson is my neighbor, and very good friend. I might have acquainted him with the business, and got him, with a file of musketeers, to secure us all.

*W.* But this would not secure your honor. What would the world have judged.

*C.* Let the world have judged what it would! Have we not had many precedents of late? and the world knows not what to judge.

It may be observed here, that Sir Nicholas may be supposed to be alluding to such men as Hans Behr, who was much addicted to firing printed broadsides at his adversaries, who advertised him as "*poltroon*" in return. There are some placards having reference to this matter, in the British Museum, which admirably display the caution of the wordsmen and the spirit of the swordsmen of that day. But to resume. Cully, observing that his adversary has not arrived, suggests that his own duty has been fulfilled, and that he "will be going," the more particularly, says the knight, as "the air is so bleak, I can no longer endure it."

*W.* Have a little patience. Methinks I see two making toward us in the next close.

*C.* Where? Where? 'Tis them!

*W.* Bear up bravely, now, like a man.

*C.* I protest I am the worst dissembler, now, in cases of this nature.

*W. Allons!* Look like a man of resolution. Whither, whither go you?

*C.* But to the next house to make my will, for fear of the worst. Tell them I'll be here again, presently.

The provident knight is, however, detained, and on Palmer and that gentleman's second appearing, the swords are measured, "and all strip but Cully, who fumbles with his doublet."

*P.* Come, sir! are you ready for this sport?

*C.* By-and-by, sir. I will not rend the buttons from my doublet for no man's pleasure.

And so "Oliver's Knight" continues to procrastinate; he can not be either pricked or pinked into action; and at length, pleading that his conscience will not let him fight in a wrong cause, he purchases a whole skin, at the price of a promissory note for a thousand pounds.

I have said that there is no comic situation for the actor who represents Sir Nicholas, but the scene from which the above passages are taken may, perhaps, be an exception to the rule. That Sheridan has profited by it, will be clear to any reader who will take the trouble to compare this scene with the fighting scene in the "Rivals." The latter is far richer in humor, and while we care very little what becomes of Sir Nicholas, we should regret that any harm should befall poor Acres—although he prefers fighting at forty paces, would stand sidewise to be shot at, feels that he would be horribly afraid if he were alone, and confesses that valor oozes out at the palms of his hands when his adversary appears in sight, with pistols for two.

Sir Nicholas is in spirits again when making love to one whom he considers a woman of rank and fortune. No cavalier could then vie with him in finery. "I protest," he says, "I was at least at sixteen brokers, before I could put myself exactly in the fashion." But with all this, he is a craven again when he is called upon to enter and address her who awaits the wooing with impatience. "Come!" he exclaims, "I will go to the tavern and swallow two whole quarts of wine instantly; and when I am drunk, ride on a drawer's back, to visit her." Wheadle suggests that "some less frolic will do, to begin with."—"I will cut three drawers over the pate, then," says the knight, "and go with a tavern-lanthorn before me at noonday;"—just as very mad gallants were wont to do.

The liquor has not the effect of rendering Oliver's knight decent, for in proposing the health of "my lord's sister," he does it in the elegant form of "Here's a brimmer to her then, and all the fleas about her;" offers to break the windows to show his spirit, and in the lady's very presence exclaims, "Hither am I come to be drunk, that you may see me drunk, and here's a health to your flannel petticoat." The latter *gentillesse* is by way of proof of the knight's quality, for it was of the very essence of polite manners, when a spirited gentleman drank to a spirited lady, to strain the wine through what the Chesterfields and Mrs. Chapones of that day, if such were to be found, would not have blushed to call "their smocks."

But enough of the way in which the stage represented "one of Oliver's knights." He is not worse than the courtiers and gentlemen by whom he is swindled out of his money and into a wife. Nay, nearly the last sentence put into his mouth is, at least, a complimentary testimony to the side of which Sir Nicholas is but an unworthy member. "If I discover this," he remarks, "I am lost. I shall be ridiculous even to our own party."—The reader will, probably, not require to be reminded that before Etherege drew Cully, Jonson had depicted Sogliardo, and that the latter, in the very spirit of Oliver's knight, remarks:—"I do not like the humor of challenge; it may be accepted."

The stage, from about the middle of the seventeenth century to nearly the middle of the succeeding century, was uncommonly busy with knights as heroes of new plays. The piece which brought most money to the theatrical treasury, after the "Comical Revenge," was the "Sir Martin Mar-all," an adaptation by Drydren, from the "Etourdi" of Molière. Such adaptations were in fashion, and the heroes of the French author were invariably knighted on their promotion to the English stage. Such was the case with "Sir Solomon, or the Cautious Coxcomb," adapted by

Carill, from Molière's "Ecole des Femmes." The same course was adopted by Mrs. Behn when she transferred Molière's "Malade Imaginaire" to the stage at Dorset Gardens, and transformed *Argon* into *Sir Patient Fancy*. One of the characters in this intolerably indecent play instructs the city knight's lady how to divide her time according to the fashion set by "the quality." "From eight to twelve," he says, "you ought to employ in dressing. Till two, at dinner. Till five, in visits. Till seven, at the play. Till nine, in the park; and at ten, to supper with your lover."

In the "Sir Barnaby Whig, or No Wit like a Woman's," one of D'Urfey's comedies, and produced in 1681, we have again a hero who is described as one of Oliver's knights. The play is avowedly a party piece, and the author, in his prologue, remarks,

> "That he shall know both parties now, he glories;
> By hisses, Whigs; and by their claps, the Tories."

The audience at the "Theatre Royal," in the days of Charles II., was made especially merry by this poor jest. Sir Barnaby is represented as a Cromwellian fanatic, who will not drink the King's health; is in an agony of terror at hearing that an army of twenty thousand men is about to sweep every rebel from the land; turns traitor; sings a comic song against the Roundheads; is saluted as Rabbi Achitophel; offers to turn Roman Catholic or Mohammedan; and is finally consigned to Newgate.

Mrs. Behn, in the same year, had *her* political knight as well as D'Urfey. In this lady's more than usually licentious play, the "City Heiress," performed at Dorset Gardens, she has a Sir Timothy Treat-all for her comic hero. She boasts in her introduction that her play is political, loyal, true Tory all over; and as "Whiggism has become a jest," she makes a caricature of Sir Timothy, an old, seditious, Oliverian knight, who keeps open house for commonwealth-men and true-blue Protestants. He is contrasted with two Tory knights, Sir Anthony and Sir Charles Meriwill, and a Tory gentleman, named Wilding. The old Whig knight, however, is by far the least disreputable fellow of the lot. The Tory knights and their friends are rogues, perjurers, and something worse. When they are not on the stage, Mrs. Behn is not afraid to tell what they are about, and *that* in the very plainest language. "D—n the City!" exclaims the courtly Sir Charles. "Ay, ay!" adds his uncle, Sir Anthony, "and *all* the Whigs, Charles, d—n all the Whigs!"—And in such wise did Mrs. Afra Behn take vengeance upon political enemies, to the infinite delight of loyal audiences. How the Whig knights ever kept their own against the assaults made on them in plays, prologues, and epilogues, is, as Mr. Slick says, "a caution!" It is a fact, however, that these political plays were far more highly relished than those which merely satirized passing social follies. Audiences roared at the dull jokes against the Oliverian knights, but they had no relish for the rhyme-loving Sir Hercules Buffoon, of Lacy.

For one stage knight we may be said to be indebted to Charles II. himself. It was from a hint from him that Crowne wrote his "Sir Courtly Nice," produced at the Theatre Royal shortly after the death of Charles. Sir Courtly alludes to the death of one, and the accession of a new, king, in very flattering terms:—

> "What nation upon earth, besides our own,
> But by a loss like ours had been undone?
> Ten ages scarce such royal worth display
> As England lost and found in one strange day."

Of all the comedies with knights for their heroes, this one of Sir Courtly Nice retained a place longest on the stage. The hero was originally played by handsome, but hapless Will Mountfort. Cibber played it at the Haymarket in Queen Anne's time, 1706, and again at Drury Lane, and before George I. at Hampton Court. Foote and Cibber, jun., and Woodward, were there presentatives of the gallant knight, and under George II. Foote played it, for the first time, at Drury Lane, and the younger Cibber at Covent Garden, in 1746, and Woodward, at the latter house, in 1751. The last-named actor was long the favorite representative of the gentlemanly knight, retaining the character as his own for full a quarter of a century, and being succeeded, but not surpassed in it, by sparkling Lewis, at Covent Garden, in 1781.

The satire in this piece against the Puritans is of a more refined character than in any other play of the period; and the contrast between the rash and ardent cavalier and the cautious Puritan is very fairly drawn. "Suppose I see not many vices, says the Roundhead, Testimony, "morality is not the thing. The heathens had morality; and, forsooth, would you have your footman or your coachman to be no better than Seneca?" This is really complimentary to the Cromwellians; and there is but a good-natured dash of satire in the answer of Testimony, when asked what time of day it may be, that—"Truly, I do believe it is about four. I can not say it positively, for I would not tell a lie for the whole world."

I find little worthy of notice in other dramatic pieces having knights for their heroes. Southeran produced one entitled, "Sir Anthony Love" at the Theatre Royal in 1691, for the purpose of showing off Mrs. Mountfort as an errant lady in male attire.

In the eighteenth century, the knights gave name to a few historical pieces not worth recording. The only exceptions are scarcely worthy of more notice. Dodsley's "Sir John Cockle at Court" made our ancestors, of George the Second's time, laugh at the sequel of the "King and the Miller of Mansfield;" and "Sir Roger de Coverley" was made the hero of a pantomime at Covent Garden in 1746. By this time, however, the fashion was extinct of satirizing living politicians under knightly names. To detail the few exceptions to the rule would only fatigue the perhaps already wearied reader.

To what a low condition knight and squire could fall may be seen in the Sir Joseph Wittol and Captain Bluffe, in Congreve's comedy, the "Old Batchelor." The only redeeming point about this disreputable pair is, that, cowards and bullies as they are, they have both read a little. The Captain has dipped into history, and he remarks that "Hannibal was a pretty fellow in his day, it must be granted; but, alas, sir! were he alive now, he would be nothing; nothing on the earth." Sir Joseph, the knight, *in comitatu Bucks*, has also indulged in a little reading, but that of a lighter sort than the Captain's. When the gallant Captain affects not to be frightened at the aspect of Sharper, and exclaims, "I am prepared for him now, and he shall find he might have safer roused a sleeping lion," the knight remarks, "Egad, if he should hear the lion roar, he'd cudgel him into an ass, and his primitive braying. Don't you remember the story in Æsop's Fables, Bully?

Egad, there are good morals to be picked out of Æsop's Fables, let me tell you that; and 'Reynard the Fox' too;" to which the deboshed Captain can only reply, " D—n your morals !" as though he despised fiction when compared with history.

Some of the stage knights are wonderfully great boasters, yet exceedingly dull fellows. I do not know that in the mouth of any one of them there is put so spirited a remark as the great Huniades made to Ulderick, Count of Sicily. The latter asked for a conference with the great governor of Hungary. Huniades bade him come to the Hungarian camp. The offended Ulderick, in a great chafe, replied that it was beneath him to do such a thing, seeing that he was descended from a long line of princely ancestors; whereas Huniades was the first of his family who had ever been raised to honor. The Hungarian very handsomely remarked, " I do not compare myself with your ancestors; but *with you!*" This has always appeared to me as highly dramatic in spirit. There is nothing half so spirited in the knightly pieces brought on the stage during the reign of George III., and which caused infinite delight to very easily-pleased audiences. It is well known that the good-natured Sovereign of England, although unassuming in his domestic character, was exceedingly fond of display in public ceremonies. He used to arrange the paraphernalia of an installation of the Garter with all the energy and care of an anxious stage-manager. The people generally were as anxious to have an idea of the reality. On one occasion, in the preceding reign, they so nearly forced their way into the banqueting-room, where the knights were holding festival, that the troops fired over their heads in order to frighten them into dispersing. Under George III. they were more content to view these splendors through a dramatic lens.

In 1771, accordingly, the splendors of the then late installation of the Garter were reproduced on the stage, in a masque, called " The Institution of the Garter, or Arthur's Round Table Restored." The show was as good as the piece was bad. The former was got up to profit the managers, the latter to flatter or do homage to the King and Queen. It was at once cumbersome and comic. A trio of spirits opened the delectable entertainment by summoning other spirits from every nook and corner of the skies, the moon's horns included, to the work of escorting the car of the Male Genius of England, the husband probably of Britannia, down to earth. Nothing can exceed the alacrity with which the spirits and bards of the empyreal heaven obey the summons. They descend with the car of the Genius, singing a heavy chorus, ponderous as the chariot they help to "waft down,"—in which, not the chariot, but the chorus, there is the assurance that

> "The bliss that spotless patriots feel
> Is kindred to the bliss above,"—

so that we may hope, though we can not feel certain, that there are some few persons here below, who are not unconscious of an antepast of heaven.

The Genius is a civil and polished personage, who with due remembrance to metropolitan fogs, very courteously apologizes to the spirits, that he has been the cause of bringing them down

> "To this grosser atmosphere awhile."

After such celestial compliments as these, he despatches them to shed heavenly influences over Windsor, while he remains to hold a little colloquy with the Druids, "Britain's old philosophers," as he calls them. He adds an assertion that may, probably, have startled the Society of Antiquaries of that day, namely, that the aforesaid Druids—

> "Still enamored of their ancient haunts,
> Unseen of mortal eyes, do hover round
> Their ruined altars and their sacred oaks,"

which may account for that loose heterodoxy which marked the period when Druids exercised these unseen influences.

The Genius requests the Druids to have the kindness to repair to Windsor, where the order is in the act of being founded by Edward, and there direct his choice in the selection of members. This is a very heathenish idea, but Druids and Bards are alike delighted at it; for, as the Genius remarks, Edward's perspicuity, his intellectual eyes, needed charming

> "from the mists
> It haply hath contracted from a long
> Unebbing current of prosperity."

The heathen priests are flaming patriots, and express their eagerness to leave Heaven for England, seeing that the new order may be the means to propagate

> "The sovereignty of England, and erect
> Her monarchs into judges of mankind."

As this expressed end has not been accomplished, and the order has not propagated the sovereignty of England, we may logically conclude that the Druids themselves hardly knew much of the subject upon which they were singing to their tuneless harps. Meanwhile, the first Bard, in a bass song, petitions the south gales to blow very mildly, and bring blue skies and sweet smells to the installation.

The ceremony of the installation then opens to the view when all the knights have been created, except the King's son, Edward the Black Prince, who really was not created knight when the order was founded. How far the Druids have succeeded in influencing the choice of the King, there is no possibility of knowing. No one utters a word, save royal father and son: and the commonplace prose which they deliver does not give us a very exalted idea of the Druidic inspiration. The old sages themselves, however, are perfectly satisfied with the result; and in a noisy chorus, they make an assertion which might well have frightened the Archbishop of Canterbury—had he cared about the matter. After vaticinating that the name of the Prince should roll down through the tide of ages, they add, that glory shall fire him, and virtue inspire him,

> "Till blessed and blessing,
> Power possessing,
> From earth to heaven he lifts his soul,"—

a feat which one would like to see put upon canvass by a Pre-Raphaelite.

While the Knights are supposed to be preparing to pass to the hall, the scene takes us to the front of the castle, where crowds of liege and loyal people are assembled. First Citizen, "very like a whale indeed," sings a comic song, which, as a specimen of the homage offered to monarch and consort, more than fourscore years ago, is worth transcribing—for both its imagery and syntax:—

> "Oh, the glorious installation!
> Happy nation!
> You shall see the King and Queen:
> Such a scene!
> Valor he, sir;
> Virtue she, sir;
> Which our hearts will ever win.
> Sweet her face is,
> With such graces
> Show what goodness dwells within.
>
> "Oh, the glorious installation!
> Happy nation!
> You shall see the noble knights:
> Charming sights!
> Feathers wagging,
> Velvet dragging,
> Trailing, sailing, on the ground;
> Loud in talking,
> Proud in walking,
> Nodding, ogling, smirking round."

The banquet over, and more comic business, as dreary as the song above quoted, being concluded, King Edward walks forth into the garden for refreshment—and there the Genius of England takes him by the hand. Edward, we are sorry to say, knows so little of this Genius, that he boldly asks him, "What art thou, stranger?" We should, only with reluctance, trouble our readers with all this unrecognised Genius says in reply to the royal inquirer, but one passage may be transcribed to show what the popular spirit was thought to be in the last century.

> "Know that those actions which are great and good,
> Receive a nobler sanction from the free
> And universal voices from all mankind,
> Which is the voice of Heaven, than from the highest,
> The most illustrious act of royal power."

This maxim of the Genius of England further shows that the individual in question not only passed off prose for blank verse, but stole the phrase of " Vox populi vox Dei," and tried to render it unrecognisable by indefinite extension.

That the sentiment is not very much to the taste of the Monarch may be conjectured from the fact that he sulkily lets it pass without any comment, and very naturally falls asleep of being talked-at by so heavily-pinioned a Genius. The latter avails himself of the opportunity to exhibit to the slumbering Monarch a vision of the future of England, down to the era of George and Charlotte. The spectacle soothes him still less than the speech, though oppressive ecstacy may be sweet, and Edward springs into wakefulness, and loudly exclaiming that

" This is too much for human strength to bear,"

the loquacious Genius flies at him again with some remarkable figures of speech, to which the worn-out Edward answers nothing. The Genius, unwilling to attribute his taciturnity to rudeness, finds a satisfactory solution in the conclusion that

"Astonishment seals up his lips."

The founder of the " Garter" will not provoke the eloquence of the heavenly visiter by unsealing the lips which astonishment is supposed to have sealed up, and the remainder of the piece is left to Genius and chorus, who unite in a musical asseveration, to the effect that the reigning Sovereign of England is

"The great miracle on earth, a patriot king,"

and so terminates, amid the most vociferous plaudits, the scenic story of the Garter, enacted in celebration of the great installation of 1771.

The real installation was, by far, a more cheerful matter than its theatrical counterfeit. It took place on the 25th of July. At this ceremony the King raised to the dignity of Knights of the illustrious order, his sons the Prince of Wales and the Bishop of Osnaburg, his brother the Duke of Cumberland, with the Queen's brother, the Duke of Mecklenburgh, and Prince Henry of Brunswick, the Dukes of Marlborough and Grafton, and the Earls of Gower and Albermarle. The festival occupied the entire day. Four mortal hours in the morning were consumed in making the Knights, after which Sovereign and chapter dined together in St. George's Hall. While the banquet was progressing, Queen Charlotte sat in a gallery, looking on. She was brilliantly surrounded, and had at her right side the pretty Princess Royal, and the infant Prince Ernest at her left. One of her Majesty's brothers stood by each royal child. On the right of the canopy under which the King dined, was a long table, at which were seated all the Knights, in full view of the occupants of raised seats and a gallery in front. At the end of the first course, the good-natured Monarch was determined to make a Knight Bachelor of some deserving individual present, and he rendered good Mr. Dessac (clerk of the check, belonging to the band of Gentlemen Pensioners) supremely happy by selecting *him*. As soon as the other courses had been served, and the banquet was concluded, which was not till between six and seven o'clock, the whole of the cavaliers and company separated in haste, hurrying to their respective rooms or hotels, to dress for the ball which was to be held in the Great Guard-Room. When all the guests were there assembled, the King and Queen entered the apartment about nine o'clock. Whereupon the Duke of Gloucester danced a couple of minuets with a brace of duchesses — Grafton and Marlborough. The minuets were continued till eleven o'clock. No one seemed to tire of the stately, graceful dance, and it was only during the hour that followed, that any young lady, as anxious as the elegant American belle, who told Mr. Oliphant at Minnesota that "she longed to shake the knots out of her legs," had a chance of indulging in her liveliness. During one hour — from eleven to midnight — country dances were accomplished. I say accomplished, for only three were danced — and each set procured twenty minutes of very active exercise. Midnight had scarcely been tolled out by the castle clock when the festive throng separated — and thus closed one of the most brilliant installations that Windsor had ever seen, since Edward first became the founder of the order. If there was any drawback to the gratification which the King felt on this occasion, it was at beholding Wilkes and his daughter conspicuously seated among the spectators in the courtyard; whither the man whom the King hated had penetrated by means of a ticket from Lord Tankerville. It was at this period that Mr. Fox revived, for a few court-days, the fashion of appearing at the drawing-room in red-heeled shoes. To the public, these matters were far more comic than the comic portion of the "Installation," in which (setting aside the Edward III. of Aikin, and the Genius of England, played by Reddish) King enacted Sir Dingle, a court fool knighted; Parsons, Nat Needle; and Weston, Roger. Never was foolish knight played by an actor so chivalrous of aspect as King.

I will avail myself of this opportunity to state that at solemn ceremonies, like that above named, four of our kings of England were knighted by their own subjects. These were Edward III., Henry VI. and VII., and Edward VI. The latter was dubbed by the Lord Protector, who was himself empowered to perform the act by letters patent, under the great seal. At a very early period, priests, or prelates rather, sometimes conferred the honor on great public occasions. The Westminster Synod deprived them of this privilege in 1102.

It has been said that English knights wearing foreign orders, without permission of their own sovereign, are no more knights in reality than those stage knights of whom I have been treating. This, however, is questionable, if so great an authority as Coke be not in error. That great lawyer declares that a knight, by whomsoever created, can sue and be sued by his knightly title, and that such is not the case with persons holding other foreign titles, similar to those of the English peerage. Let me add that, among other old customs, it was once common in our armies for knighthood to be conferred previous to a battle, to arouse courage, rather than afterward, as is the case now—after the action, in order to reward valor. Even this fashion is more reasonable than that of the Czar, who claps stars and crosses of chivalry on the bosoms of beaten generals, to make them pass in Muscovy for conquerors.

In connection with the stage, knights have figured sometimes before, as well as behind the curtain. Of all the contests ever maintained, there was never, in its way a fiercer than that which took place between Sir William Rawlings, and young Tom Dibdin. The son of "tuneful Charlie," born in 1771, and held at the font, as the "Lady's Magazine" used to say, by Garrick, was not above four years of age when he played Cupid to Mrs. Siddons' Venus, in Shakespeare's Jubilee. It was hardly to be expected that after this and a course of attendance as choir-boy at St. Paul's, he would settle down quietly to learn upholstery. This *was* expected of him by his very unreasonable relatives, who bound him apprentice to the city knight, Sir William Rawlings, a then fashionable upholsterer in Moorfields. The boy was dull as the mahogany he had to polish, and the knight could never make him half so bright in business matters. "Tom Dibdin," thus used to remark the city cavalier—"Tom Dibdin is the stupidest hound on earth!" The knight, however, changed his mind when his apprentice, grown up to man's estate, produced "The Cabinet." Sir William probably thought that the opera was the upholstery business set to music. But before this point was reached, dire was the struggle between the knight and the page, who would not "turn over a new leaf." When work was over, the boy was accustomed to follow it up with a turn at the play—generally in the gallery of the Royalty Theatre. On one of these occasions the knight followed him thither, dragged him out, gave him a sound thrashing, and, next morning, brought him before that awfully squinting official, John Wilkes. The struggle ended in a drawn battle, and Tom abandoned trade: and instead of turning out patent bedsteads, turned out the "English Fleet," and became the father of "Mother Goose." He would have shown less of his relationship to the family of that name, had he stuck to his tools; in the latter case he might have taken his seat as Lord Mayor, in a chair made by himself, and in those stirring times he might have become as good a knight as his master.

As it was, the refuse of knighthood had a hard time of it. He was actor of all work, wrote thousands of songs, which he sold as cheap as chips, and composed four pieces for Astley's Theatre, for which he received fourteen pounds—hardly the price of a couple of arm-chairs. How he flourished and fell after this, may be seen in his biography. He had fortune within his grasp at one time, but he lost his hold when he became proprietor of a theatre. The ex-apprentice of the old knight-upholder could not furnish his own house with audiences, and the angry knight himself might have been appeased could his spirit have seen the condition into which "poor Tom" had fallen just previous to his death, some twenty years ago.

But I fear I have said more than enough about stage knights; may I add some short gossip touching real knights with stage ladies? Before doing so, I may just notice that the wedded wife of a *bona fide* knight once acted on the English boards under the chivalric name—and a time-honored one it is in Yorkshire—of her husband, Slingsby. Dame, or Lady Slingsby, who had been formerly a Mrs. Lee, was a favorite actress in the days of James II. She belonged to the Theatre Royal, resided in St. James's parish, and was buried in Pancras church-yard in March 1693-4. In the list of the Slingsbys, baronets, of Scriven, given in Harborough's "History of Knaresborough," Sir Henry Slingsby, who died in 1692, is the only one of whose marriage no notice is taken. But to our stage ladies and gallant lovers.

## STAGE LADIES AND THE ROMANCE OF HISTORY.

> "Our happy love may have a secret church,
> Under the church, as Faith's was under Paul's,
> Where we may carry on our sweet devotion,
> And the cathedral marriage keep its state,
> And all its decencies and ceremonies."
>
> CROWNE, *The Married Beau.*

AFTER the loose fashion of Master Crowne's Married Beau, it was no uncommon thing for gallants once to woo the mimic ladies of the scene.

From the time that ladies first appeared upon the stage, they seem to have exercised a powerful attraction upon the cavaliers. Under date of the 18th October, 1666, Evelyn says in his Diary: "This night was acted my Lord Broghill's tragedy, 'Mustapha,' before their majesties at court, at which I was present, very seldom going to the public theatres, for many reasons, now, as they are abused to an atheistical liberty, foul and undecent women now (and never till now) permitted to appear and act, who, inflaming several young noblemen and gallants, became their misses, and to some their wives; witness the Earl of Oxford, Sir R. Howard, Prince Rupert, the Earl of Dorset, and another greater person than any of them, who fell into their snares, to the reproach of their noble families, and ruin of both body and soul. I was invited by my Lord Chamberlain to see this tragedy, exceedingly well written, though in my mind I did not approve of any such pastime in a time of such judgments and calamities."

A year and a half earlier than the date of the above entry, namely, April 3, 1665, Pepys notices the same play, with some allusions to the ladies: "To a play at the Duke's of my Lord Orrery's, called 'Mustapha,' which being not good, made Betterton's part and Ianthe's but ordinary too. All the pleasure of the play was, the king and my Lady Castlemaine were there; and pretty witty Nell of the King's House, and the younger Marshall sat next us, which pleased me mightily." The play, however, is not so poor a one as Pepys describes it, and the cast was excellent. Betterton played Solyman the Magnificent. Mustapha and Zanga, the sons of Solyman, were played by Harris and Smith; and Young made a capital Cardinal. Mrs. Betterton was the Roxalana; and Mrs. Davies, one of those ladies who, like her sisters, the two Marshalls, Hughes and Nelly, exercised the fatal attraction over young noblemen and gallants, deplored by Evelyn, was the magnificent Queen of Hungary. Mustapha continued to be the favorite play until the theatre closed, when the plague began to spread. Pepys's "Ianthe" was Mrs. Betterton, of whom he says, on the 22d October, 1662, "the players do tell me that Betterton is not married to Ianthe, as they say; but also that he is a very sober, serious man, studious and humble, following of his studies, and is rich already with what he gets and saves." Betterton, however, married the lady, Miss Saunderson, in 1663. She had been famous for her Ianthe in Davenant's "Siege of Rhodes;" and she played Shakespeare's heroines with great effect. Pepys rightly designates the author of the play, Lord Orrery. Lord Broghill was made Earl of Orrery, five years before Evelyn saw his play. I may add that Mustapha has appeared in half-a-dozen different versions on the stage. Probably the worst of these was Mallet's; the latter author created great amusement by one of his passages, in which he said:—

"*Future* sultans
*Have* shunned the marriage tie;"—

a confusion of tenses which has been compared with a similar error in the sermons of so correct a writer as Blair (vol. v., third edition, page 224), "in *future* periods the light *dawned* more and more."

Although Evelyn, in 1666, says that "never till now" were women admitted to assume characters on the stage, he is not quite correct in his assertion. There were actresses full thirty years previous to that period. Thus, in 1632, the "Court Beggar" was acted at the Cockpit. In the last act, Lady Strangelove says:—
"If you have a short speech or two, the boy's a pretty actor, and

his mother can play her part: women-actors now grow in request." Our ancestors wisely followed a foreign fashion when they ceased to employ boys in female characters. Prynne says, in 1633, "They have now their female players in Italy and other foreign parts;" and in Michaelmas 1629, they had French women-actors in a play personated at Blackfriars, to which there was a great resort. Geneste quotes Freshwater as writing thus of French actresses in Paris, in 1629: "Yet the women are the best actors; they play their own parts, a thing much desired in England."

In Davenant's patent for opening Lincoln's-inn Fields, in 1661, permission was given for the engaging of women as actresses, on the ground that the employment of men in such parts had given great offence. I more particularly notice this matter, because it was a knight who first opened a theatre with a regular female *troupe* added to the usual number of male actors. Sir William's ladies were Mrs. Davenport, Mrs. Saunderson, Mrs. Davies, Mrs. Long, Mrs. Gibbs, Mrs. Norris, Mrs. Holden, and Mrs. Jennings. The first four were Sir William's principal actresses, and these were boarded in the knight's own dwelling-house. Their title of "Mistress" does not necessarily imply that they were married ladies, but rather that they were old enough to be so.

This knight, too, was the first who introduced scenery on the stage. I will add (*par parenthèse*) that it was a priest who first suggested the levelling of the pit with the stage, for the purpose of masquerades and balls.

Prynne was not among those who fancied that morality would profit by the introduction of actresses. He had his misgivings as to the effects likely to be produced on the susceptible young gallants of his day. Touching the appearance of the French actresses at the Blackfriars Theatre, noticed above, he calls it "an impudent, shameful, un-womanish, graceless, if not more than w———ish attempt." The fashion was, undoubtedly, first set by the court, and by no less a person than a queen. Anne of Denmark, wife of James I., acted a part in a pastoral. They who remember some of the incidents of the training she gave her son, the princely knight young Henry, will hardly think that Anne gave dignity to the occupation she temporarily assumed.

Mrs. Saunderson is said to have been the first regularly-engaged actress who opened her lips on the English stage. Had she and her compeers only half the charms which report ascribed to them, they must have afforded far more pleasure to audience and spectators than the "beautiful woman-actor," Stephen Hamerton Hart, with his womanly dignity; Burt, with his odious female sprightliness; or Goffe, who was as hearty and bustling as old Mrs. Davenport. King Charles himself and his cavaliers, too, must have been especially delighted when they were no longer kept waiting for the commencement of a play, on the ground that the *Queen* was not yet shaved."

It is curious that there were some people not near so strait-laced as Prynne, who considered that public virtue would suffer shipwreck if actresses were permitted to establish themselves in the general favor. The opposite party, of course, went to an opposite extreme; and in 1672, not only were "Philaster," and Killigrew's "Parson's Wedding," played *entirely* by women, but one of the "Miss" Marshalls, gay daughter of a Presbyterian minister, on both occasions spoke the prologue and epilogue in male attire. "Philaster" is simply an absurd piece, which was rendered popular by Hart and Nell Gwyn; but with respect to Killigrew's piece, it is so disgusting, from the commencement to the finale, that I can hardly fancy how any individuals, barely alive to their humanity, could be brought to utter and enact the turpitudes which Killigrew set down for them, or that an audience could be kept from fleeing from the house before the first act was over.

But the gallants could endure anything rather than a return to such effects as are alluded to by a contemporary writer, who, by way of introducing a female Desdemona, said in his prologue:—

> "Our women are defective and so sized
> You'd think they were some of the guard disguised;
> For, to speak truth, men act that are between
> Forty and fifty, wenches of fifteen;
> With brow so large, and nerve so uncompliant,
> When you call *Desdemona* — enter *Giant*."

Half a century elapsed before knight or gentleman took an actress from the stage, for the purpose of making her his wife. The squires, in this case, had precedence of the knights; and the antiquary, Martin Folkyes, led the way by espousing Lucretia Bradshaw, the uncorrupted amid corruption, and the original Corinna in the "Confederacy," Dorinda in the "Beaux Stratagem," and Arabella Zeal in the "Fair Quaker of Deal." This marriage took place in 1713, and there was not a happier hearth in England than that of the antiquary and the actress. A knight of the Garter followed, with an earl's coronet, and in 1735 the great Lord Peterborough acknowledged his marriage with that daughter of sweet sounds, Anastasia Robinson. This example at once flattered, provoked, and stimulated the ladies, one of whom, the daughter of Earl de Waldegrave, Lady Henrietta Herbert, married young Beard the actor. This was thought "low," and another knight's daughter was less censured for marrying her father's footman. The "Beggars' Opera" gave two coronets to two Pollys. Lavinia Fenton (Betswick), the original Polly at Lincoln's Inn, in 1728, became Duchess of Bolton a few years later; and in 1813, no less a man than Lord Thurlow married Mary Catherine Bolton, who was scarcely an inferior *Polly* to the original lady, who gave up *Polly* to become a Bolton.

The squires once more took their turn when Sheridan married Miss Lindley; but before the last century closed, Miss Farren gave her hand to "the proudest earl in England," the Earl of Derby, Knight of the Bath. In 1807, knight and squire took two ladies from the stage. In that year Mr. Heathcote married the beautiful Miss Searle; and Earl Craven married Louisa Brunton. We have still among us five ex-actresses who married men of the degree of noble, knight, or squire. These are Miss Stephens, the widowed Countess of Essex; Miss Foote, the widowed Countess of Harrington; Miss O'Neill the widow of Sir William Beecher, Bart.; Mrs. Nisbett, the relict of the bold Sir Felix Boothby; and Miss M. Tree, whose late husband, Mr. Bradshaw, was at one time M. P. for Canterbury.

There is something romantic in the lives of all these ladies, but most in that of "Lizzy Farren," and as the life of that lady of a Knight of the Bath has something in common with the career of a celebrated legal knight and judge, I will take some of its incidents as the chief points in the following sketch, which is a supplementary chapter to the Romance of History, and perhaps not the least interesting one in such a series.

If gayety consists in noise, then was the market-place of Salisbury, toward the close of Christmas Eve, 1769, extremely joyous and glad. In the centre, on a raised stage, his Worship the Mayor was inaugurating the holyday-time, by having a bout at single-stick with an itinerant exhibitor of the art of self-defence from London. The "professor" had been soliciting the magisterial permission to set up his stage in the market-place, and he had not only received full license, but the chief magistrate himself condescended to take a stick and try his strength with the professor.

It was an edifying sight, and bumpkins and burgesses enjoyed it consumedly. The professional fencer allowed his adversary to count many "hits" out of pure gratitude. But he had some self-respect, and in order that his reputation might not suffer in the estimation of the spectators, he wound up the "set-to" by dealing a stroke on the right-worshipful skull, which made the mayor imagine that chaos was come again, and that all about him was dancing confusedly into annihilation.

"I am afraid I have accidentally hurt your worship's head," said the wickedly sympathizing single-stick player.

"H'm!" murmured the fallen great man, with a ghastly smile, and Iris's seven hues upon his cheek, "don't mention it: there's nothing in it!"

"I am truly rejoiced," replied the professor to his assistant, with a wink of the eye, "that his worship has not lost his senses."

"Oh, ay!" exclaimed the rough aide, "he's about as wise as ever he was."

The single-stick player looked like Pizarro, who, when he *did* kill a friend occasionally—"his custom i' th' afternoon"—always went to the funeral in a mourning suit and a droop of the eye—intended for sympathy. In the meantime the mayor, who had been fancying himself in a balloon, and that he was being whirled away from his native town, began to think that the balloon was settling to earth again, and that the representation of chaos had been indefinitely deferred. He continued, however, holding on by the rail, as if the balloon was yet unsteady, and he only complained of a drumming in the ears.

At that moment the not-to-be-mistaken sound of a real drum fell in harsh accompaniment upon his singing-ears, and it had one good effect, that of bringing back the magistrate and the man. Both looked through the rather shaken windows of the one body, and indignation speedily lighted up from within.

The sound came from the suburb of Fisherton, but it swelled insultingly nearer and nearer, as though announcing that it was about to be beaten in the borough, despite the lack of magisterial sanction. The great depository of authority began to gaze in speechless horror, as the bearer of the noisy instrument made his appearance in the market-place at the head of a small procession, which was at once seen to consist of a party of strolling actors.

The drummer was a thick-set man, with nothing healthy looking about him but his nose, and that looked *too* healthy. He was the low comedian, and was naturally endowed to assume that distinctive line.

He was followed by three or four couple of "the ladies and gentlemen of the company," of some of whom it might be said, that shoes were things they did not much stand upon. They had a shabby genteel air about them, looked hungry and happy; and one or two wore one hand in the pocket, upon an economizing principle in reference to gloves. The light comedian cut jokes with the spectators, and was soon invited to the consequence he aimed at — an invitation to "take a glass of wine." The women were more tawdry-looking than the men, but they wore a lighthearted, romping aspect — all, except the young lady who played Ophelia and Columbine, who carried a baby, and looked as if she had not been asleep since it was born, which was probably the case.

The *cortége* was closed by a fine, gentleman-like man, who led by the hand a little girl some ten years old. No one could look for a moment at them, without at once feeling assured that there was something in them which placed them above the fellows with whom they consorted. They were father and daughter. *He* manager; *she* a species of infant phenomenon. In his face were to be traced the furrows of disappointment, and in his eye the gleam of hope. *Her* face was as faces of the young should ever be, full of enjoyment, love, and feeling. The last two were especially there for the father, whose hand she held, and into whose face she looked, ever and anon, with a smile which never failed to be repaid in similar currency.

The refined air of the father, and the graceful bearing of the modest daughter, won commendations from all beholders. He was an ex-surgeon of Cork, who had given up his profession in order to follow the stage. People set him down as insane, and so he was, but it was an insanity which made a countess of his daughter. His name was Farren, and his child, pet daughter of a pretty mother, was the inimitable Lizzy.

If the mayor could have read into history, he would have knelt down and kissed Lizzy Farren's shoe-buckles. As he could not so read, he only saw in the sire a vagabond, and in the child a mountebank. On the former he hurled down the whole weight of his magisterial wrath. It was in vain that the manager declared he was on his way to solicit the mayor's license to act in Salisbury. That official gentleman declared that it was an infraction of the law to pass from the suburb of Fisherton into the borough of Salisbury before the mayor's permission had been previously signified.

"And that permission I will never give," said his worship. "We are a godly people here, and have no taste for rascal-players. As his majesty's representative, I am bound to encourage no amusements that are not respectable."

"But our young king," interrupted Mr. Farren, "is himself a great patron of the theatre."

This was worse than a heavy blow at single-stick; and the mayor was the more wrath as he had no argument ready to meet it. After looking angry for a moment, a bright thought struck him.

"Ay, ay, sir! You will not, I hope, teach a mayor either fact or duty. We know, sir, what the king (God bless him!) patronizes. His majesty does not patronize strollers. He goes regularly to an *established* church, sir, and to an *established* theatre; and so, sir, I, as mayor, support only establishments. Good heavens! what would become of the throne and the altar, if a Mayor of Sarum were to do otherwise?"

As Mr. Farren did not well know, he could not readily tell; and as he stood mute, the mayor continued to pour down upon the player and his vocation, a shower of obloquy. At every allusion which he made to his predilection for amusements that were respectable and instructive, the single-stick player and his man drew themselves up, cried " *Hear ! hear !*" and looked down upon the actors with an air of burlesque contempt. The actors, men and women, returned the look with a burst of uncontrollable laughter. The mayor took this for deliberate insult, aimed at himself and at what he chose to patronize. His protégés looked the more proud, and became louder than ever in their self-applauding "*Hear ! hear !*" The players, the while, shrieked with laughter. Even Mr. Farren and Lizzy could not refrain from risibility, for the stick-player and his man were really members of the company. The former was Mr. Frederick Fitzmontague, who was great in *Hamlet*. His man was the ruffian in melodramas, and the clown in pantomimes, and as he did a little private business of his own by accepting an engagement from a religious society, during the dull season of the year, to preach on the highways against theatricals, Mr. Osmond Brontere was usually known by the cognomen of Missionary Jack.

The magisterial refusal to license this wandering company to play in Salisbury, was followed by altercation; and altercation by riot. The multitude took part with the actors, and they hooted the mayor; and the latter, viewing poor Farren as the cause and guilty mover of all that had occurred, summarily ordered his arrest; and, in spite of all remonstrance, resistance, or loudly-expressed disgust, the manager was ultimately lodged in the cage. The mob, then, satisfied at having had a little excitement, and caring nothing more about the matter, at length separated, and repaired to their respective homes. They went all the quicker that the rain had begun to descend in torrents; and they took little notice of poor Lizzy, who went home in the dusk, weeping bitterly, and led by the hands of the matronly Ophelia and Missionary Jack.

Ere morning dawned, a change had come over the scene. The rain had ceased. A hard frost had set in. All Salisbury looked as if it were built upon a frozen lake. The market-place itself was a *mer de glace*. Christmas-day was scarcely visible when a boy of early habits, standing at the door of an upholsterer's shop, which bore above it the name of Burroughs, fancied he saw something moving with stealthy pace across the market-place; and he amused himself by watching it through the gloom. It was developed, after a while, into the figure of a thinly-clad girl, bearing in her arms a bowl of hot milk. She trod cautiously, and looked now down at her feet, now across the wide square, to measure the distance she had yet to go. Each little foot was put forward with hesitation, and so slowly was progress made, that there was good chance of the boiling milk being frozen, before it had been carried half-way to its destination.

The girl was Lizzy Farren, and in the bowl, which between her arms looked as graceful as urn clasped by Arcadian nymph, lay the chief portion of a breakfast destined, on this sad Christmas morning, for her captive sire in the cage.

"She'll be down!" said young Burroughs, as he saw her partially slip. Lizzy, however, recovered herself; but so alarmed was she at her situation, so terrified when she measured the distance she had to accomplish by that which she had already traversed, that she fairly stood still near the centre of the market-place, and wept aloud over the hot bowl and her cold position. It was then that the young knight recognised the crisis when he was authorized to interfere. He made a run from the door, shot one leg in advance, drew the other quickly after him, and went sliding, with express-train speed, close up to Lizzy's feet. *She* no sooner saw the direful prospect of collision than she shrieked with an energy which roused all the rooks in the close.

"Hold hard!" exclaimed the merry-faced boy; "hold hard! that's myself, you Lizzy, and the milk. Hold hard!" he continued, as he half held her up, half held on to her. "Hold hard! or we shall all be down together."

"Oh, where do you come from? and how do you know my name is Lizzy?"

"Well! Mr. Fitzmontague lodges in our house, and he told us all about you, last night. And he said, as sure as could be, you would be awake before anybody in Salisbury. And sure enough, here you are, almost before daylight."

By the help of the young cavalier, the distressed damsel was relieved from her perplexity. Young Burroughs offered to carry the bowl, which she stoutly refused. "No one," she said, "shall carry my father's breakfast to him, but myself, on such a morning."

And so, her deliverer walked tenderly by her side, holding her cautiously up, nor ceased from his care, until Lizzy and her burden had safely reached the cage. Through the bars of the small window, Farren had watched her coming; and he hailed her arrival with a "God bless you, my own child!"

"Oh, papa!" said Lizzy, weeping again, and embracing the bowl as warmly as if it had been her father himself; "oh, papa! what would mamma and my little sisters, and all our friends in Liverpool say, if they knew how we are beginning our Christmas day?"

"Things unknown are unfelt, my darling. We will tell them nothing about it, till Fortune gilds over the memory of it. But what do you bring, Lizzy?—or rather, why do I ask? It is my breakfast; and Lizzy herself has had none."

A pretty altercation ensued; but Lizzy gained her point; and not one drop would she taste till her sire had commenced the repast. Aided by young Burroughs, she held the lip of the bowl through the bars of the cage; and the little English maiden smiled, for the first time since yesterday, at beholding her sire imbibe the quickening draught. It was not till three years after that Barry and his wife played Evander and Euphrasia in the Grecian Daughter, or Farren would have drawn a parallel suitable to the occasion. He was not so well up in history as in theatricals; and on the stage, history has a terrible time of it. Witness this very tragedy in which Murphy has made Evander, King of Sicily, and confounded Dionysius the elder, with his younger namesake. To be sure, pleasant Palmer, who played the character, was about as wise as Murphy.

When the primitive breakfast was concluded, Lizzy stood sad and silent; and the father sadly and silently looked down at her; while young Burroughs leaned against the wall, as sad and silent as either of them. And so a weary two hours passed; at the end of which, a town-constable appeared, accompanied by a clerical gentleman, and empowered to give liberty to the captive. When the constable told the manager that his liberation was owing to the intercession made in his behalf, by the Reverend Mr. Snodgrass, who had just arrived in Salisbury, Lizzy clapped her hands with agitation, for she saw that the clerical interceder was no other than Missionary Jack. "Oh, Mr. Brontere," said the curious girl, when they had all reached home together, "how did you ever manage it?"

"Well!" said the enterprising actor, with a laugh; "I called on his worship, to inquire what Christmas charities might be acceptable; and if there were any prisoners whom my humble means might liberate. He named your papa, and the company have paid what was necessary. His worship was not inexorable, particularly as I incidentally told him his Majesty patronized, the other day, an itinerant company at Datchet. As for *how* I did it. I rather think I am irresistible in the dress in which poor Will Havard, only two years ago, played 'Old Adam.' A little ingenuity, as you see, has made it look very like a rector's costume; and, besides," said Missionary Jack, "I sometimes think that nature intended me for the church."

Three years had elapsed. On the Christmas eve of 1772, all the play-going people of Wakefield were in a state of pleasant excitement, at the promise made in bills posted over the town announcing the immediate appearance of the "Young Queen of Columbines." All the young bachelors of the town were besieging the box-office. In those days there were not only theatres in provincial towns, but people really went to them. Amid the applicants, was a sprightly-looking articled clerk, who, having achieved his object, had stopped for a moment at the stage-door to read the programme of the forthcoming pantomime. While thus engaged the Columbine Queen, the most fairy-looking of youthful figures, brilliant as spring, and light as gossamer, sweet fifteen, with a look of being a year or two more, tripped into the street, on her way home from rehearsal. Eighty years ago the gallantry of country towns, with respect to pretty actresses, was much like that which characterizes German localities now. It was of a rudely enthusiastic quality. Accordingly, the fairy-looking Columbine had hardly proceeded a dozen yards, when she had twice as many offers made her of arms, whereon to find support over the slippery pavement. It was an old-fashioned winter in Wakefield, and Columbine's suitors had as many falls in the course of their assiduities, as though they had been so many "Lovers", in the pantomime, and the wand of Harlequin was tripping them up as they skipped along. Columbine got skilfully rid of them all in time, except one ; and *he* became at last so unwelcomely intrusive, that the articled clerk, who was the very champion of distressed damsels, and had been a watcher of what was going on, went up to the young lady, took her arm in his, without any ceremony, and bade her persecutor proceed any further, at his peril. The gentleman took the hint, and left knight and lady to continue their way unmolested. They no sooner saw themselves alone, when, looking into each other's faces, they laughed a merry laugh of recognition, and it would be difficult to say which was the merrier — Miss Farren or Mr. Burroughs, the young actress and the incipient lawyer.

When boxing-night came, there was a crowded house, and Lizzy created a *furore*. Like Carlotta Grisi, she could sing as well as dance, and there was a bright intellect, to boot, pervading all she did. On the night in question, she sang between the acts; and young Burroughs, ever watchful, especially marked the effect of her singing upon a very ecstatic amateur who was seated next to him. "What a treasure," said the amateur, "would this girl be in Liverpool!" "Well," remarked Burroughs, "I am ready to accept an engagement for her. State your terms. Thirty shillings a-week, I presume, will not quite exhaust your treasury." "I will certainly," said the stranger, "tell our manager, Younger, of the prize which is to be acquired so cheaply; and the affair need not be delayed; for Younger is at the Swan, and will be down here to-night, to see the pantomime."

In five minutes, Burroughs was sitting face-to-face with Younger at the inn, urging him to go at once, not to see Columbine dance, but to hear her sing. "I wonder," said the manager, "if your young friend is the child of the Cork surgeon who married the daughter of Wright, the Liverpool brewer. If so, she's clever; besides, why———"

"Why she'll make your fortune," said the lawyer's clerk. "She is the grand-daughter of your Liverpool brewer, sings like a nightingale, and is worth five pounds a week to you at least. Come and hear her."

Younger walked leisurely down, as if he was in no particular want of talent; but he was so pleased with what he did hear that when the songstress came off the stage, Burroughs went round and exultingly announced that he had procured an engagement for her at Liverpool, at two pounds ten per week; and to find her own satin shoes and silk stockings. In prospect of such a Potosi, the Columbine danced that night as boundingly as if Dan Mercury had lent her the very pinions from his heels.

"Mr. Burroughs," said Lizzy, as he was escorting her and her mother home, "this is the second Christmas you have made happy for us. I hope you may live to be Lord Chief Justice."

"Thank you, Lizzy, that is about as likely as that Liverpool will make of the Wakefield Columbine a countess."

A few years had again passed away since the Christmas week which succeeded that spent at Wakefield, and which saw Lizzy Farren the only *Rosetta* which Liverpool cared to listen to, and it was now the same joyous season, but the locality was Chester.

There was a custom then prevailing among actors, which exists nowhere now, except in some of the small towns in Germany. Thus, not very long ago, at Ischl, in Austria, I was surprised to see a very pretty actress enter my own room at the inn, and putting a play-bill into my hand, solicit my presence at her benefit. This was a common practice in the north of England till Tate Wilkinson put an end to it, as derogatory to the profession. The custom, however, had not been checked at the time and in the locality to which I have alluded. On the Christmas eve of the period in question, Lizzy Farren was herself engaged in distributing her bills, and asking patronage for her benefit, which was to take place on the following Twelfth Night. As appropriate to the occasion she had chosen Shakespeare's comedy of that name, and was to play *Viola*, a part for which Younger, who loved her heartily, had given her especial instruction.

Miss Farren had not been very successful in her "touting." She had been unlucky in the two families at whose houses she had ventured to knock. The first was that of an ex-proprietor of a religious periodical, who had a horror of the stage, but who had a so much greater horror of Romanism, that, like the Scottish clergy of the time, he would have gone every night to the play during Passion week, only to show his abhorrence of popery. This pious scoundrel had grown rich by swindling his editors and supporting any question which paid best. His household he kept for years, by inserting advertisements in his journal for which he was paid in kind. He was a slimy, sneaking, mendacious knave, who would have advocated atheism if he could have procured a dozen additional subscribers by it. His lady was the quintessence of vulgarity and malignity. She wore diamonds on her wig, venom in her heart, and very-much-abused English at the end of her tongue.

Poor Lizzy, rebuffed here, rang at the garden-gate of Mrs. Penury Beaugawg. She was a lady of sentiment who drank, a lady of simplicity who rouged, a lady of affected honesty who lived beyond her income, and toadied or bullied her relations into paying her debts. Mrs. Penury Beaugawg would have graciously accepted orders for a private box; but a patronage which cost her anything, was a vulgarity which her gentle and generous spirit could not comprehend.

Lizzy was standing dispirited in the road at the front of the house, when a horseman rode slowly up; and Lizzy, not at all abashed at practising an old but not agreeable custom, raised a bill to his hand as he came close to her, and solicited half-a-crown, the regular admission-price to the boxes.

"Lizzy!" cried the horseman, "you shall have such a house at Chester, as the old town has not seen since the night Garrick was here, and played *Richard* and *Lord Chalkstone*."

The equestrian was Mr. Burroughs, then in training for the bar, and as willing to help Miss Farren now as he was to aid her and her bowl of milk across the market-place at Salisbury. The incipient barrister kept his word. The Chester theatre was crammed to the ceiling; and, as Lizzy said, Mr. Burroughs was her Christmas angel, the thought of whom was always associated in her mind with plumbs, currants, holly——

"And mistletoe," said the budding counsellor, with a look at which both laughed merrily and honestly.

On the Christmas eve of 1776, Miss Farren was seated in Colman's parlor in London, looking at him while he read two letters of introduction; one from Burroughs, the other from Younger; and both in high praise of the young bearer, for whom they were especially written. My limits will only allow me to say that Lizzy was engaged for the next summer-season at the Haymarket, where she appeared on June 9, 1777, in "She Stoops to Conquer." She was *Miss Hardcastle*, and Edwin made his first appearance in London with her, in the same piece. Colman would have brought out Henderson too, if he could have managed it. That dignified gentleman, however, insisted on reserving his *debût* for *Shylock*, on the 11th of the same month. And what a joyous season did Lizzy make of it for our then youthful grandfathers. How they admired her double talent in *Miss Hardcastle!* How ecstatic were they with her *Maria*, in the "Citizen!" How ravishedly did they listen to her *Rosetta!* How they laughed at her *Miss Tittup*, in "Bon Ton!" and how they extolled her playfulness and dignity as *Rosina*, of which she was the original representative, in the "Barber of Seville!" It may be remarked that Colman omitted the most comic scene in the piece, *that* wherein the Count is disguised as a drunken trooper — as injurious to morality!

When, in the following year, she played Lady Townley, she was declared the first, and she was then almost the youngest of living actresses. And when she joined the Drury Lane company in the succeeding season, the principal parts were divided between herself, Miss Walpole, Miss P. Hopkins, and *Perdita* Robinson. Not one of this body was then quite twenty years of age! Is not this a case wherein to exclaim —

"O mihi præteritos referat si Jupiter annos?"

Just twenty years did she adorn our stage; ultimately taking leave of it at Drury Lane, in April, 1797, in the character of Lady Teazle. Before that time, however, she had been prominent in the Christmas private plays at the Duke of Richmond's, in which the Earl of Derby, Lord Henry Fitzgerald, and the Honorable Mrs. Dormer acted with her; and that rising barrister, Mr. Burroughs, looking constantly at the judicial bench as his own proper stage, was among the most admiring of the audience. It was there that was formed that attachment which ultimately made of her, a month after she had retired from the stage, Countess of Derby, and subsequently mother of a future countess, who still wears her coronet.

Not long after this period, and following on her presentation at Court, where she was received with marked kindly condescension by Queen Charlotte, the countess was walking in the marriage procession of the Princess Royal and the Duke of Wurtemberg; her foot caught in the carpeting, and she would have fallen to the ground, but for the ready arms, once more extended to support her, of Mr. Burroughs, now an eminent man indeed.

Many years had been added to the roll of time, when a carriage, containing a lady was on its way to Windsor. It suddenly came to a stop, by the breaking of an axle-tree. In the midst of the distress which ensued to the occupier, a second carriage approached, bearing a goodnatured-looking gentleman, who at once offered his services. The lady, recognising an old friend, accepted the offer with alacrity. As the two drove off together in the gentleman's carriage toward Windsor, the owner of it remarked that he had almost expected to find her in distress on the road; for it was Christmas Eve, and he had been thinking of old times.

"How many years is it, my lady countess," said he, "since I stood at my father's shop-door in Salisbury, watching your perilous passage over the market-place, with a bowl of milk?"

"Not so long at all events," she answered with a smile, "but that I recollect my poor father would have lost his breakfast, but for your assistance."

"The time is not long for memory," replied the Judge, "nor is Salisbury as far from Windsor as Dan from Beersheba; yet how wide the distance between the breakfast at the cage-door at Salisbury, and the Christmas dinner to which we are both proceeding, in the palace of the king!"

"The earl is already there," added the countess, "and he will be happier than the king himself to welcome the legal knight who has done such willing service to the Lady of the Knight of the Bath."

To those whose power and privilege it is to create such knights, we will now direct our attention, and see how kings themselves behaved in *their* character as knights.

# THE KINGS OF ENGLAND AS KNIGHTS.

## FROM THE NORMANS TO THE STUARTS.

"Un roi abstrait n'est ni père, ni fils, ni frère, ni parent, ni chevalier, ami. Qu'est il donc ? *Roi*, même quand il dort."— DIDEROT.

IF we judge some of our kings by the strict laws of chivalry, we shall find that they were but sorry knights after all. They may have been terrible in battle; but they were ill-mannerly in ladies' bower.

William the Conqueror, for instance, had none of the tender sentiment of chivalry; in other words he showed little gentleness in his bearing toward women. It is said by Ingerius, that after Matilda of Flanders had refused his hand, on the ground that she would not have a bastard for a husband, he waylaid her as she was returning from mass in one of the streets of Bruges, dragged her out from among her ladies, pommelled her brutally, and finally rolled her in the mud. A little family difference arose in consequence; but as it was less bitter than family quarrels usually are, a reconciliation took place, and Matilda gave her hand to the knight who had so terribly bruised her with his arm. She loved him, she said, because he had shown more than the courage of common knights, by daring to beat her within sight of her father's own palace. But all's well that ends well; they were not only a handsome but a happy couple, and Matilda was head of the household at the Conqueror's hearth. The general's wife was *there* the general.

How William bore himself in fight is too well known to need recapitulating here. He probably never knew fear but once, and that was at the sounds of a tumult in the street, which reached his ears as he was being crowned. Then, indeed, "'tis true this god did shake," for the first and only time. His successor, who was knighted by Archbishop Lanfranc, was in the field as good a knight as he, and generous to an adversary, although he was never so to any mortal besides. But Rufus was nothing of a knight in his bearing toward ladies. His taste with regard to the fair sex was of the worst sort; and the court of this royal and reprobate bachelor was a reproach at once to kingship and knighthood, to Christianity and civilization. He had been accused, or rather the knights of his time and country, with having introduced into England the practice of a crime of which the real introducer, according to others, was that Prince William who was drowned so fortunately for England, on the sea between Calais and Dover. The chivalrous magnanimity of Rufus is exemplified in the circumstance of his having, in disguise, attacked a cavalier, from whom he received so sound a beating, that he was at length compelled to avow himself in order to induce his conqueror to spare his life. The terrified victor made an apology, in the very spirit of the French knight of the Holy Ghost to a dying cavalier of the Golden Spur, whom he had mortally wounded in mistake: "I beg a thousand pardons," said the polite Frenchman, "but I really took you for somebody else." So William's vanquisher began to excuse himself for having nearly battered the king's skull to a jelly, with his battle-axe, on the ground of his having been unacquainted with his rank. "Never heed the matter," said the king, "you are a good fellow, and shall, henceforth, be a follower of mine." Many similar instances might be cited. Further, Rufus was highly popular with all men-at-arms; the knights reverenced him as the very flower of chivalry, and I am glad that the opprobrium of having slain him in the New Forest no longer attaches itself to a knight, although I am sorry an attempt has been made to fix it upon the church. No one now believes that Sir Walter Tyrrel was the author of the crime, and chivalry is acquitted of the charge against one of its members of having slain the flaxen-haired but rubicund-nosed king.

Henry Beauclerc was more of a scholar than a knight, without, however, being so very much of the first. The English-born prince was far less chivalrous of spirit than his former brother Robert; that is, if not less brave, he was less generous, especially to a foe. When he was besieged on St. Michael's Mount by Robert, and reduced to such straits that he was near dying of thirst, Robert supplied him with water; an act for which Rufus called the doer of it a fool; but as poor Robert nobly remarked, the quarrel between him and their brother was not of such importance that he should be made to perish of thirst. "We may have occasion," said he, "for a brother hereafter; but where shall we find one, if we now destroy this?" Henry would hardly have imitated conduct so chivalrously generous. He was more knightly in love, and it is recorded to his honor, that he married Matilda, daughter of Malcolm, King of Scotland, for pure love, and not for "filthy lucre," preferring to have her without a marriage portion, than to wait till one could be provided for her. This would have been praiseworthy enough had Henry not been, subsequently, like many other persons who marry in haste — for ever looking for pecuniary assistance from other resources than his own. He especially lacked too what was enjoined on every knight, a love of truth. His own promises were violated with alacrity, when the violation brought profit. He wanted, too, the common virtue of fidelity, which men of knightly rank were supposed to possess above all others. The fact that fifteen illegitimate children survived him, speaks little for his respect for either of his consorts, Matilda of Scotland, or Adelicia of Louvain. Generally speaking, however, the character of the royal scholar may be described in any terms, according to the view in which it is taken. With some historians, he is all virtue, with others all vice.

Stephen had more of the knightly character about him. He was an accomplished swordsman, and loved the sound of battle as became the spirit of the times, which considered the king as the first knight in the land. He had as little regard as Henry for a sense of justice when disposed to seize upon that to which he had no right, but he was incontestably brave, as he was indefensibly rash. Stephen received the spurs of knighthood from his uncle, Henry I., previous to the battle of Tinchebray; and in that fray he so bore himself as to show that he was worthy of the honor that had been conferred upon him. But Stephen was as faithless to his marriage vow as many other belted knights, and Matilda of Boulogne had to mourn over the faithlessness of one who had sworn to be faithful. It is said, too, of this king that he always went into battle terribly arrayed. This was in the spirit of those birds that raise their crests to affright their enemies.

Henry II., like his brother kings, we can only consider in his character of knight. In this character he is almost unexceptionable, which is more than can be said of him generally as king or as man. He was brave and generous, two chief characteristics of knighthood. He it was who abolished that burdensome and unprofitable feudal military service, which brought the barons or military tenants into the field, for forty days. The camp consequently abounded in unskilful and disorderly men. Henry accordingly introduced the practice of commuting their military service for money, by levying scutages from his baronies and knights-fees, or so much for every shield or bearer of it that *should* attend but had purchased exemption.

Henry II., not only loved knightly practice himself, but he loved to see his sons exercising knight-errantry, and wandering about in disguise from court to court, displaying their prowess in tournaments, and carrying off prizes from all adversaries. To the stories of these adventures of his by no means exemplary sons he would listen with delight. He was himself, however, a sire who set but indifferent example to his children; and his two sons, of whom fair Rosamond was the mother, were brought up and educated with his children by Eleanor. He received much knightly service and true affection from his illegitimate children. William, Earl of Salisbury, is known by his chivalric surname of "Longsword," but Geoffrey, Bishop of Lincoln, the second son of Henry and Rosamond, was not the less a knight for being a bishop before he was twenty. It was this prelate who, at the head of an armed force put down the first great northern insurrection. He was on his triumphant way back, at the head of one hundred and forty knights, when he was met by his royal sire, who embraced him warmly, exclaiming the while, "Thou alone art my legitimate son, the rest are all bastards." That he himself could endure much was evinced when he submitted to correction at the shrine of Becket. He was flagellated by the prelates, abbots, bishop, and eighty monks; and the first refreshment he took after the long penance. was some water in which a portion of Becket's blood was mingled. His claim to be considered chivalrous never suffered, in the mind of the church at least, because of this humiliating submission.

But in the dissensions which led to this humiliation, the church incurred perhaps more disgrace than the king. Nothing could possibly be more disgraceful than the conduct of the pope and the diplomacy of the Roman government throughout the continuation of the quarrel between Becket and the king. Double-dealing, atrocious deceit, and an unblushing disregard for truth, marked every act of him who was looked upon as the spiritual head of Christendom. Comparing Becket with the king, it is impossible to avoid coming to the conclusion that, in many of the requirements of knighthood, he was superior to the sovereign. His death, that is the way in which he met it, was sublime. Throughout the great quarrel, of which that death was a consequence, Becket never, like Henry, in his moments of defeat and discouragement, gave way to such impotent manifestations of rage as were shown by his royal antagonist. The latter forgot the dignity, not only of knight, but of manhood, when he was seen casting his cap violently to the earth, flinging away his belt, tearing his clothes from his body, and dragging the silk coverlet from his bed, on which, in presence of his captains, he rolled himself like a maniac, grasping the mattress in his mouth, and gnawing the wool and the horsehair which he drew out with his teeth.

Richard I. has a brilliant reputation as a knight, and if valor were the only virtue required, he would not be undeserving of the pre-eminence which is claimed for him. But this was his sole virtue. Of the other qualifications for, or qualities of chivalry, he knew nothing, or little cared for them. He was faithless in love; regardless of his pledged word; cruel, extravagant, dishonest; and not even always brave, when away from the clamor and excitements of war. But John lacked the one rough quality of Richard, and was not even brave—that is to say, he was not distinguishedly brave. When he stole away Isabella of Angoulême from her first lover, Sir Hugh de Lusignan, it was not done with the dashing gallantry of Young Lochinvar. John, in fact, was a shabby and recreant knight; and when stout Sir Hugh challenged him to single combat, because of his crime of abduction, John offered to accept it by deputy, and to fight also by deputy. Sir Hugh knew the craven prince thoroughly, and truly enough remarked that the deputy would be a mere assassin, and he would have nothing to do with either principal or representative. John kept the lady; and, if there be any persons curious to see how niggardly he kept her, they are referred to the duly published chronicles wherein there are full details.

Henry III. was the most pacifically-minded of the kings of England who had hitherto reigned. He had little of the knight about him, except the courtesy, and he could occasionally forget even that. Devotion to the fair, too, may fairly be reckoned among his knightly qualities; but he lacked the crowning virtue of fidelity. He wooed many, was rejected by several, and jilted the few who believed in him. He exhibited, it must be allowed, a chivalrous generosity in at last marrying Eleanor of Castile, without dowry; but he was not the more true to her on that account. Mild as he was by nature, he was the especial favorite of the most warlike of the orders of knighthood—the Templars. They mourned for him when dead, as though he had been the very flower of chivalry, and the most approved master of their order. They buried him, too, with a pomp which must have drawn largely even on their well-lined purses, and the Knights of the Temple deposited the king in the tomb of the most pious of monarchs — Edward the Confessor. It is difficult to say why the Templars had such love for the weak king, for he was not an encourager of knightly associations and observations. At the same time he may be said to have lowered the estimation in which knighthood had been held, by making the honor itself cheap, and sometimes even less than that — unwelcome. Henry III. issued a writ in the twenty-ninth year of his reign, summoning tenants in chief to come and receive knighthood at his hands: and tenants of mesne lords to be knighted by whomsoever they pleased. It may be believed that this last permission was abused, for soon after this period "it became an established principle of our law that no subject can confer knighthood except by the king's authority." So says Hallam. The most extraordinary law or custom of this reign with respect to chivalry was, that any man who possessed an annual income of fifteen pounds derived from land, was to be *compelled* to receive the honor of knighthood.

## THE KINGS OF ENGLAND AS KNIGHTS 335

The successor of Henry, Edward I., was of a far more knightly quality. Faithful in love, intrepid in battle, generous to the needy, and courteous to all—except when his temper was crossed—he may pass muster as a very respectable knight. He was active and strong, and, with one hand on the back of his steed, could vault, at a single bound, into the saddle. Few men cared less for finery. He was even reproved on one occasion by a bishop, for being dressed beneath his dignity of either king or knight. "Father," said Edward, "what could I do more in royal robes than in this plain gaberdine?"

Edward would have acted little in the spirit of a true knight if he had really acted toward the Bards, according to the cruel fashion recorded in history. I am inclined to believe with Davies, in his "Mythology of the Druids," that this king has been calumniated in this respect. "There is not the name," says Davies, "of a single bard upon record who suffered either by his hand or by his orders. His real act was the removal of that patronage, under which the bards had, hitherto, cherished the heathenish superstition of their ancestors, to the disgrace of our native princes." This king showed a feeling common with many knights, that however indifferently they might look living, in rusty armor or faded mantle, they should wear a decent and comely covering when dead. Thus he ordered that every year his tomb should be opened, and his remains covered with a new cere-cloth or pall. It was a pride akin to that of Mrs. Oldfield's, in the days of our grandmothers, who was buried in a Brussels lace head-dress, a Holland shift with tucker and double ruffles of the same lace, and a pair of new kid gloves. The same weakness of nature marked both the tragedy-queen and the actual king; and it marks many more than they. There was more humility, however, in the second Duke Richard of Normandy, who was far more chivalrous than Edward I., and who ordered his body to be buried at the church-door, where passengers might tread upon it, and the spouts from the roof discharge their water upon it.

It was in the religious spirit of chivalry that Edward I. expelled the Jews. One curious result is said to have followed. Report alleges that many of the Jewish families fled into Scotland, where "they have propagated ever since in great numbers; witness the aversion this nation has above others to hog's flesh."

Of the unfortunate Edward II., it may be said that he was an indifferent knight, who gave the honors of chivalry to very indifferent persons, and committed great outrages on knightly orders themselves. In the annals of knighthood he is remembered as the monarch who abolished the Order of Knights Templars in England. He treated the luckless chevaliers with far more generosity than Henry VIII. observed toward the ejected monks and abbots. He allowed two shillings per day to the deprived master of the Temple, and fourpence each daily to the other knights for their support, out of their former confiscated property. Edward himself loved carousing and hunting, more than any other pastime. There were other pleasures, indeed, in which he greatly delighted, and these are well catalogued in one of Gaveston's speeches in Marlowe's tragedy, called by this king's name:—

> "I must have wanton poets, pleasant wits,
> Musicians, that with touching of a string,
> May draw the pliant king which way I please;
> Music and poetry are his delight,
> Therefore I'll have Italian masks by night,
> Sweet speeches, comedies, and pleasing slaves;
> And in the day, when he shall walk abroad,
> Like sylvan nymphs my pages shall be clad;
> My men, like satyrs grazing on the lawns,
> Shall with their goats' feet dance the antic hay.
> Sometimes a lovely boy, in Dian's shape,
> With hair that gilds the water as it glides
> Coronets of pearl about his naked arms,
> And in his sportive hands an olive-tree,
> To hide those parts which men delight to see,
> Shall bathe him in a spring; and there hard by
> One, like Actæon, peeping through the grove,
> Shall by the angry goddess be transformed,
> And running in the likeness of a hart,
> By yelping hounds pulled down, shall seem to die;
> Such things as these best please his majesty."

How dearly he paid for indulgence in such pleasures, and how meekly he accepted his fierce destiny or retribution, need not be detailed here.

Whatever may be thought of the character of Edward II. himself, his chivalry wrought little good for the realm. The crown of England during his reign was weaker; and as the knight-historian, Sir J. Davies, remarks in his History of Ireland, "suffered more dishonor in both kingdoms than at any time since the Norman Conquest." There were few such honest knights, too, in that reign, as in that of the third Edward, when Sir Thomas Rookesby, an eminent law-knight and judge, was wont to say that he "would eat in wooden dishes, but would pay gold and silver for his meat." In this speech a blow was dealt at the extravagant people who in order "to eat off plate," made no scruple of cheating their butcher.

In Edward III. we have a king who is more closely connected with knightly associations in our memory than any other sovereign of England. He it was who, by reviving or reconstructing the ancient order, founded by Richard I., of "The Blue Thong"—a leather knee-band, worn by certain of the English crusaders—formed that brilliant Order of the Garter, which has been conferred on so few who are deserving, and on so many whose claims were not so great as their "pretensions."

How far gallantry to the Countess of Salisbury had to do with the renewing of the Order of the Blue Thong, under the name of the Garter, is still an unsettled rather than a disputed point. Froissart's account is: "You have all heard how passionately King Edward was smitten with the charms of the noble Lady Katherine, Countess of Salisbury. Out of affection to the said lady, and his desire to see her, he proclaimed a great feast, in August, 1343. He commanded all his own lords and knights should be there without fail, and he expressly ordered the Earl of Salisbury to bring his lady, his wife, with as many young ladies as she could collect to attend her. The Earl very cheerfully complied with the king's request, for he thought no evil, and his good lady dared not to say nay. She came, however, much against her will, for she guessed the reason which made the king so earnest for her attendance, but was afraid to discover it to her husband, intending by her conduct to make the king change his opinion. . . All the ladies and damsels who assisted at the first convocation of the Order of the Garter came superbly dressed, excepting the

Countess of Salisbury, who attended the festival, dressed as plainly as possible; she did not wish the king to admire her, for she had no intention to obey him in anything evil, that might tend to the dishonor of her dear lord." The repetition of the word *evil* here, has probably nothing to do with the motto of the Garter, but I may notice that when Froissart calls the above festival a convocation of the order, he is in error, for, the first *chapter* of the Garter was held at Windsor, on St. George's Day, 1344. At this chapter Queen Philippa was present in the robes of the order; for every knight's lady in the olden time shared in the knightly honors of her lord.

How Edward bore himself in tournament and battle we all know. Both historians and poets have rejoiced to exhibit this chivalrous monarch as a lover, and he is even more interesting as a knight in love than as one in war, and moreover as the account of him in the former character reveals some other incidents of knightly life, I will borrow Froissart's historical picture of Edward in a lady's bower, and contrast therewith the picture of the same monarch in the same circumstances, as depicted by the hands of a poet. It is only necessary to premise that the lady who was the object of Edward's homage was Katherine de Granson, daughter of a handsome, penniless knight, and a rich Wiltshire heiress named Sibyl. "Katherine the fair," says Miss Strickland, "was the only child of this couple, and was richly endowed with her mother's wealth and her father's beauty. She bestowed *both* on the brave Earl of Salisbury"— who, if he was ugly as he was valiant, must have been grateful for the gift of the beauty of William de Granson.

When Edward wooed the countess, the earl was a prisoner in France, and the lady's castle of Wark had just been relieved from siege laid against it by an army of Scots. "The moment the countess heard the king's approach she ordered all the gates to be thrown open, and went out to meet him most richly dressed, insomuch that no one could look at her, but with wonder and admiration at her noble deportment and affability of behavior. When she came near King Edward she made her obeisance to the ground, and gave him thanks for coming to her assistance, and then conducted him into the castle, to entertain and honor him, as she was very capable of doing. Every one was delighted with her; but the king could not take his eyes from her; so that a spark of fine love struck upon his heart, which lasted for a long time, for he did not believe that the whole world produced another such a lady, so worthy of being beloved. Thus they entered the castle, hand in hand. The countess led him first to the hall, and then to the best chamber which was very richly furnished as belonging to so fine a lady. King Edward kept his eyes so fixed upon the countess that the gentle lady was quite abashed. After he had sufficiently examined his apartment, he retired to a window, and leaning on it, fell into a profound revery.

"The countess left him, to order dinner to be made ready, and the table set, and the hall ornamented and set out; likewise to welcome the knights and lords who accompanied the king. When she had given all the orders to her servants she thought needful, she returned with a cheerful countenance to King Edward and said: 'Dear sir, what are you musing on? Such meditation is not proper for you, saving your grace! You ought rather to be in high spirits, having freed England from her enemy without loss of blood.' The king replied, 'Oh, dear lady, you must know since I have been in this castle, some thoughts have oppressed my mind that I was not before aware of, so that it behooves me to reflect. Being uncertain what may be the event, I can not withdraw my attention.' 'Dear sir,' answered the lady, 'you ought to be of good cheer, and feast with your friends to give them more pleasure, and leave off pondering, for God has been very bountiful to you in your undertakings, so that you are the most feared and renowned prince in Christendom. If the king of Scotland have vexed you by the mischief he hath done in your kingdom, you will speedily be able to make reprisals in his dominions. Therefore, come, if it please you, into the hall to your knights, for your dinner will soon be served.' 'Oh, sweet lady,' said King Edward, 'there be other things which touch my heart and lie heavy there, than what you talk of. For in good truth, your beauteous mien, and the perfection of your face and behavior have wholly overcome me, and so deeply impress my heart, that my happiness wholly depends on meeting a return to my flame, which no denial from you can ever extinguish.' 'Oh, my dear lord,' replied the countess, 'do not amuse yourself by laughing at me with trying to tempt me; for I can not believe you are in earnest as to what you have just said. Is it likely that so gallant and noble a prince, as you are, would ever think of dishonoring either me or my husband, a valiant knight, who has served you so faithfully, and who now lies in a doleful prison on your account? Certainly, sir, this would not redound to your glory, nor would you be the better if you could have your wayward will.'

"The virtuous lady then quitted the king, who was astonished at her words. She went into the hall to hasten dinner; afterward she approached the king's chamber, attended by all the knights, and said to him, 'My lord king, your knights are all waiting for you, to wash their hands, for they, as well as yourself, have fasted too long.' King Edward left his apartment, and came to the hall, where, after he had washed his hands, he seated himself with his knights at the dinner, as did the lady also; but the king ate very little, and was the whole time pensive, casting his eyes, whenever he had the opportunity, on the countess. Such behavior surprised his friends, for they were not accustomed to it, never having seen the like before in the king. They supposed it was his chagrin at the departure of the Scots without a battle. The king remained at the castle the whole day, without knowing what to do with himself. Thus did he pass that day and a sleepless night, debating the matter within his own heart. At daybreak he rose, drew out his whole army, exercised his camp, and made ready to follow the Scots. Upon taking leave of the countess he said, 'My dear lady, God preserve you safe till I return; and I pray that you will think well of what I have said, and have the goodness to give me a different answer.' 'My gracious liege,' replied the countess, 'God of his infinite goodness preserve you, and drive from your noble heart such villanous thoughts, for I am, and ever shall be, willing to serve you, but only in what is consistent with my honor and with yours.' The king left her, quite astonished at her answers." He was, in fact, a very villanous personage in these matters, and looked for as much submission from those ladies on whom he cast his eyes, as the Czar Nicholas did from the loyal ladies whom that "copper captain" delighted to favor.

An unknown poet, of the period between 1590 and 1600, in an

## THE KINGS OF ENGLAND AS KNIGHTS.

historical play entitled "Edward III." has reproduced this incident, and worked it up for the stage—with some touches which are probably warranted by facts, and which, for that reason alone, render the passage worth transcribing.

> *Edward (solus).* She is grown more fairer far, since I came hither.
> Her voice more silver ev'ry word than other,
> Her wit more fluent; what a strange discourse
> Unfolded she of David and his Scots!
> Even thus, quoth she, he spoke; and then *spake broad
> With epithets and accent of the Scot;*
> But somewhat better than the Scot could speak:
> And then, quoth she, and answered then herself;
> For who could speak like her? but she herself
> Breathes from the wall an angel note from heaven
> Of sweet defiance to her barbarous foes—
> When she could talk of peace, methinks her tongue
> Commanded war to prison; when of war,
> It wakened Cæsar from his Roman grave,
> To hear war beautified by her discourse.
> Wisdom is foolishness, but in her tongue;
> Beauty is slander, but in her fair face;
> There is no summer, but in her cheerful looks;
> Nor frosty winter, but in her disdain.
> I can not blame the Scots that did besiege her,
> For she is all the treasure of our land;
> But call them cowards that they ran away,
> Having so rich and fair a cause to stay.
>
> \* \* \* \* \* \*
>
> *Countess.* Sorry am I to see my liege so sad;
> What may thy subject do to drive from thee
> This gloomy consort, sullen Melancholy?
>
> *Edward.* Ah, Lady! I am blunt and can not straw
> The flowers of solace in a ground of shame.
> Since I came hither, Countess, I am wronged.
>
> *Countess.* Now, God forbid that any in my house
> Should think my sov'reign wrong! Thrice gentle king,
> Acquaint me with your cause of discontent.
>
> *Edward.* How near then shall I be to remedy?
>
> *Countess.* As near, my liege, as all my woman's power
> Can pawn itself to buy thy remedy.
>
> *Edward.* If thou speak'st true, then have I my redress.
> Engage thy power to redeem my joys,
> And I am joyful, Countess; else I die.
>
> *Countess.* I will, my liege.

*Edward.* Swear, Countess, that thou wilt.
*Countess.* By Heaven, I will!
*Edward.* Then take thyself a little way aside,
And tell thyself a king doth dote on thee.
Say that within thy power it doth lie
To make him happy; and that thou hast sworn
To give him all the joy within thy power.
Do this, and tell him, when I shall be happy.
*Countess.* All this is done, my thrice-dread sovereign.
That power of love that I have power to give
Thou hast, with all devout obedience.
Employ me how thou wilt, in proof thereof.
*Edward.* Thou hear'st me say that I do dote on thee.
*Countess.* If on my beauty, take it, if thou canst.
Though little, I do prize it ten times less;
If on my virtue, take it, if thou canst;
For virtue's store, by giving, doth augment.
Be it on what it will that I can give,
And thou canst take away, inherit it.
*Edward.* It is thy beauty that I would enjoy.
*Countess.* Oh! were it painted, I would wipe it off,
And dispossess myself to give it thee.
But, sov'reign, it is soldered to my life.
Take one and both; for, like an humble shadow,
It haunts the sunshine of my summer's life.
*Edward.* But thou mayst lend it me in sport withal.
*Countess.* As easy may my intellectual soul
Be lent away, and yet my body live,
As lend my body (palace to my soul)
Away from her, and yet retain my soul.
My body is her bower, her court, her abbey,
And she an angel, pure, divine, unspotted.
If I should lend her house, my lord, to thee,
I kill my poor soul, and my poor soul me.
*Edward.* Didst thou not swear to give me what I would?
*Countess.* I did, my liege; so what you would I could.
*Edward.* I wish no more of thee than thou mayst give.
Nor beg I do not, but I rather buy;
That is thy love; and for that love of thine,
In rich exchange I tender to thee mine.
*Countess.* But that your lips were sacred, my good lord,
You would profane the holy name of love.
That love you offer me, you can not give;
For Cæsar owes that tribute to his queen.
That love you beg of me I can not give;
For Sarah owes that duty to her lord.

> He that doth clip or counterfeit your stamp
> Shall die, my lord; and shall your sacred self
> Commit high treason 'gainst the King of Heav'n,
> To stamp his image in forbidden metal,
> Forgetting your allegiance and your oath?
> In violating marriage' sacred law
> You break a greater honor than yourself.
> *To be a king* is of a younger house
> Than *to be married;* your progenitor,
> Sole-reigning Adam on the universe,
> By God was honored for a married man,
> But not by Him anointed for a king.
> It is a penalty to break your statutes,
> Though not enacted with your highness' hand;
> How much more to infringe the holy act
> Made by the mouth of God, sealed with his hand?
> I know my sovereign in my husband's love
> Doth but to try the wife of Salisbury,
> Whether she will hear a wanton's tale or no;
> Lest, being guilty therein, by my stay,
> From that, not from my liege, I turn away.

The countess, naturally, has the best of the argument, and shames the king. In this pleasant light is she presented by both chronicler and poet, and the lady, chiefly to honor whom the Order of the Garter was constructed upon the basis of the Order of the Blue Thong, was worthy of all the distinctive homage that could be rendered to her by knight or king.

Richard II., so fond of parade and pleasure, so refined and intellectual, so affable at first, so despotic and absolute at last, till he was superseded and then slain, is among the most melancholy of knights and sovereigns. He was not heroic, for he was easily elevated and easily depressed. He turned deadly pale on hearing, in Ireland, of the landing of Henry Bolingbroke in England, and that the Archbishop of Canterbury had preached in favor of the usurper. He was eminently courageous, sang a roundelay as well as any minstrel, and often made the roundelays he sung. He looked little like a knight indeed when he traversed part of Wales to Conway, disguised as a Franciscan friar; or flying from castle to castle, having sorry lodging and little food. It was in the dress and cowl of a monk that the once chivalrous Richard surrendered himself to his cousin. In the army of that cousin, sent to take

Richard and his few faithful knights and squires who refused to detach his device from their coats, was "Sir Henry Percy" (the *Hotspur* of Shakespeare), "whom they held to be the best knight in England."

It was by persuasion of Hotspur's father that Richard left Conway for Flint, where he was made prisoner, and afterward conveyed to Chester, the English knights of the opposite faction behaving to him with most unchivalric rudeness. The unsceptred monarch was first taken to Pickering, one of the most beautiful spots in England, defaced by scenes of the greatest crimes, of which place knights and nobles were the masters. Thence he passed on to Leeds and Knaresborough Castle, where the king's chamber is still pointed out to visiters. Finally, he was carried to "bloody Pomfret"—"fatal and ominous to noble peers." Never, it is said, did man look less like a knight than the unhappy king, when he appeared before the drawbridge of Pontefract Castle. Majestic still he was in feature, but the majesty was depressed by such profound melancholy, that few could look upon the weeping king without themselves shedding tears. If the picture of him at this juncture might be metrically given in outline, the following sketch might feebly render it:—

> Who enters now that gate,
> With dignity upon his pallid brow?
> Who is the man that, bending to his fate,
>     Comes hither now?
>
> A man of wo he seems,
> Whom Sadness deep hath long marked for her own.
> Hath such a form as that indulged in dreams
>     Upon a throne?
>
> Have smiles e'er wreathed that face?
> Face now so stamped with every line that's sad;
> Was joy e'er known those quivering lips to grace,
>     That heart to glad?
>
> Who is this shadow's shade?
> This type of withered majesty? this thing?
> Can it be true that knightly form decayed
>     Was once a king?

Son of a noble sire,
And of his father's virtues too, the heir;
Those eyes so dim once rivalled the sun's fire;
 None were more fair.

Gallant, and light of heart,
The rock-born eagle was less bold than he;
Formed upon earth to play each graceful part
 Enchantingly.

His joys were early crushed;
His mind perverted by most ruthless men;
Hope, like a short-lived rose, a moment blushed,
 And withered then.

His virtues were his own;
His vices forced upon him, against his will;
His weaker faults were of his age alone—
 That age of ill.

In him thou seest the truth,
How tyrannous and all-usurping night,
Heedless of means, will, acting without ruth,
 Triumph o'er Right.

Nor is this lesson sad
Void of instruction to the wary sent.
Learn from it with thy portion to be glad,
 Meek and content.

And be, where'er thy path,
Whate'er the trials life may to thee bring,
Grateful that Heaven has not, in its wrath,
 Made thee a king!

Of the chivalrous spirit of Henry IV. no one entertains a doubt, and yet he once refused to accept a challenge. The challenger was the Duke of Orleans, who had been Henry's sworn friend, accomplice in some of his deeds, and who, failing to realize all the advantages he expected, urged Henry to meet him in the marches of Guienne, with a hundred knights on each side. Henry fenced with the challenge rather than with the challenger, but when the latter called him rebel, usurper, and murderer, he gave his former friend the lie, in no very gentle terms, as regarded the charge of being accessory to the death of Richard. The little flower, the Forget-me-not, owes some of its popularity to Henry, who, previous to his being king, and when in exile, chose it for his symbol, wore it in gold on his collar, and added to it by way of device, the words "Souvenez de moi." It is worthy of observation that, after Henry's death, his widow, Joanna of Navarre, continued to be recognised as a lady of the Garter, receiving presents from Henry V. as such, and being in attendance on high festivals, in robes of the order, the gift of the new king.

That new king requires no advocacy as a knight. The simple word "Agincourt" is sufficient. His wooing of Katherine of Valois is also characteristic of the gallant, if not the amorous knight. At the betrothal of the illustrious couple, Henry presented to the lady his own favorite knight, Sir Louis de Robsart, as her personal attendant, to watch for ever over her safety; but this queen's knight was simply the queen's keeper, and his chief mission was to take care that the lady was not stolen from him, between the day of betrothal and that of the royal nuptials.

Although the reign of Henry V. formed a period of glory for knighthood, the victories obtained by the chivalrous combatants were effected at such a cost, that toward the close of the reign, there were not men enough in England qualified to competently carry on its civil business. It was still worse under Henry VI. When peace with France was negotiating, the Cardinal of Winchester represented to the French government that, during a struggle of a quarter of a century, there had been more men, of both countries, slain in these wars, for the title and claim to the crown of France, than there were then existing in the two nations. It was shocking, the Cardinal said, to think of so much Christian blood having been shed;—and there were not very many Christian knights left to cry "hear, hear," to such an assertion.

Least cavalier of any of the kings who had hitherto reigned was Henry VI., but there was chivalry enough for two in the heart of his admirable wife, the most heroic, perhaps, of English queens, Margaret of Anjou. How unlike was the destiny of this ill-matched pair to that of their successors Edward IV. and his wife Elizabeth Woodville! This king assumed one privilege of knighthood, by loving whom he pleased, and marrying whom he loved. He was the first king of England who married with a simple lady, that is, one not of princely blood. He did not prosper much the more for it, for his reign was one of a rather splendid misery, in which the luxurious king was faithful to no one, neither to the friends who upheld his cause, nor to Mistress Shore, who helped him to render his cause unworthy. Passing over Edward V., we may notice that there was much more of the knightly character in Richard III., than in the fourth Edward. Richard would be better appreciated if we judged him according to the spirit of the times in which he was born, and not by the standard of our own. A braver monarch never fronted an English force; and if heavy crimes can justly be laid to his account, it should not be forgotten, that amid the bloody struggles which he had to maintain, from the day almost of his accession, he had leisure to put in force more than one enactment by which English people profit, down even to the present period.

I have elsewhere remarked that many of us originally take our idea of Henry VII. from the dashing Richmond who opens the fifth act of Richard III. in panoply and high spirits. None of Shakespeare's characters make a more knight-like appearance than he. The fact, nevertheless, is that Henry was anything but chivalrous in mien or carriage. His mother was married, it was said, when only nine years old; and it is added that Henry was born in the year following the marriage. It is certain that the lady was not in her teens, and to this circumstance, Turner is inclined to attribute the feebleness of Henry's constitution.

If he could not so well defend himself by the sword as poets and Tudor historians have declared he could, he at least knew how to do so by the strong arm of the law. It was in his reign that benefit of clergy was taken from lay persons murdering their lord, master, or sovereign immediate.

It is as certain that, in some parts of the island at least, the chivalry of Richard, who was never nearly so black as he has been painted, was more appreciated than the cautiousness of his successful rival. In the northern counties, says Bacon, "the memory of King Richard was so strong, that it lay like lees in the bottom of men's hearts, and if the vessel was but stirred, it would come up."

The *gallant* sentiment of chivalry was really strongly impressed on the popular mind at this period. I may cite as an instance, that not only was Perkin Warbeck, who may be called an adventurous knight who has not had due justice rendered to him, familiarly spoken of by the name of "the White Rose;" but that if we may believe Bacon, the name was continued in common speech to his wife, in compliment to her true beauty.

Henry has been much censured for a vice from which all knights were bound, like friars, to be free. But there were chevaliers in his reign who were as fond of money as he. Sir William Stanley was one of them. At the period of his execution, there was found in his castle of Holt, a more than modest temporary provision for a poor knight. In ready money alone, there were forty thousand marks—to say nothing of plate, jewelry, household furniture, and live stock, all in abundance, and of the first quality. "And for his revenue in land and fee, it was three thousand pounds sterling a year of old rent, great matter in those times. The great spoil of Bosworth field came almost wholly into this man's hands, to his infinite enriching."

Bacon classes Henry VII., Louis XI., and Ferdinand of Aragon, as the three *Magi* of kings of the age in which they lived. It is a happy classification. Ferdinand, however, had more of the knight in him than his royal cousins, and not less of the statesman. He it was who first invented the resident embassador at foreign courts.

In chivalric bearing, Henry VIII., when young, was perhaps never equalled, and certainly never surpassed. He was the most courteous of knights, and the most gallant of gentlemen. As long as he had Cardinal Wolsey at his side to guide and control him, he maintained this character unimpaired; and it was not till this old Mentor died, that Henry lost his reputation as a Christian knight and gentleman.

By a decree of the 24th of this king's reign, no person below the degree of a knight could wear a collar of SS. The judges wear such collars because they are, or rank with, knights. That a decree was issued to this effect would seem to imply that previous to the period named, individuals below the knightly degree might wear the collar in question. Edward IV., therefore, when he conferred the collar on the Tanner of Tamworth, was not guilty of any anomaly. On the contrary, he evidently knew what he was about, by the remark—

> "So here I *make* thee the best Esquire
> That is in the North Countrie."

In Edward's time then, the collar may have constituted the difference between squire and knight. But it was not the only one. If there was a difference at their necks, there was also a distinction at their heels. The knight always wore golden spurs : he was the Eques Auratus. The squire could wear spurs of no more costly metal than silver, and "White-spurs," accordingly, was the generic term for an esquire. It was probably in allusion to this that the country squire mentioned by Jonson, displayed his silver spurs among his side-board plate. To return to Henry VIII.; let me add that he exhibited something of what was considered a knightly attribute, compassion for the lowly, when he suggested that due sleeping-time should be allowed to laborers during the summer.

Edward VI. was simply a youth of much promise. His father was unwilling to create him a knight before he knew how to wield arms; and if he gained this knowledge early, he was never called to put it in practice. There was more of the chivalrous character in his over-abused half-sister, Mary, and also in Elizabeth; but then queens can not of course be considered as knights: Elizabeth, however, had much of the spirit, and she was surrounded by knightly men and served with a knightly devotion. There was, I may observe, one species of knights in her time, who were known as "knights of the road." The 39th of Elizabeth, especially and curiously points to them in an act to relieve the hundred of Beynhurst from the statute of Hue and Cry (where there was no voluntary default) on account of the penalties to which that hundred was subject from the numerous robberies committed in Maidenhead Thicket. Mavor, in his account of Berkshire, says that "The vicar of Henley who served the curé of Maidenhead, was allowed about the same time an advance of salary as some compensation for the danger of passing the thicket." The vicar, like the knights of the road, at least, had purer air than the clergy and chivalry who kept house in the capital. "In London," says Euphues, "are all things (as the fame goeth) that may either please the sight, or dislike the smell; either fill the eye with delight, or fill the nose with infection."

Refreshment under such circumstances was doubly needed; and the popular gratitude was due to that most serviceable of knights, Sir Thomas Gresham, who introduced the orange as an article of trade, and who was consequently painted by Antonio More with an orange in his hand. The old Utrecht artist just named, was knighted by Charles V. who paid him poorly—some six hundred ducats for three pictures, but added knighthood, which cost the emperor nothing, and was esteemed of great value by the painter.

One would imagine that under Mary and Elizabeth, knighthood had become extinguished, were we to judge by an anonymous volume which was published in Mary's reign, and republished in that of Elizabeth. The great names of that period are proof to the contrary, but there may have been exceptions. Let us then look into the volume of this unknown writer who bewails the degeneracy of his times, and lays down what he entitles the "Institution of a Gentleman."

## "THE INSTITUTION OF A GENTLEMAN."

"Your countenance, though it be glossed with knighthood, looks so borrowingly, that the best words you give me are as dreadful as 'stand and deliver.'"—*The Asparagus Garden.*

THE unknown author of the "Institution of a Gentleman," dedicates his able treatise to "Lorde Fitzwater, sonne and heire to the Duke of Sussex." In his dedicatory epistle he does not so much mourn over a general decay of manners, as over the lamentable fact, that the lowly-born are rising to gentility, while nobility and knighthood are going to decay. These he beseeches "to build gentry up again, which is, for truth sore decayed, and fallen to great ruin, whereby such great corruption of manners hath taken place, that almost the name of gentleman is quenched, and handicraftsmen have obtained the title of honor, though (indeed) of themselves they can challenge no greater worthiness than the spade brought unto their late fathers."

The writer is troubled with the same matter in his introductory chapter. This chapter shows how, at this time, trade was taking equality with gentry. "Yea, the merchantman thinketh not himself well-bred unless he be called one of the worshipful sort of merchants, of whom the handicraftsman hath taken example; and taketh to be called 'Master,' whose father and grandfather were wont to be called 'Good Man.'"

On the question of "What is a gentleman?" the author goes back to a very remote period, that of Adam, quoting the old saying:—

> "When Adam delved and Eve span,
> Who was then the gentleman?"

and he makes the following comment upon this well-known text:

"There be many of so gross understanding that they think to

confound a gentleman, when they ask of him this question. To whom it may be said that so much grace as Adam our first father, received of God at his creation, so much nobility and gentry he received. And to understand perfectly how and after what demeanor Adam behaved himself, or how he directed the order of his life, the witnesses, I think, in that behalf are far to seek, whose behavior, if it were good and honest, then was he the first gentleman, even so much as the first earthly follower of virtues. But if there were in him no such virtue, then was he the first gentleman in whom virtues and gentle deeds did first appear."

As a training toward excellence, our anonymous author recommends severity of discipline from the cradle upward. "Neither," he says, "do I mean to allow *any* liberty to youth, for as liberty is to all eyes hurtful, so is it to youth a present poison;" but he forgets that even poisons are administered in small doses in order to cure certain diseases, and that life would be a disease, even to the young, without some measure of liberty. He is terribly afraid that freedom in childhood will spoil the man, who himself will be no man, with too much liberty, but a " Royster ;" "and a ' Royster,'" he adds, "can not do the office of a gentleman, so long I mean as a Roysterian he doth continue."

He then informs us that there had long been in England a division of classes, under the heads of " Gentle Gentle, Gentle Ungentle, and Ungentle Gentle." These were not classes of society generally, but classes of the orders of Gentlemen exclusively. The *Gentle Gentle* are those of noble birth, from dukes' sons down to esquires, provided they join to their " gentle house, gentle manners, and noble conditions, which is the cause of the addition of the other word called gentle." This is much such a definition of gentleman as might be now given, with the exception that the question of birth has little to do with the matter, and that gentle manners and noble conditions, as our author calls gentlemanlike bearing, scholarly education, and Christian principles, now make of a man a gentleman, let him be of "gentle" house or not. Indeed, the author himself is not indisposed to accept this method of definition, for on proceeding to tell us what " Gentle Ungentle" is, he says that " Gentle Ungentle is that man which is descended of noble parentage, by the which he is commonly called gentle, and hath in him such corrupt and ungentle manners as to the judgment of all men he justly deserveth the name of ungentle." His remedy again for preventing the gentle becoming ungentle is coercion in youth-time. He thinks that virtue is to be got from the human being like oils or other juices from certain vegetable substances, by ex-pression. Squeeze the human being tightly, press him heavily, he is sure to yield something. No doubt; but after the pressure he is often of little more use than a well-sucked orange.

We next come to the "Ungentle Gentle." In the definition of this term, the author, with all his reverence for nobility, is compelled to allow that there is a nobility of condition as well as a nobility of birth; but others who contested this fact, gave a new word to the English tongue, or made a new application of an old word in order to support their theory and assail those whom they sought to lower.

"Ungentle Gentle," says our author, "is he which is born of a low degree—which man, taking his beginning of a poor kindred, by his virtue, wit, policy, industry, knowledge in laws, valiancy in arms, or such like honest means, becometh a well-behaved and high-esteemed man, preferred then to great office, put in great charge and credit, even so much as he becometh a post or stay of the commonwealth, and so growing rich, doth thereby advance and set up the rest of his poor line or kindred. They are the children of such one commonly called gentleman; of which sort of gentleman we have now in England very many, whereby it should appear that virtue flourisheth among us. These gentlemen are now called 'Up-starts,' a term lately invented by such as pondered not the grounds of honest means of rising or coming to promotion." Nevertheless, says our censor, there be upstarts enough and to spare. The worshipful unworthies, he tells us, abound; and the son of good-man Thomas, or good-man John, have obtained the name of gentlemen, the degree of esquires or knights, and possessing "a little dunghill forecast to get lands, by certain dark augmentative practices," they are called "worshipful" at every assize. He dates the origin of this sort of nobility, knighthood and esquirearchy, from the time of the suppression and confiscation of abbeys and abbey-estates. He has a curious passage on this subject:—

"They have wrongfully intruded into gentry, and thrust themselves therein, as Bayard, the cart-jade, might leap into the stable of Bucephalus, and thrust his head into the manger with that worthy courser. The particular names of whom, if I should go about to rehearse, it would require long labor, and bring no fruit to the readers thereof. And it is well known that such intruders, such unworthy worshipful men, have chiefly flourished since the putting down of abbeys, which time is within my remembrance."

While allowing that gentlemanly manners help to make the gentleman, and that birth is only an accidental matter, having little to do with the subject, he still can not forbear to reverence rather good men of high birth than good men of low degree. He evidently thinks that he was enjoined by religion to do so, for he remarks: "As in times past, no man was suffered to be 'Knyght of the Roodes,' but such one as was descended of the lyne of gentleman, whereby it appeareth that no men were thought so meet to defend the right, that is to say the faith of Christ, as gentlemen, and so to have their offices agreeable with their profession, it is most meet that all gentlemen be called to such room and office as may be profitable to the commonwealth." This idea that the holy sepulchre was to be rescued from the infidels only by gentlemen, and the fact that it has not been so rescued, reminds me of that king of Spain, who, finding himself in danger of being roasted alive, from sitting in a chair which one of his great officers had placed too near the fire, chose to roast on, for the singular reason that there was no grandee at hand to draw his chair away again!

In 1555, this writer still accounted the profession of arms as the noblest, the most profitable to the professor, and the most useful to the commonwealth. Courage, liberality, and faithful observance of all promises; thus endowed, he thinks a man is a true gentleman. He draws, however, a happy parallel when admitting that if it become a gentleman to be a good knight and valiant soldier, it even more becometh him to be a great statesman. For, "although to do valiantly in the wars it deserveth great praise and recompense, yet to minister justice in the state of peace is an office worthy of higher commendation. The reason is, wars are nothing necessary, but of necessity must be defended when they fall. And contrariwise, peace is a thing not only most necessary, but it is called the best thing which even nature hath given unto man." This parallel, if indeed it may be so called, is only employed, however, for the purpose of showing that certain posts in the state should only be given to gentlemen born. There is a good deal of the red-tapist in our moralist after all; and he has a horror, still entertained in certain localities, of admitting the democratic element into the public offices. Thus we find him maintaining that, " Unto a gentleman appertaineth more fully than unto any other sort of man, embassage or message to be done between kings or princes of this earth; more fitly I say, because gentlemen do know how to bear countenance and comely gesture before the majesty of a king, better than other sorts of men." One would think that the majesty of a king was something too dazzling for a common man of common sense to look upon and live, and yet the writer is evidently aware that there is nothing in it, for he concludes his chapter on this matter by observing that " a gentleman sent of embassage unto a prince ought to think a king to be but a man, and, in reverence and humility, boldly to say his message unto him." Surely a man of good sense might do this, irrespective of his birth, particularly at a time when the unskilfulness and ignorance of gentlemen were so great as to pass into a proverb, and " He shooteth like a gentleman fair and far off," implied not only ill-shooting with bows and arrows, "but it extended farther and reached to greater matters, all to the dispraise of ignorant gentlemen."

It is so common a matter with us to refer to the days in which this author wrote, as days in which old knights and country gentlemen maintained such hospitality as has seldom been since witnessed, that we are surprised to find complaint made, in this treatise, of something just the contrary. The author enjoins these knights and gentlemen to repair less to London, and be more seen dispensing hospitality in their own houses. " In the ancient times," he says, " when curious buildings fed not the eye of the wayfaring man, then might he be fed and have good repast at a gentleman's place, so called. Then stood the buttery door without a hatch; yeoman then had no cause to carve small dishes; Flanders cooks had then no wages for their devices, nor square tables were not used. This variety and change from the old English manner hath smally enriched gentlemen, but much it hath impoverished their names, not without just punishment of their inconsistency in that behalf." Let me add, that the writer thinks the country knight or gentleman would do well were he to exercise the office of justice of the peace. He is sorely afraid, however, that there is a disqualification, on the ground of ignorance. A moralist might have the same fear just now, without coming to the same conclusion. Our author, for instance, argues that reverence is to be paid to the noble, *quand même*. Let him be ignorant and tyrannical, yet to reverence him is to give example of obedience to others. This is very poor logic, and what follows is still worse; for this writer very gravely remarks, that "We ought to bear the offences of noble men patiently, and that if these forget themselves, yet ought not smaller men to be oblivious of their duty in consequence, and fail in their respect."

We come upon another social trait, when we find the author lamenting that, however much it becometh a gentleman to be acquainted with hawking and hunting, yet that these pastimes are so abused by being followed to excess, that "gentlemen will almost do nothing else, or at the least can do that better than any other thing." To the excess alluded to does the author trace the fact that "there are so many raw soldiers when time of war requireth their help. This is the cause of so many unlearned gentlemen, which, as some say, they understand not the inkhorn terms that are lately crept into our language. And no marvel it is, though they do not understand them, whereas in their own hawking and hunting terms they be ignorants as 'Auvent' and 'Retrouvre,' which they call '*Houent*' and '*Retrires*.'" What better could be expected from men who had given up the practice of the long bow to take to the throwing of dice? But there was now as wild extravagance of dress as ignorance of uncommon things, in the class of foolish knights and gentlemen. This is alluded to in the chapter on dress, wherein it is said that "the sum of one hundred pounds is not to be accounted in these days to be bestowed of apparel for one gentleman, but in times past, a chamber gown was a garment which dwelt with an esquire of England twenty years"—

and I believe that the knights were as frugal as the esquires. "Then flourished the laudable simplicity of England," exclaims the author; "there were no conjurors and hot scholars, applying our minds to learne our new trifle in wearing our apparel." Upon the point of fashions, the author writes with a feeling as if he despaired of his country. "The Englishman," he observes, "changeth daily the fashion of his garment; sometimes he delighteth in many guards, welts and pinks, and pounces. Sometimes again, to the contrary, he weareth his garments as plain as a sack; yet faileth he not to change also that plainness if any other new fangle be invented. This is the vanity of his delight." And this vanity was common to all men of high degree in his time—to those to whom "honor" was due, from men of less degree—and these were "dukes, earls, lords, and such like, of high estate," as well as to those who were entitled to the "worship" of smaller men, and *these* were "knights, esquires, and gentlemen." There is here, I think, some confusion in the way such terms are applied; but I have not made the extract for the purpose of grounding a comment upon it, but because it illustrates one portion of my subject, and shows that while "your honor" was once the due phrase of respect to the peerage, "your worship" was the reverential one paid to knights, esquires, *and* gentlemen. We still apply the terms, if not to the different degrees named above, yet quite as confusedly, or as thoughtlessly with respect to the point whether there be anything honorable or worshipful in the individual addressed. This, however, is only a form lingering among the lower classes. As matters of right, however, "his honor" still sits in Chancery, and "your worship" is to be seen behind any justice's table.

We will now return to a race of kings who, whatever their defects, certainly did not lack some of the attributes of chivalry.

# THE KINGS OF ENGLAND AS KNIGHTS.

## THE STUARTS.

> "May't be pleasure to a reader's ear,
> That never drew save his own country's air,
> To hear such things related."
>
> HEYWOOD, *the English Traveller*

IT is an incontrovertible fact, that the king of England, who least of all resembled a knight in his warlike character, was the one who surpassed all his brother sovereigns in his knightly spirit as a lover. I allude to James I. The godson of Charles IX. of France was in his childhood, what his godfather had never been, a dirty, droll boy. He is the only king who ever added an original remark to a royal speech set down for him to deliver. The remark in question was, probably, nearly as long as the speech, for James was but four years old when he gave utterance to it. He had been rolling about on the throne impishly watching, the while, the grim lords to whom he, ultimately, recited a prepared speech with great gravity and correctness. At the end of his speech, he pointed to a split in the tiled roof of the hall, or to a rent in the canopy of the throne, and announced to the lords and others present the indisputable fact, that "there was a hole in the parliament."

The precocious lad passed no very melancholy boyhood in Stirling Castle, till the Raid of Ruthven took him from his natural protectors, and placed him in the hands of Gowrie. His escape thence exhibited both boldness and judgment in a youth of sixteen; and when Frederick II., of Denmark, gave him the choice of the two Danish princesses for a wife, no one thought that so gallant a king was undeserving of the compliment. When it was, however, discovered that the royal Dane required James either to accept a daughter or surrender the Orkney and Shetland islands, as property illegally wrested from Denmark, men began to look upon the Danish king as guilty of uncommonly sharp practice toward the sovereign of the Scots. A world of trouble ensued, which it is not my business to relate, although were I inclined to be discursive — which, of course, I am *not* — I might find great temptation to indulge therein, upon this very subject. Suffice it then to say, that a world of trouble ensued before James made his selection, and agreed to take, rather than prayed to have granted to him, the hand of Elizabeth, the elder daughter of Frederick II.

How the intrigues of Queen Elizabeth prevented this marriage I must not pause to relate. The Danish Princess espoused a reigning duke, and James was on the point of engaging himself to Katherine of Navarre, when the offer of the hand of Anne the younger daughter of Frederick being made to him, coupled with the alternative of his either taking Anne, or losing the islands, he "prayed and advised with God, for a fortnight," and wisely resolved to wed with " pretty Anne." [1]

The matter progressed anything but smoothly for a time. At length, after endless vexations, the young princess was married by proxy, in August, 1589, and set sail, soon after, for Scotland under convoy of a dozen gallant ships, and with prospects of a very unpleasant voyage.

A terrible storm blew bride and convoy on to the inhospitable coast of Norway, and although two or three witches were executed for raising this storm out of very spite, the matter was not mended. Disaster pursued the fleet, and death overtook several who sailed in it, till the coast of Scotland was fairly in sight. The Scotch witches, or perhaps other causes not less powerful than witches, in those seas, in the fall of the year, then blew the fleet back to the mouth of the Baltic. "I was commissioned," said Peter Munch, the admiral, "to land the young queen in Scotland; it is clear, therefore, that I can not return with her to Denmark. I will put her majesty ashore, therefore, in Norway." The conclusion was not logically attained, but the fact was as we have described it. Letters reached James announcing to him the deplorable condition in which his queen was lying at Upslo, on the Norwegian coast—storm-bound and half-famished. After many projects considered for her relief, James resolved to set forth and seek the princess himself. It is in this passage of his life that we have an illustration of the degree in which he surpassed all other kings who have sat on the English throne—as a gallant knight *es amours*.

Toward the end of October, of this year, in the very stormiest portion of the season, James went, privately, on board a diminutive vessel, with a very reluctant party of followers and confederates, leaving behind him, for the information of the astonished lieges, a promise to be back in twenty days; and for their especial profit, a solemn exhortation to live peaceably till he arrived again among them, with his wife.

The knightly lover landed in Norway, early in November, and made his way along the coast, now on foot, now on horseback anon in sledges, and occasionally in boats or on shipboard, until with infinite pains, and in a sorry plight, he reached Upslo, to no one's astonishment more than the queen's, about the 19th of November. Accoutred and travel-soiled as he was, he proceeded at once to her presence. He was so well-pleased with the fair vision before him, that he made as if he would at once kiss the queen, who stood gazing at him. "It is not the form of my country," said pretty Anne, not very violently holding her head aside. "It's good old Scottish fashion," said the young king: and it was observed that in less than an hour, Anne had fallen very completely into the pleasant mode from beyond seas, and quite forgotten the forms of Denmark.

The young couple were duly married in person, on the Sunday following the arrival of James. The latter, like any Paladin of romance, had perilled life, and contended with almost insurmountable obstacles, in order to win the royal lady after a less easy fashion than marks the wooing and wedding of kings generally. Such a couple deserved to have the merriest of marriage banquets, but while such a storm was raging without as Norway itself had never seen since the sea-wind first blew over her, such a tempest was raised within, by the Scottish nobles, on a question of precedence, that the king himself was chiefly occupied in soothing the quarrellers, and only half succeeded in accomplishing the desired end. Added to this was the prospect of a long winter among the melancholy huts of Upslo. James, however, again exhibited the spirit of a knight of more than ordinary gallantry. He not only resolved that the young queen should not be thus imprisoned amid the Norway snows till May, but he resolved to conduct her himself across the Norwegian Alps, through Sweden, to her Danish home. The idea of such a journey seemed to partake of insanity, but James proceeded to realize it, by means of method and judgment. He first performed the perilous journey alone, as far as Sweden, and finding it practicable, returned for his wife, and departed a second time, in her company. Much peril but small accident accompanied them on their way, and when the wedding party arrived safely at Cronenburg, toward the end of January, the marriage ceremony was not only repeated for the third time — to despite the witches who can do nothing against the luck that is said to lie in odd numbers, but there was a succession of marriage feasts, at which every gentleman drank deeper and deeper every day, until such uproar and dissension ensued that few kept their daggers in sheath except those who were too drunk to draw them. That all were not in the more disgraceful state, or were not continually in that condition, may be conjectured from the fact that James paid a visit to Tycho Brahe, and conversed with the astronomer in his observatory, in very vigorous Latin. The king, however, was not sorry to leave old Denmark, and when a Scottish fleet appeared off Cronenburg, to convey his bride and himself homeward, he could no more be persuaded to stay a day longer, than Tycho Brahe could be persuaded that Copernicus was correct in dislodging the earth from its Ptolemaic stand-point as centre of the solar system. The bridal party set sail on the 21st of April, 1590, and was safely moored in Leith harbor on May-day. A pretty bride could not have arrived at a more appropriate season. The royal knight and his lady deserved all the happiness that could be awarded to the gallantry of the one and the beauty of the other. But they did not escape the trials common to much less dignified couples; and here the knightly character of James may be said to terminate. Exemplary as he had been as a lover, and faithful as he continued to be as a husband, he was in all other respects, simply a shrewd man; and not indeed always *that*. There is little of this quality in a husband who begins and continues his married life with an indifference upon the matter of borrowing. With James it was silver spoons to-day, silk stockings to-morrow, and marks and moidores from any one who would give him credit. The old French knight who drank broth out of his own helmet rather than sip it from a borrowed bowl, was moved at least by a good principle. James rather agréed with Carlo Buffone, in Jonson's "Every Man out of his Humor," that "it is an excellent policy to owe much in these days." A policy which, unfortunately, is still deemed excellent, in spite of the ruin which attends its practice.

The grave chivalry impressed on the face and features of Charles I., is strikingly alluded to by Ben Jonson in his Masque of "The Metamorphosed Gypsies;" for example:—

> "His brow, his eye, and ev'ry mark of state,
> As if he were the issue of each grace,
> And bore about him *both his fame and fate*.

Echard says of him, that he was perfect in all knightly exercises, "vaulting, riding the great horse, running at the ring, shooting with cross-bows, muskets, and sometimes great guns; that if sovereignty had been the reward of excellences in those arts, he would have acquired a new title to the crown, being accounted the most celebrated marksman, and the most perfect manager of the great horse, of any in the three kingdoms."

It was with reference to the expression of the face, alluded to by Jonson, that Bernini the sculptor said, on executing the bust of Charles, that he had never seen any face which showed so much greatness, and withal such marks of sadness and misfortune. The knight, Sir Richard Bulstrode, tells us, that when the bust was being carried across Greenwich Park, it suffered, what Moore calls on another occasion, some "Tobit-like marks of patronage" from the sparrows. "It was wiped off immediately," says Charles's good knight—"but, notwithstanding all endeavors, it would not be gotten off, but turned into blood." No chevalier in poetic romance meets with more threatening portent than the above.

The Scotch soldiers of fortune, at this period, were as good representatives as could be found of the old knight-errant. To them, Vittorio Siri imputes many of the misfortunes of the period. Some one tells of an old Scottish knight exclaiming, in a year of universal peace, "Lord, turn the world upside-down, that gentlemen may make bread of it." So, for the sake of furthering their trade of arms, the Scottish, and, indeed, other mercenary men-at-arms, fanned the flame. The words of Siri are precise on this point, for he says, "Le Leslie, le Gordoni, le Duglas ed altri milordi della Scotia, del' Inghilterra, e dell' Irlanda."

Never had knights of romance worse fare in the dungeons of morose magicians than they who entered the bloody lists, where was fought out the quarrel between royalty and republicanism. "I heard a great officer say," remarks Blount, "that during the siege of Colchester, he dined at an entertainment, where the greatest delicacies were roast horseflesh."

The warlike spirit was, probably, never stronger than in this reign. It is well illustrated by Hobbes, who remarks that, the Londoners and citizens of other county capitals, who fought against Charles, "had that in them which, in time of battle, is more conducing to victory, than valor and experience both together; and that was *spite*."

But it is as a lover that Charles I. is chiefly distinguished when we consider him solely to discover his knightly qualities. In his early days he was strongly impressed by romance, and possessed of romantic feelings. This fact is best illustrated by his conduct in connection with the Spanish Match; and to this matter we will devote a brief space, and go back to the time when James was king, and Charles was Prince of Wales.

## THE SPANISH MATCH.

This unhappy and ill-advised affair, will ever remain one of the darkest blemishes on the uniformly pacific but inglorious reign of the royal pupil of Buchanan;—the whole detail is an ungrateful one of intrigue and ill-faith, and however justly Buckingham may be accused of exerting his baleful influence to dissolve the treaty, and that he did so in the wantonness of his power is now past doubt; the disgrace which should have attached to him, still hangs round the memory of the timid king and his weak yet gallantly-disposed son. I am more inclined to allow a high-mindedness of feeling to Charles than to his father. The king, who supposed the entire art of reigning lay in dissimulation, may not be charged with an over-scrupulous nicety in his observations of the rules of fair dealing; but the young prince, at this period, had the sentiments without the vanity of a knight-errant, his only error was in the constitutional weakness which bent to the arrogance of Buckingham's somewhat stronger mind. With such a disposition, the favorite found it as easy to persuade Charles to break off the match, as he had with facility advised him to the romantic journey —as rash as it was impolitic. It would be almost an unprofitable occupation to search for Buckingham's motives, they are quite unattainable, and, like hunting the hare in a wagon, conjecture might lead us on, but we should, at every step, be farther from our object. It is the received opinion, that the prince's visit was begun in caprice; and with caprice it ended. Buckingham viewed it, perhaps, at first as a mere adventure, and he terminated it, because his wounded pride suggested to him that *he* was not the favorite actor in the piece. His terms were, "Ego et rex meus," and a less-distinguished station would not satisfy the haughty insolence of Somerset's succession in the precarious favor of the king.

Our British Solomon who willed, but could not restore, the Palatinate to his son-in-law, had long been accustomed to consider the union of Charles with the Infanta, as the only available means left by which he could secure the object he had so much at heart. He was not made of the stern stuff, which in other kings would have set a whole army in motion. That "sagacious simpleton" was never in so turbulent a vein. His most powerful weapon was an ambassador, and the best of these were but sad specimens of diplomacy, and thus, weak as he was, both in the cabinet and field, we may guess at his rapture when the marriage was agreed to by the Court of Spain — the restoration of the Palatinate talked of as a wedding present, and the bride's dowry two millions of eight.

It was at the expiration of five years of negotiation, that James at length saw the end of what had hitherto been an ever-continuing vista. The dispensation of the Pope, an indispensable preliminary to the union of a Most Catholic princess, with a Protestant heir-apparent, had been held up as a difficulty; James immediately loosened the reins with which he had held in the Catholic recusants — he set them at liberty, for the good of the reformed religion, *he said;* then apologized to his subjects for having so set them at liberty — for the benefit of Protestantism; and finally, he exulted in having accomplished so honorable an end for England, as making her the first to enter the path of moderation. He, moreover, sent to Spain, Digby, the good and great Lord Bristol, and while *he* was negotiating with Philip IV., the Infanta's brother, George Gage, "a polite and prudent gentleman," was employed at Rome to smooth down the obstacles which the zeal of the Fourteenth Gregory raised in behalf of his mother-church. The parties were a long time at issue as to what period the presumed offspring of this marriage should remain under the guardianship of their mother; that is to say, under the Catholic tuition of her confessors. The period of "fourteen years," was suggested by the Pope, and agreed to by the Court of Spain. Now, George Gage, we are told, was both polite and prudent; George made some slight objection. The father of the faithful and the descendant of Roderic now named twelve years as the stipulated period of maternal or ecclesiastical rule. Mr. Gage, without losing sight of his prudence. retained all his civility; he treated the Pope courteously. Gregory, in return, granted the dispensation, condescended even to agree to the term of nine years, and merely asked a few privileges for the Catholic suite of the Infanta, which were not hard to grant, and would have been impolitic to refuse. James's advisers counselled him to demand the restitution of the Palatinate by a preliminary treaty. This he wisely refrained from doing; he saw that his desired object was considered inseparable from the marriage, and he was content to trust to the existing treaty which, probably, would not have been changed, had he so expressed his wish. There is a curious item in all these diplomatic relations; beside the public treaty there were various private articles, passed between and signed by the parties concerned, agreeing that more toleration should be granted to the papists, and that more of the penal laws against them should be repealed than was expressed in the public document. There appears also to have existed a yet more private treaty, of even more restricted circulation, whereby James was not to be required to act up to the very letter of that article, by which his royal word pledged what was then considered — emancipation to the Catholics.

Thus far had proceeded this tedious affair of state; the nation was beginning to consider its accomplishment with diminished aversion, and a few months would have brought a Spanish Princess of Wales to England, when all this goodly and fair-wrought edifice was destroyed by the temerity of the man who was the evil spirit of the age. Charles's youth and inexperience readily lent a willing ear to the glowing description which Buckingham recounted of the celebrated journey. His young melancholy was excited into cheerfulness, when he dwelt on the hoped-for and surprised rapture with which his destined bride would receive a prince whose unusual gallantry spurned at the laws of political interest, and whose chivalric feeling had broken through state negotiation, and, despising to woo by treaty, had brought him to her feet to win her by his merits. His blood warmed at the popularity he would acquire by such a step, from a nation famed for its knightly devotion to the fair, and whose watch-word, according to one of its poets, has ever been, "love and the ladyes." Charles would have been a dull lover, indeed, had he only, like other princes, thought his bride not worth the fetching. He would have been doubly dull and undeserving had he paused to consider the bearings, the risks, or the probable absurdity of the act. There was a certain political danger; but Charles, young, and a lover, refused to see it; he was tearing the bonds which might bind more ignoble princes, but were too weak to confine him; he rent the shackles which proxies' force on their principals, and stood in his own princely strength to win a prize which has often lost the world.

The only step subsequent to the prince's acquiescence, was to obtain the king's permission, a matter of little difficulty. They attacked the good-natured and simple James at a moment when his jovial humor would not have denied a greater boon. He had sense, however, to see something of the impropriety of the absence of Charles and Buckingham from England; but his obtusity of intellect was overpowered by the craft of his favorite, and the petitioners at length obtained his unadvised sanction to the wild enterprise, less by the strength of their arguments, than the persisting urgency of its expression. The prince and his companion further obtained a promise of secrecy; and they saw nothing more wanting than the ordinary preparations for their departure. Left to his own reflections, however, the poor king reproached his own weakness; he saw with terror that his subjects would not readily forgive him for committing so invaluable a pledge into the hands of a Catholic sovereign, who might detain Charles in order to enforce new exactions or demands; and with equal terror he saw that even success could not possibly justify the means; for there was no advantage to be obtained, and no unprejudiced censurer would consider the freak otherwise than as one played for the gratification of the will of the duke, and of an enthusiastic prince, whose abstract idea of chivalrous love had overcome his character for prudence.

There ensued, on the return of Charles and Buckingham to the royal presence for despatches, a melancholy scene. There were the objurgations and schoolboy blubbering of the monarch, the insolent imperiousness of the favorite, and the silent tears and submission of the prince. The audacious threats of the duke wrung from James the assent which Buckingham required — a second permission for their journey. A knight, Sir Francis Cottington, the prince's secretary, and Endymion Porter, a gentleman of the bedchamber, were selected as the attendants of the Prince. The duke was, however, also to be accompanied by his master of the horse, a man of knight's degree, Sir Richard Graham. There was a recapitulation of the crying scene when the two former gentlemen were appointed, for Sir Francis boldly pointed out the danger of the proceeding. Charles's countenance showed his displeasure; but Buckingham was completely carried away by his overwhelming passion. James cried, the duke swore, and the king had nothing left to do, but to wish them God speed on their amorous and knight-errant mission.

There is a work, known to many and read by few, the "Epistolæ Howelianæ," consisting of a collection of familiar letters on many subjects, by a certain James Howell. The author was a cadet of a noble family, several members of which had been on the roll of knighthood. He pushed his fortunes with all the vigor of an aspiring younger brother. His letters exhibit him as agent to a glass factory at Vienna—a tutor—a companion—a clerk—secretary to an embassy—agent again, and finally an attaché to the privy council. Master Howell, in these epistles, continually rings the changes on the importance of attending to the main chance; bewails the stagnation which non-employment throws round his fortunes; or congratulates himself on the progress they are making, through his industry. At the period of Charles's visit to Madrid, he was agent there for the recovery of a vessel taken by unlawful seizure, and he contemplates the prince's arrival with delight, viewing him as a powerful adjunct to his cause. He complains bitterly of the prince as showing more condescension to the needy Spanish poor, than politeness to the accredited agent of an English company. The agent's honor or ruin depended on the success of his mission, hence good Master Howell is occasionally and ill at ease. The success of his mission, too, hung upon the happy termination of the match; a marriage he considers as the avant-courier of his appointments, but should some unlucky reverse prevent the end he hopes for, why then, to use one of the worshipful agent's most favorite figures of speech—then "my cake is dough." His letters are the chief authority for what follows.

It is quite consistent with the whole character of this drama, that the journey should be prosecuted through France. Charles and his suite travelled incognito it is true, but Buckingham was rash enough to introduce the prince at a court-ball in Paris, where he perhaps saw and admired the lovely Henrietta Maria. From the gay court of France the errant company speedily decamped, hurried rapidly toward the south, and crossed the frontier just in time to escape the strong arm of the governor of Bayonne, stretched out to arrest their progress.

On Friday the 7th of March, 1623, Charles and his attendants arrived at Madrid, under the guise of very homely personages. Buckingham took a name which has since served to cover a fugitive king of the French—that of (Thomas) Smith, and therewith he entered Bristol's mansion, "'twixt the gloaming and the murk," with a portmanteau under his arm, while Charles waited on the other side of the street, not as the Prince of Wales, but as Thomas Smith's brother, John. Lord Bristol did not allow the son of his monarch to remain long in such a situation. Charles was conducted to the house, and on being ushered into a bedchamber, he immediately asked for writing materials, and despatched a messenger to his father, announcing his safe arrival in the Spanish capital. Cottington and Porter arrived the next day; and even so soon as this, a report was spreading through the city that James himself was in Madrid. On the evening of Saturday, Buckingham went privately to court, in his own person, and told the tale of the adventures of the knight to whom he had acted as squire. The delight of all parties was intense. Olivarez accompanied Buckingham on his return to the prince, to express how immeasurably glad his Catholic majesty was at his coming. This proud minister, who was the contemporary, and perhaps the equal, of Richelieu, knelt and kissed the prince's hand, and "hugged his thighs," says Mr. Howell, like a slave as he was. Gondomar, too, hastened to offer his respects and congratulations to the young prince. At ten that night, too, came the most distinguished as he was the most desired visiter: Philip himself appeared in generous haste to welcome the person and thank the noble confidence of his almost brother-in-law. The meeting of the parties appears to have been unaffected and cordial. After the salutations and divers embraces which passed in the first interview, *they parted late*. The stern severity of Spanish etiquette would not permit of Charles's introduction to the Infanta, and it was accordingly arranged that the princess should appear in public on Sunday, and the prince meet her on the Prado, just as the knight Guzman sees Inez, in the ancient ballad. In the afternoon of the eventful day, the whole court, neglecting for the occasion all sumptuary laws, appeared in all its bravery. Philip, his queen, two brothers, and the Infanta, were together in one carriage, and the princess, the cynosure of attraction, scarcely needed the blue riband which encircled her arm, as a sign by which Charles might distinguish her. The knightly lover, who had experienced some difficulty in making his way through the exulting multitude, who threw up their caps and cried "God bless him," was in waiting, with his diminutive court and Count Gondomar, to view the defiling of the procession. The royal carriage approached, and as the eyes of the princess first rested on her destined lord, she blushed deeply, "which," adds the calculating Mr. Howell, "we hold to be an impression of love and affection, for the face is oftentimes a true index of the heart." The Infanta, at this period, was only sixteen and tall for her age — "a very comely lady," says the agent, "rather of a Flemish complexion than Spanish, fair-haired, and carried a most pure mixture of red and white in her face: she is full and big-lipped, which is held as beauty rather than a blemish."

Charles was now honored with a complete court establishment and apartments in the palace; there was revelry in camp and city; and the gallantry of the journey so touched this high-minded people, that they declared the beautiful bride ought to have been made Charles's immediate reward. Gayety was at every heart and poesy, in the person of Lope de Vega, celebrated "the Stuart," and "Marie, his star." In all the festivals and carousals at court, Charles was not once permitted to approach "his star." The royal family sat together under a canopy, but there was ever some unwelcome intervener between the lovers, and the prince was compelled to satisfy his ardent soul with gazing. The worthy English agent records that he has seen him "have his eyes immovably fixed upon the Infanta half-an-hour together, in a thoughtful, speculative posture, which," he sagaciously adds, "would needs be tedious unless affection did sweeten it." It was on one of these occasions that Olivarez, with less poetic truth than energy of expression, said that Charles watched her *as a cat does a mouse*.

Whatever outward respect Charles may have voluntarily offered to the prejudices and observances of Spanish ceremony, he, and perhaps the blushing Infanta, thought it very cumbersome lovework for young hearts. Words had passed between them, it is true, but only through the medium of an interpreter, and always in the presence of the king, for Philip "sat hard by, to overhear all," and understand if he could, the interpretations made by Lord Bristol.

Weary of this restraint, the prince soon found means, or rather an opportunity, to break through the pompous obstacles which opposed the good old plan of love-making, and he, with Endymion Porter to attend him, did not fail to profit by the occasion. Near the city, but across the river, the king had a summer-house, called Casa di Campo. Charles discovered that the Infanta was accustomed to go very often of a morning to gather May-dew. The knight and esquire, accordingly, donning a silken suit for a spring morning, went out betimes, and arrived without let or hindrance at the Casa di Campo. Their quality was a sure passport, and doors, immovably closed to all others, opened to *them*. They passed through the house into the garden, but to their wonder and disappointment, the "light of love" was not visible. The Infanta had not arrived, or had fled, and disappointment seemed likely to be the probable reward of their labor. The garden was divided from an adjoining orchard by a high wall; the prince heard voices on the other side, perhaps heard *the* voice, and hastened to a door which formed the only communication of the two divisions. To try this outlet was the work of a moment; to find it most vexatiously locked, was the conviction of the next. The lover was at bay, and Endymion's confused brain had no resource to suggest. They looked at the wall. It was high, undoubtedly; but was ever such a barrier too high for a king's son — a knight and a gallant, when it stood between him and such a "star" as the muse of De Vega made of the Infanta? Charles was on the summit of the wall almost as soon as the thought of climbing it had first struck him; with the same eagerness he sprang lightly down on the other side, and hastily made toward the object of his temerity. Unfortunately there was an old "duenna" of a marquis with her in quality of guardian, and the Infanta, who perchance expected to see the intruder, was constrained, for the sake of appearances, to scream with well-dissembled terror. " She gave a shriek and ran back." Charles followed, but the grim marquis interfered his unwelcome person between the lovers. " Turning to the prince, he fell on his knees, conjuring his highness to retire;" he swore by his head, that if he admitted the prince to the company of the Infanta, he, the grisly guardian of the dove, might pay for it with his head. As the lady, meanwhile, had fled, and did not return, Charles was not obdurate. Maria, though she had escaped (because seen) could not but be pleased with the proof he had given of his devotion, and as the old marquis continued to talk of his head, the prince, whose business lay more with the heart, turned round and walked slowly away. He advanced toward the door, the portal was thrown open, and thus, as Mr. Howell pithily says, "he came out under that wall over which he had got in." Endymion was waiting for him, and perhaps for his story, but the knight was sad, and his squire solemn. Charles looked an embodying of the idea of gloom, and Master Porter, with some ill-will, was compelled to observe a respectful silence.

The Infanta and her governor hurried back to the palace, while her suitor and his followers were left to rail in their thoughts against the caprice of the ladies, and the reserve of royal masters; and so ends a pretty story of " how a princess went to gather May-dew."

This solitary and unsuccessful love-passage was the last effort which Charles made to engage the good-will of Maria. He, at once, retired to his apartments in the palace; whence he seldom went abroad, except for the purpose of attending a bull-fight. Buckingham was sick a-bed, his offended nobility lay ill-disposed at court, and the palace residence was gradually becoming irksome to all parties. Charles could only have bedchamber prayers, and not possessing a room where he might have attended the service of his own church, the sacred plate and vestments he had brought over were never used. Moreover, the Knights of the Garter, Lords Carlisle and Denbigh, had well nigh set the palace on fire, through leaving their lighted pipes in a summer-house. The threatened mischief, however, was prevented by the activity of Master Davies, my Lord of Carlisle's barber, who "leapt down a great height and quenched it." Perhaps a more unfortunate accident than this, in the eyes of a Catholic population, was a brawl within the royal precinct between Ballard, an English priest, and an English knight, Sir Edmund Varney. The prince had a page named Washington, lying mortally ill; to save his soul the anxious priest hastened to the death-bed of the page; here, however, he met Sir Edmund, an unflinching pillar of the English church. An unseemly scene ensued; and while knight and priest passed from words to blows, the poor suffering page silently died, and soon after was consigned to the earth under a fig-tree in Lord Bristol's Garden.

In the meantime, the Princess Infanta was publicly addressed as Princess of Wales, and as an acquaintance with the English language was a possession much to be desired by the bearer of so proud a title, the Lady Maria began "*her accidence*," and turned her mind to harsh declensions and barbarous conjugations. Though enthusiasm had somewhat cooled, the business continued to proceed; the most serious interruption was occasioned by the death of the Pontiff, as it entailed many of the ensuing obstacles which at once began to rise. The unfinished work of Gregory was thought to require a *da capo* movement from his successor Urban, and the new Hierarch commenced a string of objections and proposals, which were of no other effect than to produce mistrust and delay. Buckingham too, recovering from his sickness, longed to return to England, where it was now understood that the Pope's tardiness was founded on hopes of the prince's conversion. The people of England were alarmed and clamorous. Charles and the duke discontented and impatient. The latter urged a return, and the prince, in expressing his wishes to Philip, stated as his reasons, his father's age and infirmities, the murmurs of his people, and the fact that a fleet was at sea to meet him. He added, a most close argument, that the articles which had been signed in England bore, as a proviso, that if he did not return by a specified month, they should be of no validity. It honorably belied the suspicions against the Spanish Cabinet, that not the slightest opposition was made to the return; proxies were named, and on the termination of affairs with the Pope, Maria was to follow Charles to England. The lady is said to have remarked, that if she was not worth waiting for she was not worth having. Charles must have felt the remark, but the duke was paramount, and the wind, which favored their departure, as speedily blew away the popularity of a prince whose knightly bearing, modest gallantry, and high virtues, so particularly formed him for the favorite of a romantic nation. The treaty for the Spanish match was broken.

The secret history of the French match possesses an equal interest with that of the Spanish; but Charles only wrote to his bride on this occasion, and met her, on her way to him, at Canterbury.

As a further instance of the chivalrous gallantry of Charles I., it deserves to be recorded, that he it was who suggested a revival of the custom of inviting the ladies to participate in the honors of the Garter. I have elsewhere said, that at one time, the ladies were regularly admitted, but nothing is known as to when this gallant custom was first introduced. Dr. Barrington, in his excellent "Lectures on Heraldry," says, that "in the earliest notice of the habit of the order having been issued to the ladies, immediately after the accession of Richard II.," they are said to have been "newly received into the Society of the Garter," and were afterward called "Ladies of the Fraternity of St. George." Who were admitted to this distinguished order, or how long the practice continued, does not appear, though it is probable it had fallen into disuse in the time of Henry VIII. Charles remained content with merely suggesting the revival of the custom, and "nothing," says Dr. Barrington, "seems to have been done to carry this suggestion into effect. If any one period,"—adds the docter, most appropriately—"if any one period were more fit than another for doing it, it must surely be the present, when a *lady* is the sovereign of the order."

# THE KINGS OF ENGLAND AS KNIGHTS.

## FROM STUART TO BRUNSWICK.

CHARLES II. loved the paraphernalia of courts and chivalry. He even designed to create two new orders of knighthood — namely "the Knights of the Sea," a naval order for the encouragement of the sea-service; and "the Knights of the Royal Oak," in memory of his deliverance, and for the reward of civil merit. He never went much farther than the intention. He adopted the first idea at another's suggestion, and straightway thought no more of it. The second originated with himself, and a list of persons was made out, on which figured the names of the intended knights. The matter never went further.

At Charles's coronation, the knights of the Bath were peculiarly distinguished for their splendor. They were almost too gorgeously attired to serve as waiters, and carry up, as they did the first course to the king's own table, at the coronation banquet, after a knight of the Garter had been to the kitchen and had eaten a bit of the first dish that was to be placed before his Sacred Majesty.

If the king was fond of show, some at least of his knights, shared in the same feeling of vanity. The robes in recent times were worn only on occasions of ceremony and service. The king revived a fashion which his knights followed, and which sober people (who were not knights) called a ridiculous humor. They were "so proud of their coats," as the expression went, that they not only wore them at home, but went about in them, and even rode about the park with them on. Mr. Pepys is particularly indignant on this matter especially so, when told that the Duke of Monmouth and Lord Oxford were seen, "in a hackney-coach, with two footmen in the park with their robes on ; which," adds the censor, " is a most scandalous thing, so as all gravity may be said to be lost, among us." There was more danger of what Pepys calls " gravity" being lost, when the Order, at command of the Sovereign head, elected such men as the Elector of Saxony, who had no other distinction but that of being a good drinker.

I do not know what the rule now may be in St. George's Chapel, but in the reign of Charles II., a singular regulation is noticed by Pepys. He went in good company to the royal chapel, where he was placed, by Dr. Childe, the organist, "among the knights' stalls, and pretty the observation," he adds, " that no man, but a woman, may sit in a knight's place, where any brass plates are set." What follows is also, in some degree, germane to our purpose. " Hither come cushions to us, and a young singing boy to bring us a copy of the anthem to be sung. And here, for our sakes, had this anthem and the great service sung extraordinary, only to entertain us. Great bowing by all the people, the poor knights particularly, toward the altar."

Charles II. was the first monarch who allowed the Knights of the Garter to wear, as at present, the star of the order on the breast of the coat. Our present queen has renewed in her gracious person, the custom that was once observed, if we may believe Ashmole, by the ladies, that is, the wives of Knights of the Garter — namely, of wearing the symbol of the order as a jewelled badge, or a bracelet, on the arm. This is in better taste than the mode adopted by Lady Castlereagh, at the gay doings attendant upon the sitting of the Congress of Vienna ; where the noble lady in question appeared at court with her husband's jewelled garter, as a bandeau, round her forehead!

James II. has had not merely his apologists but his defenders. He had far more of the knightly character than is commonly supposed. For a long time he labored under the disadvantage of being represented, in England, by historians only of the Orange faction. Poor Richard the Third has suffered by a similar misfortune. He was wicked enough, but he was not the monster described by the Tudor historians and dramatists.

James, in his youth, had as daring and as crafty a spirit as ever distinguished the most audacious of pages. The tact by the employment of which he successfully made his escape from the republican guards who kept him imprisoned at St. James's, would alone be sufficient proof of this. When Duke of York, he had the compliment paid to him by Condé, that if ever there was a man without fear it was he. Under Turenne he earned a reputation of which any knight might be proud; and in the service of Spain, he won praise for courage, from leaders whose bravery was a theme for eulogy in every mouth.

Partisans, not of his own faction, have censured his going publicly to mass soon after his accession; but it must be remembered that the Knights of the Garter, in the collar of their order, complacently accompanied him, and that the Duke of Norfolk was the only knight who left him at the door of the chapel.

He had little of the knight in him in his method of love, if one may so speak. He cared little for beauty; so little, that his brother Charles remarked that he believed James selected his mistresses by way of penance. He was coarsely minded, and neither practised fidelity nor expected it in others. Whatever he may have been in battle, there was little of the refinement of chivalry about him in the bower. It was said of Louis XIV. and his successor, that if they were outrageously unfaithful to their consorts, they never failed to treat them with the greatest politeness. James lacked even this little remnant of chivalrous feeling; and he was barely courteous to his consort till adversity taught him the worth of Mary of Modena.

He was arrogant in prosperity, but the slightest check dreadfully depressed him, and it is hardly necessary to say that he who is easily elated or easily depressed, has little in him of the hero. His conduct when his throne was menaced was that of a poor craven. It had not about it the dignity of even a decent submission. He rose again, however, to the heroic when he attempted to recover his kingdom, and took the field for that purpose. This conduct has been alluded to by a zealous and impartial writer in the "Gentleman's Magazine," for November, 1855. "After the battle of the Boyne," he says, "the Orange party circulated the story that James had acted in the most cowardly manner, and fled from the field before the issue was decided. Not only was this, in a very short time believed, but even sensible historians adopted it, and it came down to us as an historical fact. Now in the secret archives of France there are several letters which passed between Queen Mary and the Earl of Tyrconnel, and these together with some of the secret papers, dispose at once of the whole story. It has now been placed beyond a doubt, that the king was forced from the field. Even when the day was lost and the Dutch veterans had routed the half-armed and undisciplined Irish, James rallied a part of the French troops, and was leading them on, when Tyrconnel and Lauzun interposed, pointed out the madness of the attempt, and seizing the reins of his horse, compelled him to retreat."

This is perhaps proving a little too much, for if the day was lost, it was not bravery, but rashness, that sought to regain it; and it is the first merit of a knight, the great merit of a general, to discern when blood may be spilled to advantage. As for the archives in France, one would like to know upon what authority the papers preserved there make their assertions. Documents are exceedingly valuable to historians, but they are not always trustworthy. The archives of France may contain Canrobert's letter explaining how he was compelled to put constraint upon the bravery of Prince Napoleon, and send him home, in consequence of severe indisposition. And yet the popular voice has since applied a very uncomplimentary surname to the Prince—quite as severe, but not so unsavory, as that which the people of Drogheda still apply to James. In either case there is considerable uncertainty. I am inclined to believe the best of both of these illustrious personages, but seeing that the uncertainty is great, I am not sure that Scarron was wrong when he said that the best way of writing history was by writing epigrams, pointed so as to prick everybody.

Cottington (Stafford's Letters) tells us of a domestic trouble in which James was concerned with one of his knights. The king's perplexities about religion began early. "The nurse is a Roman Catholic, to whom Sir John Tunston offered the oath of allegiance, and she refused it; whereupon there grew a great noise both in the town and court; and the queen afflicted herself with extreme passion upon knowledge of a resolution to change the woman. Yet after much tampering with the nurse to convert her, she was let alone, to quiet the queen." The dissension is said to have so troubled the nurse, as also to have injured the child, and never had knight or king more difficult task than James, in his desire to please all parties.

It was one of the characteristics of a knight to bear adversity without repining; and if Dodd may be believed, James II. was distinguished for this great moral courage in his adversity. The passage in Dodd's Church History is worth extracting, though somewhat long: "James was never once heard to repine at his misfortune. He willingly heard read the scurrilous pamphlets that were daily published in England against him. If at any time he showed himself touched, it was to hear of the misfortunes of those gentlemen who suffered on his account. He would often entertain those about him with the disorders of his youth, but it was with a public detestation of them, and an admonition to others not to follow his example. The very newspapers were to him a lesson of morality; and the daily occurrences, both in the field and the cabinet, were looked upon by him, not as the result of second causes, but as providential measures to chastise both nations and private persons, according to their deserts. He would sometimes say that the exalted state of a king was attended with this great misfortune, that he lived out of the reach of reproof, and mentioned himself as an example. He read daily a chapter in the Bible, and another in that excellent book, 'The Following of Christ.' In his last illness he publicly forgave all his enemies, and several of them by name, especially the Prince of Orange, whom he acknowledged to be his greatest friend, as being the person whom Providence had made use of to scourge him and humble him in the manner he had done, in order to save his soul." As something very nearly approaching to reality, this is more pleasing than the details of dying knights in romance, who after hacking at one another for an hour, mutually compliment each other's courage, and die in the happiest frame of mind possible. Some one speaking of this king, and of Innocent II., made an apt remark, worth the quoting; namely, that "he wished for the peace of mankind that the pope had turned papist, and the king of England, protestant!" How far the latter was from this desired consummation is wittily expressed in the epitaph on James, made by one of the poet-chevaliers, or, as some say, by one of the abbés who used to lounge about the terrace of St. Germains.

> "C'est ici que Jacques Second,
> Sans ministres et sans maitresses,
> Le matin allait à la messe,
> Et le soir allait au sermon."

I have noticed, in a previous page, the very scant courtesy which the queen of Charles I. met with at the hands of a Commonwealth admiral. The courtesy of some of the Stuart knights toward royal ladies was not, however, of a much more gallant aspect. I will illustrate this by an anecdote told by M. Macaulay in the fourth volume of his history. The spirit of the Jacobites in William's reign had been excited by the news of the fall of Mons.... "In the parks the malcontents wore their biggest looks, and talked sedition in their loudest tones. The most conspicuous among these swaggerers was Sir John Fenwick, who had in the late reign been high in favor and military command, and was now an indefatigable agitator and conspirator. In his exaltation he forgot the courtesy which man owes to woman. He had more than once made himself conspicuous by his impertinence to the queen. He now ostentatiously put himself in her way when she took her airing, and while all around him uncovered and bowed low, gave her a rude stare, and cocked his hat in her face. The affront was not only brutal but cowardly. For the law had provided no punishment for mere impertinence, however gross; and the king was the only gentleman and soldier in the king was the only gentleman and soldier in the kingdom who could not protect his wife from contumely with his sword. All that the queen could do was to order the park-keepers not to admit Sir John again within the gates. But long after her death a day came when he had reason to wish that he had restrained his insolence. He found, by terrible proof, that of all the Jacobites, the most desperate assassins not excepted, he was the only one for whom William felt an intense personal aversion."

The portrait of William III. as drawn by Burnet, does not wear any very strong resemblance to a hero. The "Roman nose and bright sparkling eyes," are the most striking features, but the "countenance composed of gravity and authority," has more of the magistrate than the man at arms. Nevertheless, and in despite of his being always asthmatical, with lungs oppressed by the dregs of small-pox, and the slow and "disgusting dryness" of his speech, there was something chivalrous in the character of William. In "the day of battle he was all fire, though without passion; he was then everywhere, and looked to everything. His genius," says Burnet in another paragraph, "lay chiefly in war, in which his courage was more admired than his conduct. Great errors were often committed by him; but his heroical courage set things right, as it inflamed those who were about him." In connection with this part of his character may be noticed the fact that he procured a parliamentary sanction for the establishment of a standing army. His character, in other respects, is not badly illustrated by a remark which he made, when Prince of Orange, to Sir W. Temple, touching Charles II. "Was ever anything so hot and so cold as this court of yours? Will the king, who is so often at sea, never learn the word that I shall never forget, since my last passage, when in a great storm the captain was crying out to the man at the helm, all night, 'Steady, steady, steady!'" He was the first of our kings who would not touch for the evil. He would leave the working of all miracles, he said, to God alone. The half-chivalrous, half-religious, custom of washing the feet of the poor on Maundy Thursday, was also discontinued by this prince, the last of the heroic five Princes of Orange.

Great as William was in battle, he perhaps never exhibited more of the true quality of bravery than when on his voyage to Holland in 1691, he left the fleet, commanded by Sir Cloudesley Shovel and Sir George Rooke, and in the midst of a thick fog attempted, with some noblemen of his retinue, to land in an open boat. "The danger," says Mr. Macaulay, who may be said to have *painted* the incident in a few words, "proved more serious than they had expected." It had been supposed that in an hour the party would be on shore. But great masses of floating ice impeded the progress of the skiff; the night came on, the fog grew thicker, the waves broke over the king and the courtiers. Once the keel struck on a sandbank, and was with great difficulty got off. The hardiest mariners showed some signs of uneasiness, but William through the whole night was as composed as if he had been in the drawing-room at Kensington. "For shame," he said to one of the dismayed sailors, "are you afraid to die in my company?" The *vehis Cæsarem* was, certainly, not finer than this.

The consort of Queen Anne was of a less chivalrous spirit than William. Coxe says of him, that even in the battle-field he did not forget the dinner-hour, and he appears to have had more stomach for feeding than fighting. Of George I., the best that can be said of him in his knightly capacity, has been said of him, by Smollet, in the remark, that this prince was a circumspect general. He did not, however, lack either courage or impetuosity. He may have learned circumspection under William of Orange. Courage was the common possession of all the Brunswick princes. Of some of them, it formed the solitary virtue. But of George I., whom it was the fashion of poets, aspiring to the laureatship, to call the great, it can not be said, as was remarked of Philip IV. of Spain, when he *took* the title of "Great," "He has become great, as a ditch becomes great, by losing the land which belonged to it."

One more custom of chivalry observed in this reign, went finally out in that of George II. I allude to the custom of giving hostages. According to the treaty of Aix-la-Chapelle, "two persons of rank were to reside in France, in that capacity, as sureties to France that Great Britain should restore certain of its conquests in America and the West Indies." The "Chevalier," Prince Charles Edward, accounted this as a great indignity to England, and one which, *he said*, he would not have suffered if he had been in possession of his rights.

The age of chivalry, in the old-fashioned sense of the word, went out before Burke pronounced it as having departed. I do not think it survived till the reign of George II. In that reign chivalry was defunct, but there was an exclusive class, whose numbers arrogated to themselves that nice sense of honor which was supposed, in olden times, to have especially distinguished the knight. The people alluded to were *par excellence*, the people of "fashion." The gentlemen who guarded, or who were supposed to guard, the brightest principle of chivalry, were self-styled rather than universally acknowledged, "men of honor."

The man of honor has been painted by "one of themselves."

The Earl of Chesterfield spoke with *connoissance de fait*, when he treated of the theme; and his lordship, whose complacency on this occasion, does not permit him to see that his wit is pointed against himself, tells a story without the slightest recollection of the pithy saying of the old bard, "De te fabula narratur."

"A man of honor," says Lord Chesterfield, "is one who peremptorily affirms himself to be so, and who will cut anybody's throat that questions it, even upon the best grounds. He is infinitely above the restraints which the laws of God or man lay upon vulgar minds, and knows no other ties but those of honor, of which word he is to be the sole expounder. He must strictly advocate a party denomination, though he may be utterly regardless of its principles. His expense should exceed his income considerably, not for the necessaries, but for the superfluities of life, that the debts he contracts may do him honor. There should be a haughtiness and insolence in his deportment, which is supposed to result from conscious honor. If he be choleric and wrongheaded into the bargain, with a good deal of animal courage, he acquires the glorious character of a man of honor; and if all these qualifications are duly seasoned with the genteelest vices, the man of honor is complete; anything his wife, children, servants, or tradesmen, may think to the contrary, notwithstanding."

Lord Chesterfield goes on to exemplify the then modern chivalrous guardian of honor, by drawing the portrait of a friend under an assumed name. He paints a certain "Belville" of whom his male friends are proud, his female friends fond, and in whom his party glories as a living example—frequently making that example the authority for their own conduct. He has lost a fortune by extravagance and gambling; he is uneasy only as to how his honor is to be intact by acquitting his liabilities from "play." He must raise money at any price, for, as he says, "I would rather suffer the greatest incumbrance upon my fortune, than the least blemish upon my honor." His privilege as a peer will preserve him from those "clamorous rascals, the tradesmen; and lest he should not be able to get money by any other means, to pay his "debts of honor," he writes to the prime minister and offers to sell his vote and conscience for the consideration of fifteen hundred pounds. He exacts his money before he records his vote, persuaded as he is that the minister will not be the first person that ever questioned the honor of the chivalrous Belville.

The modern knight has, of course, a lady love. The latter is as much like Guinever, of good King Arthur's time, as can well be; and she has a husband who is more suspicious and jealous than the founder of the chivalrous Round Table. "Belville" can not imagine how the lady's husband can be suspicious, for he and Belville had have been play-fellows, school-fellows, and sworn friends in manhood. Consequently, Belville thinks that wrong may be committed in all confidence and security. "However," he writes to the lady, "be convinced that you are in the hands of a man of honor, who will not suffer you to be ill-used, and should my friend proceed to any disagreeable extremities with you, depend upon it, I will cut the c——'s throat for him."

Life in love, so in lying. He writes to an acquaintance that he had "told a d——d lie last night in a mixed company," and had challenged a "formal old dog," who had insinuated that "Belville" had violated the truth. The latter requests his "dear Charles" to be his second—"the booby," he writes of the adversary who had detected him in a lie, "was hardly worth my resentment, but you know my delicacy where honor is concerned."

Lord Chesterfield wrote more than one paper on the subject of men of honor. For these I refer the reader to his lordship's works. I will quote no further from them than to show a distinction, which the author draws with some ingenuity. "I must observe," he says, "that there is a great difference between a MAN OF HONOR and a PERSON OF HONOR. By PERSONS OF HONOR were meant, in the latter part of the last century, bad authors and poets of noble birth, who were but just not fools enough to prefix their names in great letters to the prologues, epilogues, and sometimes even the plays with which they entertained the public. But now that our nobility are too generous to interfere in the trade of us poor, professed authors" (his lordship is writing anonymously, in the WORLD), "or to eclipse our performances by the distinguished and superior excellency and lustre of theirs; the meaning at present of a PERSON OF HONOR is reduced to the simple idea of a PERSON OF ILLUSTRIOUS BIRTH."

The chivalrous courage of one of our admirals at the close of the reign of George II., very naturally excited the admiration of Walpole. "What milksops," he writes in 1760, "the Marlboroughs and Turennes, the Blakes and Van Tromps appear now, who whipped into winter quarters and into ports the moment their nose looked blue. Sir Cloudesley Shovel said that an admiral deserved to be broken who kept great ships out after the end of September; and to be shot, if after October. There is Hawke in the bay, weathering this winter (January), after conquering in a storm."

George III. was king during a longer period than any other sovereign of England; and the wars and disasters of his reign were more gigantic than those of any other period. He was little of a soldier himself; was, however, constitutionally brave; and had his courage and powers tested by other than military matters. The politics of his reign wore his spirit more than if he had been engaged in carrying on operations against an enemy. During the first ten years after his accession, there were not less than seven administrations; and the cabinets of Newcastle and Bute, Grenville and Rockingham, Grafton and North, Shelburne and Portland, were but so many camps, the leaders in which worried the poor monarch worse than the Greeks badgered unhappy Agamemnon. Under the administration of Pitt he was hardly more at his ease, and in no degree more so under that of Addington, or that of All the Talents, and of Spencer Perceval. An active life of warfare could not have more worn the spirit and health of this king than political intrigues did; intrigues, however, be it said, into which he himself plunged with no inconsiderable delight, and with slender satisfactory results.

He was fond of the display of knightly ceremonies, and was never more pleased than when he was arranging the ceremonies of installation, and turning the simple gentlemen into knights. Of the sons who succeeded him, George IV. was least like him in good principle of any sort, while William IV. surpassed him in the circumstance of his having been in action, where he bore himself spiritedly. The race indeed has ever been brave, and I do not know that I can better close the chapter than with an illustration of the " Battle-cry of Brunswick."

## THE BATTLE-CRY OF BRUNSWICK.

The "Battle-cry of Brunswick" deserves to be commemorated among the acts of chivalry. Miss Benger, in her "Memoirs of Elizabeth, Queen of Bohemia," relates that Christian, Duke of Brunswick, was touched alike by the deep misfortunes, and the cheerful patience of that unhappy queen. Indignant at the neglect with which she was treated by her father, James I. of England, and her uncle, Frederick of Denmark, Duke Christian "seemed suddenly inspired by a sentiment of chivalric devotion, as far removed from vulgar gallantry as heroism from ferocity. Snatching from her hand a glove, which he first raised with reverence to his lips, he placed it in his Spanish hat, as a triumphal plume which, for her sake, he ever after wore as a martial ornament; then drawing his sword he took a solemn oath never to lay down arms until he should see the King and Queen of Bohemia reinstated in the Palatinate. No sooner had Christian taken this engagement than he eagerly proclaimed it to the world, by substituting on his ensign, instead of his denunciation of priests, an intelligible invocation to Elizabeth in the words 'For God and for her!' *Fur Gott und fur sie!*"

> "Flash swords! fly pennons! helm and shield
> Go glittering forth in proud array!
> Haste knight and noble to the field,
> Your pages wait, your chargers neigh.
> Up! gentlemen of Germany!
> Who love to be where strife is seen,
> For Brunswick leads the fight to-day,
> For God and the Queen!
>
> "Let them to-day, for fame who sigh,
> And seek the laurels of the brave;
> Or they who long, 'ere night, to lie
> Within a soldier's honored grave,
> Round Brunswick's banner take their stand;
> 'Twill float around the bloody scene,
> As long as foeman walks the land,
> 'Gainst God and the Queen.
>
> "Draw, Barons, whose proud homes are placed
> In many a dark and craig-topped tower;
> Forward, ye knights, who have been graced
> In tourney lists and ladies' bower.

> And be your country's good the cause
>   Of all this proud and mortal stir,
> While Brunswick his true sabre draws
>   For God and for her!
>
> "To Him we look for such good aid
>   As knights may not be shamed to ask,
> For vainly drawn would be each blade,
>   And weakly fitted to its task,
> Each lance we wield, did we forget
>   When loud we raise our battle-cry,
> For old Bohemia's Queen, to set
>   Our hopes with God on high."

The original superscription on the banner of Brunswick was the very energetic line: "Christian of Brunswick, the friend of God and the enemy of priests." Naylor, in his "Civil and Military History of Germany," says, that the Duke imprinted the same legend on the money which he had coined out of the plate of which he had plundered the convents, and he adds, in a note derived from Galetti, that "the greater part of the money coined by Christian was derived from twelve silver statues of the apostles, which the bigotry of preceding ages had consecrated, in the cathedral of Munster." When the Duke was accused of impiety by some of his followers, he sheltered himself under the authority of Scripture; and pretended to have only realized the ancient precept: "Go hence, into all parts of the earth!"

Having seen the English Kings as knights, let us look at a few of the men whom they knighted.

## RECIPIENTS OF KNIGHTHOOD.

"The dew of grace bless our new knights to-day."
BEAUMONT AND FLETCHER.

THE Conquest was productive of a far more than average quantity of knights. Indeed, I think it may be asserted without fear of contradiction, that the first and the last William, and James I. were more addicted to dubbing knights than any other of our sovereigns. The good-natured William IV. created them in such profusion that, at last, gentlemen at the head of deputations appeared in the royal presence with a mysterious dread lest, in spite of themselves, they should be compelled to undergo a chivalric metamorphosis, at the hands of the "sea king." The honor was so constantly inflicted, that the recipients were massed together by "John Bull" as "The Thousand and one (K)nights!"

William the Conqueror was not so lavish in accolades as his descendant of remoter days, nor was he so off-handed in the way of administering the distinction. He drew his sword with solemnity, laid it on the shoulder before him with a sort of majestic composure, and throughout the ceremony looked as calm as dignity required. William is said to have ennobled or knighted his cook. He does not stand alone in having so acted: for, unless I am singularly mistaken, the great Louis tied some small cross of chivalry to the button-hole of the immortal Vatel. William's act, however, undoubtedly gave dignity to that department in palaces, whence many princes have derived their only pleasure. It was from him that there passed into the palace of France the term "Officiers de Service," a term which has been appropriated by others of less elevated degree than those whom it originally served to distinguish. The term has led to a standing joke in such dwellings. "Qui vive?" exclaims a sentinel in one of the base passages, as one of these officials draws near at night. "Officier," is the reply of the modest official in question. "Quel officier?" asks the guard. "Officier de service!" proudly answers he who is thus questioned; whereupon the soldier smilingly utters "Passe, Caramel!" and the royal officer—*not* of the body-guard, passes, as smilingly, on his way.

But, to return from Caramel to the Conqueror, I have to observe, that the cook whom William knighted bore an unmusical, if not an unsavory, name. The culinary artist was called Tezelin. The service by which he had won knighthood consisted in the invention of a white soup for maigre days. The hungry but orthodox William had been accustomed to swallow a thin broth "à l'eau de savon;" but Tezelin placed before him a tureen full of an orthodox yet appetizing liquid, which he distinguished by the name of *Dillegrout*. The name is not promising, particularly the last syllable, but the dish could not have been a bad one. William created the inventor "chevalier de l'office," and Sir Caramel Tezelin was farther gratified by being made Lord of the Manor of Addington. Many a manor had been the wages of less honest service.

The Tiercelins are descendants of the Tezelins; and it has often struck me as curious that of two recently-deceased holders of that name, one, a cutler in England, was famous for the excellence of his carving-knives; and the other, an actor in France, used to maintain that the first of comic parts was the compound cook-coachman in Molière's "*Avare*." Thus did they seem to prove their descent from the culinary chivalry of William of Normandy.

But there are other samples of William's knights to be noticed. Among the followers who landed with him between Pevensey and Hastings, was a Robert who, for want of a surname, and because of his sinews, was called Robert le Fort, or "Strong." It would have gone ill with William on the bloody day on which he won a throne, had it not been for this Robert le Fort, who interposed his *escu* or shield, between the skull of the Norman and the battle-axe of a Saxon warrior. This opportune service made a "Sieur Robert" of him who rendered it, and on the coat-of-arms awarded to the new knight was inscribed the device which yet belongs to the Fortescues;—"Forte Scutum Salus Ducum,"—a strong shield is the salvation of dukes — or leaders, as the word implies. The Duke of Normandy could not have devised a more appropriate motto; but he was probably helped to it by the learning and ready wit of his chaplain.

The danger into which William rushed that day was productive of dignity to more than one individual. Thus, we hear of a soldier who, on finding William unhorsed, and his helmet beaten into his face, remounted his commander after cleverly extricating his head from the battered load of iron that was about it. William, later in the day, came upon the trusty squire, fainting from the loss of a leg and a thigh. "You gave me air when I lacked it," said the Conqueror, "and such be, henceforth, thy name; and for thy lost leg and thigh, thou shalt carry them, from this day, on thy shield of arms." The maimed knight was made lord of broad lands in Derbyshire; and his descendants, the Eyres, still bear a leg and a thigh in armor, for their crest. It is too pretty a story to lose, but if the account of these knight-makings be correct, some doubt must be attached to that of the devices, if, as some assert, armorial bearings were not used until many years subsequent to the battle of Hastings. The stories are, no doubt, substantially true. William, like James III. of Scotland, was addicted to knighting and ennobling any individuals who rendered him the peculiar pleasures he most coveted. Pitscottie asserts that the latter king conferred his favors on masons and fiddlers; and we are told that he not only made a knight of Cochrane, a mason, but also raised him to the dignity of Earl of Mar. Cochrane, however, was an architect, but he would have been none the worse had he been a mason — at least, had he been a man and mason of such quality as Hugh Millar and Allan Cuningham.

Although it has been often repeated that there were no knights, in the proper sense of that word, before the period of William the Conqueror, this must be accepted with such amount of exception as to be almost equivalent to a denial of the assertion. There were knights before the Conquest, but the systems differed. Thus we know from Collier's Ecclesiastical History that Athelstan was knighted by Alfred; and this is said to have been the first instance of the performance of the ceremony that can be discovered. Here again, however, a question arises. Collier has William of

Malmesbury for his authority. The words of this old author are: "Athelstane's grandfather, Alfred, seeing and embracing him affectionately, when he was a boy of astonishing beauty and graceful manners, had most devoutly prayed that his government might be prosperous; indeed, he had made him a knight unusually early, giving him a scarlet cloak, a belt studded with diamonds, and a Saxon sword with a golden scabbard." This, and similar instances which might be cited, is supposed by some to prove the existence of knights as a distinct order among the Saxons, while others think that it may amount to nothing more than the first bestowing of arms. Louis le Débonnaire, it is remarked, *ense accinctus est*, received his arms at thirteen years old. But this was in some degree "knighting," for we read in Leland's History of Ireland, of Irish knighthood being conferred on recipients only seven years old.

If William the Conqueror made many knights in order to celebrate his conquest, the gentlemen with new honors did not always obtain peaceable possession of the estates which were sometimes added to the title. Here is an instance in the case of the ancient family of the Kinnersleys. William's commissioners had appeared in Herefordshire, and in course of their predatory excursion, they came before the castle of John de Kinnersly, an old man, who is described as a knight, albeit some assert that there were no more knights in England before the conquest than there was rain on the earth before the flood. The old man who was blind, stood at his castle-gate in front of a semicircle formed by his twelve sons. Each had sword on thigh and halberd in hand. When the sheriffs and other commissioners asked him by what tenure he held his castle and estates, blind John exclaimed, "By my arms; by sword and spear; and by the same will keep them!" To which all his lively lads uttered a vigorous "Ay, ay," and the Norman commissioners were so satisfied with the title, that they did not venture to further question the same, but left the possessor of castle and land undisturbed in that possession which is said to be nine points out of the ten required by the law.

During many reigns, no man was knighted, but who was of some "quality," and generally because he was particularly useful to his own or succeeding generations. These require no notice.

Some of these introduced customs that are worth noticing, and here is a sample.

Among the lucky individuals knighted by Edward I., Sir William Baud holds a conspicuous place. Sir William gave rise to a curious custom, which was long observed in Old St. Paul's. During his lifetime, the dean and chapter had made over to him some laud in Essex. In return, or perhaps in "service" for this, the knight presented at the high altar of the cathedral, a doe "sweet and seasonable," on the conversion of St. Paul, in winter; and a buck, in equally fitting condition, on the commemoration of St. Paul in summer. The venison was for the especial eating of the canons resident. The doe was carried to the altar by one man, surrounded by processional priests, and he was to have nothing for his trouble. The buck had several bearers and a more numerous accompaniment of priests, who disbursed the magnificent sum of twelve pence to the carriers. The knight's buck made the dean and chapter so hilarious that when they appeared at the doors of the cathedral to escort it to the altar, they wore copes and vestments, and their reverences wore wreaths of roses on their solemn heads! Indeed, there was a special dress for the cathedral clergy on either day; each, according to the occasion, being ornamented with figures of bucks or does. At the altar, the dean sent the body to be baked, but the head was cut off and carried on a pike to the western door, where the huntsmen blew a *mort*, and the notes proclaiming the death of the stag were taken up and repeated by the "horners" of the city, who received a trifle from the rosy dean and chapter, for thus increasing the noisy importance of the occasion.

There is something, too, worthy of notice in the fact that Richard II. was the first king who knighted a London tradesman. Walworth, who struck down Wat Tyler, and who was knighted by that king for his good service, was engaged in commercial pursuits. This lord mayor, however, derived very considerable profits from pursuits less creditable to him. He was the owner of tenements by the water side, which were of the very worst reputation, but which brought him a very considerable yearly revenue. Sir William pocketed this with the imperially-complacent remark of "non olet." The dagger in the city arms is not in memory of this deed; it simply represents the sword of St. Paul, and it has decorated the city shield since the first existence of a London municipality.

Walworth then is not a very respectable knight. We find one of better character in a knight of ancient family name, whose deeds merit some passing record.

Sir Robert Umfreville, a knight of the Garter, who owed his honors to the unfortunate Henry VI., found leisure, despite the busy and troubled times in which he lived, to found the Chantry of Farmacrès, near Ravensworth, where two chaplains were regularly to officiate according to the law of Sarum. If the knight's charity was great, his expectations of benefit were not small. The chaplains were daily to perform service for the benefit of the souls of the founder, and of all his kith, kin, and kindred. Nay, more than this, service was to be performed for the soul's profit of all knights of the Garter, as long as the order existed, and of all the proprietors of the estate of Farmacres. The chaplains were to reside, board, and sleep, under the roof of the chapel. Once every two years the pious will of the founder allowed them a renewal of costume, consisting of "a sad and sober vest sweeping to their heels." Upon one point Sir Robert was uncommonly strict; he would not allow of the presence of a female in the chapel, under any pretence whatever—even as a servant to the chaplains—*quia frequenter dum colitur Martha, expellitur Maria.* The latter, too, were bound to exercise no office of a secular nature, especially that of bailiff. To a little secular amusement, however, the sagacious knight did not object, and two months' leave of absence was allowed to the chaplains every year; and doubtless no questions were asked, on their return, as to how it had been employed.

While touching on the matters which occurred during the reign of that unhappy Lancastrian king, Henry VI., I will observe that we have foreign testimony to the fact of our civil wars having been carried on with more knightly courtesy than had hitherto been the case in any other country. "In my humble opinion," says Comines, "England is, of all the dominions with which I am acquainted, the one alone in which a public interest is properly treated. There is no violence employed against the people, and in war-time no edifice is destroyed or injured by the belligerents. The fate and misery of war falls heaviest on those immediately concerned in carrying it on." He alludes particularly to the knights and nobles; but it is clear that, let war be carried on in ever so knightly a fashion, the people must be the chief sufferers. The warehouses may stand, but so also will commerce—very still and unproductive.

Courteous as the knights of this age may have been, they were by no means incorruptible. There were many of them in the service of Edward IV., who were the pensioners of Louis XI., who used to delight in exhibiting their names at the foot of acknowledgments for money received. One official, however, Hastings, would never attach his autograph to his receipt, but he had no scruples with regard to taking the money. The Czar buys Prussian service after the fashion of Louis XI.

Henry VIII. cared more for merit than birth in the knights whom he created. He first recognised the abilities of him who was afterward Sir John Mason, the eminent statesman of five reigns. This king was so pleased with an oration delivered in his presence by Mason, at All Souls, Oxford, that he took upon himself the charge of having him educated abroad, as one likely to prove an able minister of state. He was a faithful servant to the king. Elizabeth had one as gallant in Sir Henry Unton, who challenged the great Guise for speaking lightly of his royal mistress. The motives for the royal patronage of these knights was better than that which moved Richard I. when he raised the lowly-born Will Briewer to favoriteship and knighthood. Henry VIII. was fond of conferring the honor of chivalry on those who served him well; thus of the Cornish lawyer, Trigonnel, he made a knight, with forty pounds a year to help him to keep up the dignity, in acknowledgment of the ability with which, as proctor, he had conducted the case of divorce against Queen Katharine. It was better service than John Tirrell rendered to Richard III., who knighted him for his aid in the murder of the young princes, on which occasion he kept the keys of the Tower, and stood at the foot of the stairs, while Forest and Dighton were despatching the young victims. We have a knight of a different sort of reputation in Sir Richard Hutton, Charles I.'s "honest judge," at whose opposition against the levying of ship-money, even the king could not feel displeased. Sir Richard deserved his honors; and we may reckon among them the fact, that "when he was a barrister at Gray's Inn, he seldom or never took a fee of a clergyman."

The old crest of the Huntingdonshire Cromwells was a lion rampant, holding a diamond ring in its fore-paw. This crest has reference to an individual knighted by Henry VIII. In the thirty-second year of that king's reign, Richard Williams, *aliàs* Cromwell, with five other gentlemen, challenged all or any comers from Scotland, Flanders, France, or Spain, who were willing to encounter them in the lists. The challenge was duly accepted, and on the day of encounter, Richard Cromwell flung two of his adversaries from their horses. Henry loved the sport, and especially such feats as this exhibited by Cromwell, whom he summoned to his presence. The king said, "You have hitherto been my Dick, now be my diamond;" and taking a diamond ring from his own finger, and placing it on that of Cromwell, he bade the latter always carry it for his crest. The king, moreover, knighted Richard, and what was better, conferred on him Romney Abbey, "on condition of his good service, and the payment of £4,663 4s 2d. held in capite by the tenth part of a knight's fee, paying £29 16s."

It was in the reign of Henry VIII. that for the first time a serjeant-at-law received the honor of knighthood. This seems to have been considered by the learned body as a corporate honor, by which the entire company of sergeants were lifted to a level with knights-bachelors, at least. It is doubtless for this reason that sergeants-at-law claim to be equal in rank with, and decline to go below those said knight's bachelors.

Of Elizabeth, it is sufficient to name but one sample of her knights. She created many, but she never dubbed one who more nobly deserved the honor than when she clapped the sword on the shoulder of Spielman, the paper-maker, and bade him rise a knight. This was done by way of recompense for the improvements he had introduced into his art, at a time when printers and paper-makers were considered by Romanists anything but angels of light.

Hume, referring to the chivalry of James I.'s time, remarks that the private soldiers were drawn from a better class of men than was the case in Hume's time. They approached, he says, nearer to an equality with the rank of officers. It has been answered that no such rank existed as that from which they are chiefly drawn now. This, however, is not the case. There were then, as now, doubtless many of the peasant and working classes in the army; but there is not now, as there was then, any encouragement to men of respectable station to begin the ascent in profession of arms at the lowest round of the ladder.

One of James I.'s knights was the well-known Sir Herbert Croft. James knighted him at Theobalds, out of respect to his family, and personal merits. Some years subsequently Sir Herbert, then above fifty years of age, joined the Church of Rome, and retired to Douay, where he dwelt a lay-brother, among the English Benedictines. He died among them, after a five years' residence, in the year 1622. His eldest son William was also knighted, I think, by Charles I. He is an example of those who were both knights and clergymen, for after serving as colonel in the civil wars, he forsook catholicism, in which he had been brought up by his father, entered the Church of England, and like so many other knights who in former times had changed the sword for the gown, rose to the dignity of carrying an episcopal pastoral staff, and was made Bishop of Hereford in 1661. It was a descendant of his who wrote the very inaccurate biography of Young, in "Johnson's Lives of the Poets." Wood, in his *Athenæ*, shows that the first Sir Herbert was a literary knight, who took up pen in the service of the communion into which he had entered. These were;—1. Letters persuasive to his wife and children to take upon them the Catholic religion. 2. Arguments to show that the Church, in communion with the See of Rome, is the true Church. 3. Reply to the answers of his daughter, Mary Croft, which she made to a paper of his sent to her concerning the Roman Church." All these pieces appeared in the same year, 1619, and they seem to have been very harmless weapons in the hands of a very amiable knight.

Among the most worthy of the knights created by James I. was Leonard Holliday, who served the office of Lord Mayor in 1605, and was dubbed chevalier by a king who is said never to have conferred the honor without being half afraid of the drawn sword which was his instrument. Sir Leonard did good service in return. In his time Moorfields consisted of nothing but desolate land, the stage whereon was enacted much violence and terrible pollution. In this savage locality, Sir Leonard effected as wonderful a change as Louis Napoleon has done in the Bois de Boulogne; and even a greater; for there were more difficulties in the knight's way, and his will was less sovereign and potent to work mutation. Nevertheless, by perseverance, liberal outlay, and hard work of those employed in the manual labor, he transformed the hideous and almost pathless swamp into a smiling garden, wherein the citizens might take the air without fearing violence either to body or goods. They blessed king James's knight as they disported themselves in the rural district with their wives and children. The laborers employed were said to have been less lavish of benedictions upon the head of him from whom they took their wages. They complained bitterly of the toil, and for a long time in London, when any great exertions were necessary to produce a desired end, promptly, men spoke of the same as being mere "Holiday work."

James I. was not so perfect a knight in presence of a sword as he was in presence of a lady. He made more knights than any other king, not excepting William IV.; but he never dubbed one without some nervousness at the sight of the weapon with which he laid on the honor. Kenelm Digby states that when *he* was knighted by James, the sword, had it not been guided in the King's hand by the Duke of Buckingham, would have gone, not upon his shoulder, but into his eye. James's aversion from the sight of a sword is said to have descended to him from his mother who, a short time previous to his birth, was the terrified spectator of the murder of Rizzio. The same King used to remark that there were two great advantages in wearing armor, namely, that the wearer could neither receive nor inflict much injury. Indeed, as James sagaciously remarked, the chief inconvenience to be dreaded from armor was in being knocked down in it, and left without a squire to lend assistance. In this case the knight stood, or lay, in imminent peril of suffocation; the armor being generally too heavy to admit of a knight rising from the ground without help. If he lay on his face his condition was almost hopeless. The sentiment of chivalry was, after all, not so foreign to James as is popularly supposed. Witness the circumstance when Sully came over here as embassador extraordinary, James made the embassador lower his flag to the pennant of the English vessel sent out to receive or escort him. This, however, had been well nigh construed into an affront. The poets of this time too began to have a chivalrous feeling for the hardships of common women. The feeling used to be all for princesses and courtly dames, but it was now expressed even for shop-wives, behind counters. Thus the author of "The Fair Maid of the Inn" says:—

> "A goldsmith keeps his wife
> Wedged into his shop like a mermaid; nothing of her
> To be seen, that's woman, but her upper part."

The ladies too, themselves were growing ambitious, and as fanciful as any knight's "dame par amour" of them all. The Goldsmith's daughter in "Eastward Ho!" who wants to be made a lady, says to her "sweet knight," "Carry me out of the scent of Newcastle coal and the hearing of Bow bells!" and *à-propos* to titles, let me add that, in James's time, it was, according to Jonson—

> "——— a received heresy
> That England bears no Dukes."

Southey commenting on this passage, said that the title was probably thought ominous, so many dukes having lost their heads.

In the second year of the reign of James I., he made not less than three hundred knights; and on another occasion he is said to have made two hundred and thirty-seven in six weeks. In France, when the state was in distress, knighthood was often a marketable commodity; but it probably was never more so there, than it was in England under the first James. No one was more conscious than he, when he had an unworthy person before him; and it sometimes happened that these persons had the same uncomfortable consciousness touching themselves. Thus, we are told that when "an insigificant person" once held down his head, as the king was about to knight him, James called out, "Hold up thy head, man, I have more need to be ashamed than thou."

The indiscriminate infliction of the order caused great confusion. Knights-aldermen in the city claimed precedence of knights-commoners, and violent was the struggle when the question was agitated. Heralds stood forth and pleaded before "my lords," as lawyers do, with reference to the party by which they were retained. One party considered it absurd that a knight who happened to be an alderman should take precedence of one who was only a knight. The civic dignitary, it was said, was no more above the chivalric, than a rushlight was superior to the sun. Such an idea, it was urged, by York against Garter, was an insult to God and man. The case was ultimately gained by the chivalric aldermen, simply because the knights-commoners did not care to pursue it, or support their own privileges. York thought that knights-commoners, though tradesmen, who *had* been lord mayors, and yet were not now aldermen, ought to take precedence of mere alderman knights. The commoners lost their cause by neglect; but it has been ruled that ex-lord mayors, and provosts of Scotland, shall precede all knights, as having been the Sovereign's lieutenants.

James may be said, altogether, to have shown very little regard for the dignity of knights generally. By creating a rank above them, he set them a step lower in degree of precedence. This monarch is, so to speak, the inventor of the baronet. When money was required for the benefit of the Irish province of Ulster, a suggestion was made that they who supplied it liberally should have the hereditary title of "Sir" and "Baronet." James himself was at first a little startled at the proposition, but he soon gave it his sanction upon Lord Salisbury observing, "Sire, the money will do you good, and the honor will do *them* none." James thought that a fair bargain, and the matter was soon arranged. The knights were not pleased, but it was intimated to them, that only two hundred baronets would be created, and that as the titles became extinct, no new hereditary "Sirs" would be nominated. The successors of James did not think themselves bound by the undertaking of their predecessor. George III. the least regarded it, for during four or five years of his reign he created baronets at the rate of one a-month.

A particular annoyance to the poor knights was, that esquires could purchase the title, and so leap over them at a bound, or could be dubbed knights first, if they preferred to take that rank, by the way. But if the knights were aggrieved, much more so were their ladies, for the wife of a baronet was allowed precedence of all knights' ladies, even of those of the Garter. The baronets themselves took precedence of all knights except of those of the Garter; and their elder sons ranked before simple knights, whose distinction of "Sir" they were entitled to assume, at the age of twenty-one, if they were so minded. Few, however, availed themselves of this privilege.

This matter went so much to the satisfaction of James, that he resolved to sell another batch of baronet's titles, and thereupon followed his "Baronets of Nova Scotia." All these titles were bought of the crown, the pecuniary proceeds being applied to the improvement of the outlying province of Nova Scotia. A sneer, not altogether rightly directed, has been occasionally flung at these purchased hereditary baronetcies. No doubt a title so acquired did not carry with it so much honor as one conferred for great and glorious service rendered to the country. But there have been many titled sneerers whose own dignity stood upon no better basis than that their ancestress was a king's concubine, or the founder of their house an obsequious slave to monarch or minister. The first baronets, whether of Ulster or Nova Scotia, rendered some better service than this to their country, by giving their money for purposes of certain public good. They were not, indeed, rewarded accordingly. They were public benefactors, only on condition that they should be recompensed with an hereditary title. The morality here is not very pure; the principle is not very exalted; but a smaller outlay of morality and principle has purchased peerages before now, and the baronets, therefore, have no reason to be ashamed of the origin of their order. Least of all have those baronets of later creation, men who have made large sacrifices and rendered inestimable services to their country. On these the rank of baronet conferred no real dignity which they did not before possess, but it served as an acknowledgment of their worth in the eyes of their fellow-men. I may notice here, that when Sir Walter Scott makes record of the gallant action performed at Pinkie by Ralph Sadler, when he rallied the English cavalry so effectually as to win a battle almost lost, and seized the royal standard of Scotland with his own hand, the biographer adds that the rank to which the gallant Ralph was then raised—of knight-banneret, "may be called the very pinnacle of chivalry. Knight-bannerets could only be created by the king himself or, which was very rare, by a person vested with such powers as to represent his person. They were dubbed either before or after a battle, in which the royal standard was displayed; and the person so to be honored, being brought before the king led by two distinguished knights or nobles, presented to the sovereign his pennon, having an indenture like a swallow's tail at the extremity. The king then cut off the fished extremity, rendering the banner square, in shape similar to that of a baron, which, thereafter, the knight-banneret might display in every pitched field, in that more noble form. If created by the king, the banneret took precedence of all other knights, but if by a general, only of knights of the Bath and knights-bachelors. Sir Francis Brian, commander of the light horsemen, and Sir Ralph Vane, lieutenant of the men-at-arms, received this honor with our Sir Ralph Sadler, on the field of Pinkie. But he survived his companions, and is said to have been the last knight-banneret of England."

I suppose Washington thought that he had as much right as the English Protector to dub knights; which is not, indeed, to be disputed. But Washington went further than Cromwell, inasmuch as that he instituted an order. This was, what it was said to be, trenching on the privilege of a king. It was a military order, and was named after the agricultural patriot, who was summoned from his plough to guide the destinies of Rome; for the Romans had a very proper idea that nations created their own destinies. The order of Cincinnatus being decreed, the insignia of the order were sent to Lafayette, then in Paris, where the nobility, who could no more spell than Lord Duberly, trusting to their ears only, took it for the order of St. Senatus. A little uproar ensued. The aristocracy not only sneered at the American Dictator for assuming the "hedging" of a king, but they considered also that he had encroached upon the privileges of a pope, and, as they had searched the calendar and could not find a St. Senatus, they at once came to the conclusion that he had canonized some deserving but democratic individual of the city of Boston.

The commonwealth knights, whether in the naval or land service, had perhaps less of refined gallantry than prevailed among the " Cavaliers" *par excellence.* Thus it was a feat of which old chivalry would have been ashamed—that of Admiral Batten, when he cannonaded the house in which Queen Henrietta Maria was sleeping, at Bridlington, and drove her into the fields. But, what do I say touching the gallant refinement on the respective sides?—after all, the rudeness of Batten was civility itself compared with the doings of Goring and his dragoons. On the other hand, there was not a man in arms, in either host, who in knightly qualifications excelled Hampden—" a supreme governor over all his passions and affections, and having thereby a great power over those of other men." With regard to Cromwell himself, Madame de Sévigné has remarked, that there were some things in which the great Turenne resembled him. This seems to me rather a compliment to Turenne than to the Protector. The latter, like Hampden could conceal, at least, if he could not govern his passions. He had the delicacy of knighthood; and he was not such a man as Miles Burket, who, in his prayer on the Sunday after the execution of the king, asked the Almighty if he had not smelt a sweet savor of blood?

The fighting chivalry of Goring, let me add, was nevertheless perfect. The courtesies of chivalry were not his; but in ability and bravery he was never surpassed. His dexterity is said to have been especially remarkable in sudden emergencies; and it was this dexterity that used to be most praised in the knight of olden times. Many other cavaliers were poor soldiers, but admirable company.

The fierce but indomitable spirit of chivalry, on the other hand, that spirit which will endure all anguish without relinquishing an iota of principle, or yielding an inch of ground in the face of overwhelming numbers, was conspicuous in other men besides the martial followers of Cromwell. I will only instance the case of Prynne, who, under the merciless scourge, calmly preached against tyranny; and with his neck in the pillory, boldly wagged his tongue against cruelty and persecution. "Freeborn John" was gagged for his audacity, but when he was thus rendered speechless, he stamped incessantly with his unshackled feet, to express that he was invincible and unconvinced still. If this was not as great courage as ever was shown by knight, I know not what to call it.

Against the courage of Cromwell, Dugdale and Roger Manby say more than can ever be alleged against Prynne—namely, that his heart failed him once in his life. It is said, that when he was captain of a troop of horse in Essex's regiment, at Edgehill, "he absented himself from the battle, and observing, from the top of a neighboring steeple the disorder that the right wing sustained from Prince Rupert, he was so terrified, that slipping down in haste by a bell-rope, he took horse, and ran away with his troop, for which cowardice he had been cashiered, had it not been for the powerful mediation of his friends." This passage shows that the legendary style of the chivalrous romance still was followed as an example by historians. Indeed romance itself claimed Oliver for a hero, as it had done with many a knight before him. It was gravely told of him that, before the battle of Worcester, he went into a wood, like any Sir Tristram, where he met a solemn old man with a roll of parchment in his hand. Oliver read the roll—a compact between him and the Prince of Darkness, and was heard to say, "This is only for seven years; I was to have had one for one-and-twenty." "Then," says the Chronicler, "he stood out for fourteen; but the other replied, that if he would not take it on those terms, there were others who would. So he took the parchment and died that day seven years." This is history after the model of the Seven Champions.

The observance of knightly colors was kept up in the contest between commonwealth men and the crown. Those of Essex were deep yellow; and so acute were the jealousies of war, that they who wore any other were accounted as disaffected to the good cause.

I have remarked before, that Siri puts blame upon the Scottish men-at-arms, whose alleged mercenary conduct was said to have been the seed of a heavy crop of evil. The Scots seem to have been unpopular on all sides. Before the catastrophe, which ended king and kingdom, the French embassador, then in the north, was escorted to some point by a troop of Scots horse. On leaving them, he drew out half-a-crown piece, and asked them how many pence it contained. "Thirty," was the ready-reckoned answer of an arithmetical carabinier. "Exactly so!" replied the envoy, flinging the piece among them with as much contempt as the Prince of Orange felt respect, when he threw his cross among the Dutch troops at Waterloo. "Exactly so! take it. It was the price for which Judas betrayed his master."

If the saints were unsainted in the time of the commonwealth, they found some compensation at the hands of Mr. Penry, the author of Martin Mar-Prelate, who chose to knight the most distinguished — and this not only did he do to the male, but to the female saints. The facetious Penry, accordingly, spoke of Sir Paul, Sir Peter, and Sir Martin, and also of Sir Margaret and Sir Mary.

Passing on to later times, those of James II., I may observe that Poor Nat Lee, when mad, said of a celebrated knight of this time, Sir Roger Lestrange, that the difference between the two was that one was Strange Lee, the other Lestrange. "You poor in purse," said Lee, "as I am poor in brains." Sir Roger was certainly less richly endowed mentally than the poet, but he had *one* quality which a knight of old was bound to have, above most men who were his contemporaries — namely, intense admiration for the ladies. This gallantry he carried so far that when he was licenser of books, it is said that he would readily wink at unlicensed volumes, if the printer's wife would only smile at him.

Though not exactly germane to the immediate subject of Sir Roger, I will notice here that it was the custom for children, as as late as the reign of James II., on first meeting their parents in the morning, to kneel at their feet and ask a blessing. This was an observance seldom omitted in the early days of chivalry by knights who encountered a priest. We often hear praises of this filial reverence paid by errant knights to the spiritual fathers whom they encountered in their wanderings.

Another social custom connected with chivalry was still observed during this, and even during the reign of William III. It is noticed by Dryden, in the dedication to his "Love Triumphant," in the following words:—"It is the usual practice of our decayed gentry to look about them for some illustrious family, and then fix their young darling where he may be both well-educated and supported." The knightly courage and the education were not *always* of the highest quality, if we might put implicit faith in the passage in Congreve's *Old Bachelor*, wherein it is said, "the habit of a soldier now-a-days as often cloaks cowardice, as a black coat does atheism." But the stage is not to be taken as fairly holding the mirror up to nature; and for my part, I do not credit the assertion of that stage-knight, Sir Harry Wildair, that in England, "honesty went out with the slashed doublets, and love with the close-bodied gown." Nor do I altogether credit what is said of Queen Anne's time, in the *Fair Quaker of Deal*, that "our sea-chaplains, generally speaking, are as drunk as our sea-captains."

William III. knighted many a man who did not merit the honor, but he was guilty of no such mistake when he laid the sword of chivalry on the shoulders of honest Thomas Abney, citizen of London. Abney was one of those happy architects who build up their own fortunes, and upon a basis of rectitude and common-sense. In course of time, he achieved that greatness which is now of so stupendous an aspect in the eyes of the Parisians; in other words, he became Lord Mayor of London. The religious spirit of chivalry beat within the breast that was covered with broadcloth, and Sir Thomas Abney humbled himself on the day on which he was exalted. He had been "brought up" a dissenter, but he certainly was not one when he became sovereign of the city in the year 1700. He was none the less a Christian, and it is an exemplary and an agreeable trait that we have of him, as illustrated in his conduct on the day of his inauguration. The evening banquet was still in progress, when he silently withdrew from the glittering scene, hurried home, read evening prayers to such of his household as were there assembled on the festive day, and then calmly returned and resumed his place among the joyous company.

This knight's hospitality was of the same sterling quality. Who forgets that to him Dr. Watts (that amiable intolerant!) was indebted during thirty years for a home? The Abney family had a respect for the author of "the Sluggard," which never slept. It almost reached idolatry. I have said thirty years, but in truth,

Dr. Watts was at home, at the hearth of Sir Thomas, during no briefer a period than six-and-thirty years. The valetudinarian poet, the severity of whose early studies had compelled him to bid an eternal *vale* to the goddess of health, was welcomed by the knight, with an honest warmth born of respect for the worth and genius of a kind-hearted man who "scattered damnation" in gentle rhymes, and yet who would not have hurt a worm. In the little paradise where he was as much at ease as his precarious health would allow, it is astonishing with what vigor of spirit and weakness of phrase the good-intentioned versifier thrust millions from the gates of a greater paradise. Such at least was my own early impression of the rhymes of the knight's guest. They inspired much fear and little love: and if I can see now that such was not the author's design, and that he only used menace to secure obedience, that thereby affection might follow, I still am unable to come to any other conclusion, than that the method adopted is open to censure.

He sat beneath the knightly roof, without a want unsupplied, with every desire anticipated; exempted from having to sustain an active share of the warfare in the great battle of life, he was beset by few, perhaps by no temptations; and free from every care, he had every hour of the day wherein to walk with God. His defect consisted in forgetting that other men, and the children of men, had not his advantage, and while, rightly enough, he accounted their virtue as nothing, he had no bowels of compassion for their human failings. It is well to erect a high standard, but it is not less so to console rather than condemn those who fall short of it. "Excelsior" is a good advice, on a glorious banner, but they who are luxuriously carried on beneath its folds should not be hasty to condemn those who faint by the way, fall back, and await the mercy of God, whereby to attain the high prize which they had for their chief object. I should like to know if Sir Thomas ever disputed the conclusions adopted by his guest.

This mention of the metropolitan knight and the poet who sat at his hearth, reminds me of a patron and guest of another quality, who were once well known in the neighborhood of Metz;—"Metz *sans* Lorraine," as the proud inhabitants speak of a free locality which was surrounded by, but was never *in* Lorraine.

The patron was an old chevalier de St. Louis, with a small cross and large "ailes de pigeon." The guest was the parish priest, who resided under his roof, and was the "friend of the house." The parish was a poor one, but it had spirit enough to raise a subscription in order to supply the altar with a new *ciborium*—the vessel which holds the "body of the Lord." With the modest sum in hand, the Knight of St. Louis, accompanied by the priest, repaired to Metz, to make the necessary purchase. The orthodox goldsmith placed two vessels before them. One was somewhat small, but suitable to the funds at the knight's disposal; the other was large, splendidly chased, and highly coveted by the priest.

"Here is a pretty article," said the chevalier, pointing to the simpler of the two vessels: "But here is a more worthy," interrupted the priest. "It corresponds with the sum at our disposal," remarked the former. "I am sure it does not correspond with your love for Him for whom the sum was raised," was the rejoinder. "I have no authority to exceed the amount named," whispered the cautious chevalier. "But you have wherewith of your own to supply the deficiency," murmured the priest. The perplexed knight began to feel himself a dissenter from the church, and after a moment's thought, and looking at the smaller as well as the simpler of the two vessels, he exclaimed—"it is large enough for the purpose, and will do honor to the church." "The larger would be more to the purpose, and would do more honor to the Head of the Church," was the steady clerical comment which followed. "Do you mean to say that it is *not* large enough?" asked the treasurer. "Certainly, since there is a larger, which we may have, if you will only be generous." "*Mais!*" remonstrated the knight, in a burst of profane impatience, and pointing to the smaller ciborium, "Cela contiendroit le diable!" "Ah, Monsieur le Chevalier," said the priest, by no means shocked at the idiomatic phrase. "Le Bon Dieu est plus grand que le diable!" This stroke won the day, and the goldsmith was the most delighted of the three, at this conclusion to a knotty argument.

George I. was not of a sufficiently generous mind to allow of his distributing honors very profusely. The individuals, however, who were eminently useful to him were often rewarded by being appointed to enjoy the emoluments, if not exercise the duties of several offices, each in his own person. At a period when this was being done in England, the exact reverse was being accomplished in Spain. Thus we read in the *London Gazette* of March 29 to April 1, 1718, under the head of Madrid, March 21, the following details, which might be put to very excellent profit in England in these more modern times:—

"The King having resolved that no person shall enjoy more than one office in his service, notice has been given to the Duke d'Arco, who is Master of the Horse, and Gentleman of the Bedchamber; the Marquis de Montelegre, Lord Chamberlain and Captain of the Guard of Halberdiers; the Marquis de St. Juan, Steward of the Household, and Master of the Horse to the Queen; and one of the Council of the Harinda, the Marquis de Bedmar, the Minister of War, and President of the Council; and several others who are in the like case, to choose which of their employments they will keep. To which they have all replied that they will make no claim, but will be determined by what his Majesty shall think fit to appoint. The like orders are given in the army, where they who receive pay as General Officers, and have Colonels' commissions besides, are obliged to part with their regiments."

This regulation seriously disturbed the revenue of many a Spanish knight; but it was a wise and salutary regulation, nevertheless. At the very period of its being established, Venice was selling her titles of knighthood and nobility. In the same Gazette from which the above details are extracted, I find it noticed, under the head of "Venice, March 25," that "Signor David, and Paul Spinelli, two Geneva gentlemen, were, upon their petition, admitted this week by the Grand Council, into the Order of the Nobility of this Republic, having purchased that honor for a hundred thousand ducats." It was a large price for so small a privilege.

I have treated of knighthood under George II., sufficiently at length, when speaking of that king himself; and I will add only one trait of his successor.

It was not often that George III. was facetious, but tradition has attributed to him a compound pun, when he was urged by his minister to confer knighthood upon Judge Day, on the return of the latter from India. "Pooh! pooh!" remonstrated the king, "how can I turn a Day into night?" On the ministerial application being renewed, the king asked, if Mr. Day was married, and an affirmative reply being given, George III. immediately rejoined, "Then let him come to the next drawing-room, and I will perform a couple of miracles; I will not only turn Day into Knight, but I will make Lady-Day at Christmas."

There was a saying of George III. which, put into practice, was as beneficial as many of the victories gained by more chivalrous monarchs. "The ground, like man, was never intended to be idle. If it does not produce something useful it will be overrun with weeds."

Among the men whom James I. knighted, was one who had passed through the career of a page, and notice of whom I have reserved, that I might contrast his career with that of a contemporary and well-known squire.

## RICHARD CARR, PAGE; AND GUY FAUX, ESQUIRE.

Of all the adventurers of the seventeenth century, I do not know any who so well illustrate the objects I have in view, as the two above-named gentlemen. The first commenced life as a page; the second was an esquire by condition, and a man-at-arms. Master Faux, for attempting murder, suffered death; and Richard Carr, although he was convicted of murder, was suffered to live on, and was not even degraded from knighthood.

When the Sixth James of Scotland reigned, a poor king in a poor country, there was among his retinue a graceful boy — a scion of the ancient house of Fernyhurst, poor in purse, and proud in name. At the court of the extravagant yet needy Scottish king, there was but scant living even for a saucy page; and Richard Carr of Fernyhurst turned his back on Mid Lothian, and in foreign travel forgot his northern home.

James, in his turn, directed his face toward the English border; and subsequently, in the vanities of Whitehall, the hunting at Theobald's, the vicious pleasure of Greenwich, and the roysterings at Royston, he forgot the graceful lad who had ministered to him at Holyrood, St. Andrews, and Dunbar.

When this James I. of England had grown nearly tired of his old favorite and minister, Salisbury, for want of better employment he ordered a tilting match, and the order was obeyed with alacrity. In this match Lord Hay resolved to introduce to the King's notice a youth who enjoyed his lordship's especial patronage. Accordingly, when the monarch was seated in his tribune, and the brazen throats of the trumpets had bidden the rough sport to begin, the young squire of Lord Hay, a handsome youth of twenty, straight of limb, fair of favor, strong-shouldered, smooth-faced, and with a modesty that enhanced his beauty, rode up on a fiery steed, to lay his master's shield and lance at the feet of the monarch. The action of the apprentice warrior was so full of grace, his steed so full of fire, and both so eminently beautiful, that James was lost in admiration. But suddenly, as the youth bent forward to present his master's device, his spur pricked the flank of his charger, and the latter, with a bound and a plunge, threw his rider out of the saddle, and flung young Carr of Fernyhurst, at the feet of his ex-master, the King. The latter recognised his old page, and made amends for the broken leg got in the fall, by nursing the lad, and making him Viscount Rochester, as soon as he was well. James created him knight of the Garter, and taught him grammar. Rochester gave lessons to the King in foreign history. The ill-favored King walked about the court with his arms round the neck of the well-favored knight. He was for ever either gazing at him or kissing him; trussing his points, settling his curls, or smoothing his hose. When Rochester was out of the King's sight James was mindful of him, and confiscated the estates of honest men in order to enrich his own new favorite. He took Sherborne from the widow and children of Raleigh, with the cold-blooded remark to the kneeling lady, " I maun have it for Carr!"

Rochester was a knight who ruled the King, but there was another knight who ruled Rochester. This was the well-born, hot-headed, able and vicious Sir Thomas Overbury. Overbury polished and polluted the mind of Rochester; read all documents which passed through the hands of the latter, preparatory to reaching those of the King, and not only penned Rochester's own despatches, but composed his love-letters for him. How pointedly Sir Thomas could write may be seen in his "Characters;" and as a poet, the knight was of no indifferent reputation in his day.

Rochester, Sir Thomas, and the King, were at the very height of their too-warm friendship, when James gave Frances Howard, the daughter of the Earl of Suffolk, in marriage to young Devereux, Earl of Essex. The bride was just in her teens. The bridegroom was a day older. The Bishop of Bath and Wells blessed them in the presence of the King, and Ben Jonson and Inigo Jones constructed a masque in honor of the occasion. When the curtain fell, bride and bridegroom went their separate ways; the first to her mother; the second to school. Four years elapsed ere they again met; and then Frances, who had been ill-trained by her mother, seduced by Prince Henry, and wooed by Rochester, looked upon Essex with infinite scorn. Essex turned from her with disgust.

Rochester then resolved to marry Frances, and Frances employed the poisoner of Paternoster-row, Mrs. Turner, and a certain Dr. Forman, to prepare philters that should make more ardent the flame of the lover, and excite increased aversion in the breast of the husband. Overbury, with intense energy, opposed the idea of the guilty pair, that a divorce from Essex was likely to be procured. He even spoke of the infamy of the lady, to her lover. Frances, thereupon, offered a thousand pounds to a needy knight, Sir John Ward, to slay Overbury in a duel. Sir John declined the offer. A more successful method was adopted. Sir Thomas Overbury was appointed embassador to Russia, and on his refusing to accept the sentence of banishment, he was clapped into the tower as guilty of contempt toward the king. In that prison, the literary knight was duly despatched by slow poison. The guilt was brought home less to Rochester than to Frances, but the King himself appears to have been very well content at the issue.

James united with Rochester and the lady to procure a divorce between the latter and Essex. The King was bribed by a sum of £25,000. Essex himself did not appear. Every ecclesiastical judge was recompensed who pronounced for the divorce—carried by seven against five, and even the son of one of them was knighted. This was the heir of Dr. Bilson, Bishop of Winchester, and he was ever afterward known by the name of Sir Nullity Bilson.

Sir Nullity danced at the wedding of the famous or infamous pair; and never was wedding more splendid. King, peers, and illustrious commoners graced it with their presence. The diocesan of Bath and Wells pronounced the benediction. The Dean of St. Paul's wrote for the occasion an epithalamic eclogue. The Dean of Westminster supplied the sermon. The great Bacon composed, in honor of the event, the "Masque of Flowers;" and the City made itself bankrupt by the extravagant splendor of its fêtes. One gentleman horsed the bride's carriage, a bishop's lady made the bride's cake, and one humorous sycophant offered the married pair the equivocal gift of a gold warming-pan.

The King, not to be behindhand in distributing honors, conferred one which cost him nothing. He created Rochester Earl of Somerset.

Two years after this joyous wedding, the gentleman who had made a present to the bride, of four horses to draw her in a gilded chariot to the nuptial altar, had become a knight and secretary of state. Sir Richard (or, as some call him, Sir Robert) Winwood was a worshipper of the now rising favorite, Villiers; and none knew better than this newly-made knight that the King was utterly weary of his old favorite, Somerset.

Winwood waited on the King and informed him that a garrulous young apothecary at Flushing, who had studied the use of drugs under Dr. Franklin of London, was making that melancholy town quite lively, by his stories of the abuses of drugs, and the method in which they had been employed by Lord and Lady Somerset, Mrs. Turner (a pretty woman, who invented yellow starched ruffs) and their accomplices, in bringing about the death of Overbury. The food conveyed to the latter was poisoned by Frances and her lover, outside the tower, and was administered to the imprisoned knight by officials within the walls, who were bribed for the purpose.

There is inextricable confusion in the details of the extraordinary trial which ensued. It is impossible to read them without the conviction that some one higher in rank than the Somersets was interested, if not actually concerned, in the death of Overbury. The smaller personages were hanged, and Mrs. Turner put yellow ruffs out of fashion by wearing them at the gallows.

Lady Somerset pleaded *guilty*, evidently under the influence of a promise of pardon, if she did so, and of fear lest Bacon's already prepared speech, had she pleaded *not guilty*, might send her to an ignominious death. She was confined in the Tower, and she implored with frantic energy, that she might not be shut up in the room which had been occupied by Overbury.

Somerset appeared before his judges in a solemn suit, and wearing the insignia of the Garter. He pleaded *not guilty*, but despite insufficiency of legal evidence he was convicted, and formally condemned to be hanged, like any common malefactor. But the ex-page won his life by his taciturnity. Had he, in his defence, or afterward, revealed anything that could have displeased or disturbed the King, his life would have paid the forfeit. As it was, the King at once ordered that the Earl's heraldic arms as knight of the Garter should not be taken down. For the short period of the imprisonment of the guilty pair, both guilty of many crimes, although in the matter of Overbury there is some doubt as to the extent of the Earl's complicity, they separately enjoyed the "Liberty of the Tower." The fallen favorite was wont to pace the melancholy ramparts with the George and collar round his neck and the Garter of knighthood below his knee. He was often seen in grave converse with the Earl of Northumberland. Sometimes, the guilty wife of Somerset, impelled by curiosity or affection, would venture to gaze at him for a minute or two from her lattice, and then, if the Earl saw her, he would turn, gravely salute her, and straightway pass on in silence.

When liberated from the Tower, the knight of the Garter, convicted of murder, and his wife, confessedly guilty, went forth together under protection of a royal pardon. Down to the time of the death of Lady Somerset, in 1632, the wretched pair are said never to have opened their lips but to express, each hatred and execration of the other. The earl lived on till 1645 — long enough to see the first husband of his wife carry his banner triumphantly against the son of James, at Edgehill. The two husbands of one wife died within a few months of each other.

Such was the career of one who began life as a page. Let us contrast therewith the early career of one whose name is still more familiar to the general reader.

Toward the middle of the sixteenth century there was established at York a respectable and influential Protestant family of the name of Fawkes. Some of the members were in the legal profession, others were merchants. One was registrar and advocate of the Consistory Court of the cathedral church of York. Another was notary and proctor. A third is spoken of as a merchant-stapler. All were well to-do; but not one of them dreamed that the name of Fawkes was to be in the least degree famous.

The Christian name of the ecclesiastical lawyer was Edward. He was the third son of William and Ellen Fawkes, and was the favorite child of his mother. She bequeathed trinkets, small sums, and odd bits of furniture to her other children, but to Edward she left her wedding suit, and the residue of her estate. Edward Fawkes was married when his mother made her will. While the document was preparing, his wife Edith held in her arms an infant boy. To this boy she left her "best whistle, and one old angel of gold."

The will itself is a curious document. It is devotional, according to the good custom of the days in which it was made. The worthy old testator made some singular bequests; to her son Thomas, amid a miscellaneous lot, she specifies, "my second petticoat, my worsted gowne, gardit with velvet, and a damask kirtle." The "best kirtle and best petticoat" are bequeathed to her daughter-in-law Edith Fawkes. Among the legatees is a certain John (who surely must have been a *Joan*) Sheerecrofte, to whom, says Mistress Fawkes, "I leave my petticoat fringed about, my woorse grogram kirtle, one of my lynn smockes, and a damask upper bodie." The sex, however, of the legatee is not to be doubted, for another gentleman in Mrs. Fawkes's will comes in for one of her bonnets!

The amount of linen bequeathed, speaks well for the lady's housewifery; while the hats, kirtles, and rings, lead us to fear that the wife of Master Edward Fawkes must have occasionally startled her husband with the amount of little accounts presented to him by importunate dressmakers, milliners, and jewellers. Such, however, was the will of a lady of York three centuries ago, and the child in arms who was to have the silver whistle and a gold angel was none other than our old acquaintance, known to us as Guy Faux.

Guy was christened on the sixteenth of April, 1570, in the still existing church of St. Michael le Belfry; and when the gossips and sponsors met round the hospitable table of the paternal lawyer to celebrate the christening of his son, the health of Master Guy followed hard upon that of her gracious highness the queen.

Master Guy had the misfortune to lose his father in his ninth year. "He left me but small living," said Guy, many years afterward, "and I spent it." After his sire's decease, Guy was for some years a pupil at the free foundation grammar-school in "the Horse Fayre," adjacent to York. There he accomplished his humanities under the Reverend Edward Pulleyne. Among his schoolfellows were Bishop Morton, subsequently Bishop of Durham, and a quiet little boy, named Cheke, who came to be a knight and baronet, and who, very probably went, in after-days, to see his old comrade in the hands of the hangman.

Some seventeen miles from York stands the pleasant town of Knaresborough, and not far from Knaresborough is the village of Scotten. When Guy was yet a boy, there lived in this village a very gay, seductive wooer, named Dennis Baynbridge. This wooer was wont to visit the widowed Edith, and the result of his visits was that the widowed Edith rather hastily put away her weeds, assumed a bridal attire, married the irresistible Dennis, and, with her two daughters, Anne and Elizabeth, and her only son Guy, accompanied her new husband to his residence at Scotten.

Baynbridge was a Roman Catholic, as also were the Pullens, Percies, Winters, Wrights, and others who lived in Scotten or its neighborhood, and whose names figure in the story of the Gunpowder Plot.

At Scotten, then, and probably soon after his mother's marriage, in 1582, Guy, it may be safely said, left the faith in which he had been baptized, for that of the Romish Church. Had he declined to adopt the creed of his step-sire, he perhaps would have been allowed but few opportunities of angling in the Nidd, rabbiting by Bilton Banks, nutting in Goldsborough Wood, or of passing idle holydays on Grimbald Craig.

On the wedding-day of Edith Fawkes and Dennis Baynbridge, the paternal uncle of Guy made his will. He exhibited his sense of the step taken by the lady, by omitting her name from the will, and by bequeathing the bulk of his property to the two sisters of Guy. To Guy himself, Uncle Thomas left only "a gold ring," and a "bed and one pair of sheets, with the appurtenances."

When Guy became of age, he found himself in possession of his patrimony—some land and a farm-house. The latter, with two or three acres of land, he let to a tailor, named Lumley, for the term of twenty-one years, at the annual rent of forty-two shillings. The remainder he sold at once for a trifle less than thirty pounds. Shortly after, he made over to a purchaser all that was left of his property. He bethought himself for a while as to what course he should take, and finally he chose the profession of arms, and went out to Spain, to break crowns and to win spurs.

In Spain, he fell into evil company and evil manners. He saw enough of hard fighting, and indulged, more than enough, in hard drinking. He was wild, almost savage of temper, and he never rose to a command which gave him any chance of gaining admission on the roll of chivalry. There was a knight, however, named Catesby, who was a comrade of Guy, and the latter clung to him as a means whereby to become as great as that to which he clung.

Guy bore himself gallantly in Spain; and, subsequently, in Flanders, he fought with such distinguished valor, that when Catesby and his associates in England were considering where they might find the particular champion whom they needed for their particular purpose in the Gunpowder Plot, the thought of the reckless soldier flashed across the mind of Catesby, and Guy was at once looked after as the "very properest man" for a very improper service.

The messenger who was despatched to Flanders to sound Guy, found the latter eager to undertake the perilous mission of destroying king and parliament, and thereby helping Rome to lord it again in England. The English soldier in Flanders came over to London, put up at an inn, which occupied a site not very distant from that of the once well-known "Angel" in St. Clement's Danes, and made a gay figure in the open Strand, till he was prepared to consummate a work which he thought would help himself to greatness.

Into the matter of the plot I will not enter. It must be observed, however, that knight never went more coolly to look death in the face than Guy went to blow up the Protestant king and the parliament. At the same time it must be added, that Guy had not the slightest intention of hoisting himself with his own petard. He ran a very great risk, it is true, and he did it fearlessly; but the fact that both a carriage and a boat were in waiting to facilitate his escape, shows that self-sacrifice was not the object of the son of the York proctor. His great ambition was to rank among knights and nobles. He took but an ill-method to arrive at such an object; but his reverence for nobility was seen even when he was very near to his violent end. If he was ever a hero, it was when certain death by process of law was before him. But even then it was his boast and solace, that throughout the affair there was not a man employed, even to handle a spade, in furtherance of the end in view, who was not a gentleman. Guy died under the perfect conviction that he had done nothing derogatory to his quality!

Considering how dramatic are the respective stories of the page and squire, briefly noticed above, it is remarkable that so little use has been made of them by dramatists. Savage is the only one who has dramatized the story of the two knights, Somerset and Overbury. In this tragedy bearing the latter knight's name, and produced at the Haymarket, in June, 1723, he himself played the hero, Sir Thomas. His attempt to be an actor, and thus gain an honest livelihood by his industry, was the only act of his life of which Savage was ever ashamed. In this piece the only guilty persons are the countess and her uncle, the Earl of Northampton. This is in accordance with the once-prevailing idea that Northampton planned the murder of Sir Thomas, in his residence, which occupied the site of the present Northumberland house. The play was not successful, and the same may be said of it when revived, with alterations, at Covent Garden, in 1777. Sheridan, the actor, furnished the prologue. In this production he expressed his belief that the public generally felt little interest in the fate of knights and kings. The reason he assigns is hardly logical.

> "Too great for pity, they inspire respect,
> Their deeds astonish rather than affect.
> Proving how rare the heart *that* we can move,
> Which reason tells us we can never prove."

Guy Faux, who, when in Spain, was the 'squire of the higherborn Catesby, has inspired but few dramatic writers. I only know of two. In Mrs. Crouch's memoirs, notice is made of an afterpiece, brought out on the 5th of November, 1793, at the Haymarket. A far more creditable attempt to dramatize the story of Guy Fawkes was made with great success at the Coburg (Victoria) theatre, in September, 1822. This piece still keeps possession of the minor stage, and deservedly; but it has never been played with such effect as by its first "cast." O. Smith was the Guy, and since he had played the famous Obi, so well as to cause Charles Kemble's impersonation at the Haymarket to be forgotten, he had never been fitted with a character which suited him so admirably. It was one of the most truthful personations which the stage had ever seen. Indeed the piece was played by such a troop of actors as can not now be found in theatres of more pretensions than the transpontine houses. The chivalric Huntley, very like the chivalric Leigh Murray, in more respects than one, enacted *Tresham* with a rare ability, and judicious Chapman played *Catesby* with a good taste, which is not to be found now in the same locality. Dashing Stanley was the *Monteagle*, and graceful Howell the *Percy*, Beverly and Sloman gave rough portraits of the king and the facetious knight, *Sir Tristam Collywobble*—coarse but effective. Smith, however, was the soul of the piece, and Mr. Fawkes, of Farnley, might have witnessed the representation, and have been proud of his descent from the dignified hero that O. Smith made of his ancestor.

I have given samples of knights of various qualities, but I have yet to mention the scholar and poet knights. There are many personages who would serve to illustrate the knight so qualified, but I know of none so suitable as Ulrich Von Hutten.

## ULRICH VON HUTTEN.

*"Jacta est alea."— Ulrich's Device.*

ULRICH VON HUTTEN was born on the 21st of April, 1488, in the castle of Stackelberg, near Fulda, in Franconia. He was of a noble family—all the men of which were brave, and all the women virtuous. He had three brothers and two sisters. His tender mother loved him the most, because he was the weakest of her offspring. His father loved him the least for the same reason. For a like cause, however, both parents agreed that a spiritual education best accorded with the frame of Ulrich. The latter, at eleven years old, was accordingly sent to learn his humanities in the abbey school at Fulda.

His progress in all knowledge, religious and secular, made him the delight of the stern abbot and of his parents. Every effort possible was resorted to, to induce him to devote himself for ever to the life of the cloister. In his zealous opposition to this he was ably seconded by a strong-handed and high-minded knight, a friend of his father's named Eitelwolf von Stein. This opposition so far succeeded, that in 1504, when Ulrich was sixteen years of age he fled from the cloister-academy of Fulda, and betook himself to the noted high-school at Erfurt.

Among his dearest fellow *Alumni* here were Rubianus and Hoff, both of whom subsequently achieved great renown. In the Augustine convent, near the school, there was residing a poor young monk, who also subsequently became somewhat famous. Nobody, however, took much account of him just then, and few even cared to know his name—Martin Luther. The plague breaking out at Erfurt, Rubianus was accompanied by Ulrich to Cologne, there to pursue their studies. The heart and purse of Ulrich's father were closed against the son, because of his flight from Fulda; but his kinsman Eitelwolf, provided for the necessities of the rather imprudent young scholar.

The sages who trained the young idea at Cologne were of the old high and dry quality—hating progress and laboriously learned in trifles. At the head of them were Hogstraten and Ortuin. Ulrich learned enough of their manner to be able to crush them afterward with ridicule, by imitating their style, and reproducing their gigantic nonsense, in the famous "Epistolæ Obscurorum Virorum." In the meantime he knit close friendship with Sebastian Brandt, and Œcolampadius—both young men of progress. The latter was expelled from Cologne for being so, but the University of Frankfort on the Oder offered him an asylum. Thither Ulrich repaired also, to be near his friend, and to sharpen his weapons for the coming struggle between light and darkness—Germany against Rome, and the German language against the Latin.

At Frankfort he won golden opinions from all sorts of people. The Elector, Joachim of Brandenburg; his brother, the priestly Margrave Albert; and Bishop Dietrich von Beilow were proud of the youth who did honor to the university. He here first became a poet, and took the brothers Von Osthen for his friends. He labored earnestly, and acquired much glory; but he was a very free liver to boot, though he was by no means particularly so, for the times in which he lived. His excesses, however, brought on a dangerous disease, which, it is sometimes supposed, had not hitherto been known in Europe. Be this as it may, he was never wholly free from the malady as long as he lived, nor ever thought that it much mattered whether he suffered or not.

He was still ill when he took up for a season the life of a wandering scholar. He endured all its miserable vicissitudes, suffered famine and shipwreck, and was glad at last to find a haven, as a poor student, in the Pomeranian University of Griefswalde. The Professor Lötz and his father the Burgomaster, were glad to patronize so renowned a youth, but they did it with such insulting condescension that the spirit of Ulrich revolted; and in 1509, the wayward scholar was again a wanderer, with the world before him where to choose. The Lötzes, who had lent him clothes, despatched men after him to strip him; and the poor, half-frozen wretch, reached Rostock half starved, more than half naked, with wounds gaping for vengeance, and with as little sense about him as could be possessed by a man so ill-conditioned.

He lived by his wits at Rostock. He was unknown and perfectly destitute; but he penned so spirited a metrical narrative of his life and sufferings, addressed to the heads of the university there, that these at once received him under their protection. In a short time he was installed in comparative comfort, teaching the classics to young pupils, and experiencing as much enjoyment as he could, considering that the Lötzes of Griefswalde were continually assuring his patrons that their protegé was a worthless impostor.

He took a poet's revenge, and scourged them in rhymes, the very ruggedness of which was tantamount to flaying.

Having gained his fill of honor at Rostock, his restless spirit urged him once again into the world. After much wandering, he settled for a season at Wittenburg, where he was the delight of the learned men. By their eleemosynary aid, and that of various friends, save his father, who rejoiced in his renown but would not help him to live, he existed after the fashion of many pauper students of his day. At Wittenburg he wrote his famous "Art of Poetry;" and he had no sooner raised universal admiration by its production, than forth he rushed once more into the world.

He wandered through Bohemia and Moravia, thankfully accepting bread from peasants, and diamond rings from princes. He had not a maravedi in his purse, nor clean linen on his back; but he made himself welcome everywhere. One night he slept, thankfully, on the straw of a barn; and the next sank, well-fed, into the eider-down of a bishop's bed. He entered Olmutz ragged, shoeless, and exhausted. He left it, after enjoying the rich hospitality he had laughingly extracted from Bishop Turso, on horseback, with a heavy purse in his belt, a mantle on his shoulder, and a golden ring, with a jewel set in it, upon his finger. Such were a student's vicissitudes, in the days of German wandering, a long time ago.

The boy, for he was not yet twenty years of age, betook himself to Vienna, where he kept a wide circle in continual rapture by the excellence of his poetical productions. These productions were not "all for love," nor were they all didactic. He poured out war-ballads to encourage the popular feeling in favor of the Emperor Maximilian, against his enemies in Germany and Italy. Ulrich was, for the moment, the Tyrtæus of his native country. Then, suddenly recollecting that his angry sire had said that if his son would not take the monk's cowl, his father would be content to see him assume the lawyer's coif, our volatile hero hastened to Pavia, opened the law books on an ominous 1st of April, 1512, and read them steadily, yet wearied of them heartily, during just three months.

At this time Francis the first of France, who had seized on Pavia, was besieged therein by the German and Swiss cavalry. Ulrich was dangerously ill during the siege, but he occupied the weary time by writing sharp epitaphs upon himself. The allies entered the city; and Ulrich straightway departed from it, a charge having been laid against him of too much partiality for the French. The indignant German hurried to Bologna, where he once more addressed himself to the *Pandects* and the *Juris Codices Gentium*.

This light reading so worked on his constitution that fever laid him low, and after illness came destitution. He wrote exquisite verses to Cardinal Gurk, the imperial embassador in Bologna. where the pope for the moment resided; but he failed in his object of being raised to some office in the cardinal's household. Poor Ulrich took the course often followed by men of his impulses and condition; he entered the army as a private soldier, and began the ladder which leads to knighthood at the lowest round.

Unutterable miseries he endured in this character; but he went through the siege of Pavia with honor, and he wrote such sparkling rhymes in celebration of German triumphs and in ridicule of Germany's foes, that, when a weakness in the ankles compelled him to retire from the army, he collected his songs and dedicated them to the Emperor.

The dedication, however, was so very independent of tone, that Maximilian took no notice of the limping knight who had exchanged the sword for the lyre. Indeed, at this juncture, the man who could wield a sledge-hammer, was in more esteem with the constituted authorities than he who skilfully used his pen. The young poet could scarcely win a smile, even from Albert of Bradenburg, to whom he had dedicated a poem. Sick at heart, his health gave way, and a heavy fever sent him to recover it at the healing springs in the valley of Ems.

A short time previous to his entering the army, the young Duke Ulrich of Würtemburg had begun to achieve for himself a most unenviable reputation. He had entered on his government; and he governed his people ill, and himself worse. He allowed nothing to stand between his own illustrious purpose and the object aimed at. He had for wife the gentle Bavarian princess, Sabina, and for friend, young Johan von Hutten, a cousin of our hero Ulrich.

Now, Johan von Hutten had recently married a fair-haired girl, with the not very euphonious appellation of Von Thumb. She was, however, of noble birth, and, we must add, of light principles. The duke fell in love with her, and she with the duke, and when his friend Johan remonstrated with him, the ducal sovereign gravely proposed to the outraged husband an exchange of consorts!

Johan resolved to withdraw from the ducal court; and this resolution alarmed both his wife and the duke, for Johan had no intention of leaving his lightsome Von Thumb behind him. Therefore, the duke invited Johan one fine May morning in the year 1515, to take a friendly ride with him through a wood. The invitation was accepted, and as Johan was riding along a narrow path, in front of the duke, the latter passed his sword through the body of his friend, slaying him on the spot.

Having thus murdered his friend, the duke hung him up by the neck in his own girdle to a neighboring tree, and he defended the deed, by giving out that ducal justice had only been inflicted on a traitor who had endeavored to seduce the Duchess of Wurtemburg! The lady, however, immediately fled to her father, denouncing the faithlessness of her unworthy husband, on whose bosom the young widow of the murdered Johan now reclined for consolation.

On this compound deed becoming known, all Germany uttered a unanimous cry of horror. The noblest of the duke's subjects flung off their allegiance. His very servants quitted him in disgust. His fellow-princes invoked justice against him and Ulrich von Hutten, from his sick couch at Ems, penned eloquent appeals to the German nation, to rise and crush the ruthless wretch who had quenched in blood, the life, the light, the hope, the very flower of Teutonic chivalry.

The "Philippics" of Ulrich were mainly instrumental in raising a terrible Nemesis to take vengeance upon his ducal namesake; and he afterward wrote his "Phalarismus" to show that the tyrant excited horror, even in the infernal regions. The opening sentence —"Jacta est alea!" became his motto; and his family took for its apt device—"Exoriare aliquis nostris ex ossibus ultor!" From this time forward, Ulrich von Hutten was a public man, and became one of the foremost heroes of his heroic age. He was now scholar, poet, and knight.

His fame would have been a pleasant thing to him, but the pleasure was temporarily diminished by the death of his old benefactor, Eitelwolf von Stein. The latter was the first German statesman who was also a great scholar; and *his* example first shook the prejudice, that for a knight or nobleman to be book-learned was derogatory to his chivalry and nobility. Into the area of public warfare Ulrich now descended, and the enemies of light trembled before the doughty champion. The collegiate teachers at Cologne, with Hogstraten, the Inquisitor, Pfefierkorn, a converted Jew, and Ortuin—at their head, had directed all the powers of the scholastic prejudices against Reuchlin and his followers, who had declared, that not only Greek, but Hebrew should form a portion of the course of study for those destined to enter the Church. The ancient party pronounced this Heathenism; Reuchlin and his party called it Reason, and Germany, was split in two, upon the question.

At the very height of the contest, a lad with a sling and a stone entered the lists, and so dexterously worked his missiles, that the enemy of learning was soon overcome. The lad was Von Hutten, who, as chief author of those amusing satires, "Epistolae Obscurorum Virorum," ruined Monkery and paralyzed Rome, by making all the world laugh at the follies, vices, crimes, and selfish ignorance of both.

Leo X. was so enraged, that he excommunicated the authors,

and devoted them to damnation. "I care no more," said Von Hutten, "for the bull of excommunication than I do for a soap-bubble." The reputation he had acquired, helped him to a reconciliation with his family; but the members thereof had only small respect for a mere learned knight. They urged him to qualify himself for a chancellor, and to repair to Rome, and study the law accordingly.

Something loath, he turned his face toward the Tyber, in 1515. The first news received of the law-student was to the effect, that having been attacked, dagger in hand, at a pic-nic, near Viterbo, by five French noblemen, whom he had reproved for speaking ill of Germany and the Emperor Maximilian, he had slain one and put the other four to flight. From this fray he himself escaped with a slash on the cheek. He recounted his victory in a song of triumph, and when the law-student sat down to his books, every one in Rome acknowledged that his sword and his pen were equally pointed.

His French adversaries threatened vengeance for their humiliating defeat; and he accordingly avoided it, by withdrawing to Bologne, where he again, with hearty disgust, applied himself to the severe study of a law which was never applied for justice sake. He found compensation in penning such stirring poetry as his satirical "Nemo," and in noting the vices of the priesthood with the intention of turning his observation to subsequent profit. A feud between the German and Italian students at Bologna soon drove our scholar from the latter place. He took himself to Ferrara and Venice; was welcomed everywhere by the learned and liberal, and, as he wrote to Erasmus, was loaded by them with solid pudding as well as empty praise.

From this journey he returned to his native country. He repaired to Augsburg, where Maximilian was holding court, and so well was he commended to the emperor, that on the 15th of June, 1517, that monarch dubbed him Imperial Knight, placed a gold ring, symbolic of chivalrous dignity, on his finger, and crowned him a poet, with a laurel wreath, woven by the fairest flower of Augsburg, Constance Peutinger.

After such honors, his father received him with joy at his hearth; and while Von Hutten went from his native Stackelberg to the library at Fulda, yet hesitating whether to take service under the Emperor or under the Elector of Mayence, he bethought himself of the irrefutable work of Laurentius Valla against the temporal authority and possessions of the Popedom. He studied the work well, published an improved edition, and dedicated it, in a letter of fire and ability, to Leo X.; —a proof of his hope in, or of his defiance of, that accomplished infidel.

Luther and Von Hutten were thus, each unconscious of the other, attacking Popery on two points, about the same moment. Luther employed fearful weapons in his cause, and wielded them manfully. Von Hutten only employed, as yet, a wit which made all wither where it fell; and an irony which consumed where it dropped. In the handling of these appliances, there was no man in Germany who was his equal. Leo could admire and enjoy both the wit and the irony; and he was not disinclined to agree with the arguments of which they were made the supports; but what he relished as a philosopher, he condemned as a Pontiff. The Florentine, Lorenzo de' Medici, could have kissed the German on either cheek, but the Pope, Leo X., solemnly devoted him to Gehenna.

As a protection against papal wrath, Von Hutten entered the service of Albert, Elector-Archbishop of Mayence. Albert was a liberal Romanist, but nothing in the least of an Ultra-Montanist. He loved learning and learned men, and he recollected that he was a German before he was a Romanist. In the suite of the elector, Von Hutten visited Paris, in 1518. He returned to Mayence only to carry on more vigorously his onslaught against the begging monks. He accounted them as greater enemies to Germany than the Turks. "We fight with the latter, beyond our frontier for power; but the former are the corrupters of science, of religion, of morals—and they are in the very midst of us." So does he write, in a letter to Graf Nuenar, at Cologne.

The building of St. Peter's cost Rome what the building of Versailles cost France—a revolution. In each case, an absolute monarchy was overthrown never again to rise. To provide for the expenses of St. Peter's, the Dominican Tetzel traversed Germany, selling his indulgences. Luther confronted him, and denounced his mission, as well as those who sent him on it. Von Hutten, in his hatred of monks, looked upon this as a mere monkish squabble; and he was glad to see two of the vocation holding one another by the throat.

At this precise moment, Germany was excited at the idea of a projected European expedition against the Turks. The Imperial Knight saw clearly the perils that threatened Christendom from that question, and was ready to rush, sword in hand, to meet them. He declared, however, that Europe groaned under a more insupportable yoke, laid on by Rome, and he deprecated the idea of helping Rome with funds against the Moslem. What a change was here from the Imperial crusading knights of a few centuries earlier. "If Rome," he said, "be serious on the subject of such a crusade, we are ready to fight, but she must pay us for our services. She shall not have both our money and our blood." He spoke, wrote, and published boldly against Rome being permitted to levy taxes in Germany, on pretence of going to war with the unbelieving Ottomans. At the same moment, Luther was denouncing the monks who thought to enrich the coffers of Rome by the sale of indulgences. One was the political, the other the religious enemy of the power which sought to rule men and their consciences from under the shadow of the Colosseum.

There was little hope of aid from the emperor, but Von Hutten looked for all the help the cause needed in a union of the citizen classes (whom he had been wont to satirize) with the nobility. To further the end in view, he wrote his masterly dialogue of "The Robbers." In this piece, the speakers are knights and citizens. Each side blames the other, but each is made acquainted with the other's virtues, by the interposition of a *Deus ex machinâ* in the presence of the knight, Franz von Sickingen. The whole partakes of the spirit and raciness of Bunyan and Cobbett. Throughout the dialogue, the vices of no party in the state find mercy, while the necessity of the mutual exercise of virtue and aid is ably expounded.

The knight, Franz von Sickingen, was author of a part of this dialogue. His adjurations to Von Hutten not to be over-hasty and his reason why, are no doubt his own. By the production of such papers, Germany was made eager for the fray. This particular and powerful dialogue was dedicated to John, Pfalzgraf of the Rhine, Duke of Bavaria, and Count of Spanheim. This illustrious personage had requested Ulrich that whenever he published any particularly bold book, in support of national liberty, he would dedicate it to him, the duke. The author obeyed, in this instance, on good grounds and with right good will. There is in the dialogue an audible call to war, and this pleased Luther himself, who was now convinced that with the pen alone, the Reformation could not be an established fact.

Ulrich longed for the contact, whereby to make his country and his church free of Romanist tyranny. But he considers the possibility of a failure. He adjured his family to keep aloof from the strife, that they might not bring ruin on their heads, in the event of destruction falling on his own. The parents of Ulrich were now no more; Ulrich as head of his house was possessed of its modest estates. Of his own possessions he got rid, as of an encumbrance to his daring and his gigantic activity. He formally made over nearly all to his next brother, in order that his enemies, should they ultimately triumph, might have no ground for seizing them.

At the same time, he warned his brother to send him neither letters nor money, as either would be considered in the light of aid offered to an enemy, and might be visited with terrible penalties.

Having rid himself of what few would so easily have parted from, he drew his sword joyously and independently for the sake of liberty alone, and with a determination of never sheathing it until he had accomplished that at which he aimed, or that the accomplishment of such end had been placed beyond his power.

"Jacta est alea," cried he, viewing his bright sword, "the die is thrown, Ulrich has risked it."

In the meantime Von Hutten remained in the service of the Elector-Archbishop of Mayence. The courtiers laughed at him as a rude knight. The knights ridiculed him as a poor philosopher. Both were mistaken; he was neither poor nor rude, albeit a *Ritter* and a sage. What he most cared for, was opportunity to be useful in his generation, and leisure enough to cultivate learning during the hours he might call his own. His satirical poems, coarsely enough worded against a courtier's life, are admirable for strength and coloring. Not less admirable for taste and power are his letters of this period. In them he denounces that nobility which is composed solely of family pride; and he denounces, with equally good foundation, the life of "Robber Knights," as he calls them, who reside in their castles, amid every sort of discomfort, and a world of dirt, of hideous noises, and unsavory smells; and who only leave them to plunder or to be plundered. He pronounces the true knights of the period to be those alone who love religion and education. With the aid of these, applied wisely and widely, and with the help of great men whom he names, and who share his opinions, he hopes, as he fervently declares, to see intellect gain more victories than force—to be able to bid the old barbarous spirit which still influenced too many "to gird up its loins and be off." Health came to him with this determination to devote himself to the service and improvement of his fellow-men. It came partly by the use of simple remedies, the chief of which was moderation in all things. Pen and sword were now alike actively employed. He put aside the former, for a moment, only to assume the latter, in order to strike in for vengeance against the aggressive Duke of Wurtemburg.

The crimes of this potentate had at length aroused the emperor against him. Maximilian had intrusted the leadership of his army to the famous knight-errant of his day, Franz von Sickingen. This cavalier had often been in open rebellion against the emperor himself; and Hutten now enrolled himself among the followers of Franz. His patron not only gave him the necessary permission but continued to him his liberal stipend; when the two knights met, and made their armor clash with their boisterous embrace, they swore not to stop short of vengeance on the guilty duke, but to fight to the death for liberty and Christendom. They slept together in the same bed in token of brotherly knighthood, and they rose to carry their banner triumphantly against the duke—ending the campaign by the capture of the metropolis, Stutgardt.

Reuchlin resided in the capital, and the good man was full of fear; for murder and rapine reigned around him. His fear was groundless, for Von Hutten had urged Sickingen to give out that in the sack of Stutgardt, no man should dare to assail the dwelling of Reuchlin. The two knights left the city to proceed to the spot in the wood where still lay buried the body of the murdered John von Hutten. "It had lain four years in the grave," said Ulrich, "but the features were unchanged. As we touched him, blood flowed afresh from his wounds; recognise in this the witness of his innocence." The corpse was eventually transported to the family vault at Esslingen.

The cities of the hard-pressed duke fell, one after the other, and the guilty prince was driven from his inheritance. Von Hutten remained with the army, busily plying his pen; his sword on the table before him, his dagger on his hip, and himself encased in armor to the throat. Erasmus laughingly wrote to him to leave Mars and stick to the Muses. He scarcely needed this advice, for his letters from the camp show that fond as he was of the field, he loved far better the quiet joys of the household hearth. Amid the brazen clangor of trumpets, the neighing of steeds, the rolling of the drum, and the boom of battle, he writes to Piscator (Fischer), his longing for home, and his desire for a wife to smile on, and care for him; one who would soothe his griefs and share his labors — "One," he says, "with whom I might sportively laugh and feel glad in our existence — who would sweeten the bitter of life and alleviate the pressure of care. Let me have a wife, my dear Friederich, and thou knowest how I would love her . . . . young, fair, shy, gentle, affectionate, and well-educated. She may have some fortune, but not excess of it; and as for position, this is my idea thereon: that *she* will be noble enough whom Ulrich von Hutten chooses for his mate." As a wooer, it will be seen that the scholar-knight had as little of the faint heart as the audacious "Findlay" of Burns, and I might almost say of Freiligrath, so spiritedly has the latter poet translated into German the pleasant lines of the Ayrshire ploughman.

Well had it been for Ulrich had he found, in 1519, the wife of his complacent visions. The gentle hand would have saved him from many a cruel hour.

On his return to Mayence he had well-nigh obeyed the universal call addressed to him, to join openly with Luther against Rome. He was withheld by his regard for his liberal patron, the archbishop. He remained, partly looking on and partly aiding, on the outskirts of the field where the fray was raging. He published a superb edition of Livy, and to show that the reforming spirit still burned brightly in the bosom of the scholar, he also published his celebrated "Vadiscus, sive Trias Romana." This triple-edged weapon still inflicts anguish on Rome. Never had arrow of such power stricken the harlot before. Its point is still in her side; and her adversaries knew well how to use it, by painfully turning it in the wound.

The knight now hung up his sword in his chamber at Stackelberg, and devoted himself to his pen. In the convent library at Fulda he discovered an ancient German work against the supremacy of the Pope over the princes and people of Germany. Of this he made excellent use. His own productions against Rome followed one another with great rapidity. Down to the middle of 1520 he was incessantly charging the Vatican, at the point of a grey goosequill. He had at heart the freeing of Germany from the ecclesiastical domination of Italy, just as the men of Northern Italy have it at heart to rescue her from the cruel domination of Austria.

To accomplish his ends, Von Hutten left no means untried. Knight and scholar, noble and villain, the very Emperor Charles V. himself, Ulrich sought to enlist in the great confederacy, by which he hoped to strike a mortal blow at the temporal power of the "Universal Bishop." His books converted even some of the diocesans of the Romish Church; but Rome thundered excommunication on the books and their author, and directed a heavy weight of censure against his protector, Albert of Mayence.

The archbishop admonished Von Hutten, and interdicted his works. This step decided Ulrich's course. He at once addressed his first letter to Luther. It began with the cry of "Freedom for ever!" and it offered heart, head, soul, body, brains, and purse, in furtherance of the great cause. He tendered to Luther, in the name of Sickingen, a secure place of residence; and he established his first unassailable battery against Rome, by erecting a printing-press in his own room in the castle of Stackelberg, whence he directed many a raking fire against all his assailants. "Jacta est alea!" was his cry; "Let the enemies of light look to it!"

From Fulda he started to the court of the Emperor Charles V.

at Brussels. But his enemies stood between him and the foot of the throne, and he was not allowed to approach it. His life, too, was being constantly threatened. He withdrew before these threats, once more into Germany, taking compensation by the way, for his disappointment, by a characteristic bit of spirit. He happened to fall in with Hogstraten, the heretic-finder, and the arch-enemy of Reuchlin. Ulrich belabored him with a sheathed sword till every bone in the body of Hogstraten was sore. In return, the knight was outlawed, and Leo X. haughtily commanded that hands should be laid upon him wherever he might be found, and that he should be delivered, gagged, and bound, to the Roman tribunals.

Franz von Sickingen immediately received him within the safe shelter of his strong fortress of Ebernberg, where already a score of renowned theological refugees had found an asylum. The colloquies of the illustrious fugitives made the old walls ring again. Von Hutten reduced these colloquies to writing, and I may name, as one of their conclusions, that the service of the mass in German was determined on, as the first step toward an established reformation.

The attempt of the Pope to have Ulrich seized and sacrificed, was eagerly applied by the latter to the benefit of the cause he loved. To the emperor, to the elector, to the nobles, knights, and states of Germany, he addressed papers full of patriotism, eloquence, and wisdom, against the aggression on German liberty. Throughout Germany this scholar-knight called into life the spirit of civil and religious freedom, and Luther, looking upon what Ulrich was doing, exclaimed: "Surely the last day is at hand!"

These two men, united, lit up a flame which can never be trodden out. One took his Bible and his pen, and with these pricked Rome into a fury, from which she has never recovered. The other, ungirding his sword, and transferring his printing-press to Ebernberg, sent therefrom glowing manifestoes which made a patriot of every reader.

The lyre and learning were both now employed by Von Hutten, in furtherance of his project. His popular poetry was now read or sung at every hearth. Not a village was without a copy, often to be read by stealth, of his "Complaint and Admonition." His dialogues, especially that called the "Warner," in which the colloquists are a Roman alarmist and Franz von Sickingen himself, achieved a similar triumph. It was to give heart to the wavering that Von Hutten wrote, and sent abroad from his press at Ebernberg, those remarkable dialogues.

Franz von Sickingen, his great protector, was for a season apprehensive that Ulrich's outcry against Rome was louder than necessary, and his declared resolution to resent oppression by means of the sword, somewhat profane. Ulrich reasoned with and read to the gallant knight. His own good sense, and the arguments of Luther and Ulrich, at length convinced him that it was folly and sin to maintain outward respect for Rome as long as the latter aspired to be lord in Germany, above the kaiser himself. Franz soon agreed with Hutten that they ought not to heed even the Emperor, if he commanded them to spare the Pope, when such mercy might be productive of injury to the empire. In such cases, not to obey was the best obedience. They would not now look back. "It is better," so runs it in Von Hutten's "Warner," "to consider what God's will is, than what may enter the heads of individuals, capricious men, more especially in the case wherein the truth of the Gospel is concerned. If it be proved that nothing satisfactory, by way of encouragement, can come to us from the Emperor, they who love the Church and civil liberty must be bold at their own peril, let the issue be what it may."

The dialogue of the "Warner" was, doubtless, not only read to Sickingen during the progress of its composition, but was unquestionably a transcript of much that was talked about, weighed, and considered between the two friends, as they sat surrounded by a circle of great scholars and soldiers, for whose blood Rome was thirsting. It ends with an assurance of the full adhesion of Franz to the views of Ulrich. "In this matter," says the "Warner" to the knight of Ebernberg, "I see you have a passionate and zealous instigator, a fellow named Von Hutten, who can brook delay with patience, and who has heaped piles upon piles of stones, ready to fling them at the first adversary who presents himself." "Ay, in good sooth," is the ready answer of Franz, "and his service is a joy to me, for he has the true spirit requisite to insure triumph in such a struggle as ours."

Thus at Ebernburg the battery was played against the defences of Rome, while Luther, from his known abodes, or from his concealment in friendly fortresses, thundered his artillery against the doctrines and superstitions of Rome. The movement had a double aspect. The Germans were determined to be free both as Christians and as citizens. The conducting of such determination to its successful issue could not be intrusted to worthier or more capable hands than those of Luther, aided by the Saxon Frederick the Wise, and Ulrich von Hutten, with such a squire at his side as hearty Franz von Sickingen.

In 1521 the young emperor, Charles V., delivered a speech at Worms, which seemed to have been framed expressly to assure the reformers that the emperor was with them. It abounded in promises that the kaiser would do his utmost to effect necessary reforms within the empire. The reformers were in great spirits, but they soon learned, by the summoning of Luther to Worms, and by the subsequent conduct of the emperor, that they had nothing to expect from him which they could thankfully acknowledge.

Ulrich only wrote the more boldly, and agitated the more unceasingly, in behalf of the cause of which Luther was the great advocate. To the kaiser himself he addressed many a daring epistle, as logical as audacious, in order to induce him to shake off the yoke of Rome, and be master of the Roman world, by other sanction than that of German election and papal consent. Von Hutten was more bold and quite as logical in his witheringly sarcastic epistles addressed to the pope's legates at Worms. These epistles show that if at the time there was neither a recognised liberty of the press nor of individual expression, the times themselves were so out of joint that men dared do much which their masters dared not resent.

To the entire body of the priesthood assembled at Worms to confront Luther, he addressed similar epistles. They abound in "thoughts that breathe, and words that burn." In every word there is defiance. Every sentence is a weapon. Every paragraph is an engine of war. The writer scatters his deadly missiles around him, threatening all, wounding many, sometimes indeed breaking his own head by rash management, but careless of all such accidents as long as he can reach, terrify, maul, and put to flight the crowd of enemies who have conspired to suppress both learning and religion in Germany.

In unison with Sickingen, he earnestly entreated Luther to repair to Ebernburg rather than to Worms, as there his knightly friends would protect him from all assailants. The reply of the great reformer is well known. He would go to Worms, he said, though there were as many devils as tiles on the roofs, leagued against him to oppose his journey thither. We can not doubt but that Luther would have been judicially assassinated in that ancient city but for the imposing front assumed by his well-armed and well-organized adherents, who not only crowded into the streets of Worms, but who announced by placards, even in the very bedchamber of the emperor, that a thousand lives should pay for the loss of one hair of the reformer's head.

Had it depended on Von Hutten, the reformers would not have waited till violence had been inflicted on Luther, ere they took their own revenge for wrongs and oppressions done. But he was overruled, and his hot blood was kept cool by profuse and prosaic argument on the part of the schoolmen of his faction. He chafed, but he obeyed. He had more difficulty in reducing to the same obedience the bands of his adherents who occupied the city and its vicinity. These thought that the safety of Luther could only be secured by rescuing him at once from the hands of his enemies. The scholar-knight thought so too; and he would gladly have charged against such enemies. He made no signal, however, for the onslaught; on the contrary he issued orders forbidding it; and recommended the confederates to sheathe their swords, but yet to have their hands on the hilt. The elector of Saxony was adverse to violence, and Luther left Worms in safety, after defying Rome to her face.

Then came those unquiet times in which Charles V. so warmly welcomed volunteers to his banner. Seduced by his promises, Franz von Sickingen, with a few hundreds of strong-sinewed men, passed over to the Imperial quarters. The old brotherly gathering at Ebernberg was thus broken up; and Ulrich, who had offended both pope and emperor by his denunciations of ecclesiastical and civil tyranny, betook himself to Switzerland, where he hoped to find a secure asylum, and a welcome from Erasmus.

This amphibious personage, however, who had already ceased to laud Luther, affected now a horror against Von Hutten. He wrote of him as a poor, angry, mangy wretch, who could not be content to live in a room without a stove, and who was continually pestering his friends for pecuniary loans. The fiery Ulrich assailed his false friend in wrathful pamphlets. Erasmus loved the species of warfare into which such attacks drew or impelled him. He replied to Ulrich more cleverly than conclusively, in his "Sponge to wipe out the Aspersions of Von Hutten." But the enmity of Erasmus was as nothing compared with the loss of Von Sickingen himself. In the tumultuary wars of his native land he perished, and Ulrich felt that, despite some errors, the good cause had lost an iron-handed and a clear-sighted champion.

There is little doubt that it was at the instigation of Erasmus that the priestly party in Basle successfully urged the government authorities to drive Ulrich from the asylum he had temporarily found there. He quietly departed on issue of the command, and took his solitary and painful way to Muhlhausen, where a host of reformers warmly welcomed the tottering skeleton into which had shrunk the once well-knit man. Here his vigor cast aloft its last expiring light. Muhlhausen threw off the papal yoke, but the papist party was strong enough there to raise an insurrection; and rather than endanger the safety of the town, the persecuted scholar and soldier once more walked forth to find a shelter. He reached Zurich in safety. He went at once to the hearth of Zuinglius, who looked upon the terrible spectre in whom the eyes alone showed signs of life; and he could hardly believe that the pope cared for the person, or dreaded the intellect, of so ghostlike a champion as this.

Ulrich, excommunicated, outlawed and penniless, was in truth sinking fast. His hand had not strength to enfold the pommel of his sword. From his unconscious fingers dropped the pen.

"Who will defend me against my calumniators?" asked the yet willing but now incapable man.

"I will!" said the skilful physician, Otto Brunfels; and the cooper's son stoutly protected the good name of Ulrich, after the latter was at peace in the grave.

The last hours of the worn-out struggler for civil and religious liberty, were passed at Ufnau, a small island in the Lake of Zurich. He had been with difficulty conveyed thither, in the faint hope that his health might profit by the change. There he slowly and resignedly died on the last day of August, 1523, and at the early age of thirty-eight.

A few dearly-loved books and some letters constituted all his property. He was interred on the island, but no monument has ever marked the spot where his wornout body was laid down to repose.

Through life, whether engaged with sword or pen, his absorbing desire was that his memory might be held dear by his survivors. He loved activity, abhorred luxury, adored liberty; and, for the sake of civil and religious freedom, he fought and sang with earnest alacrity. Lyre on arm, and sword in hand, he sang and summoned, until hosts gathered round him, and cheered the burthen of all he uttered. "The die is thrown! I've risked it for truth and freedom's sake." Against pope and kaiser, priest and soldier, he boldly cried, "Slay my frame you may, but my soul is beyond you!" He was the star that harbingered a bright dawn. His prevailing enemies drove him from his country; the grave which they would have denied him, he found in Switzerland, and "after life's fitful fever," the scholar-knight sleeps well in the island of the Zurich-Zee.

From the Zurich-Zee we will now retrace our steps, and consider the Sham Knights.

# SHAM KNIGHTS.

BETWEEN Tooting and Wandsworth lies a village of some celebrity for its sham knights or mayors — the village of Garrat. The villagers, some century ago, possessed certain common rights which were threatened with invasion. They accordingly made choice of an advocate, from among themselves, to protect their privileges. They succeeded in their object, and as the selection had been originally made at the period of a general election, the inhabitants resolved to commemorate the circumstance by electing a mayor and knighting him at each period of election for a new parliament. The resolution was warmly approved by all the publicans in the vicinity, and the Garrat elections became popular festivities, if not of the highest order, at least of the jolliest sort.

Not that the ceremony was without its uses. The politicians and wits of the day saw how the election might be turned to profit; and Wilkes, and Foote, and Garrick, are especially named as having written some of the addresses wherein, beneath much fustian, fun, and exaggeration of both fact and humor, the people were led to notice, by an Aristophanic process, the defects in the political system by which the country was then governed. The publicans, however, and the majority of the people cared more for the saturnalia than the schooling; and for some years the sham mayors of Garrat were elected, to the great profit, at least, of the tavern-keepers.

The poorer and the more deformed the candidate, the greater his chance of success. Thus, the earliest mayor of whom there was any record, was Sir John Harper, a fellow of infinite mirth and deformity, whose ordinary occupation was that of an itinerant vender of brick-dust. His success gave dignity to the brick-dust trade, and inspired its members with ambition. They had the glory of boasting that their friend and brother "Sir John" sat, when not sufficiently sober to stand, during two parliaments. A specimen of his ready wit is given in his remark when a dead cat was flung at him, on the hustings during the period of his first election. A companion remarked with some disgust upon the unpleasant odor from the animal. "That's not to be wondered at," said Sir John, "you see it is a pole-cat."

But Sir John was ousted by an uglier, dirtier, more deformed, and merrier fellow than himself. The lucky personage in question was Sir Jeffrey Dunstan. He was a noted individual, hunched like Esop, and with as many tales, though not always with the like "morals." He was a noted dealer in old wigs, for it was before men had fallen into what was then considered the disreputable fashion of wearing their own hair, under round hats. Sir John was a republican; but he did not despise either his office of mayor or his courtesy title of knight. Had he possessed more discretion and less zeal, he probably would have prospered in proportion. In the best, that is, in the quietest, of times, Sir Jeffrey could with difficulty keep his tongue from wagging. He never appeared in the streets with his wig-bag on his shoulder, without a numerous crowd following, whom he delighted with his sallies, made against men in power, whose weak points were assailable. The French Revolution broke out when Sir Jeffrey was mayor, and this gave a loose to his tongue, which ultimately laid him up by the heels. The knight grew too political, and even seditious, in his street orations, and he was in consequence committed to prison, in 1793, for treasonable practices. This only increased his popularity for a time, but it tamed the spirit of the once chivalrous mayor. When he ceased to be wittily bold, he ceased to be cared for by the constituents whose presence made the electors at Garrat. After being thrice elected he was successfully opposed and defeated, under a charge of dishonesty. The pure electors of Garrat could have borne with a political traitor; but as they politely said, they "could not a-bear a petty larcenist," and Sir Jeffrey Dunstan was, metaphorically and actually presented "with the sack."

When Manners Sutton ceased to be Speaker, he claimed, I believe, to be made a peer; on the plea that it was not becoming that he who had once occupied the chair, should ever be reduced to stand upon the floor, of the House of Commons. Sir Jeffrey Dunstan had something of a similar sense of dignity. Having fallen from the height of mayor of Garrat, what was then left for Sir Jeffrey? He got as "drunk as a lord," was never again seen sober, and, in 1797, the year following that of his disgrace, the ex-mayor died of excess. So nice of honor was Sir Jeffrey Dunstan!

He was succeeded by Sir Harry Dimsdale, the mutilated muffin-seller, whose tenure of office was only brief, however brilliant, and who has the melancholy glory of having been the last of the illustriously dirty line of knighted mayors of Garrat. It was not that there was any difficulty in procuring candidates, but there was no longer the same liberality on the part of the peers and publicans to furnish a purse for them. Originally, the purse was made up by the inhabitants, for the purpose of protecting their collective rights. Subsequently, the publicans contributed in order that the attractions of something like a fair might be added, and therewith great increase of smoking and drinking. At that time the peerage did not disdain to patronize the proceeding, and the day of election was a holyday for thousands. Never before or since have such multitudes assembled at the well-known place of gathering; nor the roads been so blocked up by carts and carriages, honorable members on horses, and dustmen on donkeys. Hundreds of thousands sometimes assembled, and, through the perspiring crowd, the candidates, dressed like chimney-sweepers on May-day, or in the mock fashion of the period, were brought to the hustings in the carriages of peers, drawn by six horses, the owners themselves condescending to become their drivers.

The candidate was ready to swear anything, and each elector was required to make oath, on a brick-bat, "quod rem cum aliquâ muliere intra limites istius pagi habuissent." The candidates figured under mock pseudonyms. Thus, at one election there were against Sir Jeffrey, Lord Twankum, Squire Blowmedown, and Squire Gubbings. His lordship was Gardener, the Garrat grave-digger, and the squires were in humble reality, Willis, a waterman, and Simmonds, a Southwark publican. An attempt was made to renew the old saturnalia in 1826, when Sir John Paul Pry offered himself as a candidate, in very bad English, and with a similarly qualified success. He had not the eloquent power of the great Sir Jeffrey, who, on presenting himself to the electors named his "estate in the Isle of Man" as his qualification; announced his intention of relieving the king in his want of money, by abolishing its use; engaged to keep his promises as long as it was his interest to do so, and claimed the favorable influence of married ladies, on the assurance that he would propose the annulling of all marriages, which, as he said, with his ordinary logic, "must greatly increase the influence of the crown, and vastly lower Indian bonds." He intimated that his own ambition was limited to the governorship of Duck Island, or the bishopric of Durham. The latter appointment was mentioned for the purpose of enabling the usually shirtless, but for the moment court-dressed knight, to add that he was "fond of a clean shirt and lawn-sleeves." He moreover undertook to show the governors of India the way which they ought to be going, to Botany Bay; and to discover the longitude among the Jews of Duke's Place.

Courtesy was imperative on all the candidates toward each other. When Sir Jeffrey Dunstan opposed Sir William Harper, there were five other candidates, namely—" Sir William Blaze, of high rank in the army—a corporal in the city train-bands; Admiral Sir Christopher Dashwood, known to many who has *(sic)* felt the weight of his hand on their shoulders, and showing an execution in the other. Sir William Swallowtail, an eminent merchant, who supplies most of the gardeners with strawberry baskets; Sir John Gnawpost, who carries his traffic under his left arm, and whose general cry is 'twenty-five if you win and five if you lose;' and Sir Thomas Nameless, of reputation unmentionable." Sir John Harper was the only knight who forgot chivalrous courtesy, and who allowed his squire in armor to insult Sir Jeffrey. But this was not done with impunity. That knight appealed to usage, compelled his assailant to dismount, drop his colors, walk six times round the hustings, and humbly ask pardon.

Sir William Swallowtail, mentioned above, "was one William

Cock, a whimsical basket-maker of Brentford, who, deeming it proper to have an equipage every way suitable to the honor he aspired to, built his own carriage, with his own hands, to his own taste. It was made of wicker work, and was drawn by four, high, hollow-backed horses, whereon were seated dwarfish boys, whimsically dressed, for postillions. In allusion to the American War, two footmen, tarred and feathered, rode before the carriage. The coachman wore a wicker hat, and Sir William himself, from the seat of his vehicle, maintained his mock dignity, in grotesque array, amid unbounded applause." It should be added that Foote, who witnessed the humors of the election more than once, brought Sir Jeffrey upon the stage in the character of *Doctor Last;* but the wretched fellow, utterly incapable and awfully alarmed, was driven from the stage by the hisses of the whole house. Let us now look abroad for a few " Shams."

If foreign lands have sent no small number of pseudo-chevaliers to London, they have also abounded in many by far too patriotic or prudent to leave their native land. The Hôtel Saint Florentin, in Paris, was the residence of the Prince Talleyrand, but before his time it was the stage and the occasional dwelling-place of an extraordinary actor, known by the appellation of the Chevalier, or the Count de St. Germain. He was for a time the reigning wonder of Paris, where his history was told with many variations; not one true, and all astounding. The popular voice ascribed to him an Egyptian birth, and attributed to him the power of working miracles. He could cure the dying, and raise the dead; could compose magic philters, coin money by an impress of his index finger; was said to have discovered the philosopher's stone, and to be able to make gold and diamonds almost at will. He was, moreover, as generous as he was great, and his modest breast was covered with knightly orders, in proof of the gratitude of sovereigns whom he had obliged. He was supposed to have been born some centuries back, was the most gigantic and graceful impostor that ever lived, and exacted implicit faith in his power from people who had none in the power of God.

The soirées of the Hôtel St. Florentin were the admiration of all Paris, for there alone, this knight-count of many orders appeared to charm the visiters and please himself. His prodigality was enormous, so was his mendacity. He was graceful, witty, refined, yet not lacking audacity when his story wanted pointing, and always young, gave himself out for a Methuselah.

The following trait is seriously told of him, and is well substantiated. "Chevalier," said a lady to him one night, at a crowded assembly of the Hôtel St. Florentin, "do you ever remember having, in the course of your voyages, encountered our Lord Jesus Christ?" "Yes," replied the profane impostor, without hesitation and raising his eyes to heaven. "I have often seen and often spoken to Him. I have frequently had occasion to admire his mildness, genius, and charity. He was a celestial being; and I often prophesied what would befall Him!" The hearers, far from being shocked, only continued to ply the count with other questions. "Did you ever meet with the Wandering Jew?" asked a young marquiss. "Often!" was the reply; and the count added with an air of disdain:—"that wretched blasphemer once dared to salute me on the high-road; he was then just setting out on his tour of the world, and counted his money with one hand in his pocket, as he passed along." "Count," asked a Chevalier de St Louis, "who was the composer of that brilliant sonata you played to-night, on the harpsichord?" "I *really* can not say. It is a song of victory, and I heard it executed for the first time on the day of the triumph of Trajan." "Will you be indiscreet, dear count, for once," asked a newly-married baronne, "and tell us the names of the three ladies whom you have the most tenderly loved?" "That is difficult," said the honest knight with a smile, "but I think I may say that they were Lucretia, Aspasia, and Cleopatra."

The gay world of Paris said he was, at least two thousand years old; and he did not take the pains to contradict the report. There is reason to suppose that he was the son of a Portuguese Jew, who had resided at Bordeaux. His career was soon ended.

There was a far more respectable chevalier in our own country to whom the term of Sham Knight can hardly apply; but as he called himself "Sir John," and *that* title was not admitted in a court of law, some notice of him may be taken here.

There was then in the reign of George III., a knight of some notoriety, whose story is rather a singular one. When Sir John Gallini is now spoken of, many persons conclude that this once remarkable individual received the honors of knighthood at the hands of King George. I have been assured so by very eminent operatic authorites, who were, nevertheless, completely in error. Sir John Gallini was a knight of George III.'s time, but he was so created by a far more exalted individual; in the opinion, at least, of those who give to popes, who are elective potentates, a precedence over kings, who are hereditary monarchs. The wonder is that Gallini was ever knighted at all, seeing that he was simply an admirable ballet-dancer. But he was the first dancer who ever received an encore for the dexterous use of his heels. The Pope accordingly clapped upon them a pair of golden spurs, and Gallini was, thenceforth, Cavaliere del Sperone d'Oro. Such a knight may be noticed in this place.

Gallini came to England at a time when that part of the world, which was included in the term "people of quality," stood in need of a little excitement. This was in 1759, when there was the dullest of courts, with the heaviest of mistresses, and an opera, duller and heavier than either. Gallini had just subdued Paris by the magic of his saltatory movements. He thence repaired to London, with his reputation and slight baggage. He did not announce his arrival. It was sufficient that Gallini was there. He had hardly entered his lodgings when he was engaged, on his own terms. He took the town by storm. His *pas seul* was pronounced divine. The "quality" paid him more honor than if he had invented something useful to his fellow-men. He could not raise his toe, without the house being hushed into silent admiration. His *entrechats* were performed amidst thundering echoes of delight; his "whirls" elicited shrieks of ecstacy; and when he suddenly checked himself in the very swiftest of his wild career and looked at the house with a complacent smile, which seemed to say—" What do you think of that?" there ensued an explosion of tumultuous homage, such as the spectators would have *not* vouchsafed to the young conqueror of Quebec. Gallini, as far as opera matters were concerned, was found to be the proper man in the proper place. For four or five years he was despotic master of the ballet. He was resolved to be master of something else.

There was then in London a Lady Elizabeth Bertie. Her father, the Earl of Abingdon, then lately deceased, had, in his youth, married a Signora Collino, daughter to a "Sir John Collins." The latter knight was not English, but of English descent. His son, Signor Collino, was a celebrated player of the lute in this country. He was indeed the last celebrated player on that instrument in England.

Gallini then, the very head of his profession, ranking therein higher than the Abingdons did in the peerage, was rather condescending than otherwise, when he looked upon the Earl of Abingdon as his equal. The earl whom he so considered was the son of the one who had espoused the Signora Collino, and Lady Elizabeth Bertie was another child of the same marriage. When Gallini the dancer, therefore, began to think of proposing for the hand of that lady, he was merely thinking of marrying the niece of an instrumental performer. Gallini did not think there was derogation in this; but he did think, vain, foolish fellow that he was, that such a union would confer upon him the title of "my lord."

Gallini was a gentleman, nevertheless, in his way — that is, both in manners and morals. Proud indeed he was, as a peacock, and ambitious as a "climbing-boy," desirous for ever of being at the top, as speedily as possible, of every branch of his profession. He was the "professor of dancing" in the Abingdon family, where his agreeable person, his ready wit, his amiability, and the modesty beneath which he hid a world of pretension, rendered him a general favorite. He was very soon the friend of the house; and long before he had achieved *that* rank, he was the very particular friend of Lady Elizabeth Bertie. She loved her mother's soft Italian as Gallini spoke it; and in short she loved the Italian also, language and speaker. Lady and Signor became one.

When the match became publicly known the "did you evers?" that reached from box to box and echoed along the passages of the opera-house were deafening. "A lady of quality marry a dancer!" Why not, when maids of honor were held by royal coachmen as being bad company for the said coachman's sons? It was a more suitable match than that of a lady of quality with her father's footman.

Gallini happened to be in one of the lobbies soon after his marriage, where it was being loudly discussed by some angry beauties. In the midst of their ridicule of the bridegroom he approached, and exclaimed, "Lustrissima, son io! Excellent lady, I am the man!" "And what does the man call himself?" asked they with a giggle, and doubtless also with reference to the story of the bridegroom considering himself a lord by right of his marriage with a "lady"—"what does the man call himself?" "Eccelenza," replied Gallini with a modest bow, "I am Signor Giovanni Gallini, Esquire." In the midst of their laughter he turned upon his heel, and went away to dress in flesh-colored tights, short tunic, and spangles.

The marriage was not at first an unhappy one. There were several children, but difficulties also increased much faster than the family. Not pecuniary difficulties, for Gallini was a prudent man, but class difficulties. The signor found himself without a properly-defined position, or what is quite as uneasy probably in itself, he was above his proper position, without being able to exact the homage that he thought was due to him. The brother-in-law of the earl was in the eyes of his own wife, only the dancing-master of their children. Considering that the lady had condescended to be their mother, she might have carried the condescension a little farther, and paid more respect to the father. Dissension arose, and in a *tour de mains* family interferences rendered it incurable. The quarrel was embittered, a separation ensued, and after a tranquil union of a few years, there were separate households, with common ill-will in both.

He felt himself no longer a "lord," even by courtesy, but he resolved to be what many lords have tried to be, in vain, or who ruined themselves by being, namely, proprietor and manager of the opera-house. This was in 1786, by which time he had realized a fortune by means of much industry, active heels, good looks, capital benefits, monopoly of teaching, prudence, temperance, and that economy, which extravagant people call parsimony. This fortune, or rather a portion of it, he risked in the opera-house—and lost it all, of course. He commenced his career with as much spirit as if he had only been the steward of another man's property; and he made engagements in Italy with such generosity and patriotism, that the Pope having leisure for a while to turn his thoughts from divinity to dancing, became as delighted with Gallini as Pio Nono was with Fanny Cerito. We are bound to believe that his holiness was in a fit of infallible enthusiasm, when he dubbed Gallini, Knight of the Golden Spur. The latter returned to London and wrote himself down "Sir John." Cards were just come into fashion, to enable people to pay what were called "visites en blanc," and "Sir John Gallini," was to be seen in every house where the latter had friend or acquaintance. His portrait was in all the shops, with this chivalric legend beneath it, and there are yet to be seen old opera libretti with a frontispiece exhibiting to an admiring public the effigies of "Sir John Gallini."

The public liked the sound, liked the man, and sanctioned the title, by constantly applying it to the individual, without any mental reserve. They had seen so many fools made knights that they were glad to see a spirited man make one of himself, by application of "Sir" to a papally-conferred title. The law, however, no more allowed it than it did that of the Romanist official who got presented at court as "Monsignore something," and whose presentation was cancelled as soon as the pleasant trick was discovered. Gallini, however, continued in the uninterrupted title until circumstances brought him, as a witness, into the presence of Lord Kenyon. When the Italian opera-dancer announced himself in the hearing of that judge as Sir John Gallini, the sight of the judge was what Americans call "a caution." His lordship looked as disgusted as Lord Eldon used to do, when he heard an Irish Romanist Bishop called by a territorial title. As far as the wrath of Lord Kenyon could do it, metaphorically, the great judge unsir-John'd Sir John and chopped off his golden spurs in open court. Gallini was so good-natured and popular, that the public opinion would not confirm the opinion of the judge, and Sir John remained Sir John, in the popular mouth, throughout the kingdom.

He was growing rich enough to buy up half the knights in the country. He built the music-rooms in Hanover Square, for Bach and Abel's subscription concerts. That is, he built the house; and let it out to any who required any portion of it, for any purpose of music, dancing, exhibiting, lecturing, or any other object having profit in view. He lodged rather than lived in it himself, for he had reserved only a small cabinet for his own use, magnificently sacrificing the rest of the mansion for the use of others, who paid him liberally for such use. Therewith, Sir John continued his old profession as teacher as well as performer, manager at home as well as at the theatre; wary speculator, saving—avaricious, as they said who failed to cheat him of his money on faith of illusory promises, with an admirable eye for a bargain, and admirable care for the result of the bargain after he had concluded it.

Everything went as merrily with him as it did with Polycrates, and ill-fortune and he seemed never to be acquainted, till one fatal night in 1789, the Opera House was burned to the ground, and the tide that had been so long flowing was now thought to be on the ebb. Sir John was too heroic to be downcast, and he did what many a hero would never even have thought of doing, nor, indeed, any wise man either. He put down thirty thousand pounds in hard cash toward the rebuilding of the opera-house, sent to Italy for the best architectural plans, left no means unemployed to erect a first rate theatre, and worked for that object with as much integrity as if the safety of the universe depended on the building of an opera-house in the Haymarket. What the public lost in one night was thus being made good to them by another.

Meanwhile fashion was in a deplorable state of musical destitution. What was to become of London without an opera? How could the world, the infinitesimal London world, exist without its usual allowance of roulades and rigadoons? Our knight was just the champion to come in beneficially at such an extremity. He opened the little theatre in the Haymarket, and nobody went to it. Fashion turned up its nose in scorn, and kept away; nay, it did worse, it acted ungratefully, and when some speculators established an opera at the Pantheon, Fashion led the way from the Haymarket, and a host of followers went in her train to Oxford street. "I will victoriously bring her back to her old house," said Sir John. The knight was gallant-hearted, but he did not know that he had other foes besides Fashion.

Sir John got into difficulties through law, lawyers, and false friends. He ruled as monarch at the opera-house, only to fall, with ruin. But he was not a man to be dismayed. His courage, zeal, and industry, were unbounded. He applied all these to good purpose, and his life was not only a useful but an honorable and a prosperous one. It ended, after extending beyond the ordinary allotted time of man, calmly, yet somewhat suddenly; and "Sir John" Gallini died in his house in Hanover Square, leaving a large fortune, the memory of some eccentricities, and a good name and example, to his children. For my part, I can never enter the ancient concert-rooms in Hanover Square, without wishing a "Requiescat!" to the knight of the Golden Spur, by whom the edifice was constructed.

If Sir John Gallini, the dancer, could boast of having been knighted by a pope, Crescentini, the singer, could boast of having been knighted by an emperor. He received this honor at the hands of Napoleon I. He had previously been accustomed to compliments from, or in presence of, emperors. Thus, in 1804, at Vienna, he sang the *Ombra adorata* in the character of Romeo, with such exquisite grace and tenderness, that, on one occasion, when he had just finished this admirable lyric piece, the whole court forming part of his audience, two doves descended from the clouds, bearing him a crown of laurels, while on every side, garlands and flowers were flung upon the enchanted and enchanting warbler. The Austrian Emperor paid him more honor than his predecessor had ever paid to the Polish king who saved the empire from the Turks. The reputation of Crescentini gained for him an invitation, in 1809, to the imperial court of France. He played in company with Grassini, the two representing Romeo and Juliet. The characters had never been better represented, and Talma, who was present, is said to have wept—an *on dit* which I do not credit, for there is not only nothing to cry at in the Italian characters, but Talma himself was in no wise addicted to indulgence in the melting mood, nor had he even common courtesy for his own actual Juliet. But the great actor was pleased, and the great emperor was delighted; so much so, that he conferred an honor on Crescentini which he would never grant to Talma—made a chevalier of him. It is true that Talma desired to be made a knight of the Legion on Honor; but the emperor would not place on the breast of a tragedian that cross which was the reward, then, only of men who had played their parts well, in real and bloody tragedies. The French tragedian declined the honor that was now accorded to Crescentini, whom the emperor summoned to his box, and decorated him with the insignia of the knight of the Iron Crown. The singing chevalier was in ecstacies. But the Juliet of the night had more cause to be so, for to her, Napoleon presented a draft on the Treasury, for 20,000 francs. "It will be a nice little dower for one of my nieces," said the ever-generous Grassini to one of her friends, on the following day. Several years after this, a little niece, for whom she had hitherto done little, came to her, with a contralto voice, and a request for assistance. After hearing her sing, Grassini exclaimed, "You have no contralto voice, and need small help. You will have, with care, one of the finest mezzo-sopranos in the world. Your throat will be to you a mine of gold,, and you may be both rich and renowned, my dear Giulietta Grisi." The niece has excelled the aunt.

Knights of the shire are but sham knights *now*, and they originally sprung from a revolutionary movement. Previous to the reign of Henry III. the people had no voice in the selection of their legislators. In that king's reign, however, the legislators were at loggerheads. Simon de Montfort, the aristocratic head of a popular party, was opposed to the king; and the great earl and his friends being fearful of being outvoted in the next parliament, succeeded in procuring the issue of a writ in the name of the king, who was then their prisoner, directing the sheriffs of each county to send two knights, and the authorities in cities and boroughs to send citizens and burgesses, to represent them in parliament. This was a fundamental change of a long-established usage. It was, in fact, a revolution; and the foundation at least of that form of a constitution on which our present constitutional substantiality has been erected.

When the king became emancipated, however, although he continued to summon "barons and great men," he never during his reign issued a writ for the election of knights of the shire. His son, Edward I., summoned the greater and lesser barons, or his tenants in chief, according to the old usage. This he did during, at least, seven years of his reign. The last were not barons, but they were summoned as "barons' peers, and all these attended in their own persons," and not as representatives of the people. In the reign of John, indeed, the people's voice had been heard, but it may be stated generally, that until the forty-ninth of Henry III., the *constituent* parts of the great council of the nation was composed solely of the archbishops and bishops, the earls, barons, and tenants *in capite*.

It is a singular fact that, in the early elections, the knights of the shire were elected by universal suffrage; and so, indeed, they are now, in a certain way, as I shall explain, after citing the following passage from Hallam's State of Europe during the Middle Ages: "Whoever may have been the original voters for county representatives, the first statute that regulates their election, so far from limiting the privilege to tenants *in capite*, appears to place it upon a very large and democratical foundation. For (as I rather conceive, though not without much hesitation) not only all freeholders, but all persons whatever present at the county court, were declared, or rendered, capable of voting for the knight of their shire. Such at least seems to be the inference from the expressions of 7 Henry IV., c. 15, 'all who are there present, as well suitors duly summoned for that cause, as others.' And this acquires some degree of confirmation from the later statute 8 Henry VI., c. 7, which, reciting that 'elections of knights of shires have now, of late, been made by very great, outrageous, and excessive number of people dwelling within the same counties, of the which most were people of small substance and of no value,' confines the elective franchise to freeholders of lands or tenements to the value of forty shillings."

The original summons to freeholders was, without doubt, by general proclamation, so that, as Mr. Hallam remarks, "it is not easy to see what difference there could be between summoned and unsummoned suitors. And if the words are supposed to glance at the private summonses to a few friends, by means of which the sheriffs were accustomed to procure a clandestine election, one can hardly imagine that such persons would be styled 'duly summoned.' It is not unlikely, however," adds Mr. Hallam, "that these large expressions were inadvertently used, and that they led to that inundation of voters without property which rendered the subsequent act of Henry VI. necessary. That of Henry IV. had itself been occasioned by an opposite evil, the close election of knights by a few persons in the name of the county."

The same writer proceeds to observe that the consequence of the statute of Henry IV. was not to let in too many voters, or to render election tumultuous in the largest of English counties, whatever it might be in others. Prynne, it appears, published some singular indentures for the county of York, proceeding from the sheriffs, during the intervals between the acts of the fourth and sixth Henry. These "are selected by a few persons calling themselves the attorneys of some peers and ladies, who, as far as it appears, had solely returned the knights of that shire. What degree of weight," says Mr. Hallam, "these anomalous returns ought to possess, I leave to the reader."

I have said that the universal suffrage system in the election of these knights (and indeed of others) as far as it can be carried out, in allowing all persons present to have a voice, is still strictly in force. Appeal is made to the popular assembly as to the choice of a candidate. The decision is duly announced by the highest authority present, and then the rejected candidate may, if he thinks proper, appeal from the people present to those who are legally qualified to vote. The first ceremony is now a very unnecessary one, but it is, without doubt, the relic of a time when observation of it bore therewith a serious meaning.

From parliament to the university is no very wide step. Sir Hugh Evans and Sir Oliver Martext were individuals who, with their titles, are very familiar to the most of us. The knightly title thus given to clergymen, was not so much by way of courtesy, as for the sake of distinction. It was "worn" by Bachelors of Arts, otherwise "Domini," to distinguish them from the Masters of Arts, or "Magistri." Properly speaking, the title was a local one, and ought not to have been used beyond the bounds of the University: but as now-a-days with the case of "captains" of packet-boats, they are also captains at home; so, in old times, the " Sir" of the University was Sir Something Somebody, everywhere.

We laugh at the French for so often describing our knights only by their surnames, as "Sir Jones." This, however, is the old English form as it was used at Cambridge. The Cambridge "Sirs" were addressed by Christian and surname in their livings, and in documents connected therewith. This practice continued till the title itself was abandoned some time after the Reformation. The old custom was occasionally revived by the elderly stagers, much to the astonishment of younger hearers. Thus when Bishop Mawson of Llandaff was on one occasion at court, he encountered there a reverend Bachelor of Arts, Fellow of Bene't College, and subsequently Dean of Salisbury. His name was Greene. The bishop, as soon as he saw the "bachelor" enter the drawing-room, accosted him loudly in this manner: "How do you do, Sir Greene? When did you leave college, Sir Greene?" *Mr.* Greene observing the astonishment of those around him, took upon himself to explain that the bishop was only using an obsolete formula of bygone times. The most recent courtesy title that I can remember, was one given to a blind beggar who was very well known in the vicinity of Trinity College, Dublin, where, indeed, he had been a student some five-and-thirty years ago. He was invariably styled "Domine John," and he could return a suitable answer in good Latin, to the query, *Quo modo vales?* — or to any other query.

"*Vale!*" is indeed what I ought to utter to the courteous reader; nor will I detain him longer — supposing he has kindly borne with me thus far — than with one brief chapter more, which, being miscellaneous, I may not inaptly call "Pieces of Armor."

## PIECES OF ARMOR.

THE word Pieces reminds me of a curious theatrical illustration of Macedonian chivalry. When Barry used to play Alexander the Great, he made a grand spectacle of his chariot entry. But it was highly absurd, nevertheless. When he descended from the vehicle, his attendant knights, bareheaded and unarmed, placed their hands upon it, and in an instant it went to pieces, like a trick in a pantomime, and left in every warrior's possession, swords, javelins, shields, and helmets, supplied by the spokes of the wheels, the poles, the body of the car and its ornaments. This feat was very highly applauded by our intellectual sires.

This act, however, was hardly more unnatural than the sayings of some real chevaliers, particularly those of Spain.

Among the Spanish Rhodomontades chronicled by Brantome, we find none that have not reference to personal valor. There is the choleric swordsman who walks the street without his weapon, for the good reason that his hand is so ready to fly to his sword, if the wind but blow on him too roughly, he is never able to walk out armed without taking two or three lives. "I will hoist you so high," says another Spanish cavalier to his antagonist, "that you will die before you can reach the earth again." It was a fellow of the same kidney who used not only to decapitate dozens of Moorish heads every morning, but was wont afterward to fling them so high into the air, that they were half-devoured by flies before they came down again. Another, boasting of his feats in a naval battle, quietly remarked, that making a thrust downward with his sword, it passed through the sea, penetrated the infernal region, and sliced off a portion of the moustache of Pluto! "If that man be a friend of yours," said a cavalier to a companion, referring at the same time to a swordsman with whom the cavalier had had angry words, "pray for his soul, for he has quarrelled with me." The self-complacency also of the following is not amiss. A Spanish captain in Paris, saw the haughty chevalier d'Ambres pass by him. "Is he," said the Spaniard, "as valiant as he is proud?" The reply was in the affirmative. "Then," remarked the Iberian, "he is almost as good a man as myself." We hear of another, less gallant, perhaps, than brave, who made it a great favor to ladies when he put off a combat at their request, and passed a pleasant hour with them, in place of knocking out brains upon the field. It was a knight of similar notions who cudgelled his page for boasting of the knight's valor. "If thou dost such foolish things, Sir Knave," said the doughty gentleman, "the whole female sex will perish of love for me, and I shall have no leisure left to take towns and rout armies." This was a full-developed knight. It was probably his youthful squire who remarked, when some one expressed surprise that one so young had mustaches of such unusual length. "They sprung up," said the young soldier, "under the smoke of cannon; they grew thus quickly under the same influences."

Some of the old Spanish cavaliers used to maintain that their very beauty dazzled their enemies. However this may have been, it is a fact that the beauty of Galeozo Maria, Duke of Milan, was sufficiently striking to save him for a while, against the daggers of conspirators. One of these, named Lampugnano, longed to slay him, but did not dare. He was, nevertheless, resolved; and he employed a singular means for giving himself courage. He procured a faithful portrait of the handsome duke, and every time he passed it, he looked steadfastly at the brilliant eyes and graceful features, and then plunged his dagger into the canvass. He continued this practice until he found himself enabled to look the living duke in the face without being dazzled by his beauty; and this done, he dealt his blow steadily, and destroyed his great and graceful foe.

It has often been asserted that there have been few cavaliers who have carried on war with more indifference and cruelty than the Spanish knights. But war in all times and in all ages has induced the first, at least, if not the last. I may cite among what may be called the more recent instances, one that would hardly have occurred, even at Sebastopol. It is in reference to Schomberg's army at Dundalk. "The survivors," says Leland, "used the bodies of their dead comrades for seats or shelter; and when these were carried to interment, murmured at being deprived of their conveniences." While touching upon Irish matters, I will avail myself of the opportunity to notice that Irish knights were sometimes called "iron knee," "eagle knee," and "black knee," from the armor which was especially needed for that part of the body, the Irish with their dreadful battle-axes making the sorest stroke on the thigh of the horseman. The Irish appellation of the White Knight, was given to the heir of a family wherein gray hairs were hereditary. The Irish knights, it may be observed, were generally more religious than the Spanish. The latter were too ready to ascribe every success to their own might, and not to a greater hand. Even in the case of St. Lawrence, calmly roasting to death on his gridiron, the proud Spaniards would not have this patience ascribed to the grace of God, but only to the true Spanish valor. While speaking of the burning of St. Lawrence, I will add that St. Pierre quotes Plutarch in stating, that when the Roman burners had to reduce to ashes the bodies of several knights and ladies, they used to place one female body among eight or ten males, fancying that with this amalgamation they would burn better. The author of the "Harmonies of Nature" makes upon this the truly characteristic comment, that the Roman fashion was founded on the notion, that "the fire of love still burned within us after death."

Reverting, for a moment, to the Spaniards, I may notice a fashion among them which is worth mentioning. When a Spanish cavalier entered the presence of a Spanish queen, accompanied by his lady, he did not unbonnet to his sovereign. He was supposed to be so engrossed by his mistress as to forget even the courtesies of loyalty.

Brantome, on the other hand, notices kingly courtesy toward a subject. When describing the battle-acts of the famous M. de Thorannes, he states that the King in acknowledgment that the battle of Rentz had been gained chiefly through his courage, took the collar of his own order from his neck, and placed it on that of the gallant soldier. This was a most unusual act, according to the showing of Brantome, but probably not the first time of a similar occurrence. The author just named complains in piteous terms that, in his time and previously, the honors of chivalry had been bestowed for anything but knightly deeds. They were gained by favor, influence, or money. Some set their wives to exert their fascination over the Christian sovereign, and purchase the honor at any cost. M. de Chateaubriand gave a house and an estate for the order of St. Michael. Ultimately, it was conferred on single captains of infantry, to the great disgust of the better-born gentlemen who had paid dearly for the honor. Brantome declares that he knew many who had never been half a dozen leagues from their houses, who wore the insignia of the order, and who talked of the taking of Loches, as if they had really been present. He angrily adds, that even lawyers were made knights, stripping themselves of their gowns, and clapping swords on their thighs. He appears especially annoyed that the celebrated Montaigne should have followed a similar example: and he adds with a malicious exultation, that the sword did not become him half so well as the pen.

One French Marquis was persecuted by his neighbors to get orders for them, as if they were applying for orders for the theatre. He obtained them with such facility, that he even made a knight of his house-steward, and forced the poor man to go to market in his collar, to the infinite wounding of his modesty. It was, however, one rule of the order that the collar should never, under any pretence whatever, be taken from the neck. The Court had very unsavory names for these mushroom-knights; and Brantome gives us some idea of the aristocratic feeling when he recounts, with a horror he does not seek to disguise, that the order was sold to an old Huguenot gentleman, for the small sum of five hundred crowns. A cheap bargain for the new knight, seeing that membership in the order carried with it exemption from taxation. Luckily for the Huguenot he died just in time to save himself from being disgraced. Some gentlemanly ruffians had agreed to attack this "homme de peu," as Brantome calls him, to pull the order from his neck, to give him a cudgelling, and to threaten him with another, whenever he dared to wear the knightly insignia.

Brantome wonders the more at what he calls the abuse of the

order as it had been instituted by Louis XI., on the ground that the old order of the Star founded by King John, in memory of the star which guided the Kings to the Cradle of Divinity, had become so common, that the silver star of the order was to be seen in the hat and on the mantle of half the men in France. Louis XI., in abolishing the order, conferred its insignia as an ornament of dress, upon the Chevaliers de Guet, or gentlemen of the watch, who looked to the safety of Paris when the stars were shining, or that it was the hour for them to do so. It was an understood thing with all these orders that if a knight went into the service of an enemy to the sovereign head of the order, the knight was bound to divest himself of the insignia and transmit the same directly to the King.

Before the dignity of the order was humbled, the members took pride in displaying it even in battle; although they were put to high ransom, if captured. Some prudent knights, of as much discretion as valor, would occasionally conceal the insignia before going into fight; but they were mercilessly ridiculed, when the absence of the decoration testified to the presence of their discretion. In the earlier years of its formation, a man could with more facility obtain a nomination to be captain of the body-guard than the collar of the order of St. Michael. Louis XI. himself showed a wise reluctance to making the order common, and although he fixed the number of knights at six-and-thirty, he would only, at first, appoint fifteen. Under succeeding kings the order swelled to limitless numbers, until at last, no one would accept it, even when forced upon them. One great personage, indeed, sought and obtained it. He was severely rallied for his bad ambition; but as he remarked, the emblems of the order would look well, engraved upon his plate, and the embroidered mantle would make an admirable covering for his mule.

This sort of satire upon chivalry reminds me that a knight could unknight himself, when so inclined. An instance occurs in a case connected with Jeanne Darc. The chevaliers of the Dauphin's army had no belief in the inspiration of the Maid of Orleans, until success crowned her early efforts. The female knight, if one may so speak, on the other hand, had no measure whatever of respect, either for knight or friar, who appeared to doubt her heavenly mission. I may just notice, by the way, that a "board" of seven theologians assembled to consider her claims, and examine the maiden herself. One of the members, a "brother Seguin," a Limousin, who spoke with the strong and disagreeable accent of his birthplace, asked Jeanne in what sort of idiom she had been addressed by the divine voice, by which she professed to be guided: "In a much better idiom than you use yourself," answered the pert young lady, "or I should have put no trust in it." Here, by the way, we have, perhaps, the origin of the old story of the stammering gentleman who asked the boy if his m—m—magpie could speak? "Better than you," said the boy, "or I would wring his neck off." But to resume. Jeanne was quite as *nonchalante* to the knights, as she was flippant to the friars. She expressly exhibits this characteristic, in the first council held in her presence within Orleans, when she urged immediate offensive measures, contrary to the opinion of the knights themselves. One of the latter, the Sire de Gamache, was so chafed by the pertinacity of the Pucelle, that, at last, springing to his feet, he exclaimed:— "Since noble princes listen for a moment to the nonsense of a low-bred hussy like this, rather than to the arguments of a chevalier such as I am, I will not trouble myself to give any more opinions. In proper time and place, my good sword will speak, and perchance I may prevail; but the king and my honor so will it. Henceforward, I furl and pull down my banner; from this moment I am only a simple 'squire; but I would much rather have a noble man for master, than serve under a wench who, perhaps, has been a—one really does not know what!" and with these words, he rolled up his banner, placed the same in the hands of Dunois, and walked out of the tent, not Sir John de Gamache, but plain John Gamache, Esquire.

A curious result followed. The first attack on the bastion of Tourelles failed, and Jeanne was slightly wounded and unhorsed. Gamache was near, and he dismounted and offered her his steed. "Jump up," cried the good fellow, "you are a gallant lass, and I was wrong in calling you ugly names. I will serve and obey you right willingly." "And you," said Jeanne, "are as hearty a knight as ever thwacked men or helped a maid." And so were they reconciled, and remained good friends to the end;—which was not long in coming.

Knights, irregularly made so, were unknighted with little ceremony. Although each duly dubbed knight could confer the same honor on any deserving such distinction, it was necessary that the individual about to be so honored should be a gentleman. In France, if this rule was infringed, the unlucky knight had his spurs hacked off, on a dunghill. Occasionally the unknighted person was fined. It may be observed, however, that the king might make a knight of a villain, if the sovereign were so minded. That is, a king could raise any of his own subjects to the rank, if he thought proper. Not so with sovereigns and persons not their subjects. The Emperor Sigismund, for instance, when visiting Paris, in 1415, knighted a person who was below the rank of gentleman. The French people were indignant at this, as an act of sovereignty in another monarch's dominions. If this chevalier was not unknighted, the reason, probably, was that the Emperor might not be offended. It is said, that in Naples it has never been necessary for a man to be noble, a gentleman in fact, in order to be a knight. This may readily be credited. In Naples the fact of a man being a brute beast does not incapacitate him from exercising the office even of a king.

After all, there appears to have been some uncertainty in the observance of the law on the subject. In England the custom which allowed knights to dub other knights, very soon fell into disuse, so that there are fewer examples of unknighting in this country than in France, where the custom prevailed down to the middle of the sixteenth century; and its abuses, of course, rendered the unmaking of illegally constituted knights, if not common, at least an occasional occurrence. Henry III., as I have said in another page, summoned tenants *in capite* to receive knighthood from himself, and authorized tenants of mesne lords to receive the honor from whom they pleased. But there must have been considerable disrating of these last distinguished persons, or such an abuse of creation, so to speak, that the privilege was stopped, except by special permission of the king. Some places, in France, however, declared that they held a prescriptive right for burgesses to receive knighthood at the hands of noblemen, without the royal permission. Hallam, quoting Villaret, says that burgesses, in the great commercial towns, were considered as of a superior class to the roturiers, and possessed a kind of demi-nobility.

Ridiculous as modern knights, whether of town or country, have been made upon the stage, it is indisputable that in some cases the ridicule has not been what painters call "loaded," and the reality was in itself a caricature. I have read somewhere of one city gentleman, who was knighted during his shrievalty, and who forthwith emancipated himself a little from business, and aired his chivalrous "sir" in gay company. He was once, however, sorely puzzled on receiving a note of invitation from a lady whose soirées were the especial delight of her guests, and whose note ended with the initials, so absurdly placed at the termination of an invitation in English. R. S. V. P., "réponse, s'il vous plaît." The newly-coined knight, after allusions to the pressure of business, accepted the hospitality offered him through the note, remarking at the same time, that "all work and no play made Jack a dull boy," and that he knew nothing more to his taste, after a long day's application, than what her ladyship's note appeared to present to him in the initials at its foot; namely, a Regular Small Vist Party. If this anecdote be not apocryphal, I suspect that the knight's remark may have sprung less from ignorance than humor, and that his reading of the initials was meant as a censure upon an absurd fashion.

While speaking of city knights at home, and their humor, I will avail myself of the opportunity to give an instance of wit in a poor chevalier of the city of Paris, whose whole wealth consisted of a few unproductive acres near the capital, and whose son had just married a wealthy heiress of very low degree. "Il fait bien," said the old knight, "il fume mes terres!"

This was hardly courteous; but elevated courtesy was never wanting among true knights, in the very rudest of times.

Strange contrasts of feeling were sometimes exhibited. Thus, when the English were besieging Orleans, they grew suddenly tired of their bloody work, on Christmas-day, and asked for a truce while they ate their pudding. The request was not only readily granted, but the French knights, hearing that the day was dull in the English camp, obtained the permission of the bastard Dunois, to send over some musicians to enliven the melancholy leaguers. The band played lustily during the whole period of the truce, but the last notes had scarcely ceased, and the "Godons" as Jeanne Darc rather corruptively called our great sires, who were too much addicted to swearing, had hardly ceased uttering their thanks for the musical entertainment, when their cannonade was renewed by the besiegers with such vigor, that the French knights swore—harmony had never before been paid in such hard coin.

There was little ill-feeling consequent upon this. The pages in either army were allowed to amuse themselves by slaying each other in a two days' duel, presided over by the respective generals-in-chief. This was chivalrous proof that neither party bore malice, and they beat out each other's brains on the occasion, in testimony of universal good-will, with as much delighted feeling as if they had all been Irishmen. A further proof of absence of individual rancor may be seen in the fact, that Suffolk sent a gift of pigs, dates, and raisins, for the *dessert* of Dunois; and the latter acknowledged the present by forwarding to the English general some fur for his robe—Suffolk having complained bitterly of the cold of that memorable February, 1429.

This reminds me of a similar interchange of courtesy between French and English antagonists, in later times. When brave Elliot was defending Gibraltar from gallant Crillon, the former, who never ate meat, suffered greatly (as did his scurvy-stricken men) from a scarcity of vegetables. Crillion had more than he wanted, and he sent of his superabundance, most liberally, to the foe whom he respected. A whole cart-load of carrots and compliments made general and garrison glad, and Elliot was as profuse in his gratitude as he was bound to be. It may be remembered that similar exchanges of courtesy and creature-comforts took place at Sebastopol. Sir Edmund Lyons sent Admiral Nachimoff a fat buck, a gift which the large-minded hero of the Sinope butchery repaid by a hard Dutch cheese. It may be said too that the buck would have been more appropriately sent to the half-starved English heroes who were rotting in the trenches.

There were some other naval knights of old, touching whom I may here say a word.

The history of the sea-kings or sea-knights, whose noble vocation it was to descend from the north with little but ballast in the holds of their vessels, and to return thither heavily laden with plunder and glory, is tolerably well known to the majority of readers. The story of the Flemish pirates, who, nearly eight centuries ago, carried terror to, and brought spoil from the Mediterranean, is far less familiar. This story is well illustrated in the " Biographie des hommes remarquables de la Flandres Occidentale," of whom the authors are M. Octave Delepierre, the accomplished Belgian consul in this country, and Mr. Carton.

The period is a warm June evening of the year 1097. Off the coast of Cilicia, two large vessels, belonging to the Emperor Alexis Comnenus, and manned by Constantinopolitan Greeks, were surrounded and attacked by ten fast-sailing but small vessels, belonging to the dreaded " Greek Pirates," whose name alone brought terror with the sound. On the prow of each light bark was a rudely sculptured figure of a lion; from the summit of the tall mast was displayed a green pennant, which was never hauled down, for the good reason that the pirates never attacked but where success seemed certain; and if defeat menaced them they could easily find safety in flight.

There was scarcely a place on the coast which they had not, for ten years past, visited; and many merchants purchased exemption from attack by paying a species of very liberal black mail. It was beneath the dignity of an emperor to buy safety from piratical rovers, and they had little respect for his vessels, in consequence.

M. Delepierre informs us that these Flemish pirates had been, originally, merchants, but that they thought it more profitable to steal than to barter; and found " skimming the seas," as the phrase went, far more lucrative than living by the dull precepts of trade. Their three principal chiefs were Zegher of Bruges, Gheraert of Courtrai, and Wimer (whose name still lives in Wimereux) of Boulogne. The force they had under them amounted to four hundred intrepid men, who were at once sailors and soldiers, and who are described as being so skilful that they could with one hand steer the ship, and with the other wield the boarding-hatchet. It will be seen that our Laureate's exhortation to knavish tradesmen to lay down their weights and their measures, and to mend their ways by taking to the vocation of arms, had here a practical illustration. In the present case, M. Delepierre suggests that the pirates were, probably, not less honest men than the Greeks. The latter were ostensibly on their way to succor the Crusaders, but Alexis was a double dealer, and occasionally despatched forces against the infidel, which forces turned aside to assault those Christian neighbors of his, who were too powerful to be pleasant in such a vicinity, and to get rid of whom was to be devoutly desired, and, at any cost, accomplished. The foreign policy of Alexis was as villanously void of principle as that of any government under a more advanced period of Christian civilization.

The Greek crews had been summoned to surrender. Gheraert of Courtrai had called to them to that effect through his leathern speaking-trumpet. He probably knew little of Greek, and the Orientals could not have comprehended his Flemish. We may conclude that his summons was in a macaronic sort of style; in which two languages were used to convey one idea. The Hellenes replied to it, however it may have sounded, by hurling at the Flemings a very hurricane of stones.

The stout men from Flanders were not long in answering in their turn. "They put into play," says M. Delepierre, "their mechanical slings. These were large baskets full of stones fastened to the end of an elevated balance, the motion of which flung them to some distance. They had other means of destruction, in enormous engines, which hurled beams covered with iron, and monster arrows wrapped in flaming rosin. With scythe-blades attached to long poles, they severed the ropes and destroyed the sails, and then flinging out their grapnels they made off with their prize."

To this point the present battle had not yet come. It had lasted an hour, the Greeks had suffered most by the means of attack above noticed; and they had inflicted but trifling injury, comparatively, upon the men of the green pennant. They refused, however, to surrender, but prepared to fly. Wimer saw the preparatory movement, and, in a loud voice, exclaimed:—"A dozen divers!"

Twelve men, quitting their posts, leaped over the side of the boat, carrying enormous *tarières* (augers) with them. They disappeared beneath the waves; appeared for a moment or two again above the surface, in order to draw breath; once more plunged downward; and, finally, at the end of ten minutes, climbed again into their small vessel, exclaiming, "Master, it is done!"

The twelve divers had established twelve formidable leaks in the larger of the two Greek vessels, and as it began to sink, the crew agreed to surrender. The Green Pirates seized all that was on board that and the other ship. In the latter, stripped of everything of value, they allowed the two Greek crews to sail away; and then proceeded toward the coast with their booty, consisting of rich stuffs, provisions and arms. There was far more than they needed for their own wants; and so, for the nonce, they turned traders again. They sold at a good price what they had unscrupulously stolen, and the profits realized by the Flemish rovers were enough to make all honest, but poor traders, desire to turn corsairs.

Zegher ascended the Cydnus, in order to pay a professional visit to Tarsis, and was not a little surprised, on approaching the city, to see formidable preparations made to resist him. On drawing closer, however, the pirate-leader found that Tarsis was in possession of the army of Flemish crusaders under the great Count Baldwin; and each party welcomed the other with joyous shouts of "Long live Flanders!" "Long live the Lion!" The arrival of the fleet was of the greatest advantage to the Flemings, who, though they had suffered less than the French, Italian, and German legions, by whom they had been preceded, and had been progressively triumphing since they had landed, needed succors both of men and material, and lo! here were the Green Pirates ready to furnish both, for a consideration. There was abundance of feasting that night, and a very heavy sermon in the morning.

Baldwin was himself the preacher. His style was a mixture of exhorting with the threatening; and he was so little complimentary as to tell the Green pirates that they were nothing better than brigands, and were undoubtedly on their way to the devil. He added that he would have treated them as people of such a character, going such a way, only that they were his countrymen. And then he wept at the very thought of their present demerits, and their possible destiny. This practice of weeping was inherited by knights from the old Greek heroes, and a chevalier in complete steel might shed tears till his suit was rusty, without the slightest shame. The exhortation continued without appearing to make any sensible impression upon the rovers. Baldwin, however, pointed his address at the end, with an observation that if they would join him in his career of arms, he would give them lands that should make lords of the whole of them. Upon this observation the Green Pirates, with a little modest allusion to their unworthiness, declared that they were eager, one and all, to turn crusaders.

Each man attached a small green cross, in cloth, to the top of his sleeve; and joyfully followed Baldwin to the field. The count was no more able to keep his word than a recruiting sergeant who promises a recruit that he shall be made a field-marshal. Nor was he to blame, for the greater part of his new allies perished; but enough were left to make a score of very doughty knights.

Admirable sailors were the Northmen, especially the Anglo-Normans, whether with respect to manœuvring or courage. "Close quarters" formed the condition on which they liked to be with an enemy. "Grapple and board" was their system as soon as they had created a little confusion among the enemy with their cross-bows and slings. The "mariners" in those days fought in armor, with heavy swords, spears, and battle-axes. They were well furnished too with bags of quick-lime, the contents of which they flung into the eyes of their adversaries, when they could get to windward of them, an end which they always had in view.

The first regular naval battle fought between the English and the French was conducted by the former after the fashion above mentioned. It was during the reign of Henry III., when Louis of France, by the destruction of his army at "the fair of Lincoln," was shut up in London, and depended on the exertions of his wife, Blanche of Castile, for his release. Blanche sent eighty large ships, besides many smaller vessels, from Calais, under a piratical commander, the celebrated Eustace Le Moine. Hubert de Burgh had only forty vessels wherewith to proceed against this overwhelming force; and on board of these the English knights proceeded, under protest and with a world of grumbling, at being compelled to fight on the waters when they had no sea-legs, and were accustomed to no battles but those on land. No heed was taken of protest or grumbling; the forty vessels were loosened from their moorings, and away went the reluctant but strong-boned land sailors, all in shirts of mail in place of Guernsey jackets, to contend for the first time with a French fleet. The English ships contrived to get between Calais and the enemy's vessels, and fell upon the latter in their rear. The English bowmen handled their favorite weapons with a deadly dexterity; and as soon as their vessels were made fast to those of the French, out flew the quick-lime, flung by the English, and carried by the wind into the faces of the French. While these were stamping with pain, screwing their eyes up to look through the lime-dust, or turning their backs to avoid it, the English boarders made a rush, cut down men, hacked away the rigging, and so utterly defeated the French, unaccustomed to this sort of fighting, that of the great French fleet only fifteen vessels escaped. The number of Gallic knights and inferior officers captured was very large. As for Eustace le Moine, he had slunk below to avoid the lime-powder and battle-axes. He was seized by Richard Fitzroy, King John's illegitimate son. Fitzroy refused to give the recreant quarter, but hewed off his head on the taffrail, and sent it from town to town through England as a pleasant exhibition.

Errant knights in quest of adventure, and anxious to secure renown, less frequently visited England than other countries. They appear to have had a mortal dislike of the sea. This dislike was common to the bravest and greatest among them. I may cite, as an instance, the case of the Duke of Orleans and his cavaliers, captured at Agincourt, and brought over to England, from Calais to Dover, by the gallant and lucky Henry. The latter walked the deck during a heavy ground swell, with as much enjoyment as though he had been to the matter born. The French prince and his knights, on the other hand, were as ignorant of the sea and as uneasy upon it as a modern English Lord of the Admiralty. They suffered horribly, and one and all declared that they would rather be daily exposed to the peril of battle, than cross the straits of Dover once a month.

Nevertheless, stray knights did occasionally brave the dangers of the deep, and step ashore on the coast of Kent with a challenge to all comers of equal degree. We have an instance of this sort of adventurer in Jacques de Lelaing, whose story is told in this volume. We hear of another in the nameless knight of Aragon, who in the reign of Henry V. set all London and many a provincial baronial hall in commotion by his published invitation to all knights of the same rank as himself, to come and give him a taste of their quality in a bout at two-edged sword, axe, and dagger.

The challenge was promptly accepted by stout Sir Robert Cary. Sir Robert was a poor knight, with nothing to lose, for his sire had lost all he possessed before Sir Robert's time, by being faithful to poor Richard II., a virtue, for the exercise of which he was punished by forfeiture of his estates, decreed against him by Henry IV. The disinherited knight, therefore, had a chance of winning land as well as honor, should he subdue the arrogant Aragonese. The two met in the then fashionable district of Smithfield, and the Devonshire swordsman, after a bloody and long-enduring fight, so thoroughly vanquished the Spaniard, that the king, who delighted in such encounters, and who was especially glad when victory was won by the side he most favored, not only restored to Sir Robert the forfeited paternal estates, but he also authorized him to wear the arms of the much-bruised knight from beyond sea.

At a later period knightly estates went in the service of another king. Sir Henry Cary risked life and property in the cause of Charles I., and while he preserved the first, he was deprived of nearly all the latter. The head of the family, no longer a knight, if I remember rightly, was residing at Torr Bay, when the Old Chevalier was about to attempt to regain the three crowns which, according to no less than a French archiepiscopal authority, James II. had been simple enough to lose for one mass. At this period, the English king that would be, sent the Duke of Ormond to the head of the Cary family, and not only conveyed to him an assurance that his services to the Stuarts had not been forgotten; but, by way of guarantee that future, and perhaps more than knightly honors should be heaped upon him, in case of victory declaring for the Stuart cause, the chevalier sent him the portraits of James II., and of that monarch's wife, Mary of Modena. Similar portraits are to be found among the cherished treasures of many English families; and these are supposed to have been originally distributed among various families, as pledges from the giver. that for swords raised, money lost, or blood shed in the cause of the Stuarts, knighthood and honors more substantial should follow as soon as "the king" should "get his own again."

To revert to Charles I., it may be added that he was not half so energetic in trying to keep his own as his grandson was in trying to recover what had been lost. An incident connected with the battle of Rowton Heath will serve to exemplify this. Never did king have better champion than Charles had on that day, in the able knight Sir Marmaduke Langdale. The knight in question had gained a marked advantage over his adversary, the equally able Poyntz. To cheer the king, then beleaguered in Chester Castle, with the news, Sir Marmaduke despatched Colonel Shakerley. He could not have commissioned a better man. The colonel contrived to get into Chester after crossing the Dee in a tub, which he worked with one hand, while he towed his horse after him with the other. He delivered his message, and offered to convey an answer or instructions back to Sir Marmaduke, and by the same means, in a quarter of an hour. The king hesitated; some sanction required for a certain course of action proposed by Sir Marmaduke was not given, and Poyntz recovered his lost ground, defeated the royal horse, and thus effectually prevented Charles from obtaining access to Scotland and Montrose.

I have given some illustrations of the means by which knighthood was occasionally gained: an amusing illustration remains to be told. Dangeau, in his memoirs, speaks of two French peeresses who lived chiefly upon asses' milk, but who, nevertheless, became afflicted with some of the ills incident to humanity, and were ordered to take physic. They were disgusted with the prescription, but got over the difficulty charmingly by physicking the donkey. It was not an unusual thing in France for very great people to treat their vices as they did their ailments, by a vicarious treatment. Catherine de Medicis is one out of many instances of this. She was desirous of succeeding in some great attempt, and set down her failure to the account of her sins. She instantly declared that she would atone for the latter, provided her desires were accomplished, by finding a pilgrim who would go from France to Jerusalem, on foot, and who at every three steps he advanced should go back one. The wished-for success was achieved, and after some difficulty a pilgrim was found, strong enough, and sufficiently persevering to perform the pilgrimage. The royal pledge was redeemed, and there only remained to reward the pilgrim, who was a soldier from the neighborhood of Viterbo. Some say he was a merchant; but merchant or soldier, Catherine knighted, ennobled, and enriched him. His arms were a cross and a branch of palm tree. We are not told if he had a motto. It, at all events, could not have been *nulla vestigia retrorsum*. They who affirm that the pilgrim was a merchant, declare that his descendants lost their nobility by falling again into commercial ways —a course which was considered very derogatory, and indeed, degrading, in those exclusive days.

I may mention here that Heraldry has, after all, very unfairly treated many of the doers of great deeds. No person below the degree of a knight could bear a cognizance of his own. Thus, many a squire may have outdone his master in bravery; and indeed, many a simple soldier may have done the same, but the memory of it could not go down to posterity, because the valiant actor was not noble enough to be worthy of distinction. In our English army, much the same rule still obtains. Illustrious incompetence is rewarded with "orders," but plain John Smith, who has captured a gun with his own hands, receives a couple of sovereigns, which only enable him to degrade himself by getting drunk with his friends. Our heraldic writers approve of this dainty way of conferring distinctions. An anonymous author of a work on Heraldry and Chivalry, published at Worcester "sixty years since," says—"We must consider that had heraldry distributed its honors indiscriminately, and with too lavish a hand, making no distinction between gentry and plebeians, the glory of arms would have been lost, and their lustre less refulgent."

But it is clear that the rule which allowed none to bear cognizance who was not of the rank of a knight, was sometimes infringed. Thus, when Edward the Black Prince made the stout Sir James Audley, his own especial knight, with an annuity of five hundred marks, for gallant services at Poictiers, Audley divided the annuity among his four squires, Delves, Dutton, Foulthurst, and Hawkeston, and also gave them permission to wear his own achievements, in memory of the way in which they had kept at his side on the bloody day of Poictiers.

The fashion of different families wearing the same devices had, however, its inconveniences. Thus, it happened that at this very battle of Poictiers, or a little before it, Sir John Chandos reconnoitring the French army, fell in with the Seigneur de Clermont, who was reconnoitring the English army. Each saw that the device on the upper vestment of his adversary was the same as his own, blue worked with rays of gold round the border. They each fell to sharp, and not very courteous words. The French lord at length remarked that Sir John's claim to wear the device was just like "the boastings of you English. You can not invent anything new," added the angry French knight, "but when you stumble on a pretty novelty, you forthwith appropriate it." After more angry words they separated, vowing that in next day's fight, they would make good all their assertions.

As the general rule was, that squires could not bear a cognizance, so also was it a rule that knights should only fight with their equals.

> For knights are bound to feel no blows
> From paltry and unequal foes;
> Who, when they slash and cut to pieces,
> Do all with civilest addresses.

It is in allusion to this rule that Don Quixote says to Sancho Panza: "Friend Sancho, for the future, whenever thou perceivest us to be any way abused by such inferior fellows, thou art not to expect that I should offer to draw my sword against them; for I will not do it in the least; no, do thou then draw and chastise them as thou thinkest fit; but if any knight come to take their part, then will I be sure to step in between thee and danger."

Knights, as I have said, have had honor conferred on them for very strange reasons, in many countries, but in none for slighter reasons, perhaps, than in France. We may probably except

Belgium; for there is a living knight there, who obtained his order of chivalry for his pleasant little exhibition of gallantry in furnishing new-laid eggs every morning at the late queen's table, when every hen but his, in the suburban village of Laecken had ceased to lay!

Dumas, in his "Salvandire," satirically illustrates how knights were occasionally made in the days of Louis XIV. The hero of that dashing romance finds himself a captive in the prison of Fort l'Evêque; and as the king will not grant him permission to leave, he resolves to leave without permission. He makes the attempt by night, descends from the window in the dark, is caught by the thigh on a spike, and is ultimately carried to a cell and a bed within his prison-walls. The following day the governor waits upon him, and questions him upon the motives for his dangerous enterprise. The good governor's curiosity is founded solely on his anxiety to elicit from the prisoner, that the desire of the latter to escape was not caused by his dissatisfaction with any of the prison arrangements, whether of discipline or diet. The captive signs a certificate to that effect, adding, that his sole motive for endeavoring to set himself free, was because he had never done anything to deserve that he should be put under restraint. A few days after, the governor announces to the recluse that the certificate of the latter has had an excellent effect. Roger supposes that it has gained him his liberty; but the governor complacently remarks that it has done better than that, and that the king, in acknowledgment of the strict character of the governor's surveillance, has created him chevalier of the order of St. Louis. If all the prisoners had succeeded in escaping, as nearly as Roger, the governor would probably have been made Knight of the Holy Ghost! The king of France had many such faithful servants; but history affords many examples of a truer fidelity than this; particularly the old romances and legendary history — examples of faithfulness even after death; but, though there may be many more romantic in those chronicles, I doubt if there is any one so touching as the proof of fidelity which a knighted civilian, Sir Thomas Meautis, gave of his affection for Lord Bacon, to whom that ancient servant of the great lawyer, erected a monument at his own cost. Hamond Lestrange relates a curious incident, to shew that these two were not divided even after death. "Sir Thomas," says Lestrange, "was not nearer to him living than dead; for this Sir Thomas ending his life about a score of years after, it was his lot to be inhumed so near his lord's sepulchre, that in the forming of his grave, part of the viscount's body was exposed to view; which being espied by a doctor of physic, he demanded the head to be given to him; and did most shamefully disport himself with that skull which was somewhile the continent of so vast treasures of knowledge."

Other knights have been celebrated for other qualities. Thus, Sir Julius Cæsar never heard Bishop Hackett preach without sending him a piece of money. Indeed, the good knight never heard any preacher deliver a sermon without sending him money, a pair of gloves, or some other little gift. He was unwilling, he said, to hear the Word of God, gratis.

Other knights have cared less to benefit preachers, than to set up for makers or explainers of doctrines themselves. Thus the Chevalier Ramsay held that Adam and Eve begot the entire human race in Paradise, the members of which fell with their procreators; and in this way the chevalier found in an intelligible form "the great, ancient, and luminous doctrine of our co-existence with our first parents." The Chevalier deemed that in teaching such doctrine he was rearing plants for a new Paradise; but he was not half so usefully engaged as some brother knights who were practically engaged as planters. We may cite Sir John St. Aubyn, who introduced plane-trees into Cornwall in 1723; and Sir Anthony Ashley, the Dorchester knight, who enjoys the reputation of having introduced cabbages into England about the middle of the sixteenth century.

In contrast with these useful knights, the person of the once famous Chevalier de Lorenzi seems to rise before me, and of him I will now add a few words, by way of conclusion to my miscellaneous volume.

It is perhaps the tritest of platitudes to say that men are distinguished by various qualities; but it is among the strangest if not most novel of paradoxes, that the same man should be remarkable for endowments of the most opposite quality. The eccentric knight whose name and title I have given above, is, however, an illustration of the fact; namely, that a man may be at once stupid and witty. It was chiefly for his stupidity that Lorenzi was famous, a stupidity which excited laughter. I must, nevertheless, say in behalf of the brother of the once celebrated minister of France at the Court of Florence, in the days of Louis XV., that his stupidity so often looks like wit, as to induce the belief that it was a humor too refined for his hearers to appreciate.

Acute as Grimm was, he seems to have undervalued the chevalier in this respect. That literary minister-plenipotentiary of the Duke of Saxe Gotha could only see in the chevalier the most extraordinary of originals. He acknowledges, at the same time, Lorenzi's high feeling of honor, and his frank and gentle spirit. The chevalier was crammed with scientific knowledge, but so confusedly that, according to Grimm, he could never explain himself in an intelligible way, or without exciting shouts of laughter on the part of his hearers. Madame de Geoffrin, when comparing the chevalier with the ungraceful M. de Burigny, said that the latter was awkward in body, but that Lorenzi was awkward in mind. As the latter never spoke without, at least, an air of pro found reflection, and had therewith a piquant Florentine accent, his mistakes were more relished. I do not think much of his misapprehension when introduced, at Lyons, to M. de la Michaudière, in whose company he dined, at the residence of the commandant of the city. The gentleman was addressed by an old acquaintance as Le Michaudière, and Lorenzi, mistaking this for L'Ami Chaudière, persisted in calling the dignified official by the appellation of Monsieur *Chaudière*, which, to the proud *intendant* of Lyons, must have been as bad as if the chevalier had certified that the *intendant's* father was a brazier.

He was far more happy, whether by chance or design, I can not say, at a subsequent supper at M. de la Michaudière's house. At the table sat M. le Normant, husband of Madame de Pompadour, then at the height of her brilliant infamy. Lorenzi hearing from a neighbor, in reply to an inquiry, that the gentleman was the consort of the lady in question, forthwith addressed him as Monsieur de Pompadour, which was as severe an infliction as husband so situated could well have endured.

This honorable chevalier was clearly not a religious man—but among knights and other distinguished personages in France, and elsewhere, at the period of which I am treating, the two terms were perfectly distinct, and had no necessary connection. Accordingly, a lady who had called on Lorenzi one Sunday morning, before eleven o'clock, proposed, at the end of their conversation, to go with him to mass. "Do they still celebrate mass?" asked the chevalier, with an air of astonishment. As he had not attended mass for fifteen years, Grimm gravely asserts that the Florentine imagined that it was no longer celebrated. "The more," adds the epistolary baron, "that as he never went out before two o'clock, he no longer recollected that he had seen a church-door open."

The chevalier, who was Knight of the Order of St. Stephen of Tuscany, and who had withdrawn from the French Army, with the rank of colonel, after the conquest of Minorca, had a great devotion toward the abstract sciences. He studied geometry and astronomy, and had the habit, says Grimm, to measure the events of life, and reduce them to geometrical value. As he was thoughtful, he more frequently, when addressed, made reply to abstruse questionings of his own brain than to persons who spoke to him. Grimm, after saying that the Knight of St. Stephen was only struck by the true or false side of a question, and never by its pleasant or amusing aspect, illustrates his saying by an anecdote, in which many persons will fail to find any remarkable point. Grimm encountered him at Madame Geoffrin's, after his return from a tour in Italy. "I saw him embroiling his senses with the genealogies of two ladies in whose society he passes his life, and who bear the same name, although they are of distinct families. Madame Geoffrin endeavored to draw him from these genealogical snares, observing to him:—' Really, chevalier, you are in your dotage. It is worse than ever.' 'Madame,' answered the chevalier, 'life is so short!' " Grimm thought he should have done rank injustice to posterity if he had not recorded this reply for the benefit of future students of laconic wit. And again:— Grimm shows us the chevalier walking with Monsieur de St. Lambert toward Versailles. On the way, the latter asked him his age. "I am sixty," said the knight. "I did not think you so old," rejoined his friend. "Well," replied the chevalier, "when I say sixty, I am not indeed quite so old, just yet; but—" "But how old are you then, in reality?" asked his companion. "Fifty-five, exactly; but why may I not be allowed to accustom myself to change my age every year, as I do my shirt?"

One day, he was praising the figure of a lady, but instead of saying that she had the form of a nymph, he said that her shape was like that of Mademoiselle Allard. "Oh!" cried Grimm, "you are not lucky, chevalier, in your comparison. Mademoiselle Allard may be deservedly eulogized for many qualities, but nobody ever thought of praising her shape." "Likely enough," said Lorenzi, "for I do not know, nor, indeed, have I ever seen her; but as everybody talks about Mademoiselle Allard, I thought I might talk about her too."

If there was satire in this it was not of so neat a quality as that exhibited by him at Madame Greffon's, where he was spending an evening with Grimm and D'Alembert. The last two were seated, and conversing. Lorenzi stood behind them, with his back to the chimney-piece, and scarcely able to hold up his head, so overcome was he by a desire to sleep. "Chevalier," said Grimm, "you must find our conversation a horrid bore, since you fall asleep when you are on your legs." "Oh, no!" exclaimed the chevalier, "you see I go to sleep when I like." The naïveté with which he insinuated that he liked to go to sleep rather than listen to the small talk of a wit and a philosopher, was expressed with a delicious delicacy.

Of his *non-sequential* remarks Grimm supplies several. He was once speaking disparagingly of M. de St. Lambert's knowledge of chess. "You forget," said the latter, "that I gained fifteen louis to your thirty sous, during our campaign in Minorca.' "Oh, ay," answered the knight, "but that was toward the end of the siege!"

It was at this siege that he used to go to the trenches with his astronomical instruments, to make observations. He one day returned to his quarters without his instruments, having left them all in the trenches. "They will certainly be stolen," said a friend. "That can't be," said Lorenzi, "for I left my watch with them."

And yet this "distraught" knight was the cause, remote cause, of the death of Admiral Byng. He discovered, by mere chance, in his quarters at Minorca, a book of signals as used by the English fleet. He hastened with it to the Prince de Beaubeau, who, in his turn, hastened to place it before the Marshal de Richelieu. The commanders could scarcely believe in their good fortune, but when the naval combat commenced it was seen that the English observed this system of signals exactly. With this knowledge it was easy to anticipate all their manœuvres, and they were obliged to withdraw with disgrace, which Byng was made to expiate by his death. The chevalier never thought of asking for a reward, and his government entirely forgot to give him one.

When about to accompany M. de Mirepoix, who was appointed embassador to London, he packed up his own things and that so perfectly that it was not till he had sent them off that he discovered he had left himself nothing to travel in but the shirt and robe-de-chambre which he wore while employed in thus disposing of the rest of his wardrobe.

He lived in a small apartment at the Luxembourg, as persons of like rank and small means reside in the royal palace at Hampton Court. One day, on descending the staircase he slipped, and broke his nose. On looking round for the cause of his accident, he observed a whitish fluid on the steps; and, calling the porter, he rated him soundly for allowing this soapy water to remain on the staircase. "It is *barley* water," said the porter, "which a waiter from the café spilled as he carried it along." "Oh! if that be the case," replied the chevalier, in a mild tone, and with his hand up to his mutilated nose, "if that be the case, it is I who am in the wrong."

Grimm adds, in summing up his character, that he was richer in pocket handkerchiefs than any other man. As his apartment was just under the roof of the palace, and that he, almost every day on going out, forgot to take a handkerchief with him, he found it less trouble to buy a new than to ascend to his room and procure an old one. Accordingly, a mercer in his neighborhood had a fresh handkerchief ready for him every day.

The history of eccentric knights would make a volume of

itself. Here, therefore, I will conclude, grateful to the readers who may have honored me by perusing any portion of the miscellaneous pages which I have devoted to illustrations of chivalry, and, adding a remark of Johnson, who says, touching the respect paid to those who bear arms, that "The naval and military professions have the dignity of danger, and that mankind reverence those who have got over fear, which is so general a weakness."

THE END.

# ABOUT THE AUTHOR

"Notes and Queries"
Doran as caricatured by Spy
(Leslie Ward) in Vanity Fair,
December 1873.

**John Doran** (1807 – 1878), miscellaneous writer of Irish parentage, wrote a number of works dealing with the lighter phases of manners, antiquities, and social history, often bearing punning titles, e.g., *Table Traits with Something on Them* (1854), and *Knights and their Days* (1856). He also wrote *Lives of the Queens of England of the House of Hanover* (1855), and *A History of Court Fools (1858)*, and edited Horace Walpole's *Journal of the Reign of George III*. His books contain much curious and out-of-the-way information. Doran was for a short time editor of *The Athenaeum*.

www.ingramcontent.com/pod-product-compliance
Lightning Source LLC
Chambersburg PA
CBHW031247230426
43670CB00005B/79